OECD/G20 Base Erosion and Profit Shifting Project

Tax Challenges Arising from Digitalisation – Report on Pillar Two Blueprint

INCLUSIVE FRAMEWORK ON BEPS

OECD
BETTER POLICIES FOR BETTER LIVES

Please cite this publication as:
OECD (2020), *Tax Challenges Arising from Digitalisation – Report on Pillar Two Blueprint: Inclusive Framework on BEPS*, OECD/G20 Base Erosion and Profit Shifting Project, OECD Publishing, Paris, *https://doi.org/10.1787/abb4c3d1-en*.

ISBN 978-92-64-81239-0 (print)
ISBN 978-92-64-35384-8 (pdf)

OECD/G20 Base Erosion and Profit Shifting Project
ISSN 2313-2604 (print)
ISSN 2313-2612 (online)

Photo credits: Cover © ninog – Fotolia.com.

Corrigenda to publications may be found on line at: *www.oecd.org/about/publishing/corrigenda.htm*.

Foreword

The integration of national economies and markets has increased substantially in recent years, putting a strain on the international tax rules, which were designed more than a century ago. Weaknesses in the current rules create opportunities for base erosion and profit shifting (BEPS), requiring bold moves by policy makers to restore confidence in the system and ensure that profits are taxed where economic activities take place and value is created.

Following the release of the report Addressing Base Erosion and Profit Shifting in February 2013, OECD and G20 countries adopted a 15-point Action Plan to address BEPS in September 2013. The Action Plan identified 15 actions along three key pillars: introducing coherence in the domestic rules that affect cross-border activities, reinforcing substance requirements in the existing international standards, and improving transparency as well as certainty.

After two years of work, measures in response to the 15 actions were delivered to G20 Leaders in Antalya in November 2015. All the different outputs, including those delivered in an interim form in 2014, were consolidated into a comprehensive package. The BEPS package of measures represents the first substantial renovation of the international tax rules in almost a century.

Implementation is now well underway. The BEPS package was designed to be implemented via changes in domestic law and practices, and in tax treaties. With the negotiation of a multilateral instrument (MLI) having been finalised in 2016 to facilitate the implementation of the treaty related BEPS measures, over 90 jurisdictions are covered by the MLI. The entry into force of the MLI on 1 July 2018 has paved the way for swift implementation of the treaty related measures. OECD and G20 countries also agreed to continue to work together to ensure a consistent and co-ordinated implementation of the BEPS recommendations and to make the project more inclusive. Globalisation requires that global solutions and a global dialogue be established which go beyond OECD and G20 countries.

As a result, the OECD established the OECD/G20 Inclusive Framework on BEPS (Inclusive Framework) in 2016, bringing together all interested and committed countries and jurisdictions on an equal footing in the Committee on Fiscal Affairs and all its subsidiary bodies. The Inclusive Framework, which already has more than 135 members, is monitoring and peer reviewing the implementation of the BEPS minimum standards as well as completing the work on standard setting to address BEPS issues. In addition to its member jurisdictions, other international organisations and regional tax bodies are involved in the work of the Inclusive Framework, which also consults business and civil society on its different work streams.

Addressing the tax challenges arising from the digitalisation of the economy has been a top priority of the BEPS Project and the Inclusive Framework since 2015 with the release of the BEPS Action 1 Report. At the request of the G20, the Inclusive Framework has continued to work on the issue, delivering an interim report in March 2018. In January 2019, members of the Inclusive Framework agreed to examine proposals in two pillars, which could form the basis for a consensus solution to the tax challenges arising from digitalisation. Pillar One is focused on nexus and profit allocation whereas Pillar Two is focused on a global minimum tax intended to address remaining BEPS issues. A programme of work to be conducted on Pillar One and Pillar Two was adopted in May 2019 and later endorsed by the G20 in June 2019. As part of the programme of work, the OECD Secretariat was mandated to carry out an economic analysis and impact assessment of the Pillar One and Pillar Two proposals. In July 2020, the G20 mandated the Inclusive Framework to produce reports on the Blueprints of Pillar One and Pillar Two by the G20 Finance Ministers meeting in October 2020.

This report was approved by the Inclusive Framework on 8-9 October 2020 and prepared for publication by the OECD Secretariat.

Table of contents

Follow OECD Publications on:

http://twitter.com/OECD_Pubs

http://www.facebook.com/OECDPublications

http://www.linkedin.com/groups/OECD-Publications-4645871

http://www.youtube.com/oecdilibrary

http://www.oecd.org/oecddirect/

Abbreviations and acronyms

(EU) AIFMD	European Union Alternative Investment Fund Managers Directive
BEAT	Base Erosion and Anti-abuse Tax
BEPS	Base Erosion and Profit Shifting
BIAC	Business at OECD
CbC	Country-by-Country
CbCR	Country-by-Country Reporting
CFC	Controlled foreign company
GAAP	General accepted accounting principles
G20	Group of Twenty
GILTI	Global Intangible Low-Taxed Income
ETR	Effective tax rate
EU	European Union
GloBE	Global Anti-Base Erosion
IFRS	International Financial Reporting Standards
IIR	Income Inclusion Rule
IMF	International Monetary Fund
JVs	Joint Ventures
MNE	Multinational Enterprise
NFE	Non-Financial Entity
PE	Permanent Establishment
PoW	Programme of Work
OCI	Other Comprehensive Income
OECD	Organization for Economic Co-operation and Development
ORIP	Offshore receipts of intangible property
TFDE	Task Force on the Digital Economy
R&D	Research and Development
SME	Small and Medium enterprises

SOR	Switch-Over Rule
STTR	Subject to Tax Rule
UN	United Nations
UPE	Ultimate Parent Entity
UTPR	Undertaxed Payments Rule
US	United States
WB	World Bank
WHT	Withholding tax

Cover Statement by the OECD/G20 Inclusive Framework on BEPS on the Reports on the Blueprints of Pillar One and Pillar Two

Digital transformation spurs innovation, generates efficiencies, and improves services while boosting more inclusive and sustainable growth and enhancing well-being. At the same time, the breadth and speed of this change introduces challenges in many policy areas, including taxation. Reforming the international tax system to address the tax challenges arising from the digitalisation of the economy, restore stability to the international tax framework and prevent further uncoordinated unilateral tax measures has therefore been a priority of the international community for several years, with commitments to deliver a consensus-based solution by the end of 2020.

The current context of the COVID-19 pandemic makes the need for a solution even more compelling than when it was first considered. Governments have responded through increased spending on healthcare and by providing unprecedented levels of financial support to both businesses and workers to cushion them from the economic blow of this crisis. However, the time will come when governments will need to focus on putting their finances back on a fair and sustainable footing.

A consensus-based solution comprised of two pillars (Pillar One focused on nexus and profit allocation whereas Pillar Two is focused on a global minimum tax intended to address remaining BEPS issues) can not only play an important role to ensure fairness and equity in our tax systems and fortify the international tax framework in the face of new and changing business models; it can also help put government finances back on a sustainable footing. The public pressure on governments to ensure that large, internationally operating, and profitable businesses pay their fair share and do so in the right place under new international tax rules has increased as a result of the current COVID-19 pandemic. At the same time, a consensus-based solution could provide businesses with much needed tax certainty in order to aid economic recovery.

Against this background, despite their differences, and the COVID-19 pandemic, which has had an impact on the work, the members of the OECD/G20 Inclusive Framework on BEPS (Inclusive Framework) have made substantial progress towards building consensus. The Inclusive Framework is releasing today a package consisting of the Reports on the Blueprints of Pillar One and Pillar Two, which reflects convergent views on a number of key policy features, principles and parameters of both Pillars, and identifies remaining political and technical issues where differences of views remain to be bridged, and next steps.

We approve the *Report on the Pillar One Blueprint* for public release. It is designed to deliver a sustainable taxation framework reflective of today's digitalising economy, with the potential to achieve a fairer and more efficient allocation of taxing rights. The Blueprint reflects the extensive technical work that has been done. Though no agreement has been reached, the Blueprint nevertheless provides a solid foundation for a future agreement that would adhere to the concept of net taxation of income, avoid double taxation and be as simple and administrable as possible. The Blueprint offers a solid basis for future agreement and reflects that:

- in an increasingly digital age, in-scope businesses are able to generate profits through participation in a significant/ active and sustained way in the economic life of a jurisdiction, beyond the mere conclusion of sales, with or without the benefit of local physical presence and this would be reflected in the design of nexus rules while being mindful of compliance considerations;
- the solution would follow the policy rationale set out above and allocate a portion of residual profit of in-scope businesses to market/user jurisdictions ("Amount A");
- the solution would be targeted and build in thresholds so that it minimises compliance costs for taxpayers and keeps the administration of the new rules manageable for tax administrations;
- Amount A would be computed using consolidated financial accounts as the starting point, contain a limited number of book-to-tax adjustments and ensure that losses are appropriately taken into account;
- in determining the tax base, segmentation would be required to appropriately target the new taxing right in certain cases, but with broad safe-harbour or exemption rules from segmentation to reduce complexity and minimise burdens for tax administrations and taxpayers alike;
- the solution would contain effective means to eliminate double taxation in a multilateral setting;
- the work on Amount B will be advanced, (a fixed rate of return on base-line marketing and distribution activities intended to approximate results determined under the arm's length principle) recognising its potentially significant benefits including for tax administrations with limited capacity as well as its challenges;
- the Pillar One solution would contain a new multilateral tax certainty process with respect to Amount A, recognising the importance of using simplified and co-ordinated administrative procedures with respect to the administration of Amount A;
- a new multilateral convention would be developed to implement the solution, recognising that it would offer the best and most efficient way of implementing Pillar One.

We will now focus on resolving the remaining political and technical issues, including issues around scope, quantum, the choice between mandatory and safe harbour implementation, and aspects of the new tax certainty procedures with respect to Amount A, and the scope and form of new and enhanced tax certainty procedures for issues beyond Amount A.

We also approve the *Report on the Pillar Two Blueprint* for public release. It provides a solid basis for a systemic solution that would address remaining base erosion and profit shifting (BEPS) challenges and sets out rules that would provide jurisdictions with a right to "tax back" where other jurisdictions have not exercised their primary taxing rights, or the payment is otherwise subject to low levels of effective taxation. These rules would ensure that all large internationally operating businesses pay at least a minimum level of tax. We acknowledge that jurisdictions are free to determine their own tax systems, including whether they have a corporate income tax and the level of their tax rates, but also consider the right of other jurisdictions to apply an internationally agreed Pillar Two regime where income is taxed below an agreed minimum rate. Though no agreement has been reached , the Blueprint provides a solid basis for future agreement on:

- the Income Inclusion Rule (IIR), the Undertaxed Payments Rule (UTPR), the Subject to Tax Rule (STTR), the rule order, the calculation of the effective tax rate and the allocation of the top-up tax for the IIR and the UTPR, including the tax base, the definition of covered taxes, mechanisms to address volatility, and the substance carve-out;
- the IIR and UTPR as a common approach, including an acceptance of the right of all members of the IF to implement them as part of an agreed Pillar Two regime. It would nevertheless be recognised and accepted that there may be members that are not in a position to implement these rules. However, all those implementing them would apply them consistently with the agreed Pillar Two vis-à-vis all other jurisdictions (including groups headquartered therein) that also join this consensus. Furthermore, given the importance that a large number of IF members, particularly developing countries, attach to an STTR, we recognise that an STTR would be an integral part of a consensus solution on Pillar Two;
- the basis on which the United States' Global Intangible Low Taxed Income Regime (GILTI) would be treated as a Pillar Two compliant income inclusion rule as set out in the Report on the Blueprint on Pillar Two;
- the development of model legislation, standard documentation and guidance, designing a multilateral review process if necessary and exploring the use of a multilateral convention, which could include the key aspects of Pillar Two.

We welcome stakeholder input into this process on both pillars, in particular on administration and simplification rules, which would help inform the further development of the consensus-based solution.

Next steps

We agree to swiftly address the remaining issues with a view to bringing the process to a successful conclusion by mid-2021 and to resolve technical issues, develop model draft legislation, guidelines, and international rules and processes as necessary to enable jurisdictions to implement a consensus based solution.

1 Executive Summary

1.1. Introduction

1. Digital transformation spurs innovation, generates efficiencies, and improves services while boosting more inclusive and sustainable growth and enhancing well-being. At the same time, the breadth and speed of this change introduces challenges in many policy areas, including taxation. Reforming the international tax system to address the tax challenges arising from the digitalisation of the economy has therefore been a priority of the international community for several years, with commitments to deliver a consensus-based solution by the end of 2020.

2. These tax challenges were first identified as one of the main areas of focus of the OECD/G20 Base Erosion and Profit Shifting (BEPS) Project, leading to the 2015 BEPS Action 1 Report (the Action 1 Report) (OECD, 2015[1]). The Action 1 Report found that the whole economy was digitalising and, as a result, it would be difficult, if not impossible, to ring-fence the digital economy. In March 2018, the Inclusive Framework, working through its Task Force on the Digital Economy (TFDE), issued *Tax Challenges Arising from Digitalisation – Interim Report 2018* (the Interim Report) (OECD, 2018[2]) which recognised the need for a global solution.

3. Since then, the 137 members of the Inclusive Framework have worked on a global solution based on a two pillar approach (OECD, 2015[1]). Under the second pillar, the Inclusive Framework agreed to explore an approach that is focused on the remaining BEPS challenges and proposes a systematic solution designed to ensure that all internationally operating businesses pay a minimum level of tax. In so doing, it helps to address the remaining BEPS challenges linked to the digitalising economy, where the relative importance of intangible assets as profit drivers makes highly digitalised business often ideally placed to avail themselves of profit shifting planning structures. Pillar Two leaves jurisdictions free to determine their own tax system, including whether they have a corporate income tax and where they set their tax rates, but also considers the right of other jurisdictions to apply the rules contained in this report where income is taxed at an effective rate below a minimum rate.

4. Consistent with the Policy Note Addressing the Tax Challenges of the Digitalisation of the Economy (OECD/G20, 2019[3]), approved on 23 January 2019 and the Programme of Work (PoW) (OECD, 2019[4]), approved on 28-29 May, 2019, Members of the Inclusive Framework agree that any rules developed under this Pillar should not result in taxation where there is no economic profit nor should they result in double taxation. Mindful of limiting compliance and administrative burdens, Inclusive Framework Members further agree to make any rules as simple as the tax policy context permits, including through the exploration of simplification measures.

5. Following the adoption of the Programme of Work (OECD, 2019[4]) in May 2019, the Inclusive Framework worked on developing the different aspects of Pillar Two. A public consultation was held on 9 December 2019 (OECD, 2019[5]) which received over 150 written

submissions, running to over 1,300 pages submitted by a wide range of businesses, industry groups, law and accounting practitioners, and non-governmental organisations, which provided critical input into the design of many of the aspects of Pillar Two. In January the Inclusive Framework issued a progress report on the status of the technical work. Since January, and in spite of the outbreak of COVID-19, all members have progressed the work and the engagement with stakeholders continued through digital channels including through the maintenance of digital contact groups set up by Business at OECD (BIAC).

6. This is a Report on the blueprint for Pillar Two (the "Blueprint"). It identifies technical design components of Pillar Two. It also identifies those areas linked to implementation and simplification, which would benefit from further stakeholder input, and where further technical work is required prior to finalisation. The finalisation of Pillar Two also requires political agreement on key design features of the subject to tax rule and the GloBE rules including carve-outs, blending, rule order and tax rates where, at present, diverging views continue to exist.

7. The remainder of this Section sets out the overall design consideration, before focusing on administrative and compliance considerations that were important in the design of Pillar Two. It then discusses the co-existence of the United States' Global Intangible Low-Taxed Income (GILTI) regime, before providing a chapter-by chapter summary complemented by a flow chart.

1.1. Overall design considerations and high level summary

8. Pillar Two addresses remaining BEPS challenges and is designed to ensure that large internationally operating businesses pay a minimum level of tax regardless of where they are headquartered or the jurisdictions they operate in. It does so via a number of interlocking rules that seek to (i) ensure minimum taxation while avoiding double taxation or taxation where there is no economic profit, (ii) cope with different tax system designs by jurisdictions as well as different operating models by businesses, (iii) ensure transparency and a level playing field, and (iv) minimise administrative and compliance costs.

9. The principal mechanism to achieve this outcome is the income inclusion rule (IIR) together with the undertaxed payments rule (UTPR) acting as a backstop. The operation of the IIR is, in some respects, based on traditional controlled foreign company (CFC) rule principles and triggers an inclusion at the level of the shareholder where the income of a controlled foreign entity is taxed at below the effective minimum tax rate.[1] It is complemented by a switch-over rule (SOR) that removes treaty obstacles from its application to certain branch structures and applies where an income tax treaty otherwise obligates a contracting state to use the exemption method.

10. The UTPR is a secondary rule and only applies where a Constituent Entity is not already subject to an IIR. The UTPR is nevertheless a key part of the rule set as it serves as back-stop to the IIR, ensures a level playing field and addresses inversion risks that might otherwise arise.

11. The Subject to Tax Rule (STTR) complements these rules. It acknowledges that denying treaty benefits for certain deductible intra-group payments made to jurisdictions where those payments are subject to no or low rates of nominal taxation may help source countries to protect their tax base, notably for countries with lower administrative capacities. To ensure tax certainty and avoid double taxation Pillar Two also addresses questions of implementation and effective rule coordination.

Income inclusion rule and undertaxed payments rule (the "GloBE rules")

12. The IIR and the UTPR use the same rules to determine scope and the level of effective taxation. They apply to MNE Groups and their Constituent Entities within the consolidated group as determined under applicable financial accounting standards. They only apply to businesses that meet or exceed a EUR 750 million annual gross revenue threshold.[2] This creates synergies with the current BEPS Action 13 Country by Country Reporting (CbCR) rules, thereby reducing compliance costs. It also avoids adverse impacts on SME's while preserving the impact of the rules with in scope MNE Groups still earning over 90% of global corporate revenues.

13. The rules further exclude certain parent entities including investment and pension funds, governmental entities such as sovereign wealth funds and international and non-profit bodies, which typically benefit from an exclusion or exemption from tax under applicable domestic tax law. Special rules may apply to Associates, joint ventures and so called "orphan entities" that are not part of the consolidated group.

14. Both the IIR and the UTPR use a common tax base. The determination of the base starts with the financial accounts prepared under the accounting standard used by the parent of the MNE Group to prepare its consolidated financial statements. This must be IFRS or another acceptable accounting standard. The use of financial accounts as a common basis ensures a level playing field for both jurisdictions and MNEs, enhances transparency and leverages off existing systems thereby minimising compliance cost. Certain adjustments are then made to the financial accounts to eliminate specific items of income from the tax base, such as intragroup dividends and to incorporate certain expenses, such as tax deductible stock based compensation. This is necessary where the outcomes of the financial accounting rules would otherwise distort the tax policy objectives of Pillar Two.

15. The IIR and the UTPR also use a common definition of taxes. The definition of taxes, referred to as "covered taxes" is derived from the definition of taxes used for statistical purposes by many international organisations including the OECD, EU, IMF, World Bank and the UN. The definition is deliberately kept broad to avoid legalistic distinctions and accommodate different tax systems provided they substantively impose taxes on an entity's income or profits.

16. The effective tax rate (ETR) is determined by applying the tax base and covered taxes on a jurisdictional basis. This requires an assignment of the income and taxes among the jurisdictions in which the MNE operates and to which it pays taxes. The GloBE tax computation calculation also includes two important additional adjustments; a mechanism to mitigate the impact of volatility in the ETR from one period to the next and a formulaic substance carve-out.

17. The mechanism to address volatility is based on the principle that Pillar Two should not impose tax where the low ETR is simply a result of timing differences in the recognition of income or the imposition of taxes. The GloBE rules therefore allow an MNE to carry-over losses incurred or excess taxes paid in prior periods into a subsequent period in order to smooth-out any potential volatility arising from such timing differences.

18. The formulaic substance carve-out excludes a fixed return for substantive activities within a jurisdiction from the scope of the GloBE rules. Excluding a fixed return from substantive activities focuses GloBE on "excess income", such as intangible-related income, which is most susceptible to BEPS challenges.

19. If an MNE's jurisdictional ETR is below the agreed minimum rate, the MNE will be liable for an incremental amount of tax that is sufficient to bring the total amount of tax on the excess profits up to the minimum rate. The ETR calculation therefore operates both as a trigger for the imposition of the tax liability and as a measure of the amount of top-up tax imposed under the rules. This design ensures a level playing field as all MNE's pay a minimum level of tax in each

jurisdiction in which they operate while the top up mechanism coupled with the common base makes sure that they face the same level of top-up tax irrespective of where they are based. The amount of top up tax is collected either by application of the IIR, or - where no IIR applies- by the application of the UTPR.

Subject to Tax Rule

20. The Subject to Tax Rule (STTR) complements these rules. It is a treaty-based rule that specifically targets risks to source countries posed by BEPS structures relating to intragroup[3] payments that take advantage of low nominal rates of taxation in the other contracting jurisdiction (that is, the jurisdiction of the payee). It allows the source jurisdiction to impose additional taxation on certain covered payments up to the agreed minimum rate. Any top up tax imposed under the STTR will be taken into account in determining the ETR for purposes of the IIR and the UTPR.

Implementation

21. While the IIR and the UTPR do not require changes to bilateral treaties and can be implemented by way of changes to domestic law,[4] both the STTR and the SOR can only be implemented through changes to existing bilateral tax treaties. These could be implemented through bilateral negotiations and amendments to individual treaties or as part of a multilateral convention. Alternatively the Multilateral Convention to Implement Tax Treaty Related Measures to Prevent Base Erosion and Profit Shifting (the MLI) (OECD, 2016[6]), emerging from BEPS Action 15, may offer a model for a coordinated and efficient approach to introducing these changes.

Rule co-ordination and next steps

22. As a next step and to ensure rule co-ordination and increase tax certainty the Inclusive Framework on BEPS will develop model legislation and guidance, develop a multilateral review process and explore the use of a multilateral convention, which could include the key aspects of Pillar Two. Dispute prevention and resolution processes can build on the existing infrastructure, but new provisions could also be included in a multilateral convention.

23. The graphic below shows the different components of Pillar Two and identifies the chapter where each of these components is discussed.

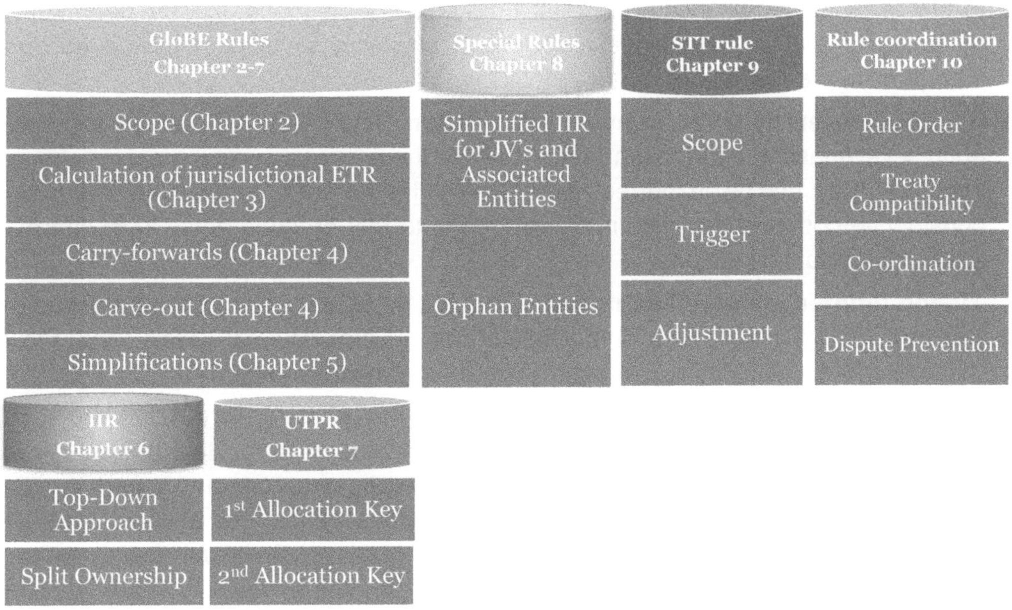

1.2. Administrative and compliance considerations

24. Within the context of the tax policy objectives of Pillar Two the design of each feature has been developed with the objective of minimising cost and resources for both tax authorities and taxpayers in applying and administering the Pillar Two rules. This has informed a number of design choices including the following:

- **Use of accounting consolidation rules for determining scope**. While from a tax policy perspective there could have been reason to go beyond the consolidated group definition, to minimise cost and complexity the Pillar Two design stays with this definition and addresses particular risk areas through targeted rules only.
- **Reliance on Country-by-Country reporting (CbCR) thresholds and definitions**. To limit compliance costs, maximise synergies, avoid adverse impacts on SME's, while preserving the overall impact of the rules, the Pillar Two design leverages off the CbCR concepts and definitions and excludes MNE's below the EUR 750 million consolidated gross revenue threshold.
- **List of excluded entities**. To provide certainty and translate the policy intent, the Pillar Two design includes a list of expressly excluded entities, including those that may, in certain circumstances, already be excluded under the operation of the consolidation rules.
- **Use of parent financial accounting standards, no book-to-book and limited book-to-tax adjustments**. The reliance on accounting information avoids the cost and complexity of having to re-compute the income and profits of each foreign group member in accordance with domestic tax accounting rules, which in practise is not something MNEs are often required to do to even where they are subject to CFC rules. In particular, a requirement to re-compute using domestic tax accounting in connection with the application of the UTPR would have resulted in disproportionate compliance burdens. Furthermore, the Pillar Two design accepts a range of accounting standards without requiring book to book adjustments, for instance between IFRS and US GAAP. The use of the accounting standards at the parent level – rather than local entity level –

further reduces compliance cost. Finally, book to tax adjustments have been kept at a minimum in part to maintain the benefit of simplicity in using financial accounting standards in the first place.

- **Reliance on entity level financial information**. The Pillar Two design accepts that entity level financial information that is used in the preparation of the parent's financial accounts may not be in perfect accord with the parent's accounting standard, but considering cost and benefits, it allows MNE's to rely on such entity level information subject to certain conditions.
- **Timing differences simplifications**. The rules provide for a simplified mechanism to address timing differences that applies on a jurisdictional basis and includes mechanisms for calculating pre-regime losses and excess taxes.
- **Rule order**. The Pillar Two design has the IIR as the primary rule with the UTPR acting as a backstop. Both rules use the same computational rules for determining low taxed income, but the primacy of the IIR is largely driven by simplicity and lower compliance costs, including the ease of obtaining the necessary income and tax information required to make an ETR determination; the fact that the IIR will generally require only one adjustment to be made by a single taxpayer and the availability of mechanisms to avoid the risk of double taxation. Equally, the general decision to use a top-down rather than a bottom-up approach for the use of the IIR in connection with multi-tier MNE Groups is driven in significant part by compliance and simplicity considerations. The top-down approach will limit the number of jurisdictions applying the IIR thereby reducing the need for co-ordination and, by extension, complexity, administrative burden, and the risk of double taxation under the rules.
- **Subject to Tax Rule using a nominal tax rate test**. The Subject to Tax Rule is limited to certain categories of payments made between members of a controlled group and is based on a nominal tax rate test, thereby avoiding the conceptual and administrative challenges of using an effective tax rate test.
- **Bright line and mechanical rule design.** Wherever possible, within the context of the tax policy objectives, Pillar Two uses bright line rules (e.g. on scope and for the determination of the tax base including any permanent adjustments) and more mechanical, formulaic approaches (e.g. the design of a formulaic substance based carve-out and in the mechanics for allocating top-up tax under the IIR and UTPR) which should make compliance easier and avoid the types of disputes that often result from more subjective rules with significant reliance on facts and circumstance tests.
- **Further simplification options in particular in light of jurisdictional blending.** During the December 2019 Public Consultation (OECD, 2019[5]), many MNEs stressed that simplification measures are needed to reduce the complexity and administrative burden associated with complying with the GloBE rules, particularly in the context of jurisdictional blending. Several submissions pointed out that large MNEs often operate in more than 100 jurisdictions and would be required to undertake the same number of ETR calculations under a jurisdictional blending approach. Other submissions expressed concern that, under jurisdictional blending, it would be necessary to compute the ETR in jurisdictions that are likely to be above the agreed minimum rate year-after-year, given the base and tax rate in these jurisdictions. These inputs informed a number of the design features already discussed above, but also led to the exploration of several further simplification measures, as set out in Chapter 5 of the Report. These simplification measures would benefit from further public consultations with stakeholders and business in particular and therefore no decision has yet been taken

on which, if any, of these simplification measures to incorporate into the final design of the rules.

1.3. GILTI co-existence

25. The United States enacted the Global Intangible Low-Taxed Income (GILTI) regime in 2017 as part of a substantial reform of the US international tax rules. The GILTI regime, which draws on elements of the BEPS Action 3 Report, provides for a minimum level of tax on the foreign income of an MNE Group. While the GILTI and GloBE rules as described in this Blueprint have a similar purpose and overlapping scope, the design of GILTI differs from GloBE in a number of important respects.

26. While GILTI results largely, but not completely, in a global blending of foreign income and taxes, in a number of other respects, the GloBE rules, as described in this Blueprint, would be more permissive than GILTI, depending also on their final design. These include the carry-forward of losses and excess taxes, a broader definition of covered taxes and a carve-out based on a broader range of tangible assets and payroll. Furthermore, GILTI applies without threshold limitations and incorporates expense allocation rules in the calculation of foreign tax credits which can result in effective rates of taxation above the minimum rate. Finally, the GILTI effective rate is currently set at 13.125% and will increase to 16.4% in 2026.

27. Given the pre-existing nature of the GILTI regime and its legislative intent there are reasons for treating GILTI as a qualified income inclusion rule for purposes of the GloBE rules provided that the coexistence achieves reasonably equivalent effects.. This treatment would need to be reviewed if subsequent legislation or regulations in the US would have the effect of materially narrowing the GILTI tax base or reducing the legislated rate of tax. The Inclusive Framework recognises that an agreement on the co-existence of the GILTI and the GloBE would need to be part of the political agreement on Pillar Two.

28. At a technical level further consideration will be given to how the interactions between the GILTI and the GloBE rules would be coordinated. That includes the coordination with the application of the GILTI to US intermediate parent companies of foreign groups headquartered in countries that apply an IIR. Moreover, considering the role of the undertaxed payments rule as a back-stop to the IIR, the Inclusive Framework on BEPS strongly encourages the United States to limit the operation of the Base Erosion and Anti-abuse Tax (BEAT) in respect of payments to entities that are subject to the IIR.

1.4. Chapter breakdown and flow-chart

29. This Pillar Two report consists of ten chapters that set out the overall design of the rules and includes an Annex with examples illustrating the operation of the rules.

30. **Chapter 1** is this executive summary and introduction.

31. **Chapter 2** contains the rules that determine the scope of the GloBE rules and includes the relevant definitions for in scope groups and Constituent Entities, as well as excluded entities. It also explains the application and computation of the consolidated revenue threshold.

32. **Chapter 3** covers the rules and explanations relating to the calculation of the ETR and top-up tax under the GloBE rules. The starting point for applying the GloBE rules is the consolidated financial statements prepared by the MNE Group. A limited number of adjustments are then made to the financial accounts to add or eliminate certain items in order to arrive at the

GloBE tax base. The Chapter then defines the covered taxes that can be taken into account in determining the ETR on a jurisdictional basis.

33. **Chapter 4** sets out a number of adjustments that may be made to the top-up tax calculation either through the carry-over of losses or excess taxes from other periods or through the application of a formulaic substance based carve-out. The carry-forward adjustments are intended to ensure that Pillar Two does not result in the imposition of additional tax where the low ETR is simply a result of differences in the timing for recognition of income or the imposition of taxes while the formulaic substance-based carve-out is intended to exclude a fixed return for substantive activities within a jurisdiction from the scope of the GloBE rules.

34. **Chapter 5** explores a number of simplification measures designed to reduce the compliance burden in particular from the use of a jurisdictional ETR calculation. As noted in that chapter these simplifications would benefit from further public consultations with business in particular and therefore no decision has yet been taken on which, if any, of these simplification measures to incorporate into the final design of the rules.

35. **Chapter 6** describes the operation of the IIR including how the IIR is applied in the context of a multi-tiered ownership structure, where Pillar Two uses a top down approach except in cases where the ownership is split with a minority holder outside the group. In the latter case the split-ownership rules require the intermediate parent entity to apply the income inclusion rule to the controlled subsidiaries of the sub-group. This chapter also explains the need for a treaty based switch over rule that would allow a jurisdiction to override the exemption method to the extent necessary to apply the IIR to the profits of a permanent establishment.

36. **Chapter 7** contains a detailed discussion of the UTPR. The UTPR only applies to those Constituent Entities in the MNE Group that are not controlled by an entity further up the chain that applies an IIR. Where the UTPR applies top-up tax is allocated proportionately among Constituent Entities applying UTPR in a co-ordinated way first to those entities making direct payments to the low-tax Constituent Entity and then amongst all entities in the group that have net intra-group expenditure.

37. **Chapter 8** discusses two special rules, one dealing with Associates and joint ventures and another dealing with so-called “orphan entities.” The first rule applies a simplified IIR to the income of an MNE Group attributable to ownership interests in entities or arrangements that are reported under the equity method. The second rule is designed to extend the application of the UTPR to “orphan” entities or arrangements that could otherwise be used to extract profit from the MNE Group for the benefit of the controlling shareholders, giving rise to a BEPS risk.

38. **Chapter 9** addresses the subject to tax rule. It sets the framework for a development of a treaty-based rule that specifically targets risks to source countries posed by BEPS structures relating to intragroup payments that take advantage of low or nominal rates of taxation in the other contracting jurisdiction (that is, the jurisdiction of the payee). The effect of the rule will be to allow the payer jurisdiction to apply a top-up tax to bring the tax on the payment up to an agreed minimum rate.

39. **Chapter 10** deals with implementation and rule co-ordination. This chapter is forward looking and explains how the Inclusive Framework will ensure rule co-ordination and increase tax certainty including through the development of model legislation and guidance, a multilateral review process and the exploration of a multilateral convention, which could also include new provision on dispute prevention and resolution.

1.2. Flow Diagram

40. The flow diagram below is intended to provide a high-level overview of the process steps for applying the GloBE rules to wholly-owned Constituent Entities of an MNE Group.

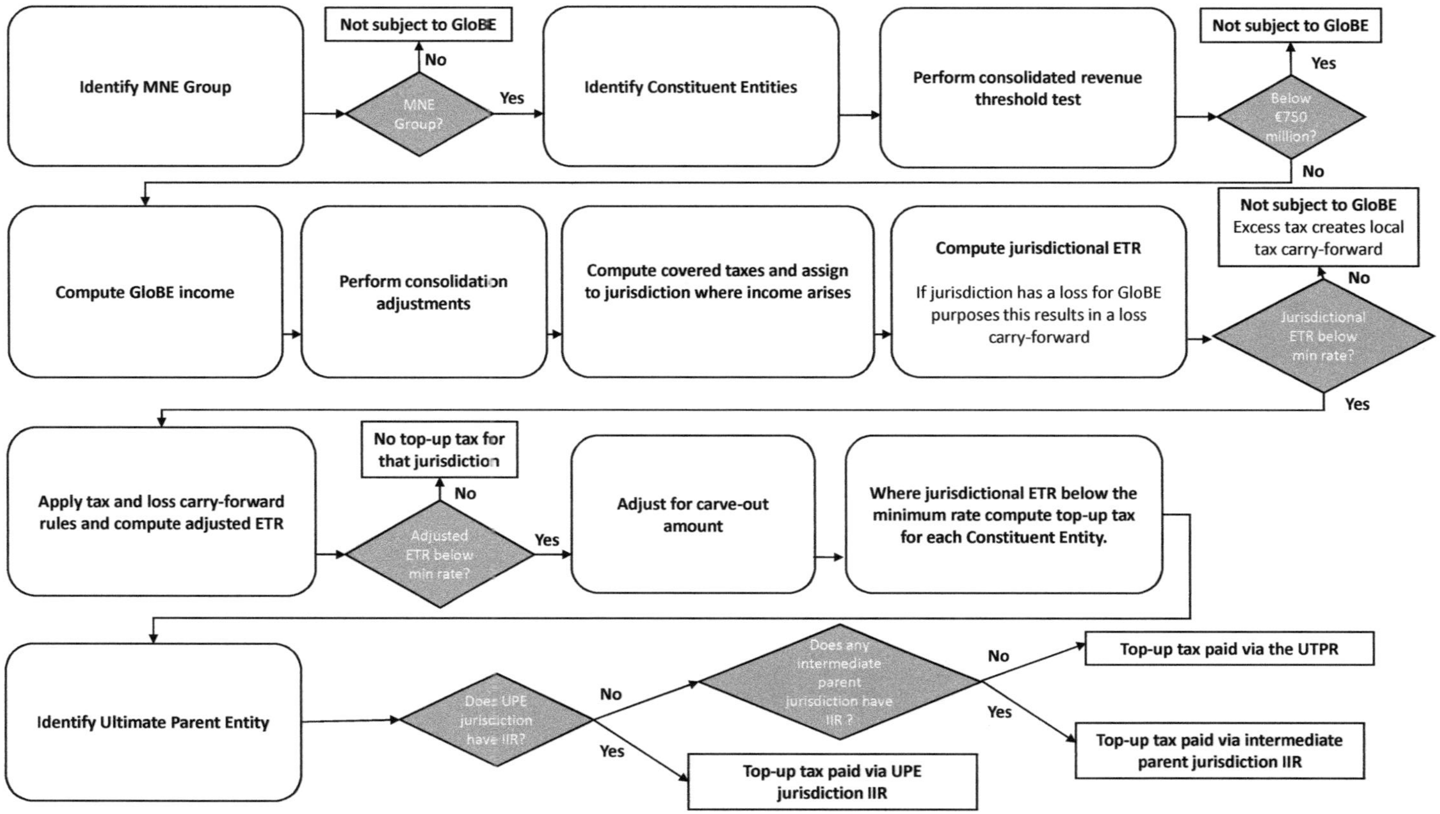

References

OECD (2019), *Global Anti-Base Erosion Proposal ("GloBE") - Pillar Two*, OECD Publishing, Paris, https://www.oecd.org/tax/beps/public-consultation-document-global-anti-base-erosion-proposal-pillar-two.pdf.pdf. [5]

OECD (2019), *Programme of Work to Develop a Consensus Solution to the Tax Challenges Arising from the Digitalisation of the Economy, OECD/G20 Inclusive Framework on BEPS*, OECD Publishing, Paris, https://www.oecd.org/tax/beps/programme-of-work-to-develop-a-consensus-solution-to-the-tax-challenges-arising-from-the-digitalisation-of-the-economy.pdf. [4]

OECD (2018), *Tax Challenges Arising from Digitalisation – Interim Report 2018: Inclusive Framework on BEPS*, OECD/G20 Base Erosion and Profit Shifting Project, OECD Publishing, Paris, https://dx.doi.org/10.1787/9789264293083-en. [2]

OECD (2016), *Multilateral Convention to Implement Tax Treaty Related Measures to Prevent Base Erosion and Profit Shifting*, OECD Publishing, Paris, https://www.oecd.org/tax/treaties/multilateral-convention-to-implement-tax-treaty-related-measures-to-prevent-BEPS.pdf. [6]

OECD (2015), *Addressing the Tax Challenges of the Digital Economy, Action 1 - 2015 Final Report*, OECD/G20 Base Erosion and Profit Shifting Project, OECD Publishing, Paris, https://dx.doi.org/10.1787/9789264241046-en. [1]

OECD/G20 (2019), *Addressing the Tax Challenges of the Digitalisation of the Economy – Policy Note*, OECD Publishing, Paris, https://www.oecd.org/tax/beps/policy-note-beps-inclusive-framework-addressing-tax-challenges-digitalisation.pdf. [3]

Notes

1 Although similar in operation, the IIR and CFC rules can co-exist because they have different policy objectives.

2 For a further discussion of the revenue threshold see Section 2.4 and 10.3 below.

3 As discussed in Section 9.1, the STTR may not in all instances be limited to intra-group payments.

4 See Section 10.5.3 on the consideration of a multilateral convention to ensure co-ordination of the IIR and UTPR.

2 Scope of the GloBE rules

2.1. Overview

41. This chapter sets out the rules for determining whether a taxpayer is within the scope of the GloBE rules. The rules set out in this Chapter build on the definitions and methodology currently used by Inclusive Framework on BEPS members under BEPS Action 13 for Country by Country Reporting (CbCR) purposes. The GloBE rules generally apply to the MNE Groups and their Constituent Entities that are subject to CbCR obligations described in the BEPS Action 13 Report (OECD, 2015[1]) however the GloBE rules specifically exclude certain Ultimate Parent Entities, such as investment and pension funds, governmental entities (such as sovereign wealth funds) and international and non-profit bodies, which typically benefit from an exclusion or an exemption from tax under the laws of the jurisdiction where they are incorporated (Excluded Entities).

42. Section 2.2 identifies the MNE Groups and entities within the scope of the GloBE rules and Section 2.3 sets out the list of Excluded Entities. Section 2.4 discusses the consolidated group revenue threshold of EUR 750 million, including the methodology used to compute it and its implications in relation to the GloBE rules.

2.2. Identifying the groups and Constituent Entities in scope

Groups and Entities within the Scope of the GloBE rules

Group

The term "Group" means a collection of enterprises[1] related through ownership or control such that it is either required to prepare consolidated financial statements for financial reporting purposes under applicable accounting principles or would be so required if equity interests in any of the enterprises were traded on a public securities exchange.[2]

MNE Group

The term "MNE Group" means any Group that includes two or more enterprises the tax residence for which is in different jurisdictions or includes an enterprise that is resident for tax purposes in one jurisdiction and is subject to tax with respect to the business carried out through a permanent establishment in another jurisdiction.[3]

Constituent Entity

The term "Constituent Entity" means

(a) any separate business unit of an MNE Group that is included in the consolidated financial statements of the MNE Group for financial reporting purposes, or would be so included if equity interests of the Ultimate Parent Entity of the MNE Group were traded on a public securities exchange;

(b) any such business unit that is, or would be, excluded from the MNE Group's consolidated financial statements solely on size or materiality grounds; and

(c) any permanent establishment of any separate business unit of the MNE Group included in (a) or (b) above provided the business unit prepares a separate financial statement for such permanent establishment for financial reporting, regulatory, tax reporting, or internal management control purposes.[4]

A Constituent Entity does not, however, include a business unit that is an Excluded Entity.

Ultimate Parent Entity (UPE)

The term "Ultimate Parent Entity" or "UPE" means a Constituent Entity of an MNE Group that meets the following criteria:

(a) it owns directly or indirectly a sufficient interest in one or more other Constituent Entities of such MNE Group such that it is required to prepare Consolidated Financial Statements under accounting principles generally applied in its jurisdiction of tax residence, or would be so required if its equity interests were traded on a public securities exchange in its jurisdiction of tax residence; and

(b) there is no other Constituent Entity of such MNE Group that owns directly or indirectly an interest described in paragraph (a) above in the first mentioned Constituent Entity.

43. The definitions set out in the box above define the entities and operations that make up an MNE Group. These definitions are the same as those that are used for CbCR with minor drafting changes to accommodate the different design of the GloBE rules,[5] which is, in turn, built on the standards used for determining whether the operation of two enterprises or business units should be consolidated for financial reporting purposes.

44. Using the consolidation standard under financial accounting to define the scope of an MNE Group and the Constituent Entities within that group has a number of advantages. The rules that determine when an MNE is required to consolidate for accounting purposes are robust, comprehensive and relatively consistent across accounting standards. The use of a financial accounting standard also has benefits from the compliance perspective, because the application of the standard will, in many cases, be subject to review by independent financial accounting auditors. A definition of an MNE Group based on the relevant financial accounting standards may even reduce the incentive for that MNE Group to adopt structures designed to artificially exclude or include subsidiaries from the group. For example, an MNE may have an incentive to include a loss-making entity within its group in order to reduce its GloBE tax base in a jurisdiction. Aligning the definition of the MNE Group with that used for financial reporting purposes would, however, mean that including such an entity for GloBE purposes would have a corresponding deleterious impact on its consolidated profit for financial reporting purposes.

45. The definitions set out in the box above are based on those agreed under BEPS Action 13.[6] The Final Report on Action 13 adopted a three-tiered approach to transfer pricing documentation consisting of the master file, the local file and the CbCR report. The CbCR report requires an MNE Group to report information such as the income earned, taxes paid, and business activities carried out in each jurisdiction,

and a list of all of its Constituent Entities. Tax authorities use the information provided in the CbCR reports to assess high-level transfer pricing and other BEPS related risks. BEPS Action 13 has a different policy objective to that of Pillar Two. CbCR is a reporting obligation that is designed to promote transparency and improve risk assessment, while Pillar Two results in the actual imposition of a tax liability. Nevertheless aligning the definitions under CbCR and the GloBE rules should reduce compliance and administrative burdens for tax authorities and taxpayers. At the same time, the use of a consolidated accounting standard as a basis for defining the MNE Group allows other design features of the GloBE rules (such as the determination of the tax base) to leverage those same accounting standards.

2.2.1. Definition of Group and MNE Group

Definition of Group

46. The definition of "Group" under the GloBE rules is the same as that used in CbCR. A group is defined as a collection of enterprises that are consolidated for financial accounting purposes. This consolidation test is, in turn, based on a control test used for accounting. In general, the effect of this test is that two entities will be treated as part of the same Group where one entity controls the other or both entities are controlled by another entity. The definition of "Group" also extends to situations where an entity or arrangement carries on business activities in foreign jurisdictions exclusively through permanent establishments because the assets, liabilities, income, and expenses of the permanent establishments are included in the financial statements of the head office as if they were consolidated on a line-by-line basis.

MNE Group

47. The definition of "MNE Group" under the GloBE rules is also consistent with, and has the same outcomes as under, the CbCR rules. The definition of MNE Group incorporates a minor drafting difference from CbCR in that the group revenue threshold, which is incorporated directly into the definition of the MNE Group for CbCR purposes, is excluded from the definition used for GloBE purposes. While the GloBE rules apply the same revenue threshold as CbCR, this requirement is dealt with separately under the GloBE rules. The purpose of the MNE Group definition set out in the box above is to identify the MNE Group and the Constituent Entities that are part of the same group, rather than determine whether an MNE Group is subject to the GloBE rules. As such, the revenue threshold is more appropriately treated as a separate design element of the GloBE rules. See Section 2.4.1.

2.2.2. Definition of Constituent Entity

48. A Constituent Entity consists of a separate business unit that it is (or would have been) included in the consolidated financial statements of the MNE Group. As with CbCR, the GloBE rules apply a "deemed consolidation" test that treats a business unit as part of an MNE Group where that business unit would have been required to be consolidated had any of the equity interests of the Ultimate Parent Entity of the MNE Group been traded on a public securities exchange.

49. Any separate business unit that is excluded from the consolidated financial statements, or that would be excluded if the MNE Group prepared such statements, solely on size or materiality grounds is also a Constituent Entity. Lastly, a permanent establishment of a Constituent Entity is treated as a separate Constituent Entity. The definition of a Constituent Entity does not include those entities specifically identified as "Excluded Entities" in Section 2.3. Further explanation of the separate limbs of the Constituent Entity definition is set out below. A flow chart based on this Section is included in the Annex (see Flow Chart set out at Example 2.2.2).

(a) Business units (other than permanent establishments)

50. A business unit means an entity or arrangement such as a company or a partnership and is intended to have the same meaning as is used in the CbCR rules. In order to meet the definition of a Constituent Entity, the business unit must be "included in the consolidated financial statements of the MNE Group". A business unit will be Constituent Entity of an MNE Group when it is consolidated with the Ultimate Parent Entity under the applicable accounting standard of that parent. These consolidation requirements apply a control test that requires the operations of the Constituent Entity to be consolidated with the rest of the MNE Group on a line-by-line basis. A non-controlled entity is not consolidated on a line-by-line basis in the consolidated financial statements of the MNE Group but rather is separately reported under the equity method. Such an entity is not considered a Constituent Entity under subparagraph (a) of the definition. A business unit that is not consolidated on a line-by-line basis because it is subject to special reporting treatment under an applicable accounting standard, for example, on the grounds that the business unit is held for sale, should continue to be treated as a Constituent Entity for tax purposes as long as it otherwise remains sufficiently within the control of the Ultimate Parent Entity to fall within the consolidation requirements of the applicable accounting standard.

Joint Operations

51. The phrase "included in the consolidated financial statements of the MNE Group" also refers to situations where an MNE Group has an investment in a joint operation such that a proportionate share of the assets, liabilities, income, and expenditures of that business unit are included in the consolidated financial statements on a line-by-line basis.[7] Therefore, a business unit that is treated as a joint operation should be treated as a separate Constituent Entity if the income and expenses of the joint operation are included in the group's consolidated financial statements in proportion to the group's ownership interest in the business unit. The Constituent Entity is comprised, however, only of the MNE Group's share of the joint operation as reflected in the consolidated financial statements.

52. For example, a Constituent Entity may be a partner of a partnership that is treated as a joint operation for financial accounting purposes and the MNE Group includes 40% of the income, expenditures, assets, and liabilities of the partnership in its consolidated financial statements. This partnership is treated as a separate Constituent Entity under the GloBE rules, however its GloBE tax base is determined based on the MNE Group's share of the partnership's income, expenditures, assets, and liabilities that are included in the consolidated financial statements and the MNE Group will be treated as controlling that Constituent Entity to the extent of that income.

Resident enterprises

53. A Constituent Entity that is a tax resident will be treated as a Constituent Entity located in its jurisdiction of tax residence. The Constituent Entity's jurisdiction of tax residence is the jurisdiction where the business unit is liable for a covered tax on its income based on its place of management, place of incorporation, or similar criteria. The legal character of the business unit is not determinative of whether it should be treated as a Constituent Entity. For example, if a partnership or trust is considered tax resident in a jurisdiction, it should be considered as a separate Constituent Entity from its owners for the purposes of these rules.

54. Where a jurisdiction does not have a corporate tax system then an entity that is incorporated in that jurisdiction (and is not tax resident in any other jurisdiction) is treated as located in its jurisdiction of incorporation. Therefore, an entity or arrangement that is incorporated or established in a jurisdiction which does not impose covered taxes is treated as a Constituent Entity in its jurisdiction of incorporation or establishment, unless it is tax resident under the laws of another jurisdiction (for example, under a place of effective management test).

Tax transparent entities or arrangements

55. An entity or arrangement that is treated as tax transparent by all of its owners and in the jurisdiction where it is created will be treated as a Constituent Entity under the GloBE rules if, as set out above, its assets, liabilities, income, and expenses are consolidated on a line-by-line basis in the consolidated financial statements of the MNE Group. This treatment of a tax transparent entity consolidated on a line-by-line basis is consistent with the requirements for CbCR. Such a tax transparent entity should be treated as a stateless entity. Under the rules of Section 3.4.2, however, all the income and expenses (and corresponding covered taxes) of that entity may be allocated to other Constituent Entities in the group. These other Constituent Entities could include the owners of the transparent entity or any permanent establishment of that entity (or the owners). The fact that a business unit does not have profit, losses, or covered taxes allocated to it under the GloBE rules does not, however, prevent a tax transparent entity from being treated as a separate Constituent Entity.

Hybrid and reverse-hybrid entities

56. Applying the above criteria, a hybrid entity (i.e. an entity that is treated as a separate entity for tax purposes in its jurisdiction of incorporation or creation, but as transparent by its owners) should be considered a Constituent Entity that is located in the jurisdiction where it is treated as resident.[8] A reverse-hybrid entity (i.e., a business unit that is treated as tax transparent in the jurisdiction where it was created but as a separate entity for tax purposes in the jurisdiction of at least one of its owners), on the other hand, is treated as a Constituent Entity that is not located in any jurisdiction (i.e., a stateless entity).

Dual resident entities

57. There may be cases where a Constituent Entity could be considered a tax resident of more than one jurisdiction. This outcome would be incompatible with the GloBE rules, which determine the ETR and top-up tax liability on a jurisdictional basis. In line with the specific instructions of the CbCR template contained in the Action 13 Final Report (OECD, 2015[1]), this potential for dual residency should be resolved, solely for purposes of the GloBE rules, in accordance with the tax treaty tie breaker rule agreed between the jurisdictions where the entity or arrangement has dual-residence (even if the rules are only relevant to a particular treaty entitlement). Further work will be undertaken to develop rules for determining a Constituent Entity's tax residence in case of no applicable tax treaty tie-breaker rule, or if the tax treaty tie-breaker rule does not solve the issue (e.g., it requires competent authorities to solve the issue through a MAP or denies tax treaty benefits).

(b) No exclusion based on size or materiality

58. The GloBE definition of Constituent Entity follows the treatment under CbCR by going beyond financial accounting to capture entities or arrangements that otherwise would be excluded from the consolidated financial statements on the grounds of size or materiality. The purpose of this extension in the CbCR rules was to capture information about business units that were excluded from the consolidated financial accounts because of their low levels of income or profitability. While these entities may not be material from a financial reporting stand point, they may still be considered to raise transfer pricing risks because the business unit may not have been adequately rewarded for the functions performed, assets used, and risks undertaken by that business unit. These entities or arrangements are also considered Constituent Entities of the MNE Group for GloBE purposes for similar reasons. The GloBE rules are applied on a jurisdictional basis and though an entity may be immaterial in the overall MNE Group context, it may be material from the perspective of a particular jurisdiction (for example, under the undertaxed payments rule). Furthermore, treating these entities as Constituent Entities will not unduly increase compliance burdens on MNE Groups as they are already required to gather and submit information for purposes of CbCR. Subparagraph (b) of the definition also addresses the situation where the MNE Group does not

prepare consolidated financial statements because it is not required to consolidate all of its subsidiaries as none of them meet the size or materiality threshold.

(c) Permanent establishments

59. Finally, paragraph (c) of the definition of Constituent Entity treats a permanent establishment as a separate Constituent Entity (that is, separate from the Constituent Entity that owns it) provided that the permanent establishment has separate financial statements for financial reporting, regulatory, tax reporting, or internal management control purposes. The need to distinguish the separate business operations undertaken in the permanent establishment and the head office is particularly relevant for jurisdictional blending. It ensures that the tax rate on income earned through permanent establishments in another jurisdiction is not blended with income of the head office in a different jurisdiction. In that sense, it ensures parity in the treatment of foreign subsidiaries and permanent establishments of the MNE Group, which is consistent with the policy and design elements of the GloBE.

60. The term "permanent establishment" is not defined in the CbCR rules. For purposes of the GloBE rules, whether a permanent establishment exists is determined in accordance with the applicable tax treaty in force. In case there is no applicable tax treaty in force, then a permanent establishment would be deemed to exist in a jurisdiction if it has a sufficient business presence in such jurisdiction that the income of the operations are taxed on a net basis pursuant to the applicable domestic law. In these cases, a taxable business presence will generally be determined by reference to factors such as whether the Constituent Entity has a place of business in a foreign jurisdiction or whether it is present for a particular period, acting through an agent or any criteria of similar nature. For example, if a Constituent Entity is a partner in a tax transparent partnership and is treated as having a permanent establishment in a jurisdiction because the partnership is managed and controlled or conducts substantial operations in the jurisdiction, then the permanent establishment of that Constituent Entity is, itself, a separate Constituent Entity. See Annex, Example 3.4.2G. Furthermore, for purposes of the GloBE rules, a permanent establishment is deemed to exist if the residence jurisdiction of the Constituent Entity that owns the branch or similar establishment treats it as a separate taxpayer from its resident taxpayer. For example, a branch would be considered as a permanent establishment and a separate Constituent Entity if its income is subject to a branch exemption in the owner's residence jurisdiction. In these situations, the permanent establishment is deemed to exist even if the jurisdiction where the branch is located does not exercise any taxing rights.

61. A branch or similar establishment of a Constituent Entity that meets the definition of a permanent establishment is treated as a separate Constituent Entity of the MNE Group in the jurisdiction in which it is located. Whether the permanent establishment is considered to be owned by another Constituent Entity under local law or tax treaties is not relevant for GloBE purposes. For example, when a UPE that is tax transparent maintains a branch in another jurisdiction that qualifies as a permanent establishment, that permanent establishment is treated as a Constituent Entity of the MNE Group for GloBE purposes, even if under local law or tax treaties it is considered a permanent establishment of the owners of the UPE.

2.2.3. Definition of the Ultimate Parent Entity

62. The definition of Ultimate Parent Entity (or UPE) is a keystone definition in the sense that it is used as a reference point for the application of other GloBE rules. For example, the definition is used to identify all the controlled entities that comprise the MNE Group including the identification of Excluded Entities and the definition is important for the mechanics of the income inclusion rule which are described below in Chapter 6.

63. The UPE is the Constituent Entity that directly or indirectly owns a controlling interest in all the other Constituent Entities that are part of the same MNE Group. The UPE is the entity that is or would be required to consolidate the financial accounts of all other Constituent Entities in the MNE Group. Paragraph (b) of the definition of Ultimate Parent Entity clarifies that an entity is not an Ultimate Parent Entity if there

is another entity in the group that owns sufficient interest in that entity that it would be required to consolidate the entity's accounts with its own. Generally, this element of the definition means that there is no entity within the MNE Group that owns a controlling interest in the Ultimate Parent Entity. However, it also applies to exclude an entity that owns the controlling interests in the Ultimate Parent Entity but that is not required to consolidate its accounts with those of the Ultimate Parent Entity. For example, investment entities such as funds may be permitted to report their investments, including majority ownership interests, in an MNE Group under the fair value method rather than consolidated accounting. These investment entities would, accordingly, not be treated as the UPE of such MNE Groups.

2.2.4. Associates and joint ventures

64. Accounting rules, such as IFRS 10, typically require the Ultimate Parent Entity to fully consolidate on a line-by-line basis, the assets, liabilities, income and expenditures of the entities or arrangements that it controls. This control test is based on de facto control and may apply to treat an entity or arrangement as consolidated even where the parent holds less than a majority stake in the equity interests of the entity or arrangement.

65. Where the Ultimate Parent Entity does not have direct or indirect control over the entity or arrangement it will not be required to consolidate the operations of an Associate or joint venture on a line–by-line basis. In this case the profit (or loss) of this entity is required to be reported under the equity method unless the investment is recognised as a non-current financial asset.[9] Entities and arrangements reported under the equity method will not be considered as Constituent Entities that are members of the MNE Group under the GloBE rules.

Associates

66. Under IFRS, an Associate is an entity or arrangement over which the investor has significant influence. An investor is presumed to have significant influence over an investment when the investor holds at least 20% of the investee's voting power.[10] Associates (entities or arrangements)[11] are typically reported under the equity method and therefore excluded from the definition of a "Constituent Entity" because that entity is not under the control of the Ultimate Parent Entity. Moreover, that same entity could be a subsidiary and fully consolidated on a line-by-line basis in the financial statements of another MNE Group, which would make it a Constituent Entity of that other group. Applying the GloBE rules to an Associate could therefore lead to significant complications in the applications of the GloBE rules where the same entity would be subject to the IIR and UTPR applied by different MNE Groups in different jurisdictions. For these reasons, an entity or arrangement should only be a Constituent Entity of the MNE Group if it is a business unit whose assets, liabilities, income, and expenditures are consolidated on a line-by-line basis in the consolidated financial statements of the MNE Group.[12] Section 8.2.2 discusses the application of a simplified income inclusion rule with respect to low-taxed income of Associate entities or arrangements.

Joint ventures

67. A joint venture is an arrangement whereby the parties that have joint control of the arrangement have rights to the net assets of the arrangement.[13] Joint ventures are excluded from the definition of a "Constituent Entity" because they do not have a single controlling equity interest holder and will generally be reported under the equity method of each MNE Group. The income of joint ventures may be subject to a simplified version of the income inclusion rule in accordance with Section 8.2.2 and may be treated as Orphan Entities under Section 8.3.

2.2.5. Use of acceptable accounting standards in defining MNE Group

68. The definitions set out above rely on the accounting principles applied, or that would be equity interests of the MNE Group were traded on a public securities exchange in its jurisdiction of tax residence, by an MNE Group in preparing consolidated financial statements for financial reporting purposes. As set out above, a Constituent Entity is any separate business unit that is included (on a line-by-line basis) in the consolidated financial statements of the MNE Group. Therefore, acceptable accounting standards and, in particular, the consolidation requirements of those standards play an important role in defining the scope of the GloBE rules.

69. The final report on Action 13 (OECD, 2015[1]) does not specify the use of any particular accounting standard for CbCR. Under CbCR, an MNE Group that is not required to prepare consolidated financial statements, may choose between its local general accepted accounting principles ("local GAAP") or the International Financial Reporting Standards ("IFRS"), except that if the Ultimate Parent Entity has its tax residence in a jurisdiction that requires a specific accounting standard for companies whose shares or interests are traded on a public securities exchange, the MNE Group must use that accounting standard. Jurisdictions with no securities exchange may specify one or more jurisdictions with a securities exchange that would be considered acceptable for these purposes. These rules apply equally to an MNE Group that prepares consolidated financial statements but is not required to do so.

70. The GloBE rules with respect to the determination of an acceptable accounting standard are set out below in Section 3.3.3. Applying the requirements of an applicable accounting standard in the context of the consolidation test will ensure consistency in the rules for determining the scope of the MNE Group. Moreover these determinations are likely to already be subject to examination by an independent financial accounting auditor. The requirements for determining acceptable accounting standards are discussed further in Section 3.3.3 below.

2.3. Excluded entities

71. Provided they meet the conditions in the definitions below, certain entities or arrangements that would otherwise be at the top of the group ownership chain are excluded from the application of the GloBE rules. These are investment funds, pension funds, sovereign wealth funds, government bodies, international organisations, and non-profit organisations. Further consideration will be given for cases where the exclusion should still apply in respect of a Constituent Entity that is not otherwise the UPE, such as certain life insurance and pension structures that are consolidated within an MNE Group and whose income is not beneficially owned by the MNE Group.

72. The entities or arrangements excluded from the scope of the GloBE rules all have a particular purpose and status under the laws of the jurisdiction in which they are created or established. This status is likely to result in that entity not being exposed to domestic income tax in order to preserve a specific intended policy outcome under the laws of that jurisdiction. The domestic tax outcome may, for example, be designed to ensure a single layer of taxation on vehicles used by investors (e.g. funds) or on retirement plans used by employees, or because the entity is carrying out governmental or quasi-governmental functions. The tax policy objectives of the domestic tax exemption for these types of entities neither are inconsistent with the tax policy objectives of the GloBE rules nor create a competitive distortion that would undermine the tax policy objectives of the GloBE proposal. Subjecting the income of such entities to tax under the GloBE rules would undermine the policy objectives that the domestic jurisdiction is seeking to achieve by granting the exemption without furthering the tax policy objectives of the GloBE rules.

73. In many cases, the entities described in this Section would not be Constituent Entities under the generally applicable rules discussed in Section 2.2. For example, investment and pension funds are likely to be "investment entities" that are not required to consolidate with investments that they control and,

therefore, would not meet the definition of a Constituent Entity. These entities will also typically be portfolio investors, often are unlikely to have foreign operations and in most cases will not hold controlling interests in foreign subsidiaries. However, in the interest of certainty, these entities have been expressly excluded, with the decision on exclusion guided by three key principles:

- Whether the tax policy rationale for the residence jurisdiction providing a nil or low rate of taxation for the sector is consistent with the GloBE tax policy rationale;
- Whether the exclusion is necessary to avoid the compliance and administration costs that might otherwise arise where such entities derive income that could fall within the scope of the rules;
- Whether an exclusion would be contrary to the policy of the GloBE rules by creating material competitive distortions as compared to other internationally operating businesses.

74. The list of Excluded Entities identified in this Section is intended to be in line with existing international tax principles and the policy of the GloBE rules, while providing certainty and consistency of treatment of these listed entities. The term "entity or arrangement" is intended to be broad and accommodate the different legal forms that such body may have, including public authorities.

75. The exclusions from the GloBE rules are specific to the entities or arrangements listed and do not extend to the entities that are controlled by the Excluded Entity but which do not themselves fall within any of the defined categories set out below. The definition can, however, extend to an entity or arrangement that is established and operated to hold assets or invest funds for the Excluded Entity (i.e. pure holding vehicles). This extension to the definition does not exclude an entity or arrangement that is carrying on or managing a commercial trade or business of the MNE Group. An entity or arrangement would not be treated as carrying on a trade or business if all or substantially all of its income is comprised of passive income (such as dividends, interest, and capital gains). Thus, for example, if an Excluded Entity such as a Governmental Entity or Non-profit Organisation holds a controlling stake in an MNE Group that otherwise exceeds the consolidated revenue threshold set out in Section 2.4 below, then the GloBE rules will continue to apply to all the members of that MNE Group other than the Excluded Entity.

Excluded Entities - Definitions

Excluded Entities

An entity that would otherwise be an Ultimate Parent Entity that is an investment fund, pension fund, governmental entity (including sovereign wealth funds), international organisation, or non-profit organisation will not be treated as a Constituent Entity of an MNE Group and will be excluded from the scope of the GloBE rules.

Investment Fund

Investment Fund means an entity or arrangement that meets all of the following criteria set out in paragraphs (a) to (f) below:

(a) it is designed to pool assets (which may be financial and non-financial) from an Excluded Entity or a number of investors (at least some of which are not connected);

(b) it invests in accordance with a defined investment policy and/or to reduce transaction costs and research and analytical costs and/or to spread risk collectively;

(c) it is primarily designed to generate investment income and/or gains or protection against a particular or general event or outcome;

(d) investors have a right to return from the assets of the fund, or income earned on those assets, based on the contributions made by those investors;

(e) the fund, or the management of the fund, is subject to the regulatory regime for investment funds in the jurisdiction in which it is established or managed (including appropriate anti-money laundering and investor protection regulation); and

(f) it is managed by fund management professionals on behalf of the investors.

The definition also includes any entity or arrangement that is wholly-owned or almost exclusively owned, directly or indirectly, by one or more Investment Funds or other Excluded Entity and that does not carry on a trade or business but is established and operated exclusively or almost exclusively to hold assets or invest funds for the benefit of such Investment Funds or other Excluded Entity.

Pension Fund

Pension Fund means an entity or arrangement that is established by a government (including any political subdivision or local authority) to provide social security, retirement or ancillary and incidental benefits or is established and operated in a jurisdiction exclusively or almost exclusively to administer or provide retirement benefits and ancillary or incidental benefits to individuals and that is regulated as such by that jurisdiction or one of its political subdivisions or local authorities.

The definition also includes any entity or arrangement that is wholly-owned, directly or indirectly, by one or more Pension Funds or established by a government (including any political subdivision or local authority) and that does not carry on a trade or business but is established and operated exclusively, or almost exclusively, to hold assets or invest funds for the benefit of Pension Funds.

Governmental Entity

Governmental Entity means an entity or arrangement that meets all of the following criteria set out in paragraphs (a) to (d) below:

(a) it is established by a government (including any political subdivision or local authority thereof);

(b) it has the principal purpose of:

  i. managing or investing that government's or jurisdiction's assets through the making and holding of investments, asset management, and related investment activities for the government's or jurisdiction's assets; or

  ii. fulfilment of a government function; and

  iii. does not carry on a commercial trade or business;

(c) it is accountable to the government on its overall performance, and provides annual information reporting to the government; and

(d) its assets vest in such government upon dissolution and to the extent it distributes net earnings, such net earnings are distributed solely to such government with no portion of its net earnings inuring to the benefit of any private person.

The definition also includes any entity or arrangement that is wholly-owned, directly or indirectly, by a Governmental Entity and that does not carry on a trade or business but is established and operated to hold assets, manage and invest funds, or conduct related investment activities for the benefit of that Governmental Entity.

International Organisation

International Organisation means any intergovernmental organisation (including a supranational organisation) or wholly owned agency or instrumentality thereof, that meets all of the following criteria set out in paragraphs (a) to (c) below:

(a) it is comprised primarily of governments;

(b) it has in effect a headquarters or substantially similar agreement (for example, arrangements that entitle the organisation's offices or establishments in the jurisdiction (e.g. a subdivision, or a local, or regional office) to privileges and immunities) with the jurisdiction in which it is established; and

(c) it is prevented by law or its governing documents from inuring its income to the benefit of private persons.

The definition includes any entity or arrangement that is wholly-owned, directly or indirectly, by an International Organisation, and that does not carry on a trade or business but is established and operated exclusively or almost exclusively to hold assets or invest funds for of the benefit of that International Organisation.

Non-profit Organisation

Non-profit Organisation means an entity or arrangement that meets all of the following criteria:

(a) it is established and operated in its jurisdiction of residence:

(i) exclusively for religious, charitable, scientific, artistic, cultural, athletic, or educational purposes; or

(ii) as a professional organisation, business league, chamber of commerce, labour organisation, agricultural or horticultural organisation, civic league or an organisation operated exclusively for the promotion of social welfare;

(b) it is wholly exempt from income tax in its jurisdiction of residence;

(c) it has no shareholders or members who have a proprietary or beneficial interest in its income or assets;

(d) the income or assets of the non-profit organisation may not be distributed to, or applied for the benefit of, a private person or non-charitable entity other than:

(i) pursuant to the conduct of the entity's charitable activities;

(ii) as payment of reasonable compensation for services rendered or for the use of property or capital; or

(iii) as payment representing the fair market value of property which the entity has purchased, and

(e) upon termination, liquidation or dissolution of the entity or arrangements, all of its assets must be distributed or revert to a Non-profit Organisation or to the government or any Governmental Entity of the entity's jurisdiction of residence or any political subdivision thereof;

but does not include any entity or arrangement carrying on a commercial trade or business that is not directly related to the purposes for which it was established.

Certain UPEs subject to tax neutrality regimes

The income of a UPE may be excluded from the GloBE rules where that income qualifies for tax neutral treatment under a tax transparency or taxable distribution regime in the jurisdiction where that entity is established or incorporated provided that the owners of the UPE are subject to an immediate tax on their share of the entity's income at a rate that equals or exceeds the minimum rate.

Investment funds

76. The need to preserve the tax neutrality in respect of investment funds is a widely recognised principle that underpins the design of the international tax rules. Under this principle, investment funds may be eligible for a special exemption, deduction, or other preferential treatment under the laws of the jurisdiction where they are established, to put the investors in the same position as if they had invested in the underlying assets of the fund directly, rather than through an investment fund vehicle.

77. The tax treatment of the investment fund is not driven by a need or desire to attract investment from one jurisdiction to another, but rather to allow collective investments to be made through the fund without imposing any additional tax burden on the investment return. This policy goal is relevant across all types of investment funds, including widely held collective investment vehicles such as mutual funds, as well as alternative investment funds generally open to a smaller group of investors. There are a range of fund vehicles that may be used to deliver tax neutral outcomes for investors and the operation of the GloBE rules should not distort these choices.

78. The tax neutrality of the fund does not mean that the investment returns earned by the fund go untaxed. The investment return will be subject to tax to the extent that the source country has chosen to impose taxation (e.g. by way of withholding tax on an investment return)[14] and a further layer of taxation may be imposed in the hands of the ultimate investor either on distribution or as the investment return accrues. The recent advances in tax transparency, such as through the Standard for Automatic Exchange of Financial Account Information in Tax Matters, have further strengthened the ability of tax administrations to access the information necessary to ensure that fund income is subject to the correct amount of taxation under the laws of the investor's jurisdiction of residence.

79. The fact that the fund itself is not exposed to tax for the above policy reasons does not therefore trigger the concerns that underpin the policy rationale for the GloBE rules. The neutrality of funds is a specific and generally supported tax policy rationale, which would be undermined if the GloBE rules were applied to the income of the fund resulting in an otherwise tax neutral investment vehicle being subject to an additional layer of taxation under the laws of another state. Given this approach is already widely adopted in domestic taxation systems, an exclusion for investment funds from the GloBE rules also does not provide a competitive advantage or create economic distortions. It is therefore appropriate to preserve the tax neutrality policy, by ensuring that fund vehicles are not exposed to the GloBE rules.

80. The definition of investment fund draws on the definition of "investment entity" in IFRS 10, European Union Alternative Investment Fund Managers Directive 2011/61/EU (AIFMD), and the IMF definition of collective investment schemes used in the Balance of Payment statistics. As set out in the box above, an investment fund is an entity or arrangement that is designed to pool assets from unrelated investors (or an Excluded Entity or Entities) and that is managed by professionals on behalf of those investors. The assets of a fund include both financial and non-financial assets including rights to such assets such as options. The definition applies only to an entity or arrangement established for the purpose of collective investment which is regulated as such, whether directly in the jurisdiction where the fund is established, or indirectly through a requirement in the jurisdiction of the investment fund that it be managed by a regulated fund manager (which may be established and regulated in a different jurisdiction). The definition does not apply to unregulated investment vehicles such as family held companies.

81. The exclusion does not require that the fund benefit from a special tax status under the laws of the jurisdiction where it is established but requires that the entity or arrangement has the hallmarks of a collective investment vehicle, which include a professional manager investing under a defined investment policy. Fund management professionals may include custodians or brokers that are responsible for implementing the fund's investment policy and executing transactions on behalf of the fund. The definition requires that there be an Excluded Entity as an investor, or at least two unconnected investors in the entity or arrangement but does not otherwise limit the types or number of investors.

82. The final part of the definition recognises that an Investment Fund may use special purpose vehicles to hold assets or to make certain investments. Such entities or arrangements essentially function as part of the infrastructure of the fund itself, and should be treated as part of the Excluded Entity. The exclusion for special purpose vehicles does not extend to entities that carry on or otherwise have responsibility for managing a trade or business of the MNE Group itself. The definition also provides for cases where the entity or arrangement is held by more than one separate Investment Fund, or by one or more Investment Funds together with another Excluded Entity such as a pension fund. The definition also accommodates cases where, for regulatory or commercial reasons, the fund manager may be required to hold a de minimis shareholding in the entity or arrangement.

83. The definition of Excluded Entity set out in the box above applies to entities in the MNE Group that are at the top of the ownership chain. This definition, however, does not comprehensively address the issues associated with controlled investment funds (i.e. a fund that is controlled by a Constituent Entity of an MNE Group that is not an Excluded Entity). For example, further technical rules may be required to avoid the potential application of the IIR to a controlled fund under the top-down approach and the split-ownership rules. Further guidance may also be required as to the treatment of controlled investment funds under the UTPR. The Inclusive Framework will undertake further technical work regarding the treatment of investment funds to identify whether further rules are needed to preserve the tax neutral outcomes for investment funds under Pillar Two and to consider the application of the GloBE rules to controlled investment funds and the outcomes of this work will be incorporated into the model rules.

2.3.1. Pension funds

84. In many jurisdictions, pension funds are tax exempt in respect of the income they generate for the beneficiaries of the fund. A significant number of jurisdictions use the approach of "exempt – exempt – taxed", where the contribution to the fund is tax exempt, the income generated by the pension fund is tax exempt, and the return is taxed in the hands of the beneficiary upon distribution. The tax exemption of a pension fund may be achieved through a number of mechanisms, for example, by treating the pension fund as a transparent entity for domestic tax purposes, or by granting a specific exemption or preference under domestic tax law.

85. The policy rationale for this treatment is to encourage employees and firms to put in place structures that allow the employee to spread their employment earnings more evenly over their lifetime and to do this in a way that achieves consistency in the tax treatment for the employee. In an economic sense, these vehicles bring taxes on employment income closer to the design of a consumption tax by deferring the imposition of tax until income is actually spent. The "exempt – exempt – taxed" model encourages employees to defer a portion of their employment earnings by allowing them to capture, in full, the untaxed value of any investment returns that accrue up to the time of distribution. This tax policy is viewed as increasingly important by a number of Inclusive Framework members that consider such investment vehicles to be an important tool in addressing the need to support ageing populations. In the case of pension plans for government employees, taxation of the pension fund would simply result in an inefficient circular flow of taxation and expenditures as the government would need to increase the contributions to the fund to meet the pension's tax liabilities. A similar logic applies in respect of private pension funds, where there is a public interest in ensuring a stable retirement income to reduce the

pressure on the public social security system, and where imposing taxation in the short term would raise revenue from one source to fund another.

86. The exclusion of Pension Funds from the IIR and UTPR preserves the ability of governments to meet their domestic tax policy goals, which have informed the tax treatment of their pension funds. To do otherwise would undermine the policy of maximising the returns earned by the pension fund structure for the beneficiaries. Pension Funds, which effectively operate as a tax preferred personal savings account do not otherwise compete with other internationally operating business. It is therefore appropriate to preserve that policy, by ensuring that Pension Funds are not exposed to the minimum tax.

87. The definition of pension fund follows the definition of "recognised pension fund" used in the OECD Model Tax Convention (OECD, 2017[2]), Article 3, paragraph (i). The definition has been modified to remove reference to the fund being taxable as a separate person in the jurisdiction of formation, to allow for pension funds formed in a different legal arrangement such as a trust. The definition applies to both public and private Pension Funds provided it is a regulated investment vehicle providing services to individual members of the public (or a defined category thereof). The definition has been modified to accommodate cases where an entity that performs the function in sub-paragraph (b) of holding assets or investing funds for the pension fund is not owned by that pension fund but is established by a government.

2.3.2. Governmental Entities

88. In some cases, a government entity may hold an investment in an MNE Group. In most cases, these investments of government entities will be held through a sovereign wealth fund. Sovereign wealth funds are commonly established out of balance of payments surpluses, official foreign currency operations, the proceeds of privatisations, fiscal surpluses or receipts resulting from commodity exports. [15] The function of a sovereign wealth fund is to invest these amounts for the purpose of managing a country's future fiscal needs, stabilising a country's balance of payments and in order to strike an appropriate balance between domestic consumption and savings.

89. Different approaches to the taxation of sovereign wealth funds are taken around the world. They are generally treated as tax exempt in the jurisdiction where they are established, although in some countries, sovereign wealth funds are not tax exempt and otherwise pay ordinary tax in respect of their income. In the source jurisdiction, the practice is more varied. In some source jurisdictions, the income of a foreign sovereign wealth fund may be entirely exempt from tax or only in respect of certain types of income (such as being limited to non-commercial investment income). This exemption may apply by virtue of domestic tax law or only where such treatment is granted under a double tax treaty. The different approaches to the taxation of sovereign wealth funds reflect different domestic national interests and mutual arrangements between jurisdictions. It also reflects that there is a variety of policy views, such as different concepts of sovereign immunity.

90. Where a Governmental Entity such as a sovereign wealth fund has a low ETR under the GloBE this is likely to reflect the specific tax treatment granted to that entity because of the exercise of its government functions. In such a case, it would seem counter-intuitive to require a top-up tax. If it were otherwise, the GloBE rules could have the effect that the government in the residence jurisdiction would be incentivised to impose taxation on itself in order to prevent its own revenue being exposed to a top-up tax by other governments through the UTPR.

91. The reference in the definition to "established by government" limits the scope to governmental entities that are public in nature, including where established by specific statute or as a wholly-owned government corporation. To ensure that the exclusion for governmental entities does not result in competitive distortions with respect to internationally operating businesses, the exclusion only applies to entities that have the principal purpose of managing or investing that government or jurisdiction's assets and / or fulfilment of a government function such as the administration of programmes for the general public

with respect to the common welfare. It does not apply if the entity is carrying on or managing a commercial trade or business. For the avoidance of doubt, carrying out the principal purpose of the entity (as described in (b)(i) and b(ii) of the definition above) does not constitute carrying on a commercial trade or business.

2.3.3. International organisations

92. The rationale for excluding international organisations is similar to that which applies to the exclusion for Governmental Entities. International organisations such as supranational organisations or development finance organisations are funded by governments. Taxing these organisations on their low tax profit would undo the benefit of the tax exemptions granted to these organisations by agreement under international law. The definition of international organisation follows the definition used in the Standard for Automatic Exchange of Financial Account Information in Tax Matters (OECD, 2014[3]). The language in paragraph (b) includes an explanation of a "substantially similar agreement" which is taken from Commentary to that Standard.

2.3.4. Non-profit organisations

93. There is a range of non-profit organisations that work for a public purpose, without a view to returning profit to shareholders. Jurisdictions generally provide a tax exemption to such entities, recognising their public purpose, to encourage contributions to such entities, and to maximise the returns available for the intended public good. The provision of these tax exemptions is generally subject to a series of domestic law conditions that must be satisfied, and which are scrutinised by the tax administration.

94. The definition of non-profit organisation follows the definition of "Active Non-Financial Entity (NFE)" (paragraph (h)) used in the Standard for Automatic Exchange of Financial Account Information in Tax Matters. Where non-profit organisations have been granted a domestic tax exemption, the GloBE rules would not operate to reverse this treatment. Given the non-profit purpose of such entities, the exclusion of these entities from the GloBE rules should not give rise to a risk of competitive distortion between non-profit organisations and internationally operating business.

95. The exclusion does not apply to an MNE that is headed by a non-profit foundation or similar type entity that simply serves as the holding company for an internationally operating commercial business. A non-profit organisation that engages in business activity unrelated to the charitable purpose will also not qualify for this exception from the GloBE rules. Moreover, the exclusion is restricted to entities that do not distribute their income or assets to private persons or non-charitable organisations other than in particular situations described in the box above.

2.3.5. UPEs subject to certain tax neutrality regimes

96. In order to provide a tax neutral outcome for investors, a jurisdiction may treat certain entities or arrangements as transparent for tax purposes or permit that entity or arrangement to make taxable distributions to its investors. Under these tax transparency and taxable distribution regimes, the tax on the entity's income is effectively paid at the level of the owner, either by taxing that owner directly on its allocable share of the entity's income (in the case of a tax transparent vehicle) or by taxing the owners on a deductible dividend or other distribution paid by the entity (in the case of a taxable distribution regime).

97. The treatment of tax transparent and taxable distribution entities that are Constituent Entities is discussed in Sections 3.4.2 and 3.3.4. These rules ensure that any covered tax paid on allocated or distributed income at the shareholder level is taken into account under the GloBE rules and is treated as tax paid on such income.

98. However, where the entity subject to these tax transparency or deductible dividend regimes is the Ultimate Parent Entity, then the owners that pay the tax on the underlying income will not be Constituent

Entities of the MNE Group and therefore their tax liability will not be taken into account in computing the entity's ETR under the GloBE rules and accordingly could give rise to a UTPR adjustment. Accordingly, special rules are required to address these regimes.

99. The rules set out in the box above allow an entity that is the UPE of the MNE Group to exclude its own income from the potential application of the UTPR where that income qualifies for tax neutral treatment under a tax transparency or taxable distribution regime in the jurisdiction where that entity is established or incorporated. In order for a UPE to benefit from this exclusion, the regime must meet the following criteria:

a. the owners are subject to tax in that jurisdiction on their share of the entity's income,

b. the owner's tax liability arises immediately, and

c. the owners are subject to tax at a rate that equals or exceeds the minimum rate.

100. These criteria are described in further detail below.

Tax transparency regimes

101. Tax transparency regimes represent the most common approach to single level taxation. Under these regimes, the entity or arrangement is not subject to tax on its income. Instead, the income of the entity is passed through to the owners proportionally and taxed at the owner level. Because the entity is not itself subject to tax, absent special rules, its income would, in many cases, be subject to tax under the GloBE rules because the ETR on that income would generally be zero.

102. The owners of the UPE are not Constituent Entities, and therefore, any taxes paid by the owners would not ordinarily be taken into account in the computation of the ETR under the GloBE rules. Absent a special rule, tax transparency at the level of the UPE would produce a GloBE tax liability because the income of the UPE would be subject to a nil rate of tax. The UPE's income may be subject to tax in the hands of the owners and thus not subject to low rates of tax overall. However, the GloBE rules generally do not take account of tax paid by owners that are not Constituent Entities for two reasons. First, they are not taxes paid by the MNE Group and the GloBE rules apply to MNE Groups and seek to ensure that they are subject to a minimum level of tax on their income, not that owners of MNE Groups are subject to a minimum level of tax on their income. Second, assigning tax paid by non-Constituent Entity owners to Constituent Entities is not feasible, in part, because the UPE does not control its owners and cannot demand that they provide the necessary information. Even if such owners were willing to provide such information, it would be difficult to separate their tax liability on the entity's income from their liability with respect to other income unless the jurisdiction applied a schedular regime for the entity's income.

103. Nevertheless, there may be circumstances where tax administrations can be confident that the owners of a tax transparent entity are subject to tax above the minimum rate on the entire income of the entity. An illustration of this type of tax transparency regime is given in Example 2.3.6A in relation to the treatment of "S corporations" under Sections 1361 – 1379 of the US Federal Revenue Code.

104. An S corporation has three characteristics that indicate its income will be subject to tax in the hands of the shareholders at above the minimum rate:

a. The first is that the owners of the S Corp must be US tax residents.

b. The second is that the owners are subject to immediate taxation on their share of the income as if they earned the income directly.

c. The third is that the owners are generally subject to tax on their share of the income.

105. These characteristics mean that, by virtue of the design of the S Corporation regime, the owners of the S corporation can be expected to be subject to an immediate US tax on their share of the entity's

income at a rate that equals or exceeds the minimum rate. The S corporation regime is therefore an example of tax neutrality regime where the income that is attributable to the shareholders should be excluded from the calculation of GloBE income. The same principles set out in the paragraph above can be applied to determine whether other tax transparency regimes should benefit from this exception.

106. The treatment of tax transparent regimes described in this Section is limited to the income of the UPE and the treatment is limited to income taxable under the laws of the UPE jurisdiction. In most instances, the income allocated to the owner will be taxable in the UPE jurisdiction on the basis of the residency of the owner, however where the income is allocated to a non-resident but remains taxable in the UPE's jurisdiction at or above the minimum rate on the basis of source then this income would similarly be excluded from the GloBE rules. Further technical work will be undertaken to determine whether and to what extent taxes levied under the law of UPE jurisdiction on the income of a foreign Constituent Entity (such as domestic tax on a foreign branch) should also be included within the ETR calculation under the GloBE rules.

Distribution deduction regimes

107. Jurisdictions may provide tax regimes that are designed to produce a single level of taxation on certain cooperative or pooled activities of taxpayers. Under these regimes, the corporation is generally subject to tax on its income, but is allowed a deduction for certain distributions to owners or participants in the collective enterprise. Distribution deduction regimes are generally available for investment funds and other passive investment vehicles which are excluded from the scope of the GloBE rules. Corporations subject to distribution tax regimes that qualify as investment funds under Section 0 will be excluded from the definition of UPE under the exclusion for investment funds and no special rule is needed. However, in a narrow range of cases an active businesses may be entitle to make deductible distributions to its shareholders. For example, an agricultural cooperative corporation that buys apples from its members and markets them collectively may be allowed a deduction for distributions of profits from apple sales to each member in proportion to the corporation's purchases of apples from the member. In most cases, co-operative companies are unlikely to meet to consolidated revenue threshold necessary to bring them within the scope of the GloBE rules. However where a company that benefits from a distribution deduction regime is the UPE[16] of an MNE Group that is not an Excluded Group.

108. The income of the entity should only be exempt from the GloBE rules if the owners are subject to tax in the jurisdiction on their share of the entity's income, the owners' tax liability arises immediately, and the owners are subject to tax on the distributions at a rate that equals or exceeds the minimum rate. Typically, to qualify for the distribution deduction, distributions must be made during the entity's tax year or within a brief period after the end of the year. For GloBE purposes, the second criteria is considered met if the distribution occurs within a reasonable period following the end of the entity's tax year. Under these circumstances, a UPE subject to a distribution deduction regime is permitted to deduct distributions in the same manner as permitted under local tax law in computing its income for GloBE purposes.

109. The principles discussed above have been used to inform the treatment of tax regimes that are intended to preserve tax neutrality. The foregoing discussion broadly describes the types of tax regimes to which the rules apply but does not describe or address all the design features of tax neutrality regimes that may fall within the rules. For those Inclusive Framework on BEPS members that introduce the GloBE rules it is expected that they will assess their own tax neutrality regimes against the principles discussed in this Section. As described further in Section 10.5.2 the same multilateral process for determining whether a jurisdiction has introduced an IIR in line with GloBE requirements could be used to assess whether a jurisdiction's tax neutrality regime was consistent with the principles set out in this Pillar Two Blueprint.

2.3.6. Application of the GloBE rules to international shipping

110. The GloBE rules are designed to apply to all operating businesses. The exclusion of any specific sector could raise additional BEPS risks and fairness issues among different business sectors and jurisdictions. This could undermine the effectiveness of the GloBE rules. However, the unique features of the international shipping industry will require further work on whether, and to what extent, the GloBE rules should apply to this industry.

111. The international shipping industry is subject to special tax rules. The capital intensive nature, the level of profitability and long economic life cycle of international shipping has led a number of jurisdictions to introduce alternative or supplementary taxation regimes for this industry. Taxes, such as tonnage taxes, may result in less volatile outcomes for shipping and provide a more stable basis for long term investment. The widespread availability of these alternative tax regimes means that international shipping often operates outside the scope of corporate income tax. Including international shipping within the scope of the GloBE rules would therefore raise policy questions in light of the policy choices of these jurisdictions.

112. Additionally, if international shipping was included within the scope of Pillar Two, questions have been raised regarding the implications of this, noting that the revenue effect may be limited given the design includes an unlimited loss carry-forward, a formulaic substance-based carve-out and tonnage taxes would constitute covered taxes. Finally, the typical operating model of an international shipping firm is such that most shipping income is sourced from third parties or other group members that are subject to low or alternative taxation regimes. This operational structure may render the undertaxed payments rule an ineffective back-stop to the income inclusion rule meaning that applying the GloBE rules could lead to competitive distortions and unstable outcomes.

2.4. Consolidated Revenue Threshold

Excluded MNE Groups

MNE Groups having total consolidated group revenue below EUR 750 million or equivalent in the immediately preceding fiscal year of the Group, are excluded from the application of the GloBE rules. For the purposes of this rule:

(a) The consolidated group revenue threshold is applied to all those Constituent Entities that are owned and controlled by the same Ultimate Parent Entity.

(b) The term "fiscal year" means the annual accounting period with respect to which the Ultimate Parent Entity of the MNE Group prepares its financial statements.

113. The GloBE rules will apply to MNE Groups that have annual consolidated revenue of EUR 750 million or more in the immediately preceding fiscal year or a near equivalent in domestic currency. This is the same threshold that applies under the CbCR rules.[17]

2.4.1. Consolidated revenue threshold

114. The general rule set out in the box above limits the application of the GloBE rules to MNE Groups whose consolidated group revenue is at least EUR 750 million. The EUR 750 million threshold has several advantages.

115. **Synergies with the CbCR rules**, which are used for other elements of the GloBE rules, such as the definitions set out above that deal with the composition of the MNE Group. Furthermore MNE's that are not subject to CbCR have no independent financial reporting reason to separately report the income of the branch and head office of the same entity as they are required to under the GloBE rules. The use of the same threshold may also facilitate the use of simplification options.

116. **Use of financial accounts.** A number of design elements of the GloBE rules rely on consolidated financial accounts. A significant majority of in-scope MNE Groups are publicly accountable (listed) companies that are already required to report consolidated financial information to investors under IFRS or an equivalent standard.[18] A lower threshold would pick up more private companies that are not required to prepare consolidated financial accounts (or where they do it may be in local GAAP).

117. **Avoid adverse impacts on SMEs.** The use of the CbCR reporting threshold will exclude small and medium enterprises (SMEs) operating in more than one jurisdiction, where the application of these rules could be a significantly greater burden. A EUR 750 million revenue threshold will mean that between 85% and 90% of MNE Groups will be outside the scope of the rules. This, in turn, reduces the pressure on Inclusive Framework on BEPS members to provide carve-outs from the GloBE rules for SMEs that benefit from targeted domestic tax incentives.

118. **It preserves the impact of the GloBE rules**. MNE Groups that are within the scope of CbCR earn over 90% of global corporate revenues. Accordingly the threshold preserves the impact of GloBE rules.

2.4.2. Previous fiscal year

119. The EUR 750 million threshold is determined by reference to the total consolidated group revenue of the MNE Group during the immediately preceding fiscal year. This mirrors the rules for determining the MNE Groups to which the CbCR rules apply.[19] Therefore, whether an MNE Group is required to apply the GloBE rules is based on the preceding year's consolidated revenue regardless of whether its consolidated revenue is below or above the threshold in the year for which it is applying the rules.

120. Paragraphs 1 and 2 of the rule make reference to a "fiscal year". Taxable years can vary from one jurisdiction to another. Some jurisdictions use the calendar year as their taxable year, while others use a different period (e.g., some jurisdictions allow taxpayers to choose their taxable year). A fiscal year could also have an irregular duration because the entity or arrangement was created and/or started business operations in that calendar year. These differences justify the need to define fiscal year for purposes of the GloBE rules. An MNE Group may have Constituent Entities in jurisdictions with different required or permitted taxable years. However, the MNE Group will use the same fiscal year for all of its Constituent Entities in its consolidated financial reports because the GloBE tax base is determined primarily based on the MNE Group's consolidated financial statements. Given that CbCR Model Legislation already has a definition of "Fiscal Year" and the similarities between the CbCR and GloBE rules, the rule mirrors the CbCR definition, which is based on the MNE Group's fiscal year for consolidated financial accounting purposes.

2.4.3. Calculating the consolidated revenue threshold

121. The threshold set out above applies based on the consolidated revenue of the MNE Group. As explained in Section 2.2, the definition of MNE Group under the GloBE rules, like CbCR, relies on the UPE's applicable financial accounting standard to determine whether a subsidiary's accounts are consolidated and thus whether it is a Constituent Entity. The consolidated revenue of all Constituent Entities is included in the determination of the threshold irrespective of whether the MNE Group owns all of the equity interests in the Constituent Entity. Stated differently, no deduction for amounts that accrue to minority interest holders in a Constituent Entity should be made in the determination of the MNE Group's

total revenue. However, the revenue of two MNE Groups or different standalone entities that are not part of the same consolidated financial statement should not be aggregated even if they are controlled by the same person (e.g. an individual).

122. This situation could arise in the case of investment entities that control two different MNE Groups. According to IFRS 10, investment entities are not required to consolidate an investment in a subsidiary, unless the main purposes and activities of the subsidiary is to provide services related to the investment entity's activities. Thus, an investment entity that is the controlling shareholder of two or more MNE Groups would typically not consolidate these groups into its financial statements and would not be considered as the Ultimate Parent Entity of these groups.

123. This is illustrated in Example 2.4.3 of Annex A where an investment fund controls two separate MNE Groups with annual consolidated revenue of EUR 500 million each. If the investment entity meets the definition of an investment entity in accordance with IFRS 10 or similar financial accounting standards, the entity will not be required to consolidate the MNE Groups. In these cases, each MNE Group would typically have separate consolidated financial statements, and these groups would be considered as separate MNE Groups. As such, they would separately determine whether they meet the threshold described in this Section.

124. The approach set out in the previous paragraphs is in line with CbCR rules. CbCR rules do not consider investment funds or entities as the Ultimate Parent Entity of an MNE Group unless accounting rules instruct them to consolidate with investee companies. The Guidance on the Implementation of CbCR states that investment funds or entities that are investees are not considered as Constituent Entities or part of a Group or an MNE Group unless they are consolidated by the Group.

125. The entities that are excluded from the GloBE rules are not considered as Constituent Entities of an MNE Group. Therefore, the revenue of these entities is excluded from computation of the threshold even if they are consolidated on a line-by-line basis in the financial statements of an MNE Group. Furthermore, given that these entities would not qualify as the Ultimate Parent Entity of an MNE Group, the subgroups that they control would be accounted as if the Excluded Entity was not the parent entity for consolidation purposes. This is also illustrated in Example 2.4.3 of Annex A, in which FUND can be an entity excluded in accordance to Section on excluded entities. Moreover, the consolidated revenue of the remaining Constituent Entities of MNE Group may need further adjustments for purposes of the threshold computation. For example, any intragroup payments from the Excluded Entity to the rest of the MNE Group should be reflected for purposes of the revenue threshold because these payments are eliminated in the consolidated financial statements.

126. Further work could be undertaken to consider whether the consolidation threshold should be supplemented with a targeted anti-avoidance rule to avoid the fragmentation of a single MNE Group into different subgroups in order to avoid the EUR 750 M threshold. This work would need to take into account the on-going work on the 2020 Country-by-Country (BEPS Action 13 Minimum Standard) review process and the outcomes from this work would be incorporated into the development of model rules (see Section 10.5.1 below).

References

IWG (2008), *Generally Accepted Principles and Practices — "Santiago Principles"*, IWG, https://www.ifswf.org/sites/default/files/santiagoprinciples_0_0.pdf. [5]

OECD (2019), *Guidance on the Implementation of Country-by-Country Reporting – BEPS Action 13*, OECD Publishing, Paris, https://www.oecd.org/ctp/guidance-on-the-implementation-of-country-by-country-reporting-beps-action-13.pdf. [4]

OECD (2017), *Model Tax Convention on Income and on Capital*, OECD Publisher, Paris, https://doi.org/10.1787/mtc_cond-2017-en. [2]

OECD (2015), *Transfer Pricing Documentation and Country-by-Country Reporting, Action 13 - 2015 Final Report*, OECD/G20 Base Erosion and Profit Shifting Project, OECD Publishing, Paris, https://dx.doi.org/10.1787/9789264241480-en. [1]

OECD (2014), *Standard for Automatic Exchange of Financial Account Information in Tax Matters*, OECD Publishing, Paris, https://doi.org/10.1787/9789264216525-en. [3]

Notes

1 The term "enterprise" is used in definitions of "Group" and "MNE Group" in the CbCR Model Legislation. This term is included in the definition to maintain consistency between GloBE and CbCR definitions. For these purposes, the term "enterprise" is broadly equivalent to the term "business unit" which is used as part of the definition of Constituent Entity.

2 See BEPS Action 13 Report (p. 39) (OECD, 2015[1]).

3 See BEPS Action 13 Report (p. 39) (OECD, 2015[1]).

4 See BEPS Action 13 Report (p. 39) (OECD, 2015[1]).

5 In brief, and as described further below, the differences between the definitions under CbCR and GloBE are: 1) the reference to "Excluded Group" (subsection (ii)) was eliminated from the definition of "MNE Group" because the GloBE rules deal with the EUR 750 million threshold in a separate rule; 2) the term "business unit" was eliminated from subparagraph (a) from the definition of "Constituent Entity" to clarify the operation of the deemed consolidation test; 3) a last sentence was added to the definition of "Constituent Entity" to make reference to the excluded entities in accordance with the Section 0. Minor formatting changes have also been made to align with the overall design of the GloBE rules.

6 The definitions for CbCR are currently being evaluated as part of the 2020 Country-by-Country Reporting (BEPS Action 13 Minimum Standard) review process.

7 This is in line with paragraph 20 of IFRS 11 as well as the Guidance on the Implementation of Country-by-Country Reporting (December 2019) (OECD, 2019[4]). See *Treatment of an entity owned and/or operated by more than one unrelated MNE Groups* (p.19).

8 Under this section, an entity or arrangement is created in a jurisdiction if it was incorporated, organized, or created based on the domestic laws of such jurisdiction.

9 Typically, where the MNE's stake in a company is less than 20%, it would report its investment in its consolidated financial statements as a non-current financial asset e.g., IFRS 9 – Financial Instruments.

10 Paragraph 3 of IAS28. IFRS Foundation.

[11] "Associate" is an accounting term which is different to the term "associated enterprise" as used in the context of transfer pricing.

[12] This includes joint operations where a portion of its assets, liabilities, income, and expenditures are consolidated on a line-by-line basis. See section 2.2.2.

[13] Paragraph 16 of IFRS 11. IFRS Foundation.

[14] Double taxation treaties typically limit the source country's taxing rights over dividends, interest and capital gains derived by a resident of another country. However for procedural reasons, investment funds and / or fund investors cannot always effectively claim the withholding tax relief to which they are entitled under such treaties, leading to over-taxation.

[15] See International Working Group of Sovereign Wealth Funds, Sovereign Wealth Funds — Generally Accepted Principles and Practices — "Santiago Principles" (IWG, 2008[5]), October 2008, Annex 1; also replicated in 2017 Model Tax Convention (OECD, 2017[2]), Commentary on Article 4, paragraph 8.5

[16] Special rules are prescribed in section 3.3.4 for the treatment of dividends distributed by Constituent Entities that are subject to distribution tax regimes and for dividends received by Constituent Entities from corporations subject to distribution tax regimes. Those rules would ensure that the Constituent Entity's income would not be subject to the GloBE rules at the entity level simply due a dividends paid deduction, thus preserving the jurisdiction's single level of tax policy, while simultaneously ensuring that the MNE Group's share of the entity's income remains subject to the GloBE rules.

[17] See further discussion in Section 10.3.

[18] See section 3.3.1 below on *Profit or loss determined in accordance with financial accounting standard.*

[19] This rule is currently under review as part of the 2020 Review of Country-by-Country Reporting.

3 Calculating the ETR under the GloBE rules

3.1. Overview

127. This chapter sets out the rules for determining an MNE's effective tax rate (ETR) under the GloBE rules. The Globe ETR is determined by dividing the amount of covered taxes by the amount of income as determined under the GloBE rules. Section 3.2 below sets out the definition of covered taxes and Section 3.3 describes the methodology for calculating an MNE's income for GloBE purposes. As described in further detail in Section 3.3, the GloBE rules start with the financial accounts that are prepared under the same accounting standard that is used by the parent of the MNE to prepare its consolidated financial statements. The rules then require certain adjustments to be made to those financial accounts to eliminate specific items of income from the tax base, such as intra-group dividends, and to incorporate certain expenses, such as tax deductible stock-based compensation. Section 3.3 also describes a number of modifications that can be made to the tax base to address differences in the timing in the recognition of income and taxes. The first modification, described in Section 3.3.5, addresses timing issues that can arise through immediate expensing and accelerated depreciation of assets for local law purposes. The second modification, described in Section 3.3.6, addresses the timing issues raised by distribution-based corporate income tax systems. Finally, Section 3.3.8 describes an exclusion from the GloBE tax base for emergency government assistance.

128. The GloBE ETR is calculated on a jurisdictional basis as described further in Section 3.4. The jurisdictional ETR computation requires assignment of the income and taxes among the jurisdictions in which the MNE operates and to which it pays taxes. Generally, the income of the MNE is assigned to the jurisdiction of the Constituent Entity that earned the income with each permanent establishment being treated as a separate Constituent Entity. The corresponding covered taxes on that income are then assigned to the jurisdiction that has been allocated the income. Special rules address the treatment of entities that are tax transparent and that do not have any tax jurisdiction of residence.

3.2. Covered taxes

Definition of covered taxes

Covered taxes means any tax on an entity's income or profits (including a tax on distributed profits), and includes any taxes imposed in lieu of a generally applicable income tax. Covered taxes also includes taxes on retained earnings and corporate equity.

A tax is a compulsory unrequited payment to general government.

129. The definition of covered taxes aligns the numerator (i.e. the measure of covered taxes) and the denominator (i.e. the measure of net income) in the GloBE's ETR calculation so that the taxes imposed on income included in the GloBE tax base are treated as a covered tax for the purposes of determining the GloBE ETR. The definition of covered taxes is developed solely for the purposes of the GloBE rules and has no direct interaction with Article 2 (Taxes Covered) of the OECD Model Tax Convention (OECD, 2017[1]), which is developed for the distinct purpose of eliminating double taxation. Taxes that do not qualify for the definition of covered taxes under the GloBE, such as excise taxes and payroll taxes, will be treated as deductible in the computation of the GloBE tax base (i.e. as reductions to the denominator in the GloBE's ETR calculation).

130. The definition of covered taxes applies not only to taxes imposed on income at the time such income is derived but also on taxes that are imposed on a subsequent distribution of profits. The definition further applies to any tax that is imposed in lieu of a generally applicable income tax. The definition of covered taxes also includes taxes on retained earnings and corporate equity. In determining whether a tax is a covered tax, the focus is on the underlying character of the tax. The name that is given to a tax or the mechanism used to collect it (such as through a withholding mechanism) is not determinative of its character. Whether a tax charge is levied under a jurisdiction's corporate income tax rules or under a separate regime or statute does not have any bearing on its underlying character. Whether a tax is deductible is not relevant to determining whether it is a covered tax.

131. The definition of tax is based on the OECD's longstanding definition of taxes used for statistical purposes, with the same definition equally used by many international organisations (IMF, World Bank, United Nations, European Union) (OECD, 2018[2]), and which defines taxes as any compulsory unrequited payment to general government. General government is a defined term in the UN-OECD National Accounts that includes the central administration, agencies whose operations are under its effective control, state and local governments and their administrations (OECD, 2018[2]). Taxes are unrequited in the sense that any benefits provided by government to the taxpayer are not in proportion to their payments. Thus, fees and payments for privileges, services, property, or other benefits provided by government do not qualify as taxes. Similarly, taxes do not include fines and penalties nor do they include interest or similar charges with respect to payments of tax liabilities after the applicable due date.

3.2.1. Design principles

132. The agreement on a definition of covered taxes under the GloBE rules has been guided by a number of principles:

- **Align with the GloBE tax base and avoid double taxation.** Because the GloBE tax base covers a wide range of income and gains, it is imperative that the GloBE ETR calculation similarly adopts an expansive definition of covered taxes in order to accommodate the present and future design of tax systems and to avoid the risk of double taxation.
- **Provide for clear and consistent outcomes.** To enhance compliance and administration, and to ensure a level playing field, the GloBE demands a definition of covered taxes that is transparent and clear in its application, and produces consistent and predictable outcomes.
- **Avoid the need for a legalistic analysis of the specific technical design features of taxes in various jurisdictions.** The definition of covered taxes focuses on the underlying character of the tax and avoids the need to engage in a legalistic analysis of the technical nuances of particular taxes imposed by each jurisdiction to determine whether those taxes qualify as a covered tax.
- **Accommodate differences in the timing of the imposition of tax under local law.** The definition of covered taxes is designed to take account of the effects of temporary differences so that the GloBE does not result in incremental taxation in respect of temporary mismatches between the recognition of income and the imposition of tax on that income.

133. The principles set out above underpin the definition of covered taxes that has been developed for the purposes of the GloBE, and which is further elaborated in the commentary below. The commentary explains how this definition is applied to certain common design features of taxes in many Inclusive Framework on BEPS jurisdictions. The commentary does not describe or address every design feature of all the taxes that may fall within the definition. In order to provide certainty to MNEs and ensure the rules are consistently applied, Inclusive Framework on BEPS members have adopted a common definition of covered taxes. Consistency in the application of that definition could be co-ordinated through additional guidance, as necessary, as part of the development of model rules (see Section 10.5.1).

3.2.2. Taxes on income

134. While there is no internationally agreed definition of an income tax, income taxes are generally levies on a flow of money or money's worth that accrue to a taxpayer during a period of time. Income taxes take into account related expenses of producing the flow of money to measure the taxpayer's net increase in wealth for the period. A definition of covered taxes that applies to income calculated on a net (rather than gross) basis is in line with the definition of income tax used for financial accounting purposes and therefore it is expected that a tax recognised as an income tax for financial accounting purposes should generally qualify as a covered tax under the GloBE rules.

135. It is clear, however, that a tax need not determine the taxpayer's precise change in wealth to qualify as an income tax. A definition of covered taxes that required taxpayers and administrators to undertake further technical analysis of the precise terms of each type of tax in order to determine whether a particular tax took into account an appropriate amount of relevant expenses incurred in the generation of that income would be cumbersome to apply and lead to uncertainty in the determination of the ETR. Accordingly, the definition of covered taxes includes taxes that allow for a simplified estimate of net profit. For example, a tax that allows deductions for some but not all expenses of earning the relevant income, would be considered an income tax provided the deductible expenses can reasonably be considered to have been incurred in connection with deriving that income. Similarly, a tax on income that allows a standardized deduction in place of actual expenses is generally considered an income tax if such standardised deduction is based on a reasonable method for estimating such expenses. A tax imposed on gross income or revenue without any deductions (i.e. a tax on turnover) would not be considered an income tax. The design and substantive character of such turnover taxes generally have more similarities to consumption or sales taxes. The definition of covered taxes therefore does not apply to a tax on a gross amount unless such a tax is in lieu of an income tax (see Section 3.2.3).

136. Taxes or surcharges imposed on the net income from specific activities, such as banking or the exploration and production of oil and gas, irrespective of whether or not they apply in addition to a generally applicable income tax, would also fall within the general definition of a covered tax. That would include a separate resource levy that is imposed on the net income or profits from the extraction activity (or a component of a multi-component levy that is imposed on net income or profits). However, resource levies closely linked to extractions, for example, those that are imposed on a fixed basis or on the quantity, volume or value of the resources extracted rather than on net income or profits, would not be treated as covered taxes except where these levies satisfy the "in lieu of" test described below.

137. A supplementary tax which applies a top-up tax to the net income of domestic entities would also fall within the definition of a covered tax. Supplementary taxes that apply on an alternative basis - that is other than net income - would not, however, fall within the general definition of a covered tax as they are not taxes imposed on net income. As set out above, taxes on net income imposed at state and local government level are covered taxes, even where they are deductible for the purposes of income taxes imposed at national government level. Tax paid on net income allocated to a jurisdiction under Pillar One would also be treated as a covered tax under the GloBE (see Section 3.3.4. on *Adjustment for Pillar One Outcomes* for discussion of adjustments to the GloBE tax base).

138. Under an imputation credit regime, the tax that is imposed by a jurisdiction on a corporation's income gives rise to a credit, which can be attached to a subsequent distribution and used by a resident shareholder to shelter or reduce the tax payable under the laws of the same jurisdiction on that distribution. An imputation system is designed to ensure a single level of tax on corporate income whereby a portion of the tax paid by the corporation is creditable against the shareholder's tax liability arising from dividend distributions. Thus, in a sense, part of the tax paid by the corporation can be thought of as the pre-payment of the shareholder's tax liability. However, the fact that a shareholder may subsequently be entitled to an indirect credit for the tax paid by the corporation on the underlying income, does not prevent the corporation tax from being treated as a covered tax. Imputation regimes that protect resident shareholders from the imposition of economic double taxation under the laws of the same jurisdiction on the same income are equivalent, in this sense, to other mechanisms, such as foreign tax credits, exemptions and preferential rates, designed to protect domestic shareholders from economic double taxation on distributions of previously taxed income. Corporation tax paid under an imputation system that seeks to prevent economic double taxation at the resident shareholder level (and does not provide credits or refunds to non-residents) is properly treated as a covered tax provided the resident shareholder is subject to tax. Where, however, the imputation regime allows for a refund of taxes to be paid in respect of distributions made to a non-resident shareholder who is not subject to tax under domestic law, the regime has gone beyond relieving economic double taxation of the same income under the laws of the same jurisdiction, rather it is providing a refund of covered taxes paid in prior years. Accordingly, a distribution paid to a non-resident that gives rise to a refund of covered taxes (either to the company or to the shareholder) that relates to a distribution paid to a non-resident should be treated as a refund or reduction in covered taxes in the year such distribution is made. Similarly, where an imputation regime allows for a refund of taxes to be paid in respect of distributions made to a resident corporate shareholder which is not generally subject to tax on such distributions (e.g. due to a participation exemption) and is not an Excluded Entity[1], it should be treated as a reduction in covered taxes in the year such distribution is made. However, where an imputation regime allows a refund of taxes to be paid in respect of distributions made to a resident shareholder that is generally subject to tax, or which is an Excluded Entity, it should not be treated as a reduction in covered taxes under the GloBE.

3.2.3. Taxes in lieu of a generally applicable income tax

139. The definition of covered taxes includes taxes in lieu of a generally applicable corporate income tax. A generally applicable corporate income tax could be one that applies to all resident corporations or one that typically applies to those resident corporations that are members of a large multinational group. A generally applicable corporate income tax would also include an income tax imposed on a corporation but which also applies to other taxable persons such as individuals. The "in lieu of" test includes taxes that are not covered under the generally applicable income tax definition but which operate as substitutes for such taxes. This test, which will be familiar to some tax administrations in the context of their foreign tax credit rules, would generally include withholding taxes on interest, rents and royalties, and other taxes on other categories of gross payments such as insurance premiums, provided such taxes are imposed in substitution for a generally applicable income tax.

140. The "in lieu of" concept also covers taxes that are imposed on an alternative basis, such as taxes based on number of units produced or commercial surface area, and which are used as substitutes for a generally applicable income tax under the laws of the jurisdiction. Where, for example, a jurisdiction imposes a simplified methodology for calculating the income on a particular category of business or investment and this tax is imposed in substitution for a generally applicable income tax then that tax should be treated as falling within the definition of a covered tax. This includes a tax on deemed return for investments in foreign equity. It also includes taxes such as tonnage taxes that use income earning capacity as a proxy for income and are designed to act as a substitute for corporation tax. Generally when a taxpayer elects into a tonnage tax regime, the taxpayer opts out of the normal corporate income tax

rules.[2] A tax imposed on an alternative basis (i.e. other than net income) levied at state or local government level, which is creditable against a generally applicable income tax levied at national government level, would also qualify as a covered tax under the "in lieu of" test to the extent that it is credited against income tax in the same jurisdiction. Such local taxes can be considered as being in substitution (partially or fully) for a generally applicable income tax and an administratively efficient way of transferring resources from national to local government within the same jurisdiction. A tax that is imposed on an alternative basis that applies in addition to, and not as substitute for, a generally applicable income tax under the laws of the jurisdiction would not fall under the "in lieu of" test for covered taxes.

3.2.4. Taxes on retained earnings and corporate equity

141. Some jurisdictions impose taxes on the net equity of a corporation in addition to corporate income tax. The equity or capital of a corporation is composed of its retained earnings (i.e. the undistributed portion of the after-tax income in the Profit and Loss statement) and the contributions made by shareholders. Taxes on corporate equity may be inherently interlinked with the design of the corporate income tax systems. For example, it may be possible under the laws of a jurisdiction to credit corporate income tax against a corporate equity tax so that a company is allowed to reduce the corporate equity tax up to the amount of corporate income tax that it pays in that jurisdiction. Taxes on corporate equity may also act as a supplement to corporate income tax as part of a jurisdiction's overall approach to the taxation of a corporation's activities in that jurisdiction. For example, some taxes on corporate equity may incorporate a minimum tax element to their design. Such taxes on corporate equity are therefore an integral part of the overall system of corporate taxation in those jurisdictions. From an economic perspective, a tax on net equity can be seen as an ex ante income tax on the company. For these reasons, these type of taxes based on corporate equity should be treated as covered taxes under the GloBE rules.

3.2.5. Taxes based on multiple components

142. Some jurisdictions impose taxes that have multiple components to the base. Where all the components of the tax base fall within the definition of income or profit covered by the GloBE rules then the tax should as a whole, be included within the definition of covered taxes. Other taxes may be levied in respect of a corporation's activities in a jurisdiction, and are administratively and conceptually part of the system of corporate taxation in these jurisdictions but may include both an income and a non-income element. Where such taxes are predominately a tax on an entity's income and it would be administratively burdensome to split the tax into separate income and non-income components then such taxes should be treated as fully covered under the GloBE rules. This approach would minimise the complexity of the GloBE rules and avoid the additional administrative and compliance burden of requiring the different components of such taxes to be split out for the purposes of the ETR calculation. Furthermore, it is consistent with the general principle that the definition of covered taxes should focus on the underlying character of the tax and avoid the need for a legalistic analysis of the technical nuances of particular taxes imposed by each jurisdiction.

143. An example of a covered tax with multiple components is the corporate Zakat levied by the Kingdom of Saudi Arabia, which is described in Example 3.2.5-1A. As described in that example, the Zakat operates as a tax on income or equity or both and is therefore properly considered a covered tax for the purposes of the GloBE rules.

3.2.6. Taxes on distributed profits

144. In line with the principle to address temporary differences, the timing of a levy does not have any bearing on the definition of covered taxes. Accordingly, taxes imposed on the income of a distributing corporation at the time it distributes the income are covered taxes, irrespective of whether the income distribution is attributable to current or previously accumulated retained earnings (see Section 3.3.6 for

more detail on the modification to the GloBE ETR computation for entities subject to a distribution-based corporate income tax).

3.2.7. Taxes paid under CFC rules

145. Taxes paid in accordance with Controlled Foreign Corporation (CFC) rules are considered covered taxes for the purposes of the GloBE provided that they are imposed on the income of the CFC that is attributed to shareholders in the parent jurisdiction. Such CFC taxes should be assigned, where possible, to the jurisdiction in which the underlying income arises (i.e. to the jurisdiction of the CFC) and should be excluded from the ETR computation if the underlying income is excluded (see Section 3.4.2 on *Assignment of income and taxes of entity to each jurisdiction* for the approach for the treatment of CFC income and related taxes in the ETR calculation under the GloBE).

3.2.8. Non-covered taxes

Consumption and sales taxes

146. Consumption taxes, such as sales taxes and value-added taxes (VATs), are not covered taxes under the GloBE rules. Such taxes are calculated by reference to the consideration for a defined supply and are not taxes on the net income of a taxpayer.

Excise taxes

147. Excise and other taxes on inputs are not covered taxes under the GloBE rules. Such taxes arise in relation to a specific input which do not represent an accretion of income.

Digital services taxes

148. Digital services taxes (DSTs), as currently contemplated by a number of Members of the Inclusive Framework, are generally designed to apply to the gross revenues from the provision of certain digital services and so would not be considered an income tax. DSTs are generally designed to apply in addition to, and not as substitutes for, a generally applicable income tax under the laws of a jurisdiction, and so would not fall under the "in lieu of" test for covered taxes either.

Stamp and other transfer taxes

149. Stamp duty, ad valorem taxes and other taxes that are imposed on a particular transaction are not taxes on income or taxes in lieu of an income tax. They are therefore outside the scope of the covered tax definition.

Payroll taxes and social security contributions

150. Payroll taxes and other employment based taxes, as well as social security contributions, are not covered taxes under the GloBE rules. Payroll taxes and social security contributions are not imposed on the employer in respect of its income. This follows the well-established view of payroll taxes and social security contributions as being levied on labour income (i.e. wages and in some cases personal income) as opposed to business profits. Rather, payroll taxes and social security contributions are typically deductible from business profits in the same way that wages are deducted from business profits. Payroll taxes and social security contributions will also be included in the payroll component of the proposed formulaic substance-based carve-out from the GloBE (see Section).

Property taxes

151. Taxes based on ownership of specified items or categories of property are distinguishable from taxes based on a corporation's equity and should not be covered taxes under the GloBE rules. Taxes on corporate equity are generally levied on a broader range of assets than property taxes. Property taxes are based on the assessed value of the property, often without regard to whether the property is subject to a liability. They are not based on income, retained earnings, or corporate equity. Neither are they taxes imposed in lieu of a generally applicable income tax.

152. Furthermore, including property taxes in covered taxes would give a preference to owned assets over leased assets. In many cases, ownership versus lease of assets are business structure or finance decisions. In other cases, the treatment of a financing arrangement as a purchase or lease depends on accounting rules that do not implicate the policy of the GloBE. There is no apparent reason to favour ownership of assets over leasing of assets under the GloBE.

153. A property tax that reduced the assessed value of taxable property based on liabilities associated with the property might be considered similar to corporate equity taxes because corporate equity is the difference between the value of an entity's assets and its liabilities. However, equity taxes are not generally based on the specific assets held by a company, although the equity tax base could be reduced by certain categories of assets. Moreover, corporate equity is determined by taking into account all liabilities of the corporation, not just liabilities associated with specific assets. Adjustments to the assessed value of property for liabilities against the property is more akin to a valuation method under a property tax than a tax that is predominantly on previous income. Accordingly, property taxes are not included in the definition of covered taxes under the GloBE rules.

3.3. Tax base

GloBE tax base calculated by reference to consolidated financial accounts

Profit or loss determined in accordance with financial accounting standard

The starting point for determining the GloBE tax base is the profit (or loss) before income tax as determined using the relevant financial accounting standard, which may include items previously included in other comprehensive income. Certain items of income are removed from and certain items of expense are added back to the profit (or loss) before income tax to arrive at the GloBE tax base.

Financial accounting standard

The relevant financial accounting standard for calculating the GloBE tax base is the financial accounting standard used by the parent in the preparation of its consolidated financial statements.

Acceptable accounting standards

The acceptable financial accounting standards are IFRS and any equivalent financial accounting standard. Equivalent financial accounting standards include the generally accepted accounting principles of Australia, Canada, Hong Kong (China), Japan, New Zealand, the People's Republic of China, the Republic of India, the Republic of Korea, Singapore, and the United States.

In addition, an MNE should be permitted to use any generally acceptable accounting standard permitted by the body with legal authority in the Ultimate Parent Entity's tax jurisdiction to prescribe, establish, or accept accounting standards for financial reporting purposes, provided the use of that standard will not result in material competitive distortions in the application of the GloBE rules.

Determining profit (or loss) before tax of each entity

Entity-level financial information that is used in preparing the parent's consolidated financial accounts can be used, even if such financial information is not prepared in strict accordance with the parent's financial accounting standard where (a) it is reasonable to do so, (b) the information is reliable, and (c) the use of such information does not result in material permanent differences from the accounting standard of the parent.

Determining income of permanent establishment and head office

Profit (or loss) before tax of a permanent establishment is determined based on the income and expenses that are treated as arising for tax purposes in the jurisdiction where the permanent establishment is located. Transactions between the permanent establishment and the head office that are taken into account in determining the taxable income of the permanent establishment are taken into account in determining the profit (or loss) before tax of the permanent establishment and the head office under the GloBE rules.

Intercompany items

Income, gains, expenses, and losses attributable to transactions between members of the GloBE tax group should be recorded in the entity level financial accounts in accordance with the arm's length principle. Intercompany items can be excluded, however, to the extent the transaction is between group members in the same jurisdiction.

Items held in consolidation

Purchase accounting adjustments held in consolidation should not be pushed down or otherwise allocated to specific entities. Other items maintained at the consolidated level should only be taken into account in the GloBE tax base of a Constituent Entity where those items can be reliably and consistently traced to that entity.

Dividends and equity method profit (or loss)

The GloBE tax base excludes dividends received from a corporate entity, except dividends on stock in corporations in which the MNE Group owns a low percentage of the equity interests, and profit (or loss) attributable to an investment in an entity accounted for using the equity method of accounting..

Dispositions of stock and fair value accounting gain (or loss)

The GloBE tax base generally excludes gain (or loss) arising from dispositions of stock, including mergers. The acquired entity is required to use the historical carrying value of its underlying assets to compute its GloBE tax base after the acquisition. An exception to these rules applies to stock transactions between parties tax resident in the same jurisdiction that are treated as taxable asset sales in that jurisdiction. Gains and losses arising under fair value accounting for stock should be excluded from the GloBE tax base to the same extent gain or loss on actual sale of the stock would be excluded.

Covered taxes

Covered taxes, including taxes that are not treated as income taxes for financial accounting purposes, are not deductible in the computation of the GloBE tax base.

Stock-based compensation expense

Stock-based compensation expense is only allowed as a deduction in the GloBE tax base computation for a jurisdiction to the extent it is allowed as a deduction in the local tax base of the jurisdiction of the entity that employed or contracted with the party receiving the stock-based compensation. However, MNEs may reduce the GloBE tax base by stock-based compensation expense as recognised for financial accounting purposes (rather than local tax purposes), in those jurisdictions that do not have a corporate income tax system.

Bribes, kickbacks and other illegal payments

Bribes, kickbacks (and other illegal payments) are not allowed as a deduction to the GloBE tax base.

Fines and penalties

A fine or penalty imposed by government on an entity is not allowed as a deduction to the GloBE tax base of a jurisdiction if the fine or penalty, including a periodic penalty, incurred by the entity in the jurisdiction equals or exceeds EUR 50,000.

Investment returns of life insurance policy holders

Any earnings on assets beneficially owned by a life insurance policy holder that are included in the income of an insurance company pursuant to the financial accounting standard used by the company for GloBE purposes must be removed from the insurance company's GloBE tax base.

Adjustment for Pillar One Outcomes

Pillar One applies before Pillar Two. Depending upon the final design of Pillar One, an adjustment may be required to the GloBE tax base to properly reflect Pillar One outcomes.

Modification to determination of annual depreciation expense

Depreciation expense allowed with respect to tangible property of a Constituent Entity in computing the GloBE tax base may be determined based on depreciation rules applicable in the computation of taxable income in the Constituent Entity's tax jurisdiction.

Modification to tax expense computation for entities subject to a distribution-based corporate income tax

A shareholder of a Constituent Entity that is subject to a corporate income tax on distribution of its income may elect to increase the tax expense included in the numerator of the GloBE ETR computation of the jurisdiction up to the minimum tax rate, but not more than the amount of distribution tax that would be due if all of the income for the year were distributed (deemed minimum tax). The subsidiary must recapture the amount of such deemed minimum tax to the extent that corporate income tax is not paid upon distribution of income within [X] years after the year in which the income was derived.

3.3.1. Profit or loss determined in accordance with financial accounting standard

154. As directed in the Programme of Work, the Inclusive Framework first considered the possibility of calculating the GloBE tax base using the parent jurisdiction's rules for computing domestic taxable income or the income of controlled foreign companies (CFC). Leveraging the existing tax base calculation rules that a country uses for CFC purposes might initially seem to have the advantage of facilitating a tax administrations implementation and administration of the rules. However, CFC rules typically do not apply to all the subsidiaries in an MNE Group and, when they do apply, they usually only capture certain types of low-tax passive income.[3] In contrast, the GloBE rules will apply to all the subsidiaries in the group and

all types of income. Therefore, Members of the Inclusive Framework considered that using the tax base calculation rules in the Parent's jurisdiction of residence would entail significant compliance costs due to the need for each foreign subsidiary to re-calculate all of its income in accordance with the tax base of another jurisdiction. These re-calculations could lead to situations where technical and structural differences between the calculation of the tax base in the parent and subsidiary jurisdiction could result in an otherwise highly-taxed subsidiary being treated as having a low ETR for reasons unrelated to the policy underlying the GloBE rules. For example, differences between jurisdictions in the treatment of carry-forward losses and in the timing of the recognition of income and expenses could impact the calculation of the ETR in different jurisdictions. Such differences could result in the application of the rule in cases that do not give rise to the policy concerns that are intended to be addressed by the GloBE rules.

155. Structural differences in the calculation of the tax base between jurisdictions could also complicate the application of the GloBE rules and undermine its policy objectives, including the policy of ensuring transparent outcomes. For example, two jurisdictions may apply the same minimum tax rate to the income of entities pursuant to their income inclusion rules. However, if one jurisdiction has a different tax base from the other, this could result in significantly different outcomes for similarly situated entities, undermining the policy intent of creating a transparent and level playing field already reflected in the agreement on a minimum ETR equal to a fixed percentage. Finally, from the perspective of the application of the undertaxed payments rule it would be impossible to design an effective tax rate test that required a group entity making a related party payment to re-compute the recipient's income according to the tax base rules in the paying entity's tax jurisdiction. This could result in requiring taxpayers to re-compute the income many times over, possibly hundreds of times for larger groups.

156. In order to improve compliance and administration and to neutralise the impact of structural differences in the calculation of the tax base, the Programme of Work called for the exploration of simplifications to help address the issues arising from the use of the tax base in the parent jurisdiction. One simplification identified in the Programme of Work was to start with the relevant financial accounting rules. The net income calculated for financial accounting purposes could then be subject to any necessary and agreed adjustments to arrive at the GloBE tax base.

157. Use of financial accounts as a starting point for determining the tax base under the GloBE rules offers numerous advantages. From a compliance and administration perspective, it facilitates the coordination of the GloBE rules operating in different jurisdictions and eliminates the need to re-calculate the taxable income of each foreign subsidiary under the rules of the jurisdiction applying the GloBE rules. It also improves the transparency of outcomes under the GloBE rules and reduces distortions among jurisdictions based on differences in the tax base.

158. Importantly, the use of financial accounts to determine the GloBE tax base builds on existing internationally agreed standards. Although there are variations in financial accounting standards among jurisdictions, International Financial Reporting Standards (IFRS) and the generally accepted accounting principles (GAAP) of many Inclusive Framework jurisdictions have far more commonalities than differences. Moreover, there are no other uniform international standard methods of measuring the income of an entity, and it is not feasible to create, from the ground up, a new international accounting standard for computing profit (or loss) before tax under the GloBE rules.

159. The financial accounts of the entity are used to determine the entity's profit (or loss) before tax. Profit (or loss) before tax is the preferred profit measure under the GloBE rules for several reasons. First, it takes into account the actual costs of doing business, including all operating and non-operating expenses. Second, it is the most comparable financial accounting measure to taxable income, but, critically, it is computed without regard to special local tax exclusions, deductions and tax accounting conventions that would undermine the policy objectives of the GloBE rules. Therefore, using profit (or loss) before tax as a measure of profit for computing the GloBE tax base should limit the risk of the GloBE tax

base diverging significantly from the tax base of the MNE Group under local corporate income tax rules, where such a divergence would be inconsistent with the policy objectives of the GloBE rules.

160. Most commonly used accounting standards, including IFRS, do not strictly define profit (or loss) before tax. Profit measures other than net income, such as profit (or loss) before tax, are typically referred to as non-GAAP measures, and MNE Groups have some flexibility in how to calculate them.

161. For the purposes of the GloBE rules, it will be necessary to establish a consistent way for MNE Groups to determine profit (or loss) before tax using their separate entity financial accounts. One option would be to adopt an additive approach, which would define the various income and expense items that should be included. Alternatively, a deductive approach would assume that all items included in the computation of net income for purposes of the group's consolidated financial accounting statements should be included in the computation of profit (or loss) before tax, but would identify specific items that should be excluded for specific policy reasons. Inclusive Framework on BEPS members have agreed that the latter approach is the preferred one as it is likely to be simpler for MNE Groups to apply given that it merely requires exclusion of a limited number of items.

Other comprehensive income

162. Generally, financial accounting profit (or loss) does not include other comprehensive income (OCI). However, some items of income or loss reported in OCI are "recycled" through the profit and loss statement. OCI is reported on a company's balance sheet, under the equity section. The items included in OCI may include gains and losses on certain debt and equity investments, foreign currency exchange gains and losses, and changes in liabilities under pension plans. Certain revenue, expenses, gains, and losses appear in OCI before a third-party transaction has been completed. For example, if a company has invested in an interest-bearing bond and the value of that bond changes due to changes in market interest rates, then the company might be required to recognise that change in value as a gain (or loss) in OCI. Once the company sells or redeems the bond, it will then realise the transactional gain (or loss) associated with the bonds, and the realised gain (or loss) will be reported in the income statement and impact profit (or loss) before tax. Some items that are included in OCI may also be subject to tax in the local jurisdiction. In most cases, however, this will only be expected to give rise to a temporary or timing difference between local tax base and the GloBE tax base.[4]

163. In other cases, the corresponding gain (or loss) can generally be expected to be excluded from the GloBE tax base. The GloBE rules do not directly recognise items of OCI as includible in the GloBE tax base. However, such items will be included in the GloBE tax base if and when they are recognised as profit (or loss) for financial accounting purposes, provided they are not otherwise excluded from the calculation of the GloBE tax base under another rule. In this regard, an adjustment may be necessary to ensure that all of the gain (or loss) is included in the GloBE tax base in cases where only the current portion of the total gain (or loss) on disposition is included in the profit (or loss) for financial accounting purposes. This situation could arise where an asset is disposed and previous increases or decreases in fair value in respect of that asset have already been reflected in the OCI. These corresponding carrying value adjustments should be taken into account in determining the gain or loss in the year of disposition.

3.3.2. Use of parent entity's consolidated financial accounting standard

164. The starting point for the GloBE tax base is the financial accounts of each Constituent Entity of the MNE Group prepared in accordance with the financial accounting standard used by the parent entity of the group in the preparation of its consolidated financial statements.

165. There are two advantages to using the parent entity's accounting standard. First, the use of a single standard helps minimise mismatches in the treatment of transactions between Constituent Entities that may arise due to the use of different accounting standards in different jurisdictions. Second, the

standards used to prepare financial accounts for Constituent Entities will, in many cases and particularly for those MNE Groups that are listed, follow the standard used in the parent jurisdiction. This is because, in many cases, maintaining financial accounts for all Constituent Entities using a single standard facilitates the preparation of consolidated financial statements and quarterly reporting for those groups. In those cases where a Constituent Entity's accounts are not regularly maintained in accordance with the accounting standard of the parent entity there will typically be mechanisms in place that allow those accounts to be converted into or derived from the parent entity's standard as part of the consolidation process.

3.3.3. Acceptable financial accounting standards

166. The use of any accounting standard for purposes of the GloBE rules, including the standard used by the parent entity in preparing its consolidated financial statements, is always subject to the caveat that the standard, itself, must be a reliable and acceptable financial accounting standard.

167. Agreement on acceptable accounting standards is an important part of the consensus on the GloBE rules. It is recognized that financial accounting standards promulgated by independent accounting standard setting bodies tend to converge over time. Inclusive Framework on BEPS members expect that the financial accounting standards that are acceptable for use in determining the GloBE tax base will increase in the future and that a financial accounting standards could lose that status only in rare and unusual circumstances.

IFRS and equivalents

168. The rule accepts IFRS as adopted by the parent jurisdiction. IFRS is the most commonly used and accepted financial accounting standard worldwide. IFRS were established by the International Accounting Standards Board (IASB) in order to create a common accounting language, so that financial statements can be consistent and reliable from company to company and country to country. Jurisdictions adopt IFRS by conforming their local generally accepted accounting principles (GAAP) to IFRS. However, some jurisdictions have adopted IFRS with minor modifications, including different effective dates for the application of specific IFRS rules.

169. In addition, the GloBE rule accepts any financial accounting standard that is equivalent to IFRS. Equivalency with IFRS can be assessed based on the work of the IASB as well as the work of securities regulators that allow other accounting standards in financial reports of publicly accountable companies.

170. The IASB works with accounting standard authorities of different jurisdictions in an effort to converge these different accounting standards. The IASB provides information on the status of IFRS adoption and convergence projects in many jurisdictions on its website. For example, the IASB notes on its website that the accounting standards used for publicly listed entities in the People's Republic of China, the Republic of India, the Republic of Korea, and Singapore are substantially converged with IFRS standards. Similarly, the IASB notes that Australia, Hong Kong (China), and New Zealand have adopted IFRS "nearly word for word as their national accounting standards".[5] IFRS as adopted by all of these jurisdictions are considered IFRS for purposes of the GloBE proposal. However, the IASB generally does not undertake an evaluation of the overall comparability of each jurisdiction's local financial accounting standards with IFRS. Thus, assessments of equivalency to IFRS for purposes of the GloBE rules cannot be based solely on the work of the IASB.

171. Securities regulators in Inclusive Framework jurisdictions may issue guidance authorising foreign issuers of securities to use financial statements that are prepared under an accounting standard different from the accounting standards generally applicable to domestic issuers. Each regulator has its own process for authorising the use of an alternative accounting standard and the basis on which this authorisation is made may not be publicly disclosed. However, in general, the regulator will consider

whether the alternative accounting standard provides investors with substantially similar financial information about the issuer such that an investor acting on such information is likely to make the same decisions about the acquisition or disposal of the issuer's securities. For example, European Union securities regulators have recognised that the GAAP of Canada, Japan, the People's Republic of China, the Republic of India, the Republic of Korea, and the United States are generally equivalent to IFRS. Determinations by securities regulators for a significant number of jurisdictions that use IFRS as the primary reporting standard to allow foreign issuers to use financial statements prepared under an alternative financial accounting standard provides a strong indication that the alternative financial accounting standard is equivalent to IFRS.

172. The assessments made by the IASB and the reciprocal recognition of accounting standards by different regulators provide a strong indication that any differences between IFRS and the GAAP of Australia, Canada, Hong Kong (China), Japan, New Zealand, the People's Republic of China, the Republic of India, the Republic of Korea, Singapore, and the United States would not provide a material competitive advantage or disadvantage to an MNE Group using any of these standards vis-à-vis an MNE Group using IFRS. Furthermore, Inclusive Framework members are not aware of any differences between IFRS and these standards that would create material competitive distortions in the GloBE tax base, nor did the December Public Consultation (OECD, 2019[3]) bring to light any material distortions in response to this specific point. Accordingly, these accounting standards are considered equivalent to IFRS.

Other generally accepted financial accounting standards

173. As a result of the EUR 750 million consolidated revenue threshold described above in Section , a significant majority of MNEs subject to the GloBE rules are expected to be publicly accountable or listed companies (i.e. companies whose shares or debt is traded on a public securities exchange) that prepare consolidated financial statements under IFRS or an equivalent standard. There will, however, be some MNE Groups that are listed but prepare consolidated financial reports based on standards other than IFRS or an equivalent and MNE Groups that are not listed. Non-listed MNE Groups may be headquartered in a jurisdiction that requires IFRS for listed companies, but they may prepare their financial statements using the local accounting standard. It is not proportionate or reasonable to require such MNE Groups to prepare financial accounts under a different accounting standard solely for purposes of complying with the GloBE rules if their existing accounting standard is recognised by an appropriate authority and it does not result in material competitive distortions under the GloBE rules. Thus, the rule would permit an MNE Group to use any generally acceptable accounting standard permitted by the body with legal authority in the tax jurisdiction of its Ultimate Parent Entity to prescribe, establish, or accept accounting standards for financial reporting purposes, provided the use of that standard would not result in a material competitive distortion in the application of the GloBE rules.

174. In an accounting context, a material competitive distortion is an outcome that departs significantly from the result that would be realised under IFRS in a way that materially affects the ETR under the GloBE. In the case an IF member identifies a potential material competitive distortion associated with a certain element of a particular accounting standard, a review process would be initiated within the Inclusive Framework. If the relevant element was in fact deemed to be a material competitive distortion, then that particular element would be required to be brought into line with IFRS for purposes of the GloBE rules. The review process and relevant criteria will be established as part of the implementation of the model rules described in Section.

3.3.4. Adjustments for permanent differences

175. Section 3.3.1 above sets out a basic approach for computing profit (or loss) before tax for each Constituent Entity under the accounting standard of the parent entity as the starting point for the GloBE tax base. This Section sets out the adjustments to net income that are required in order to more closely

align the GloBE tax base with the computation of taxable income under the rules of the jurisdiction where the MNE operates. Adjustments may be required where differences between tax and financial accounting could have a disproportionate impact on the outcomes under the GloBE rules.

176. Differences between the relevant financial accounting standard and tax accounting rules generally can be categorized as giving rise either to permanent differences that will not reverse in a future period or temporary (i.e., timing) differences that will reverse in a future period. This chapter is focused on permanent differences. Temporary differences are addressed through the use of carry-forwards as described below in Chapter.

Evaluating permanent differences

177. Each Inclusive Framework jurisdiction has its own unique combination of additions to and exclusions from financial accounting income to arrive at taxable income. It is therefore implicit in the decision to use financial accounts as the starting point for determining the GloBE tax base that certain permanent differences will arise between that local tax base and the GloBE tax base. If there is agreement on a common tax base for the GloBE rules it follows that such permanent differences are to be expected and it would not be possible or desirable, from either a policy or a design perspective, to develop a comprehensive set of adjustments that will bring the GloBE tax base fully into line with the tax base calculation rules of all Inclusive Framework members. Nevertheless, some adjustments to financial accounts are appropriate based on the policies of the GloBE rules and tax policy more generally.

178. In order to justify adopting or rejecting potential adjustments to the financial accounts to arrive at the GloBE tax base, it is necessary to evaluate permanent differences using an agreed set of principles. The pertinent principles for evaluating permanent differences are materiality and commonality. Specifically, in order to avoid disproportionate outcomes that are out of line with the intended outcomes under GloBE, a Constituent Entity's profit (or loss) before tax, as determined under the applicable financial accounting standard, should only be adjusted to exclude material items that are commonly excluded from the tax base of Inclusive Framework jurisdictions. Furthermore any adjustments should be kept to a minimum in order to minimise complexity. Set forth below is an exclusive list of adjustments to financial accounts that have been agreed by the Inclusive Framework as being necessary and appropriate for calculating the GloBE tax base. In keeping with the desire to minimise both the number and complexity of required adjustments, the adjustments described in this Section that exclude income do not require a correlative exclusion of expenses, other than some covered taxes, attributable to that income.

Dividends and equity method accounting

179. The GloBE rules generally require the GloBE tax base and covered taxes of Constituent Entities to be determined on a separate entity basis. Dividends received from other Constituent Entities would ordinarily be included in the separate entity computation of profit (or loss) before tax and thus would be included in the starting point of the GloBE tax base. Similarly dividends received from a corporate entity in which the shareholder holds a minority interest, commonly referred to as "portfolio dividends", will also be included in the profit (or loss) before tax of the subsidiary receiving the dividend. In many jurisdictions, dividends are wholly or partially excluded, from the taxable income of a corporate shareholder. This permanent difference between the financial accounting treatment and the rules for taxing dividends under local law could give rise to a GloBE tax liability in respect of dividends unless the GloBE rules permit the taxpayer to make a corresponding adjustment for the purposes of calculating the GloBE tax base.

Intra-group dividends

180. Dividends distributed from one Constituent Entity of an MNE Group to another Constituent Entity of the same MNE Group must be excluded from the GloBE tax base because they represent income that has already been included in the GloBE tax base. Failure to exclude such dividends from the recipient's GloBE tax base could result in double taxation of the same income, which would be inconsistent with the policies of the GloBE rules. This rule applies irrespective of whether the Constituent Entity receiving the dividend owns a controlling interest in the distributing Constituent Entity.

Portfolio dividends

181. In many Inclusive Framework jurisdictions, dividends are excluded, in whole or in part, from the taxable income of a corporate shareholder (including through the use of a dividends received deduction). These dividend exclusion rules are often referred to as participation exemptions. Dividend exemptions, exclusions, or credits are usually granted under local law in recognition of the fact that the dividend is generally paid out of retained earnings that have already been subject to tax in the hands of the distributing company. Taxing these dividends under the GloBE rules would therefore give rise to the risk of over taxation.

182. However, some Inclusive Framework on BEPS jurisdictions do not apply their dividend exemption to all dividends received by taxpayers in their jurisdictions. Some Inclusive Framework on BEPS jurisdictions exempt dividends only if the shareholder owns a certain percentage of the equity interests in the distributing corporation (for example, 10% or more). Other jurisdictions also include a holding period requirement to their exemption qualification criteria. In addition, dividend exemptions in a number of Inclusive Framework on BEPS jurisdictions do not extend to trading securities held by financial services businesses, securities dealers and securities traders.

183. Accordingly, in many cases portfolio dividends received by an MNE Group will be subject to income tax under local law. If these dividends were excluded from the GloBE tax base, the corresponding taxes would need to be excluded as well. In addition, dividends and gains from sales of securities represent a core business activity of financial services businesses and securities traders and dealers. If such income were excluded from the GloBE tax base, it would also be appropriate to exclude the expenses incurred in deriving that income to prevent such expenses from reducing income otherwise appropriately included in the GloBE tax base. Accordingly, exclusion of dividends and gains on trading stock held by these enterprises would likely create a need to develop expense allocation rules.

184. The dividend exclusion rule under the GloBE rules contains an exception for dividends received from a corporation in which the MNE Group owns a low percentage of the equity interests. A percentage ownership test is more administrable than an exception that relies on a definition of financial services business or securities dealers and traders. However, it is anticipated that an exception based on a low percentage of equity ownership will also apply to most of the trading stocks in a financial services businesses or securities dealer. This exception eliminates the need to exclude taxes associated with these dividends and the allocable expenses.

185. Recognising the need for certainty and consistency and the advantages of bright-line mechanical rules, the Inclusive Framework on BEPS considers that a general dividend exclusion based on the holder's percentage ownership is the most straight-forward option and one that is in line with the policy outcomes under the GloBE rules. Further work is necessary, however, to decide the appropriate ownership threshold, both for the exclusion of dividends and the exclusion for gains and losses on the disposition of stock described below. The determination of the threshold will be based on a survey of existing participation exemptions of various Inclusive Framework on BEPS jurisdictions. Consideration will also be given to whether there should be different rules for dividends on stock in domestic and foreign corporations. In addition, depending on the final design of rules for excluding dividends and gains on portfolio from the

GloBE tax base, the Inclusive Framework on BEPS needs to consider whether the related expenses should also be excluded and how those expenses should be measured.

Use of equity method

186. As explained in Chapter, Associate entities and joint ventures are not Constituent Entities. Ownership interests in Associate entities and joint ventures are generally accounted for using the equity method. Under the equity method, the owner includes in income its proportionate share of the entity's after-tax income or loss and increases or decreases the carrying cost of the investment by the same amount. The income included by the owner under the equity method is thus equal to the amount of dividends the owner would have received if the entity had distributed its annual income. Actual distributions reduce the carrying cost of the investment but are not included in the owner's financial accounting profit (or loss).

187. For tax purposes, a shareholder with a significant interest in a foreign corporation will not ordinarily be required to include the income of that entity in the shareholder's taxable income until distribution, absent a CFC or similar rule. The equity method, however, includes the owner's proportionate share of the entity's after-tax income or loss in the year earned by the Associate entity of joint venture. Nonetheless, the equity method income is more like dividend income than consolidated income because the amount included in the shareholder's income is the net income of the entire investment on an aggregate basis.

188. Accordingly, the rule generally excludes both income and loss attributable to an interest in an entity that is accounted for by the MNE Group under the equity method from the income of the shareholder. Section. sets out special rules for the treatment of investments in Associate entities and joint ventures under a simplified income inclusion rule.

189. The determination of whether an entity is an Associate or joint venture is based on the ownership of that entity held by the MNE Group. Thus, if twenty Constituent Entities of the same MNE Group each own 5% of the same entity, that entity is a Constituent Entity of the MNE Group, not an Associate entity of each Constituent Entity shareholder.

Gain (or loss) from the disposition of stock

190. In many Inclusive Framework jurisdictions, gains arising from the disposition of stock are exempt from tax. The rationale for excluding such gains from taxation is similar (but not identical) to the rationale for excluding tax on dividends. To the extent the gain on the stock represents retained earnings, these amounts may have already been subject to tax in the issuer's jurisdiction. Similarly, to the extent the gain on the stock represents unrealised gains in assets held by the company it may be subject to tax in the issuer's jurisdiction in the future. Gain or loss on the disposition of stock that is included in the financial accounting income of the seller but excluded from the seller's taxable income would represent a permanent difference. If the difference is not adjusted for under the GloBE rules, gains on disposition will result in a lower GloBE ETR for the seller (and potential tax liability under the GloBE rules) and losses will result in a higher GloBE ETR. The rule eliminates this permanent difference by excluding from the seller's GloBE tax base all gains (or losses) arising in connection with dispositions of stock, including mergers.

191. However, similar to the treatment of dividends, gains and losses on the disposition of stock in a corporation in which the MNE Group owns less than a certain percentage of the equity interests are included in the GloBE tax base.

192. In a stock acquisition, the purchaser acquires the target entity's stock from the selling shareholders. After the acquisition, the underlying assets of the target entity are neither "stepped-up" nor reduced to fair value for tax purposes. Instead, the target entity accounts for its underlying assets using their historical carrying value. However, for financial accounting purposes, the purchaser recognises the acquired assets at fair value. If the target entity prepares separate financial statements, a question arises as to whether the historical carrying value of the target entity's underlying assets or the stepped-up carrying

value should be reflected in the target entity's separate financial statements. Pushdown accounting refers to the latter. Pushdown accounting is not permitted under IFRS, but other accounting standards, including US GAAP, allow pushdown accounting in certain circumstances.

193. Pushdown accounting results in the carrying values of some of the target entity's underlying assets being stepped-up to fair value for financial accounting purposes, which usually results in higher depreciation and amortization expense, which, in turn, leads to lower financial accounting income for the acquired entity. Because financial accounting income is the starting point for the GloBE tax base, the target entity's profit will generally be lower if pushdown accounting is permitted, which will increase the target entity's ETR, perhaps above the minimum rate.

194. For example, assume the same facts as described in the example above. After the acquisition, Corp C will account for Target B's underlying assets at their stepped-up carrying value (i.e., EUR 200) for purposes of preparing its consolidated financial accounts. In the case that Corp C pushes down the purchase accounting adjustments to Target B, Target B's stand-alone financial accounts will be based on the stepped-up carrying value of its underlying assets (i.e., EUR 200). However, for local tax purposes, Target B will compute its taxable income based on the historical carrying value of its underlying assets (i.e., EUR 50). This difference will result in more depreciation and amortization expense for financial accounting purposes than for tax purposes, which will result in a smaller GloBE tax base and a higher GloBE ETR for Target B.

195. The stock gain exclusion rule neutralises this effect by requiring the target entity to use the historical carrying value of its underlying assets to compute its GloBE tax base after the acquisition. The justification for this rule is that the purchase price of the target entity is equal to the present value of the estimated future income of its underlying assets. If the target entity was not sold then all the income generated by its underlying assets would be included in its GloBE tax base. On the other hand, if the target entity is sold, and a stepped-up carrying value is permitted, then the target entity's GloBE income will be reduced by higher depreciation and amortization expense, which would result in a portion of the income generated by its underlying assets being excluded from the GloBE tax base. The rule ensures that all the income generated by the target entity's underlying assets is included in the GloBE tax base. Furthermore, the rule eliminates a potentially material difference between different accounting standards (i.e., those that permit push-down accounting and those that do not).

196. However, if the seller and purchaser of a target entity and the entity itself are tax resident in the same jurisdiction and that jurisdiction treats the disposition of stock as a deemed asset sale for tax purposes in the target entity's jurisdiction (for both the seller and the purchaser) and imposes tax on the deemed asset sale at or above the minimum rate, then the target entity can use the stepped-up carrying value of its assets for purposes of computing its GloBE tax base. The justification for this exception is the gain (or loss) from the deemed asset sale has been subject to tax at or above the minimum rate.

Equity interests accounted for under the fair value accounting method

197. Some equity interests, usually interests below a 20% threshold, are accounted for using the fair value method. The fair value method re-values the equity interest periodically and changes in value are reported as gain or loss, either in the profit and loss statement or in the other comprehensive income section of the balance sheet. These gains and losses should also be excluded from the GloBE tax base to the extent gains and losses from actual sales of such securities would be excluded from the GloBE tax base.

Covered taxes

198. As noted above in Section 3.3.1, the GloBE tax base will be determined by starting with net income of the relevant entities and removing certain items of income and adding back certain expenses to arrive

at a profit (or loss) before tax. Covered taxes are the most obvious expense that needs to be added back to net income to determine profit (or loss) before tax. Moreover, because covered taxes are included in the numerator of the ETR fraction, it would be inconsistent with the policy of GloBE to also allow them as a deduction in the computation of the denominator of the fraction. Accordingly, covered taxes are not treated as an expense in the computation of the GloBE tax base.

199. Financial accounting distinguishes between income taxes and other taxes. Income taxes, as defined for financial accounting purposes, are typically separately reported in the profit and loss statement. Taxes that are not considered income taxes are treated like operating expenses and may not be separately identified in the income statement. The definition of covered taxes under the GloBE rules is broader than the definition of income taxes for financial accounting purposes, and therefore, both covered taxes identified as income taxes in the financial accounts and other covered taxes must be added back to the net income to determine profit (or loss) before tax.

Stock-based compensation

200. Generally, for tax purposes, a corporation is entitled to deduct the value of stock-based compensation based on the ultimate market value of the stock. For example, a corporation may be able to deduct the present value of the stock option at the time of issuance or over the term of the option and then the difference between the present value at the time of issuance and the ultimate market value when the option is exercised by the holder. For financial accounting purposes, companies generally account for stock based compensation based on the present value of the stock option at the time of issuance and amortize that amount over the vesting period. In this case, if the market value of the stock increases over the life of the option, the corporation will deduct an amount for tax purposes that is higher than the amount expensed for financial accounting purposes, which is a permanent difference. This difference between financial accounting income and the local tax base will generally result in a lower GloBE ETR, perhaps below the minimum tax rate.

201. There is a different policy behind the treatment of stock-based compensation for financial accounting and tax purposes. Financial accounting rules focus on the economic position of the reporting entity, where changes to the ownership of the entity are reflected in adjustments in respect of earnings per share. Tax policy tends to treat the issue of stock-based compensation as an expense of the company and as income of the option holder, similar to other compensation for services rendered to the company. The tax policy justification for allowing the corporation to deduct the ultimate market value of the stock option is that the option holder will include the same amount in its taxable income.

202. The rule eliminates the permanent difference by allowing stock-based compensation as a deduction in the GloBE tax base computation to the extent it is allowed and at the same time applied as a deduction in the local tax base computation. In other words, the rule conforms the treatment of stock-based compensation to the local tax treatment. In principle, the rule applies to stock-based compensation for employees and non-employees. However, if the local tax base applies different rules for employees and non-employees, the GloBE tax base would conform to those rules. This rule is consistent with the principles for evaluating permanent differences. In particular, stock-based compensation can be material and some form of deduction is commonly allowed by Inclusive Framework jurisdictions. Furthermore, the deduction is consistent with ensuring a single level of taxation in respect of these instruments.

203. However it is recognised that allowing stock-based compensation to reduce the GloBE tax base only to the extent it is deductible for local tax purposes means that stock-based compensation would never be deductible from the GloBE tax base for jurisdictions that do not impose a corporate income tax, even if the compensation income is subject to tax in the local jurisdiction. As a result, MNEs are allowed to reduce the GloBE tax base by stock-based compensation expense as recognised for financial accounting purposes (rather than local tax purposes), in those jurisdictions that do not have a corporate income tax

system. This special rule is subject to the condition described in Section 3.4.1 below that the item of expense must be able to be reliably and consistently traced to the entity in the relevant jurisdiction.

Bribes

204. Bribes are treated as expenses under financial accounting rules but are not deductible for tax purposes in most Inclusive Framework jurisdictions. A tax deduction for this item is disallowed for public policy reasons. Bribery hinders competition, distorts trade and harms consumers and taxpayers. It can also undermine public support for government. Denying a tax deduction serves as a strong symbol of a common international commitment to combat bribery. Therefore, members of the Inclusive Framework consider that a bribe should not be deductible under the GloBE rules.

205. To the extent a bribe reduces financial accounting income but is disallowed for tax purposes it represents a permanent difference. This difference between financial accounting income and the tax base will result in a higher GloBE ETR. The rule eliminates this permanent difference by disallowing a deduction for bribes in the GloBE tax base.

206. Bribes may be relatively easy to identify as they are commonly disallowed for local tax purposes. Furthermore, adjusting for this item is not expected to result in any significant added complexity and compliance costs because bribes are generally rare and non-recurring items.

207. As a practical matter, bribes may not be identified as such by local tax authorities until several years after the payment is actually made. The rules applicable to post-filing adjustments to local tax liability would apply when the bribe is discovered and disallowed for local tax purposes.[6]

208. Consistent with the principles for evaluating permanent differences, this rule recognises that bribes, while rare, can be material and a deduction for this expense is commonly disallowed in Inclusive Framework jurisdictions.

Fines and penalties

209. Similar to bribes, fines and penalties imposed by a government are commonly disallowed for tax purposes. However, the policy rationale is slightly different. The policy rationale for denying a deduction for bribes is primarily to show a common international commitment to combat bribery and therefore under no circumstance should a bribe be deductible, for any purpose, and in any amount. Whereas the policy rationale for denying a deduction for fines and penalties is to limit the economic cost to only the person that committed the act; which would be diluted if the taxpayer were allowed to share the burden of the penalty with all taxpayers (by way of tax deduction for it).

210. However, fines and penalties, particularly those for minor offenses such as traffic tickets, are more frequent than bribes and vary widely in amount. They can range from a EUR 50 traffic ticket incurred by a trucking company to a multi-million euro fine for securities law violations incurred by a large bank. Recognising the de minimis nature of many fines and penalties, the GloBE tax base excludes deduction of only fines and penalties of EUR 50,000 or more. The exclusion therefore applies only to large fines (EUR 50,000 or more in equivalent currency) but it includes fines that may be levied in respect of the same activity on a periodic basis (e.g. daily fines) that in the aggregate equal or exceed EUR 50,000 in a single year. A periodic fine or penalty includes a fine or penalty that is assessed periodically until corrective action is taken, but does not include separate fines that are for the same type of offense committed upon multiple occasions, such as traffic tickets. The purpose of the threshold is to continue to allow deductions for smaller fines that may not be specifically recorded as separate items in the accounts of the Constituent Entity. This approach avoids the complexity of tracking small fines and penalties for GloBE purposes while at the same time preventing MNEs from escaping a top-up tax because of a few large, non-deductible, fines or penalties. It is also in line with the public policy considerations supporting an adjustment for bribes and consistent with the principles for evaluating permanent differences, including materiality. Interest charges

for late payment of tax or other liabilities to a governmental unit are not considered fines or penalties for this purpose.

Gains and losses on restructuring

211. Transfers of assets among Constituent Entities in connection with a restructuring or reorganisation of the MNE Group commonly benefit from a tax deferral provision. Generally, the gains and losses on transfers of assets in connection with a reorganisation are deferred by requiring the acquiring entity to take the same carrying cost in the asset as the transferor of the asset. This preserves the built-in gain or loss on the asset at the time of the reorganisation and will be realised through use of the asset in the production of income or upon sale or other disposition outside the group. Transactions between group members are similarly eliminated in consolidation under financial accounting rules. Under the GloBE rules, however, gains and losses on transactions between Constituent Entities will generally be recognised under separate company accounting. The difference between the local tax deferral rules and the GloBE separate company accounting rules would tend to lower the ETR in jurisdictions from which the assets are transferred, possibly creating GloBE tax liability.

212. Given the commonality of tax rules in Inclusive Framework on BEPS jurisdictions that allow for gain and loss deferral in connection with reorganisations as well as the materiality of the differences between these local tax rules and the GloBE rules, Inclusive Framework on BEPS members consider it appropriate to provide a mechanism to mirror the local tax deferral under the GloBE rules. In general, it is anticipated that an MNE Group would exclude the gain or loss on a transfer of property, including intangible property, between two Constituent Entities and reduce (increase) the basis of the property in the hands of the acquiring Constituent Entity by the amount of the excluded gain (loss) if the transfer was made in connection with a non-taxable reorganisation or re-structuring. Further work, however, is required to develop and refine the mechanisms that will achieve the appropriate outcomes and to delineate the circumstances under which the rules will apply.

Covered taxes on excluded income

213. Intra-group dividends may be subject to a net basis tax in the shareholder's jurisdiction or subject to a withholding tax in the jurisdiction of the distributing Constituent Entity. Although the dividend is excluded from the GloBE tax base, such taxes represent new or additional taxes on the income of the distributing Constituent Entity that has been included in the GloBE tax base. Thus, such taxes are properly taken into account in computing the ETR of the Constituent Entity that earned the underlying income. See Section 3.4.2.

214. In some cases, a Constituent Entity of an MNE Group may be liable for covered taxes on income from an ownership interest in an entity that is not a Constituent Entity. For example, a Constituent Entity may be subject to a withholding tax on portfolio dividends received from an investment in a corporation or subject to tax under a CFC regime on a minority ownership interest in a CFC.

215. Similarly, a Constituent Entity that owns a minority interest in a partnership or other tax transparent entity or arrangement that is accounted for using the equity method for financial accounting purposes may be subject to net basis tax on its share of a partnership's, entity's, or arrangement's net income. Because income the interest is accounted for using the equity method of accounting, however, it is generally excluded from the Constituent Entity owner's GloBE tax base.

216. Any tax paid in connection with excluded income must be excluded from the numerator of the GloBE ETR computation for the jurisdiction of the owner. The rationale for this exclusion is that these items of income are permanently excluded from the GloBE tax base and hence the denominator of the GloBE ETR calculation. Therefore, it is appropriate to correspondingly exclude any taxes on these items of income from the numerator of the GloBE ETR calculation. The key distinction between taxes imposed on intra-

group dividends and taxes imposed on other excluded dividends and equity method income is that the underlying income that funded the intra-group dividend was previously included in the MNE Group's GloBE tax base when earned, whereas the income that funded the other dividends and equity method income is excluded from the GloBE tax base. Taxes paid on any dividends included in the GloBE tax base are included in the numerator of the ETR computation.

217. Like taxes on dividends, taxes on stock gains may arise in connection with sales of stock in a Constituent Entity or a non-Constituent Entity. Because of the rule that excludes gains (or losses) from the seller's GloBE tax base arising in connection with the disposition of stock, any corporate taxes imposed on the seller's gain generally should be excluded from the numerator of the GloBE ETR calculation in the seller's jurisdiction.

Investment returns of life insurance policy holders

218. Certain life insurance products provide both an insurance policy and an investment return to the owner of the policy. The life insurance company manages the investment component for the benefit of the policy owner. The investment assets are nominally owned by the life insurance company but the assets or the earnings on, and proceeds from disposition of, the assets are beneficially owned by the policy owners. Some accounting standards may require the life insurance company to include the investment returns on the policy holders' assets in its profit (or loss) statement with an adjustment to the equity section of the balance sheet to reflect the fact that the earnings do not belong to the company. Investment earnings that inure exclusively to the benefit of policy holders should not be included in the insurance company's GloBE tax base. Accordingly, if an insurance company's financial accounting standards include earnings beneficially owned by policy holders in the income of the insurance company, a permanent adjustment to the insurance company's GloBE tax base is required with respect to those earnings. Any covered taxes arising in respect of such income must also be excluded from the GloBE ETR computation.

Adjustment for Pillar One Outcomes

219. Pillar One applies before Pillar Two. Depending upon the final design of Pillar One, an adjustment may be required to the GloBE tax base of one or more jurisdictions to properly reflect Pillar One outcomes.[7] Covered taxes associated with that income would need to be assigned accordingly.

3.3.5. Modification to address immediate expensing and accelerated depreciation of assets

220. Immediate expensing and accelerated depreciation of business assets is one of the most common income tax incentives offered by jurisdictions. Consequently, these tax incentives likely will be a common cause of significant temporary differences. These tax incentives may cause the ETR in the jurisdiction to fall below the minimum tax rate, producing tax liability under the income inclusion rule, and resulting in significant and frequent IIR tax paid and ultimately IIR tax credits. The GloBE tax liability arising from this temporary difference will disgorge the tax benefits intended by the tax incentive. Furthermore, in capital-intensive businesses, there is a significant risk that continuous re-investments in assets may prevent the use of the IIR tax credits for an extended period of time and perhaps for the life of the business, potentially leading to over-taxation.

221. The carry-forward rules described in Chapter ensure that tax is paid up to the minimum rate *over time*. However, they can also reverse, in whole or in part, the timing benefit intended to be produced by domestic tax rules allowing immediate expensing and accelerated depreciation for tax purposes. A solution to prevent the GloBE rules reversing these timing benefits will be developed as part of the development of model rules (see Section). This solution must, however, be workable and keep complexity to a minimum.

Broadly, the Inclusive Framework on BEPS has considered two potential solutions, as described in the paragraphs below.

222. One approach considered would leverage deferred tax accounting used by the Constituent Entity with respect to depreciable property that is eligible for immediate expensing or accelerated depreciation for tax purposes. Deferred tax accounting neutralises the effect on the ETR of immediate expensing and accelerated depreciation for tax purposes, just like any other temporary difference. Leveraging from deferred tax accounting principles, the carry-forward approach could be modified such that the numerator of the ETR fraction (i.e., taxes paid) is increased by the deferred tax liability associated with an investment in property or accelerated depreciation during the year. To avoid the tax being double-counted in the numerator, however, a corollary rule would be needed to reduce the covered taxes otherwise computed in each subsequent year by the annual decrease in the deferred tax liability with respect to the asset. However, this approach suffers from the problem of allowing the tax expense to be determined based on estimates of taxes to be paid in the future as well as the other shortcomings associated with deferred tax accounting.

223. Another approach would be to compute the GloBE tax base using the cost recovery allowance or depreciation rates and conventions that the MNE used for local tax purposes in place of the depreciation rates and rules used for financial accounting purposes. Under this approach, the local tax depreciation rules would be applied to the carrying cost of assets as determined for financial accounting purposes. The relevant depreciation rules would include depreciation rates, depreciation periods, and placed in service conventions. It would not, however, permit deductions in excess of the actual cost of the asset. This approach would significantly reduce temporary differences in respect of the carrying cost of depreciable property.[8]

224. The use of the tax depreciation rules rather than the financial accounting depreciation introduces additional complexity into the computation of the GloBE tax base and represents a departure from the policy of determining the GloBE tax base using financial accounts. However, using the tax depreciation rules would eliminate a significant temporary difference and reduce both the frequency and amount of IIR tax paid due solely to temporary differences. Overall, this modification to the financial accounts to determine the GloBE tax base may be less burdensome from a compliance and administration perspective than a proliferation of IIR tax credits.

225. An additional complexity associated with immediate expensing and accelerated depreciation arises from the capitalisation of depreciation to inventory costs. Differences between book and tax accounting for inventoriable depreciation expense and how those differences could be mitigated must be considered as part of the design and implementation of this special rule.

3.3.6. Modification to address distribution-based corporate income tax systems

226. Some members of the Inclusive Framework have income tax regimes that impose an income tax on a corporation when the corporation's income is distributed to its shareholders, rather than when it is earned. The tax rates in these jurisdictions may equal or exceed the agreed minimum rate of tax on the GloBE tax base, thereby ensuring that ultimately the income is not subject to a low rate of tax when the earnings are eventually distributed. Absent a distribution, however, the income is not subject to the distribution tax in the year it is earned and included in the financial accounts.[9] This means that the income would be subject to tax under the GloBE rules as the covered tax expense for the year will be below the minimum tax rate in respect of the financial income. Exempting such income from the GloBE rules entirely, however, would be inappropriate because the tax may not in fact be paid for an extended period of time, which would have the effect of permitting near permanent deferral of tax on income generated in these jurisdictions. Allowing indefinite deferral of tax on income would lead to BEPS concerns equivalent to those raised by stateless income structures.

227. Absent special rules, to avoid tax liability under the GloBE rules, MNE Groups with Constituent Entities subject to a corporate distribution tax regime would need to correctly estimate the amount of the GloBE tax base in the jurisdiction for the year before year-end and distribute enough earnings so that the local tax liability incurred on those earnings equalled or exceeded the minimum tax rate. For example, if the distribution tax rate were 20% and the minimum tax rate were 10%, the Constituent Entities in the jurisdiction would need to distribute an amount equal to half of the GloBE tax base before year-end in order to incur a local tax liability equal to the minimum tax liability on the relevant income. In practice, MNE Groups with Constituent Entities in these jurisdictions would often be liable for tax under the GloBE rules, although subsequent distributions could produce IIR tax credits that could be used to satisfy other tax liabilities.

228. In order to avoid these results, the rule allows a corporation that is subject to a distribution-based corporate income tax regime to increase its covered taxes for the year by the amount of the distribution tax that would be due on the income for the year up to the minimum tax liability for purposes of the GloBE ETR computation in the jurisdiction, but requires the corporation to recapture the increase to the extent an equal amount of distribution tax is not paid within a reasonable period of time, e.g. 2-4 years. The specified time period would be truncated on a per share basis if shares of the entity were disposed by the MNE Group before the end of the specified number of years. Corporate income taxes paid upon distribution would be charged against the annual tax increases in chronological order. Distribution taxes paid in excess of the outstanding balance of annual tax increases in prior years would go into the ETR computation for the tax year in which paid and may create a local tax carry-forward.

229. Mechanically, the numerator of the ETR fraction (i.e., covered tax expense) is increased by the amount of the distribution tax necessary to bring the tax paid during the year (in excess of the outstanding balance of accrued minimum tax) to the minimum tax on the current year's GloBE tax base, except that the increase cannot exceed the amount of distribution tax that would be paid with respect to any undistributed portion of the current year's GloBE tax base. The annual increase in covered taxes up to the minimum tax would be recorded in a memorandum account and tracked by year. Corporate income taxes paid in connection with distributions would reduce the outstanding balance of annual increases, if any, in chronological order. If the corporate income taxes paid in connection with distributions during a year exceeded the outstanding balance of annual increases at the beginning of that year, the excess would increase the numerator of the ETR fraction and reduce the amount that needed to be accrued to achieve a minimum level of tax in that year. At the end of the specified period, any outstanding balance of an annual increase would reduce the numerator of the ETR fraction, but not below zero. The reduction to the numerator of the ETR fraction essentially imposes GloBE tax liability on the unpaid accrual of minimum tax at the end of the specified period. Any amount of the outstanding balance in excess of the numerator of the ETR fraction would create an equal amount of IIR tax liability for that year. The modification to address distribution based corporate income taxes is illustrated in Annex, Example 3.3.6A and Example 3.3.6B.

3.3.7. Treatment of government grants and tax credits

230. This Section addresses how government cash grants and tax credits should be taken into account in the ETR calculation under the GloBE rules (IIR and UTPR). Specifically, an approach is set out for determining whether, and under what circumstances, the grant or credit should be treated as part of the recipient's income or as a reduction in a covered tax liability.

Accounting treatment of government grants and tax credits

231. Consistent with the general approach for determining the GloBE tax base, the starting point for determining whether the grant or tax credit should be recognised as income or a reduction to tax liability is to look to existing financial accounting rules.

232. Under IFRS the accounting treatment for government grants and other forms of government assistance is prescribed by IAS 20. That accounting standard provides that government grants should be recognised as income on a systematic basis over the periods in which the entity recognises expenses for the related costs for which the grants are intended to compensate.

233. Government grants are defined broadly under IAS 20 as assistance by government in the form of transfers of resources to an entity in return for past or future compliance with certain conditions relating to the operating activities of the entity. Government is understood broadly in IAS 20 and includes central and local government bodies as well as all sorts of government agencies and similar bodies, including at the international level. Grants are usually provided as an incentive for an entity to engage in an activity that would not be commercially justified without those grants. This includes, for example, a forgivable loan when there is reasonable assurance that the entity will meet the terms for forgiveness of the loan (IAS 20.10). The benefit of a government loan at a below-market rate of interest is also treated as a government grant (IAS 20.10A). IAS 20 also covers other forms of government assistance whereby the action by government is designed to provide an economic benefit that is specific to an entity or range of entities qualifying under certain criteria. Excluded from the scope of IAS 20 are transactions with government which cannot be distinguished from the normal trading transactions of the entity (e.g. government procurement policy that is responsible for part of an entity's sales) and those forms of government assistance which cannot reasonably have a value placed on them, such as free technical or marketing advice and the provision of guarantees (IAS 20.35).[10] Other forms of government assistance affecting only general conditions, such as the provision of transportation or communication infrastructure available on an ongoing basis to the general public or the imposition of trading constraints on competitors, are also out of scope of IAS 20. Given that the GloBE tax base is based on the financial accounts, government assistance that is excluded from the scope of IAS 20 is not included as income in the GloBE tax base.

234. The accounting treatment of expenditure based tax credits, commonly referred to as investment tax credits (ITCs), is significantly less clear. In fact the accounting treatment of ITCs is specifically scoped out of IAS 20 (Government Grants) and IAS 12 (Income Taxes). In practice, this means that MNEs commonly account for ITCs by analogy with the requirements of IAS 20 or IAS 12. ITCs are provided by many jurisdictions to incentivise a range of business investments. ITCs can take different forms and be subject to different conditions, and entitlement to receive the ITC can be determined in a variety of ways. Some ITCs may relate to direct investment in property, plant and equipment. Other entities may receive ITCs relating to R&D or other activities. Some credits are not restricted to being realised as a reduction in current CIT. For example, where a credit exceeds the current year CIT liability, the unused credit may be carried forward to reduce future CIT or may be carried back. For some credits, the remaining portion of the credit can be used to offset other non-CIT liabilities, such as VAT or payroll taxes. Other credits may be settled directly in cash if the entity does not have sufficient taxes payable to access the credit within a certain period.

235. It is a matter of judgement to determine the most appropriate accounting treatment for an ITC based on a qualitative analysis of the legal requirements that must be met in order to generate the credit rather than a quantitative assessment of the economic outcomes for how a particular ITC is realised in practice. An ITC that is determined or limited by reference to an entity's income tax liability or provided in the form of an income tax deduction is likely to be accounted for under IAS 12 (Income Taxes) and recorded in the financial accounts as a reduction in current tax expense. If the realisation of the ITC is not dependent on the amount of taxable profit or on any past or future income tax liability generated by an entity, then it is likely to be accounted for under IAS 20 (Government Grants) and recorded in the financial accounts as other income.

236. Therefore, it is expected that generally under IFRS and equivalent accounting standards any "refundable" ITCs would be treated as income, whereas any non-refundable ITCs would be treated as a reduction in a tax liability. The term "refundable" is understood in a broad sense and covers ITCs that may become payable as cash or available as cash equivalents, including being available to be used to

discharge liabilities other than a covered tax liability. The rationale, from an accounting perspective, for treating refundable tax credits in the same way as grants is that, similar to grants, the taxpayer's entitlement to a refundable tax credit is not tied to its income or tax liability, and so in terms of economic substance grants and refundable tax credits are equivalent.

237. IFRS may treat a credit as "refundable" even if it is eligible to be refunded only after a number of years or where the taxpayer has the option to offset the credit against a non-CIT liability, such as a payroll tax or VAT liability. Most importantly, IFRS generally takes an "all-in" approach to refundability by which if a credit has some feature of potential refundability (e.g. the credit is required to be carried forward and only the unused / excess portion of the credit is refundable after a certain number of years), the entire amount of the credit is treated as income even if in practice the credit is used to offset a CIT liability, and thus may never actually be refunded.

Treatment under the GloBE *rules based on the financial accounting rules with safeguards for refundable tax credits to address risk areas*

Treatment of government grants and tax credits under the GloBE

General rule

The treatment of government grants and tax credits will be based on the financial accounting rules with safeguards for refundable tax credits to address risk areas:

(a) Where a refundable tax credit meets certain conditions, i.e. a "qualified refundable tax credit", the entire amount of the credit is treated as income (in line with the financial accounting treatment for refundable tax credits).

(b) Where a refundable tax credit does not meet the conditions, i.e. a "non-qualified refundable tax credit", the entire amount of the credit is treated as reducing a covered tax liability.

(c) For non-refundable tax credits, the entire amount of the credit is treated as reducing a covered tax liability (in line with the financial accounting treatment for non-refundable tax credits).

(d) For all government grants, the entire amount of the grant is treated as income (in line with the financial accounting treatment for government grants).

Conditions for a "qualified refundable tax credit" under the GloBE:

In order to be treated as a "qualified refundable tax credit" under the GloBE, the tax credit regime must be designed in a way so that a credit becomes refundable within 4 years from when it is first provided. Where the tax credit regime under the laws of a jurisdiction provides for partial refundability such that only a fixed percentage or portion of the credit is refundable, in order for the refundable portion of the credit to be treated as a qualified refundable tax credit, it must become refundable within 4 years from when it is first provided.

Furthermore, if a refundable tax credit regime is determined to give rise to a material competitive distortion under the review process described below, a credit granted under such a regime will not be treated as a "qualified refundable tax credit" under the GloBE.

Review process:

(a) Specific: As part of the review process for testing financial accounting standards for "material competitive distortions" described in Section 3.3.3., if an Inclusive Framework on BEPS member identifies a specific risk associated with a certain jurisdiction's refundable tax credit regime, it can be brought to the Inclusive Framework on BEPS for review on a case-by-case basis. This specific review process would seek to identify whether the tax credit regime has been designed in a way that made it unlikely, at the time it is introduced into law, that there will be significant refunds paid to taxpayers.

(b) General: As part of a multilateral review process described in Section. looking at the operation of the GloBE rules after a certain number of years of their application, if Inclusive Framework on BEPS members identify risks associated with the treatment of tax credits and government grants that lead to unintended outcomes, the Inclusive Framework on BEPS will be asked to consider designing further conditions for a "qualified refundable tax credit" or alternative rules for the treatment of tax credits and government grants.

238. The approach treats all government grants as income and treats refundable tax credits as income where they meet certain conditions (referred to as "qualified refundable tax credits"). The conditions are intended to reduce the particular risk areas identified specifically in relation to refundable tax credits. Refundable tax credits that do not meet the conditions (referred to as "non-qualified refundable tax credits") and all other tax credits are treated as a reduction in a covered tax liability. This approach is based on the principle underpinning the approach to the design of the GloBE rules to start with the relevant financial accounting rules subject to any agreed adjustments as necessary.[11]

239. The approach generally aligns with the financial accounting treatment for government grants and non-refundable tax credits, and, therefore, does not require adjustments for these under the GloBE rules. It also follows the accounting treatment for refundable tax credits where the terms of the credit satisfied the conditions of a qualified refundable tax credit, and only departs from the financial accounting treatment for non-qualified refundable tax credits. For a non-qualified refundable tax credit that is recorded as income for financial accounting purposes, an adjustment will be required to remove the full amount of the credit from the measure of net income in the GloBE tax base (denominator) and instead treat this as a reduction in the GloBE covered tax liability (numerator). An adjustment may also be required for a qualified refundable tax credit, to the extent that such a credit reduces corporate income tax payable for domestic tax purposes, to add this amount back to the GloBE covered tax liability (numerator) as the full amount of the credit will be treated as income in the GloBE tax base (denominator).

Conditions for a "qualified refundable tax credit"

240. Refundable tax credits are typically used by governments to incentivise activities, such as R&D, where there is significant uncertainty as to whether the expenditure will ultimately result in a net return for the investor. By making these credits refundable, the government reduces the risk associated with these types of investments and puts large and small taxpayers on an equal footing, by ensuring the subsidy is available regardless of whether the person undertaking the activity is paying taxes.

241. The conditions that a refundable tax credit would need to satisfy to be treated as a qualified refundable tax credit are intended to reduce the risk that tax credits could be used as a mechanism for distorting the GloBE ETR calculation by being legally constructed as "refundable" but with terms that make it unlikely, in practice, that the credit will actually be refunded. In particular, this risk can be specifically identified when a tax credit regime is designed in a way so that a credit is only refundable after a long period of time.

242. The primary condition to safeguard against this particular risk is to stipulate that, in order to be treated as a "qualified refundable tax credit" under the GloBE, the tax credit regime under the laws of a

jurisdiction is designed in a way so that a credit must become refundable within four years from when it is first provided. This condition is intended to be a bright-line test that should be easy to apply in order to provide certainty to taxpayers and tax administrations and minimise compliance costs. The analysis would be based on a qualitative assessment of the tax credit regime as a whole, and not on a taxpayer specific basis. Where the tax credit regime under the laws of a jurisdiction provides for partial refundability, such that only a fixed percentage or portion of the credit is refundable, in order for the refundable portion of the credit to be treated as a qualified refundable tax credit, it must become refundable within 4 years from when it is first provided. Refundable means either payable as cash or cash equivalents, including being available to be used to discharge liabilities other than a covered tax liability. Furthermore, as part of a multilateral review process set out below, further conditions could be developed to mitigate specific risks identified where refundable tax credit regimes are introduced in a way that result in material competitive distortions in the application of the GloBE rules.

Review process

243. A multilateral review process will be established to address any residual risk that refundable tax credit regimes could be designed to circumvent the condition set out above to manipulate the GloBE ETR outcomes. This review process will be designed to identify risks associated with the design of a jurisdiction's refundable tax credit regime, in particular where the terms of the tax credit are designed in a way that makes it unlikely, at the time such credit is introduced into law, that there will be significant refunds paid to taxpayers. The review process could identify hallmarks for those features of a tax credit regime that indicate risks under the GloBE rules, such as where the tax credit regime is targeted at a particular taxpayer or small group of taxpayers.

244. A specific review process focused on refundable tax credit regimes could be incorporated into the same review process that allows Inclusive Framework on BEPS members to consider whether a financial accounting standard "results in material competitive distortions in the application of the GloBE rules".[12] That is, if an Inclusive Framework on BEPS member identifies a specific risk associated with a certain country's refundable tax credit regime, it is brought to the Inclusive Framework on BEPS for review on a case-by-case basis. The logic of dealing with the review of refundable tax credit regimes as part of the same process is that the core concern is the financial accounting treatment of those refundable tax credits. Criteria will be developed to determine when a refundable tax credit regime can be brought to Inclusive Framework on BEPS for review to provide clarity and certainty to taxpayers and to minimise burdens on tax administrations. The guiding principle for this review process will be focused on identifying refundable tax credit regimes that have the effect of distorting the GloBE ETR calculation.

245. In addition to a specific review process for refundable tax credit regimes as set out above, as part of a general multilateral review of the operation of the GloBE rules after a certain number of years of their operation[13], if Inclusive Framework on BEPS members identify risks associated with the treatment of tax credits and government grants that lead to unintended outcomes, Inclusive Framework on BEPS could be asked to consider designing further conditions for a "qualified refundable tax credit" or, if necessary, explore alternative rules for the treatment of tax credits and government grants. This analysis would be based on empirical and historical data with respect to the tax credit regime as a whole, and not on a taxpayer specific basis.

246. The specified conditions for qualified refundable tax credits combined with a review process should provide sufficient disincentives to neutralise potential distortive behaviour.

3.3.8. Emergency government assistance

247. The provision of emergency government assistance (e.g. government grants and tax credits designed to mitigate the impact of Covid19) may lead to a lower GloBE ETR calculation that could trigger a top-up tax under the GloBE rules. Further consideration will be given to whether there should be a special

exemption as part of the development of the model rules (see Section) to ensure that emergency government assistance should not give rise to a tax liability under the GloBE. Such rules would establish the criteria for excluding emergency government assistance from the GloBE ETR calculation, including, for example, where the benefit is:

(a) provided by a government;

(b) limited in duration, for example the assistance is available for no longer than [x] years;

(c) intended to provide financial support in response to an external shock; and

(d) provided to a certain category of taxpayers or industry that has been, or is expected to be, materially affected by such an external shock.

3.4. Jurisdictional blending

248. The Sections above deal with the general determination of an MNE's income for GloBE purposes and the covered taxes on that income. The next Sections describe how to determine an MNE's ETR under the GloBE rules on a jurisdictional basis. Under a jurisdictional blending approach, a GloBE tax liability will arise when the ETR of a jurisdiction in which the MNE Group operates is below the agreed minimum rate. To determine the jurisdictional ETR, the MNE Group must first determine the income of each entity and then assign that income and the covered taxes paid in respect of that income to the relevant jurisdiction. More specifically, the jurisdictional ETR computation involves two steps: the first step is to determine the income of each entity in the group and make adjustments, at the entity level, in respect of consolidated items (Consolidation Adjustments); and the second step is to assign the income of and taxes paid by each entity to a jurisdiction. This Section describes the rules for making these determinations and assignments.

3.4.1. Consolidation adjustments

Consolidation adjustments

Reliance on entity level financial information

MNEs can rely on the entity-level financial information that is used in preparing the parent's consolidated financial accounts to determine the profit (or loss) before tax of each Constituent Entity, even if such financial information is not prepared in strict accordance with the parent's accounting standard where (a) it is reasonable to do so, (b) the information is reliable, and (c) the use of such information does not result in material permanent differences from the accounting standard of the parent.

Treatment of intercompany items

Income, gains, expenses, and losses attributable to transactions between Constituent Entities should not be eliminated and should be recorded in accordance with the arm's length principle. Intercompany items can be excluded, however, to the extent the transaction is between Constituent Entities in the same jurisdiction. Items recognised in consolidation

Other items maintained at the consolidated level should only be taken into account in determining the profit and loss of a Constituent Entity where those items can be reliably and consistently traced to that entity.

Reliance on entity level financial information

249. Even where a subsidiary maintains financial accounts using the parent entity's accounting standard, the subsidiary is unlikely, in many cases, to be able to produce an income statement on a stand-alone basis that would meet the rigorous standards an independent financial auditor would apply in assessing compliance with the parent entity's accounting standard. There are several reasons for this.

250. First, the materiality threshold for a subsidiary on a stand-alone basis would generally be much lower than the materiality standard of the consolidated group. The accounting treatment of a transaction or item that is out of step with the parent entity's accounting standard may be acceptable in the context of the consolidated group's financial accounts. However, on a stand-alone company basis, the transactions or items may be material such that deviation from a strict application of the accounting standard would be unacceptable.

251. Second, in the case of an acquisition, the purchaser is required to record the assets and liabilities of the acquired business at fair value based on an allocation of the purchase price (this practice is commonly referred to as "purchase accounting"). Purchase accounting commonly results in increased or decreased carrying values for fixed assets previously included in the acquired entity's financial accounts and recording new intangible assets that were not previously included in the acquired entity's financial accounts. The purchaser uses these fair value measures to prepare its consolidated financial accounts. In many cases, however, the fair value adjustments are not "pushed-down" to the acquired entity's stand-alone financial accounts. In fact, push-down accounting is not permitted under some accounting standards, including IFRS. Instead, many MNE Groups hold purchase accounting adjustments at the consolidated level, i.e., in financial accounts that are used exclusively to prepare the group's consolidated financial statements. Adjustments for purchase accounting items is further discussed below.

252. Third, similar to purchase accounting adjustments, certain other financial accounting items are maintained at the consolidated accounting level, rather than the financial accounts of stand-alone legal entities. Common examples include stock-based compensation expenses, foreign currency gain and loss, and fair value accounting adjustments related to derivatives and pension liabilities. Adjustments for stock based compensation expenses, and other items held in consolidation are discussed below.

253. Finally, it is recognised that not every MNE Group will prepare entity-level accounts. Some businesses prepare their accounts on a business line rather than an entity basis. When entity level accounts are required for local statutory or tax purposes, then these are prepared based on the business line accounts. Thus, while these local statutory accounts are derived from those that are used for consolidation purposes, they are not the basis for preparing the consolidated accounts.

254. For the reasons described above, the profit (or loss) before tax of a particular subsidiary that is used in the preparation of or derived from the preparation of the MNE Group's consolidated financial statements may not be, on a stand-alone entity basis, in perfect conformity with the parent's financial accounting standard. In fact, on a stand-alone basis, the differences could be sufficiently significant that a financial accounting auditor would require adjustments.

255. The gap between financial accounts prepared in perfect accord with the parent's accounting standard and the financial accounts that are likely to be maintained by the subsidiaries of an MNE raises a question of what it means to compute a subsidiary's profit (or loss) before tax using the "financial accounting standard used by the parent entity in the preparation of its consolidated financial statements." In other words, does the requirement mean that each subsidiary must compute its profit (or loss) before tax in strict accordance with the parent entity's financial accounting standard as if it were a stand-alone entity? Alternatively, does the requirement mean more generally that each subsidiary must start with the profit (or loss) before tax that is used in the preparation of the parent entity's consolidated financial statements?

256. The rule set out above adopts the latter interpretation. A significant benefit of using financial accounts as a starting point for the GloBE tax base is the efficiency of beginning with an income measure that has already been computed for other purposes. A requirement to compute the profit (or loss) before tax of each Constituent Entity under the more rigorous application of the parent entity's financial accounting standard than is required for that entity in the preparation of the MNE Group's consolidated financial statements would impose significant additional compliance costs. In addition, that income computation would not be subject to scrutiny by the financial accounting auditors. In contrast, the Constituent Entity's profit (or loss) before tax that is computed in connection with the preparation of consolidated financial statements under the parent entity's accounting standard is subject to audit, albeit with a materiality threshold established on a consolidated group basis.

257. As already noted above, the profit (or loss) before tax that is used in consolidation may not be a perfect application of the parent entity's accounting standard. However, if an independent auditor reviewing the consolidated financial statements would not require any adjustments to the income from that subsidiary, the same approach would be acceptable for computing the GloBE tax base. Of course, if an independent auditor required adjustments in respect of the subsidiary's financial accounts, those adjustments would be required for purposes of computing the GloBE tax base as well, unless they are related to income or expense excluded from the GloBE tax base.

258. The rule permits the profit (or loss) before tax that is used in the preparation of the consolidated financial accounts to be used in the computation of the GloBE tax base in lieu of a strict application of the Parent's financial accounting standard, but only under certain conditions that ensure data integrity. First, it must be reasonable, meaning that better financial information (i.e., financial information kept in strict accordance with the parent's accounting standard) is unavailable. This criterion could be met if the local subsidiary has no compliance or regulatory obligation to prepare stand-alone financial accounts in line with the parent's accounting standard. Second, the information must be reliable, meaning that there must be appropriate mechanisms in place to ensure that the information is recorded accurately. In this regard, the financial accounting internal controls and accounting processes employed by the subsidiary must be tested and deemed acceptable to the financial accounting auditor pursuant to Generally Accepted Auditing Standards of the parent's or subsidiary's jurisdiction. A good set of generally accepted auditing standards requires a review not only of the financial statements, but also a review of the company's internal controls and other processes which bear on the integrity of the underlying data. Third, the financial information used must not result in material permanent differences from the financial accounting standard of the parent, determined by reference to the relevant entity and not with respect to the group's consolidated materiality threshold.[14]

Treatment of intercompany items

259. Using a jurisdictional approach to blending under the GloBE rules will require transactions between Constituent Entities in different jurisdictions to be treated in the same manner as transactions with unrelated entities in order to determine the GloBE tax base for each jurisdiction. Therefore, under the rule set out above, income, gains, expenses, and losses attributable to transactions between Constituent Entities should not be eliminated and should be recorded in accordance with the arm's length principle. This has implications for both the timing and location of income.

260. In terms of timing, by not eliminating the effect of transactions between group members, a portion of the group's income or loss will be accelerated as compared to consolidated income when the buyer does not deduct its expense in the same year that the seller recognises the related income. For example, a manufacturing Constituent Entity's gain on sale to a distribution member will be offset by the distribution Constituent Entity's cost of goods sold when the latter sells those goods to a third party. If the distribution entity does not resell the goods in the same year, the combined income of all group entities on a separate company basis will exceed the group's consolidated income in that year because intercompany

transactions are eliminated in the consolidation process. When the distribution entity recognises the cost of goods sold in the subsequent year, the aggregate separate company income will be less than the group's consolidated income by the same amount. Thus, the timing of the MNE Group's income is affected by the separate company treatment, but the overall amount of income remains the same. In terms of location, by not eliminating intra-group income or loss, the MNE Group's consolidated income will be allocated between the two jurisdictions when the buying and selling entities are in different jurisdictions.[15]

261. However, jurisdictions adopting the GloBE rules may permit elimination of transactions between Constituent Entities resident in the same jurisdiction. The modification could be required or permitted at the election of the taxpayer. This would prevent a timing difference attributable to transactions between Constituent Entities resident in the same jurisdiction and likely conforms more closely to the tax accounting, consolidation, or group relief rules applicable in the jurisdiction, which would more closely align the GloBE tax base in a jurisdiction with the local tax rules. This exception is particularly beneficial in a system that addresses timing differences using a carry-forward approach.

262. If intra-group transactions are not recorded in the Constituent Entities' financial accounts based on the arm's length principle, the income and expense of each party to the transaction must be adjusted to conform to the arm's length principle. Application of the arm's length principle in the computation of the GloBE tax base is necessary to prevent misallocation of income among jurisdictions, ensure that the income of entities in each jurisdiction is taken into account at the proper time, and prevent the recognition of non-economic loses from transactions between entities in the same jurisdiction. In addition, the counterparties to an intercompany transaction are required to apply the same arm's-length price. This rule is necessary to prevent counterparties avoiding GloBE tax liability by applying transfer prices at different points within the arm's length range.

263. Transfer pricing adjustments based on the arm's length principle will often be required for tax purposes. The GloBE rules focus only on transactions between Constituent Entities within the same MNE Group and should generally follow the obligations that are imposed on those Constituent Entities under local law. Thus, requiring intra-group transactions to be reported based on the arm's length principle and at the same price under the GloBE rules may require an adjustment to the financial accounts but should not create significant additional compliance burden overall.

Items recognised in consolidation

264. Purchase accounting adjustments represent the largest and most common items of income and expense that may not be reflected in the relevant entity's separate financial accounts. When a corporation becomes a member of a consolidated financial group as the result of a stock acquisition, financial accounting rules generally require the assets of the newly acquired member to be re-valued based on their fair market values. The re-valuation results in either an increase or decrease in the carrying cost of each asset for financial accounting purposes. If the acquisition price[16] exceeds the fair market value of the tangible assets less the liabilities assumed, the relevant financial accounting rule typically will require the recording of some new intangible assets, such as goodwill. In terms of recordkeeping, however, the acquiring corporation generally will not "push down" the adjustments to the carrying value of pre-existing assets or any new intangible assets to the acquired members financial accounting records or systems. The acquiring corporation may instead account for the adjustments in its financial accounting system that is used in connection with the preparation of consolidated financial accounts, sometimes referred to as the "consolidation reporting package." This creates a potential source of discrepancy between the consolidated profit (or loss) before tax and the stand-alone profit (or loss) before tax of the acquired entity.

265. However, purchase accounting adjustments may be unnecessary for GloBE purposes given one of the rules discussed above in Section 3.3.4 in the context of adjustments for permanent differences. In particular, one of the rules is to exclude gains and losses arising from the disposition of stock. The corollary to this rule is that the acquired entity is required to use the historical carrying value of its underlying assets

to compute its GloBE tax base after the acquisition, not the post-acquisition carrying value. Therefore, the fact that the acquiring corporation may not push down purchase accounting adjustments to the acquired subsidiary is not problematic; in fact, it facilitates the correct computation of the GloBE tax base. The rule that excludes the gain (or loss) on the disposition of stock is described above in Section 3.3.4. Similarly, impairments and impairment recoveries of assets that are themselves maintained at the consolidated level should not be traced to the Constituent Entity that owns the underlying asset if the depreciation or amortisation of such assets (or the portion of the carrying cost of such assets that is held in consolidation) is not traced to the entity.

266. The parent entity of an MNE Group commonly issues stock-based compensation to employees that are on the payroll of foreign subsidiaries. In some cases, the parent will push down the compensation expense to the relevant subsidiary via a stock recharge agreement or similar arrangement. Under these agreements, the foreign subsidiary reimburses the parent entity for the costs associated with stock-based compensation issued to its employees. The foreign subsidiary may be able to claim a local deduction for the payment under a stock recharge agreement. However, local tax and accounting requirements differ in what forms of compensation are eligible, the value of the compensation that can be deducted, and accounting requirements. Some jurisdictions may allow a local tax deduction even without a recharge agreement. Other jurisdictions may not allow a local tax deduction even when a recharge agreement exists. The result is that the cost associated with stock-based compensation is pushed down to the relevant subsidiary in some cases, for example when it is required in order to receive a local deduction, but not in all cases, for example, when a local deduction is not conditioned on the existence of a re-charge.

267. Similar to purchase accounting adjustments, whether an MNE pushes down the cost of stock-based compensation may not matter for GloBE purposes given the stock-based compensation rule discussed above in Section 3.3.4 in the context of adjustments for permanent differences. In particular, the rule for stock-based compensation allows a deduction in the GloBE tax base of a jurisdiction to the extent it is allowed as a deduction in the local tax base of the subsidiary in the jurisdiction that employed or contracted with the party receiving the stock-based compensation. In other words, the treatment of stock-based compensation for financial accounting purposes is irrelevant because the rule relies on tax accounts for this particular item of expense. The use of tax accounts for stock-based compensation would be required for all Constituent Entities of the MNE Group in order to ensure consistency across group members.

268. Other financial accounting items may also be maintained at the consolidated level, rather than the financial accounts of stand-alone entities. These items may include foreign currency gain and loss and fair value accounting adjustments related to certain items. Such items should only be taken into account in determining the profit (or loss) of a group entity where those items can be reliably and consistently traced to that entity. An item can be reliably traced to an entity where it relates wholly or exclusively to that entity or it relates to a group of entities and there is a clear basis for apportioning that amount between them. This tracing method must be applied consistently by the MNE Group to items and Constituent Entities within the group and across accounting periods.

3.4.2. Assignment of income and taxes of entity to each jurisdiction

Assignment of income and taxes

Income of permanent establishments and Constituent Entities with a tax jurisdiction of residence

Profit (or loss) before tax earned by a Constituent Entity that is a permanent establishment is assigned to the jurisdiction where the permanent establishment is located. In other cases the profit (or loss) before tax earned by the Constituent Entity is assigned to its tax jurisdiction of residence.

Income of Constituent Entities without a tax jurisdiction of residence

In the case of a Constituent Entity that does not have a tax jurisdiction of residence (a stateless entity):

(a) the share of profits of each owner that is a Constituent Entity is assigned to the owner's tax jurisdiction of residence if that owner's jurisdiction treats the entity as tax transparent, and

(b) any remaining profits, including the share of profits of any owner that is a Constituent Entity whose jurisdiction does not treat the entity as tax transparent, are assigned to the stateless jurisdiction.

An owner's tax jurisdiction treats an entity as tax transparent if the owner is subject to tax on its share of the entity's income or loss in its tax jurisdiction in the same manner as if the owner directly earned its share of the entity's income or loss.

Covered taxes

Any covered tax paid by a Constituent Entity with respect to its income or income of a tax transparent entity that it owns is assigned to the same jurisdiction as the related income.

Covered taxes paid by a Constituent Entity with respect to dividends distributed by another Constituent Entity are assigned to the jurisdiction of the Constituent Entity that paid the dividend.

Overview

269. A jurisdictional blending approach under the GloBE rules requires the MNE to allocate its foreign income and taxes between the different tax jurisdictions in which it operates.[17] Generally, an MNE would be subject to tax under a jurisdictional blending approach where the tax on the income allocated to a jurisdiction was below the minimum rate. The MNE's liability for additional tax under the GloBE rules would be the aggregate of the amounts necessary to bring the total amount of tax on the income in each jurisdiction up to the minimum tax rate.

270. In order to determine, on a jurisdictional basis, whether an MNE's income is subject to a minimum level of taxation, the income earned by Constituent Entities and the covered taxes that are paid or shown as payable on the relevant return filed in respect of that income need to be correlated and assigned to the appropriate jurisdiction. Generally, the income earned by an MNE should be assigned to the jurisdiction of the Constituent Entity that earned the income, whether that Constituent Entity is a corporation or similar juridical entity or a permanent establishment of such entity, and the covered taxes paid by the MNE should be associated with the income that was the subject of the tax.

271. The starting point for determining the jurisdictional ETR is the assignment of income to jurisdictions. The rules for assigning income among jurisdictions build on the rules applicable to country by country reporting (CbCR). As noted above, the GloBE rules adopt, with some modifications, the CbCR definition of MNE Group and Constituent Entity.[18] The CbCR rules generally require MNE Groups to report

certain information in respect of Constituent Entities based on the entities' respective tax jurisdictions of residence. A permanent establishment is considered a Constituent Entity separate from its head office. For purposes of jurisdictional blending, the same approach should apply to the assignment of income among tax jurisdictions. Covered taxes in respect of a Constituent Entity's income likewise should be assigned to the Constituent Entity's tax jurisdiction. Profit (or loss) of an entity and the taxes associated therewith can only be assigned to one jurisdiction.

Assigning income

272. The income assignment rule is straightforward in the case of permanent establishments. Profit (or loss) before tax earned by a Constituent Entity that is a permanent establishment is assigned to the jurisdiction where the permanent establishment is located. This rule is consistent with CbCR. In order to avoid the risk of over-taxation, special rules may be required in respect of taxable branches, where a loss in the permanent establishment jurisdiction is taken into account in calculating the taxable income of the head office.

273. The income assignment rule is also straightforward in the case of Constituent Entities that have a tax jurisdiction of residence under the CbCR rules. Profit (or loss) before tax of such Constituent Entities are assigned to the entity's tax jurisdiction of residence. Generally, a Constituent Entity other than a permanent establishment is considered a resident in a tax jurisdiction under the CbCR rules if, under the laws of that tax jurisdiction, the member is liable to tax (other than a source-based withholding tax) therein based on place of management, place of organisation, or another similar criterion. A corporation created in a jurisdiction that does not have a corporate income tax is considered tax resident in the jurisdiction of creation, unless it is managed and controlled in a jurisdiction that does impose an income tax on the corporation on a residence basis.

274. Assigning income of Constituent Entities that do not have a tax jurisdiction of residence (stateless entities) is more challenging. As discussed in Section, this category of Constituent Entities is comprised generally of tax transparent entities and reverse-hybrid entities. A tax transparent entity is an entity or arrangement that is tax transparent in the jurisdiction of the owner and in the jurisdiction of the entity.[19] Building on the analysis in the BEPS Action 2 Report (OECD, 2015[4]), a reverse-hybrid entity is an entity or arrangement that is not tax transparent in the jurisdiction of the owner but is tax transparent in the jurisdiction in which the entity is created. An owner's tax jurisdiction treats an entity as tax transparent if the owner is subject to tax on its share of the entity's income or loss in its tax jurisdiction in the same manner as if the owner directly earned its share of the entity's income or loss. In some cases, the owner of the stateless entity may be a permanent establishment located in the tax jurisdiction in which the stateless entity conducts its business activities.

275. Under the CbCR rules, an entity that does not have a jurisdiction of tax residence is treated as a stateless entity, and, in the CbC report, its income is assigned to the "stateless" jurisdiction, which is a hypothetical jurisdiction treated as a tax jurisdiction for CbCR purposes. If the tax jurisdiction of an owner or owners of the entity treats the entity as tax transparent, the owner's share of its income is also assigned to the jurisdiction(s) of those owners. For purposes of jurisdictional blending, however, income can only be assigned to a single jurisdiction. Nonetheless, CbCR provides a useful template for assigning the income of stateless entities.

276. Adapting the CbCR approach to the GloBE rules requires the creation of a stateless jurisdiction for purposes of the GloBE rules. This stateless jurisdiction is treated the same as a tax jurisdiction for purposes of applying the GloBE rules on a jurisdictional basis. Thus, all of the income assigned to the stateless jurisdiction under this rule and the corresponding covered taxes should be aggregated for purposes of a stateless jurisdiction ETR computation and top-up tax computation.

277. The types of Constituent Entities that are treated as stateless under the rules of Section include tax transparent entities and reverse-hybrid entities. Each owner's share of the income of a stateless

Constituent Entity is assigned to that owner's tax jurisdiction, unless the owner is a Constituent Entity and its tax jurisdiction does not treat the entity as tax transparent. Thus, in the case of a tax transparent entity that is owned exclusively by Constituent Entities that are tax resident in (or, in the case of a Constituent Entity that is a Permanent Establishment, located in) jurisdictions that treat the entity as tax transparent, all of the entity's income will be assigned to the jurisdictions of those Constituent Entity owners. If the jurisdiction of a Constituent Entity owner does not treat the entity as tax transparent, the entity is a reverse-hybrid with respect to that owner and that owner's share of the entity's income will be assigned to the stateless jurisdiction. The rule also deals with situations in which non-Constituent Entities hold a minority interest in a stateless Constituent Entity of the MNE Group. The non-Constituent Entity owner's share of the income will be assigned to the jurisdiction of those owners and not taken into account by the MNE Group in the computation of the ETR or top-up tax of the stateless jurisdiction. If an owner of a stateless entity is itself a stateless entity, the rule is applied to that owner's share of the income as if that owner directly earned its share of the income.

278. As explained in Section, a business unit that is treated as a joint operation will be treated as a separate Constituent Entity if the income and expenses of the joint operation are included in the group's consolidated financial statements in proportion to the group's ownership interest in the business unit. The Constituent Entity is comprised, however, only of the MNE Group's share of the entity or arrangement as reflected in the consolidated financial statements. A joint operation may be subject to tax in a jurisdiction or may be a tax transparent entity. The general rules for determining tax residency apply to a joint operation that is treated as a Constituent Entity. Thus, the joint operation may be tax resident in a jurisdiction if it is subject to tax in that jurisdiction or, if it is tax transparent, it may be stateless. If the joint operation is a stateless entity, its income is assigned pursuant to the rules described above for stateless entities.

Assigning covered taxes

279. Covered taxes generally follow the income to which they relate under the rules for assigning covered taxes. In other words, the covered taxes associated with income assigned to a particular jurisdiction, including the stateless jurisdiction, generally are assigned to that jurisdiction.

280. Covered taxes paid with respect to the income of a permanent establishment, including taxes paid in the headquarters jurisdiction, are assigned to the location of the permanent establishment. Covered taxes paid with respect to the income of a Constituent Entity with a tax jurisdiction of residence are assigned to the Constituent Entity's tax jurisdiction. These covered taxes may be imposed by the Constituent Entity's tax jurisdiction or another tax jurisdiction. For example, withholding taxes paid in respect of a royalty received from a licensee in another jurisdiction would be assigned to the tax jurisdiction of the Constituent Entity that received the royalty. Similarly, taxes imposed on a shareholder of a Constituent Entity in respect of a dividend or under a controlled foreign company (CFC) regime should be assigned to the jurisdiction of the distributing Constituent Entity or CFC because those taxes are paid in respect of the Constituent Entity's or CFC's income. See Annex, Examples 3.4.2A, 3.4.2B, 3.4.2C, 3.4.2D, and 3.4.2G.

281. Ideally, covered taxes paid with respect to distributions of a Constituent Entity's income, including net basis taxes and withholding taxes, should be assigned to the tax jurisdiction of the Constituent Entity that earned the underlying income. However, tracking and tracing distributions through the ownership chain would be extremely complex and burdensome. Accordingly, such taxes should be assigned to the jurisdiction of the Constituent Entity that distributed the dividend that triggered the tax liability. However, a distribution from a Constituent Entity in a low-tax jurisdiction could be funded by distributions made from lower-tier subsidiaries. In such cases, net basis taxes paid by the shareholder would shelter other income of the low-taxed Constituent Entity because the distribution itself is excluded from the GloBE tax base. Targeted rules may be needed to ensure these taxes are appropriately assigned in order to address these

structures. This issue will be further considered in connection with the development of the model rules as described in Section.

282. Covered taxes arising from the sale of Constituent Entity stock are excluded from the ETR computation. Covered taxes arising from the sale of other stock are assigned to the jurisdiction of the seller to the extent the seller's gain or loss on sales of stock is included in the GloBE tax base.

283. As with other Constituent Entities, covered taxes paid or incurred on an owner's share of the income of a stateless entity are assigned to the same jurisdiction as the corresponding income. Typically, this will mean that tax imposed on each owner's share of a tax transparent entity's income will be assigned to each respective owner's tax jurisdiction. For example, partners of a partnership that is a Constituent Entity may be taxable in their jurisdiction on their share of the partnership's income. However, if the owner is located in a tax jurisdiction that does not treat the stateless entity as tax transparent it may impose tax on distributions from the stateless entity or impose tax on the owner's share of the stateless entity's income under a CFC regime. In such cases, the covered taxes paid by the latter should be assigned to the stateless jurisdiction along with the income. The assignment of income and related taxes for stateless entities is illustrated in Annex, Examples 3.4.2E, 3.4.2F, and 3.4.2G.

284. Under the jurisdictional blending approach, covered taxes are assigned to the jurisdiction of the Constituent Entity that earned and recorded the related income. Consequently, covered taxes collected by the tax authority in one jurisdiction, such as withholding taxes and CFC taxes, may be taken into account in the ETR computation of another jurisdiction. These "cross-jurisdictional" taxes present some challenges for the GloBE rules, because they are typically levied at high rates and in respect of passive (and therefore highly-mobile) income. The income that triggers these types of taxes can be shifted easily to an otherwise low-taxed jurisdiction together with the associated covered taxes, to the extent the assigned income and taxes exceed the minimum rate, the excess tax credits can be used to reduce the amount of top-up tax on other income arising in the jurisdiction. Anti-avoidance rules would prevent MNE group's structuring transactions that allowed high-tax passive income to be used to shelter other income arising in a low-tax jurisdiction. Further work on the treatment of withholding taxes and CFC taxes will be done in considering the development of a targeted rule that is consistent with the policy outcomes of the GloBE and is administrable and minimises compliance costs with the outcome of this further work being incorporated into the model rules described in Section.

Computing the jurisdictional ETR

285. Generally, the ETR of each jurisdiction will be computed by dividing the aggregate of adjusted covered taxes assigned to the jurisdiction by the aggregate of the profit (or loss) before tax assigned to the jurisdiction. Where the aggregate profit before tax assigned to a jurisdiction is zero or negative (i.e. loss-making), there will be no GloBE income and no GloBE tax liability with respect to that jurisdiction for the MNE Group for that year. Adjusted covered taxes are all covered taxes reduced by covered taxes attributable to income and gains that are excluded from the GloBE tax base, such as taxes paid on dividends and gains from dispositions of stock. The amount of covered taxes included in the ETR computation of a jurisdiction under the carry-forward approach for addressing temporary differences is discussed further below in Section.

References

OECD (2019), *Global Anti-Base Erosion Proposal ("GloBE") - Pillar Two*, OECD Publishing, Paris, https://www.oecd.org/tax/beps/public-consultation-document-global-anti-base-erosion-proposal-pillar-two.pdf.pdf. [3]

OECD (2019), *Programme of Work to Develop a Consensus Solution to the Tax Challenges Arising from the Digitalisation of the Economy, OECD/G20 Inclusive Framework on BEPS*, OECD Publishing, Paris, https://www.oecd.org/tax/beps/programme-of-work-to-develop-a-consensus-solution-to-the-tax-challenges-arising-from-the-digitalisation-of-the-economy.pdf. [5]

OECD (2018), *Revenue Statistics 1965-2017 Interpretative Guide, Annex A*, OECD Publishing, OECD, https://www.oecd.org/tax/tax-policy/oecd-classification-taxes-interpretative-guide.pdf. [2]

OECD (2017), *Model Tax Convention on Income and on Capital*, OECD Publisher, Paris, https://doi.org/10.1787/mtc_cond-2017-en. [1]

OECD (2015), *Neutralising the Effects of Hybrid Mismatch Arrangements, Action 2 - 2015 Final Report*, OECD Publishing, https://doi.org/10.1787/9789264241138-en. [4]

Notes

1 See Section 2.3 Excluded Entities

2 If there is an exclusion from the GloBE rules for MNEs operating in the international shipping industry (see Section 2.3.6) then further consideration should be given to whether tonnage taxes should be treated as covered taxes under the GloBE.

3 The scope of CFC rules vary among countries, and, in any case, the design of a CFC rule, even one with a broader scope than described in this paragraph, means that such a rule will not be considered similar to GloBE rules.

4 See below Chapter 4 on *Carry-forwards and carve-out.*

5 https://www.ifrs.org/use-around-the-world/use-of-ifrs-standards-by-jurisdiction/#analysis

6 Rules for addressing post-filing adjustments to local tax liability are discussed in section 4.2.2.

7 See Section 3.2.2 for discussion on covered taxes. Tax paid on net income allocated to a jurisdiction under Pillar One would be treated as a covered tax under the GloBE.

8 The rule simply applies the tax depreciation rules to the carrying value of assets as determined for financial accounting purpose. It would not conform the cost capitalisation rules of the financial accounts to the cost capitalisation rules of the jurisdiction. Thus, the depreciable base of the property for GloBE tax purposes and local tax purposes may still differ, which will result in some difference in the amount of depreciation computed for each period. Conforming the capitalisation of costs to depreciable assets with the tax cost capitalisation would, in some cases, require numerous other adjustments to the timing of various expenses.

[9] These tax regimes also contain rules intended to protect the jurisdiction's tax base from tax avoidance through the use of transactions, such as loans to shareholders, that are the economic equivalent of a distribution.

[10] Disclosure of these benefits is required under IAS 20.39(b).

[11] See para 71 of the PoW (OECD, 2019[5]).

[12] See the discussion on *'Other generally accepted financial accounting standards'* in Section 3.3.3.

[13] See the discussion on '*Multilateral review process*' in section 10.5.2.

[14] A review process for evaluating material differences and providing additional guidance on material differences could be undertaken as part of the multilateral review process envisioned in section 10.5.2.

[15] The timing of income between constituent entities in the same jurisdiction may be deferred until sale to a third party for local tax purposes under a group relief or consolidation regime. However, income from transactions with related parties outside the jurisdiction is likely to be recognised at the same time as income from transactions with third parties for local tax purposes. Thus, separate entity accounting for purposes of jurisdictional blending would conform in this respect to local taxation of the entities subject to the GloBE proposal.

[16] In the case of an acquisition of less than all the ownership of an entity, the value of the minority interest is also taken into account in determining the existence and amount of goodwill or other intangible assets of the acquired entity or entities.

[17] A worldwide blending approach under the GloBE proposal requires a similar allocation of the MNE's income and taxes, except that the income and taxes only need to be allocated between the tax jurisdiction of the Ultimate Parent Entity and a foreign tax jurisdiction. This section of the note assumes a jurisdictional blending paradigm. However, the principles apply equally to the assignment of income and taxes to the relevant jurisdictions under a worldwide blending model.

[18] It is recognised that no decision has yet been taken by the Inclusive Framework on whether the GloBE rules will adopt relevant definitions from the CbCR rules. However, given the strong correlation between the intended scope of the GloBE rules and the Country-by-Country reporting (CbCR) rules, this report assumes that the CbCR definitions will be adopted.

[19] For this purpose, the entity's jurisdiction may be the jurisdiction under the laws of which the entity was created if it is a juridical entity or the jurisdiction in which it conducts its activities if it is a contractual entity or arrangement.

4 Carry-forwards and carve-out

4.1. Overview

286. This Chapter sets out two adjustments that may be made to an MNE Group's top-up tax calculation for a particular jurisdiction.

(a) The first adjustment described in Section 4.2 allows an MNE to carry-forward losses incurred or excess taxes paid in prior periods into a subsequent period in order to smooth-out any potential volatility arising from the mix of taxes imposed under local law or resulting from timing differences. This adjustment is intended to ensure that Pillar Two does not result in the imposition of additional tax where the low ETR in a jurisdiction in a particular period is simply a result of the timing of the imposition of covered taxes on items of GloBE income or differences in the timing of the recognition of income under financial accounting and local tax law.

(b) The second adjustment described in Section 4.3 is a formulaic substance-based carve-out which is intended to exclude a fixed return for substantive activities within a jurisdiction from the scope of the GloBE rules. Excluding a fixed return from substantive activities focuses the GloBE rules on "excess income", such as intangible-related income, which is most susceptible to BEPS risks.

287. Section 4.4 describes the methodology to be used in calculating a jurisdictional ETR and top-up tax in light of the adjustments for timing differences and the application of the formulaic substance based carve-out.

Carry-over of losses and excess taxes

Loss carry-forward

Losses in a jurisdiction may be carried forward and allowed as a deduction in the computation of the GloBE tax base in a subsequent year, thereby reducing the GloBE tax base in that year. Losses are defined as the excess of expenses over income included in the GloBE tax base of the jurisdiction for a year.

Pre-regime losses

Losses also include qualified pre-regime losses that are incurred by a Constituent Entity prior to the MNE Group becoming subject to the rules.

Excess taxes

Excess taxes in a jurisdiction for a year may create an IIR tax credit, a local tax carry-forward, or both. Excess taxes are defined as the amount of covered taxes reflected as due and payable in the tax returns of Constituent Entities in respect of a year in excess of the minimum tax rate on the aggregate GloBE tax base for a jurisdiction for that year. If the GloBE tax base computation for a jurisdiction results in zero income or a loss for a year, any covered tax paid in respect of the year would be excess taxes for that year and would be included in a local tax carry-forward.

IIR tax credit

Excess taxes in a jurisdiction create an IIR tax credit to the extent of IIR tax paid in the preceding years in respect of the same jurisdiction that has not given rise to an IIR tax credit. An IIR tax credit can be used to reduce the shareholder's IIR tax liability in respect of any jurisdiction arising in the year the IIR tax credit was created or any subsequent year.

Local tax carry-forward

Excess taxes in a jurisdiction that do not create an IIR tax credit create a local tax carry-forward that may be carried forward an agreed number of years and treated as tax expense for that jurisdiction in a subsequent year in which the local tax paid by the Constituent Entities falls below the minimum tax rate on their aggregate income.

Post-filing adjustments to tax liability

For purposes of computing the GloBE ETR of the income assigned or allocated to a jurisdiction, post-filing increases (or decreases) to a Constituent Entity's liability for a covered tax are treated as adjustments to the entity's tax expense or carry-forwards in the year in which the tax increase (or decrease) is finally determined.

Transfers of tax attributes

Losses and local tax carry-forwards are tax attributes of the MNE Group and cannot be transferred or used by a person outside the Group. However where there is a change in the control of a Constituent Entity in a transaction that includes a transfer of deferred tax assets, the buyer and seller may agree an adjustment to the amount of their losses or local tax carry-forwards in the jurisdiction of that Constituent Entity provided such adjustment is consistent and in line with the actual effect of the transfer for local tax purposes.

288. Temporary differences are differences in the timing of the recognition of income and expense under financial accounting and tax accounting rules. They are not differences in the types of income or expense allowed in the calculation of net income. Instead, they are differences in the proper time for including those items in the calculation of net income.

289. Temporary differences can be the sole cause of a low ETR at the beginning of the temporary difference and a high ETR upon reversal, and vice versa. They have an effect on the periodic measurement of the ETR but do not affect the average ETR over the life of the entity.

290. Temporary differences should not give rise to permanent tax liability under the GloBE rules. Therefore, a mechanism to address the effects of temporary differences on the ETR and the GloBE tax liability are necessary.

291. While the discussion focuses on the application of the income inclusion rule, similar principles can be applied in the context of the undertaxed payments rule. Generally, the loss carry-forwards and local tax carry-forwards will be taken into account to determine the jurisdictional ETR under the undertaxed

payments rule as well. However, a tax credit similar to the IIR tax credit will not be available to recoup taxes paid in prior years due to the undertaxed payments rule.

292. Temporary differences can be addressed under the GloBE rules using a carry-forward approach or a deferred tax accounting approach. From a time value of money perspective, deferred tax accounting generally is more favourable to taxpayers because it leaves in place the benefits of immediate expensing of assets, accelerated depreciation, and other tax deferral mechanisms that are commonly adopted by jurisdictions to encourage capital investment and for other reasons. The basic carry-forward approach with some modifications can preserve the most significant of those benefits but does not wholly align with the tax deferral benefits allowed in every local jurisdiction.

293. The principal policy risk of deferred tax accounting, however, is that it relies on a taxpayer's estimate of future liability for tax in a subsidiary jurisdiction to determine its current liability under the GloBE rules. The carry-forward approach, in contrast, relies on actual tax liabilities existing at the time tax liability under the GloBE rules is determined.

294. The carry-forward and deferred tax accounting approaches both impose some compliance and administration burdens. On the surface, the deferred tax accounting approach appears to be simpler because taxpayers use deferred tax accounting for financial purposes already. However, differences between the policies of the GloBE rules and financial reporting will likely mean that modifications would need to be made to certain deferred tax accounting outcomes in order to adapt deferred tax accounting to the GloBE rules. These modifications would add a significant amount of additional complexity and may lead to uncertainty. Although maintaining memorandum accounts in respect of carry-forwards is somewhat burdensome, it is a familiar exercise for both taxpayers and tax administrations. Accordingly, while there appear to be some advantages with a deferred tax accounting approach the members of the Inclusive Framework do not consider that such an approach would serve as an appropriate mechanism to address timing differences. They do consider, however, that financial information on deferred tax accounting could play a useful role in the development of simplification options described below in Section 5.

4.2. Carry-forwards

4.2.1. The carry-forward approach

295. The basic operation of the carry-forward approach relies on two carry-forwards and a credit to address the various effects of temporary differences on the GloBE tax base and ETR computation. Both carry-forwards would be tracked using memorandum accounts maintained on a jurisdictional basis. The credit is tracked using memorandum accounts for each Parent of the MNE Group that applies an IIR.

296. Under the carry-forward approach, the covered tax expense included in the numerator of the ETR computation for a particular tax year includes only the amount of taxes reported as due and payable in the tax returns of Constituent Entities filed with respect to their income for that tax year. Thus, the covered taxes in the numerator for a tax year include the taxes paid in respect of that year both during the year and with the tax return for that year to the extent those taxes are payable with respect to the income for that tax year. However, any covered taxes reported in a tax return that is not paid, for example due to an administrative practice of allowing loss carry-forwards in the administrative assessment of tax rather than as part of the self-assessment in the tax return, is not included in the numerator of the ETR fraction. The covered taxes in the numerator do not include any amount of tax expense that is accrued for financial accounting purposes and that is not reported in the tax returns filed with respect to income of the relevant tax year, for example, uncertain tax positions, contested tax liabilities, and deferred tax liabilities. Finally, any amount of tax that is reported in the tax returns with respect to the income for a year that is not paid within a certain period (for example 2 years) should be treated as a reduction in covered taxes in the subsequent year.

297. Limiting the covered taxes expense in the numerator of the ETR fraction to taxes reported in the tax returns for the relevant year could, in some situations, result in an MNE Group being subject to both the IIR or UTPR and the STTR in respect of a single transaction. For example, a Constituent Entity could be resident in a jurisdiction that is generally low-taxed and thus likely subject to a Withholding Tax (WHT) under the STTR on payments received from another Constituent Entity. A timing difference between the accrual of the income and the payment, however, could result in an ETR below the minimum rate in the year of accrual, which would result in a top-up tax liability in the payer's jurisdiction under the IIR or UTPR. Assuming the income is actually received the year after, the Constituent Entity would be subject to the STTR as well when it received the income because it is resident in a low-taxed jurisdiction. However, if the income accrual and receipt had occurred in the same tax year, the WHT imposed under the STTR would have been taken into account to compute the ETR of the jurisdiction, which could have raised the ETR above the minimum tax rate and prevented application of the IIR or UTPR. The IIR tax credit can adequately address this situation. However, in the absence of a similar mechanism available under the UTPR, frequent instances of double taxation could occur on transactions subject to a withholding tax.

298. The GloBE rules ameliorate this mismatch between the income accrual and tax payment by allowing accrual of withholding taxes for income that are expected to be paid shortly after the year in which the related income accrues. Specifically, any withholding tax accrued by a Constituent Entity for financial accounting purposes on an item of income other than a distribution from another Constituent Entity that will be paid within 12 months following the end of the taxable year in which the Constituent Entity accrues the related item of income for financial accounting purposes may be included in the covered taxes expense for the year in which the income is accrued. Under this rule, a Constituent Entity that knows it will be liable for withholding tax under an STTR in the year following the accrual of the relevant income will be able to include the accrued WHT levied under the STTR in its covered tax expense for purposes of the jurisdictional ETR computation, with the likely result that the IIR/UTPR will not apply. The rule not limited to withholding taxes imposed under an STTR rule. It does not apply, however, to withholding taxes that are accrued on distributions from other Constituent Entities.

299. In some jurisdictions, loss carry-forwards are limited to a number of years. Imposing a time restriction on the use of carry-forwards can reduce the compliance and administration burdens associated with maintaining the relevant memorandum accounts. Other jurisdictions allow loss and other tax attribute carry-forwards to be carried forward for an unlimited time period.

300. The GloBE loss carry-forward is crafted so that it is effectively unlimited in duration. The GloBE rules apply to a wide range of industries and business sectors. These industries have business cycles of different lengths, with some industries, such as the mining industry, experiencing very long business cycles. Some MNE Groups or Constituent Entities of an MNE Group that are profitable over the business cycle may be profitable in some years and not profitable in other years during the cycle. Unlimited carry forward of losses ensures that MNE Groups will not be subject to tax under the GloBE rules on more than their economic income due to an expired loss carry-forward.

301. The ability to use excess local taxes to create an IIR tax credit in respect of IIR tax paid in prior years and the local tax carry-forward are limited in duration, however. This limitation does two things. First, it effectively treats a long-term deferral as a permanent difference for purposes of the GloBE rules. In other words, if a carry-forward attributable to a timing difference expires before the timing difference resolves itself, the timing difference will produce the same result under the GloBE rules as if it were a permanent difference. Second, it limits the period for which taxes that are imposed at a rate above the minimum rate can be used to shield income taxed below the minimum rate from GloBE tax liability. However, the IIR tax credit is not limited in duration, which eliminates, or significantly reduces, the possibility that IIR tax paid due to a timing difference will result in taxation under the GloBE rules.

Loss carry-forward

302. The loss carry-forward is needed to prevent taxation in excess of economic income under the GloBE rules. Financial accounting does not have a loss carry-forward concept. The financial accounting income for each year is determined without regard to any losses incurred in prior years. The annual GloBE tax base computation starts with financial accounts and thus may also include income in excess of the economic income over a period. The loss carry-forward is allowed as a deduction to prevent taxation in excess of economic income.

303. The loss carry-forward under the GloBE rules is relatively straight-forward and will be familiar to many taxpayers and tax administrations. A loss carry-forward is created for a jurisdiction in any year in which the expenses taken into account in computing the jurisdictional GloBE tax base, including prior losses carried forward from previous years, exceed the amount of income taken into account in computing the jurisdictional GloBE tax base. Losses can be carried forward indefinitely under the GloBE rules. A loss arising in a jurisdiction may be carried back to the same extent that it is carried back under the rules of that tax jurisdiction. Consistent with the jurisdictional blending model, loss carry-forwards arising in a jurisdiction can only be used as a deduction in the computation of the adjusted GloBE tax base in that same jurisdiction. A loss carry-forward is only used to reduce the GloBE tax base if the jurisdiction has an ETR below the minimum tax rate determined without regard to the loss carry-forward.

304. The loss carry-forward under the GloBE rules will not generally be expected to align with rules governing loss carry-forwards in the local jurisdiction. Rather, the GloBE loss carry-forward is intended to prevent taxation in excess of economic income and recognises that an MNE should not be subject to tax under the GloBE rules on the mere recovery of prior period losses. The loss carry-forward allowed under GloBE may be inconsistent with the rules governing loss carry-forwards in the jurisdiction in which the loss arises. For example, the tax rules in the local jurisdiction may place a limitation on the amount of loss that may be carried forward or the time period for which it can be carried forward. Alternatively, the local jurisdiction may allow losses to be carried back and used against tax liabilities arising in prior years, which may generate a tax refund. Under those circumstances, the loss carry-forward for GloBE purposes may be a different amount than the loss carry-forward for local tax purposes. In addition, losses in one subsidiary may be used to offset the income of another subsidiary in the same jurisdiction in the computation of the jurisdictional GloBE tax base, while a similar type of offset may not be allowed under local tax rules. In that case, one subsidiary could have a loss carry-forward for local tax purposes even though the loss was fully deducted in computing the GloBE tax base for the jurisdiction. No adjustment is necessary to address these differences because the GloBE tax base is not trying to mirror the local tax base and any GloBE tax consequences resulting from the differences will be addressed by the local tax carry-forward and the IIR tax credit described below.

IIR tax credit and local tax carry-forward

305. The carry-forward rules are designed to smooth the ETR of the jurisdiction over a period of time, irrespective of whether fluctuations in the ETR arise from temporary or permanent differences. The GloBE rules apply when the ETR in a jurisdiction is below the minimum tax rate. Temporary or permanent differences between the local tax base and the GloBE tax base may cause the ETR in a jurisdiction to be above or below the minimum tax rate in a particular year. Over time, the temporary differences will reverse and various permanent differences may have opposite effects on the ETR. The rules effectively smooth the ETR for the jurisdiction over a period of time by allowing a shareholder to recoup GloBE taxes paid previously or avoid paying GloBE taxes in the future whenever the ETR in the jurisdiction exceeds the minimum tax rate. Specifically, whenever the tax in a jurisdiction exceeds the minimum tax rate, a shareholder that previously has paid IIR tax in respect of the jurisdiction is allowed to create an IIR tax credit to the extent the previously paid IIR tax has not already been treated as an IIR tax credit. An IIR tax credit can be used to satisfy a current or future IIR tax liability with respect to any jurisdiction. If the

shareholder has not previously paid IIR tax in respect of a jurisdiction, tax paid in that jurisdiction in excess of the minimum tax rate on the aggregate GloBE tax base is treated as a local tax carry-forward that the shareholder can use in the computation of its ETR for that jurisdiction in a future taxable year, which may increase the ETR of the jurisdiction up to the minimum rate in that year.

306. There will be many cases in which the tax rate in a jurisdiction exceeds the minimum rate by an amount sufficient to avoid GloBE tax liability even after taking into account a permanent difference. By incorporating mechanisms that take into account the effects of temporary and permanent differences on the computation of income and tax liabilities over a period of years, the rules neutralise the consequences stemming from application of the annual accounting concept under the GloBE rules. Although the rule is primarily aimed at temporary differences that reverse over time, it also ameliorates the effect of permanent differences because their effect on GloBE tax liability may also be due to their timing. For example, equal and offsetting, but otherwise unrelated, permanent differences would have no effect on the GloBE tax liability if they arise in the same tax year but would produce a GloBE tax liability if they arose in separate tax years. While this is not a temporary difference, it does have a timing aspect and is therefore appropriately addressed by a carry-forward of excess local taxes. In addition, rules designed to separate the amount of excess local taxes attributable exclusively to temporary differences would be very complex and unduly complicate the GloBE rules.

307. Both the IIR tax credit and the local tax carry-forward hinge on excess taxes paid in respect of a jurisdiction. The rule defines excess taxes as the amount of covered taxes reported as due and payable in the tax returns of the Constituent Entities in the jurisdiction filed with respect to the income of a particular tax year, in excess of the minimum tax rate on the aggregate GloBE tax base for that jurisdiction for that year. If the GloBE tax base computation for a jurisdiction results in zero income or a loss for a year, any local tax paid in respect of the year would be excess taxes for that year and would be included in a local tax carry-forward. This situation could arise where, for example, the local tax base denied certain deductions that were recognised under the GloBE tax base. The definition of excess taxes is intended to ensure that the ETR is computed based on the taxes actually paid in respect of the relevant year. It does not include income taxes that are accrued, for example based on the likely disallowance of an uncertain tax position, but that are not reflected as due in the tax return filed for the year.

308. Under the IIR tax credit rule, in any year in which there are excess taxes in respect of a jurisdiction, the shareholder first looks back to see if it previously has paid IIR tax in respect of that jurisdiction.[1] If the shareholder has paid IIR tax in respect of the preceding taxable years (the lookback period), an IIR tax credit is created. The IIR tax credit created for a year is equal to the lesser of the excess taxes for the year and the IIR tax paid during the lookback period that has not already given rise to an IIR tax credit. The IIR tax credit is illustrated in Annex, Example 4.2.1B. In most cases it is expected that the IIR tax credit will be available to reduce IIR tax liabilities arising in the year the credit is created or any year thereafter.[2] Although an IIR tax credit results from a payment of IIR tax and a subsequent payment of excess taxes in the same jurisdiction, IIR tax credits can be used to reduce an IIR tax liability arising with respect to any jurisdiction. The use of the IIR tax credit in respect of IIR tax liabilities arising in respect of other jurisdictions is illustrated in Annex, Example 4.2.1C.

309. It is possible, given the design of the rules, that a parent with an accrued entitlement to an IIR tax credit will not have, and is not expected to have in the foreseeable future, an IIR tax liability to offset that IIR tax credit against. The mechanics of the IIR and the IIR tax credit are novel and their operation will depend on the structure and operations of the MNE and the point in the ownership chain where the IIR is applied. Rather than creating incentives for an MNE Group to restructure its operations simply in order to take advantage of an unused IIR tax credit, tax administrations could contemplate introducing a mechanism that allowed the MNE Group to offset such credits against other domestic tax liabilities of the Parent or another Constituent Entity of the MNE Group that is resident in the Parent's jurisdiction due to difficulties in recovering the IIR tax credit that could persist over time, for example, where that credit had

not been used to offset an IIR tax liability within a reasonable period of years following the period in which the credit arose.[3]

310. To effectively address timing differences, the local tax carry-forward period and the lookback period for creating an IIR tax credit need to be long enough for the timing difference that caused the original IIR tax or the carry-forward to reverse. The period in which a timing difference will reverse varies based on the timing rules of each tax jurisdiction. Nonetheless, the GloBE rules should establish a period that will adequately cover the period required for most timing differences to reverse without creating significant compliance and administrative burdens of tracking and verifying excess taxes claimed in respect of years long past. The GloBE rules will also include specific adjustments to minimize the most significant of timing differences arising in most businesses, i.e. timing differences attributable to immediate expensing and accelerated depreciation. In light of the overall design of the rules and the economic cycle of most businesses, a period of seven years may, depending on other design features of the rules, be a reasonable period for both the lookback period and carry-forward period. Further consideration will be given to whether extended time limits, including for the transitional carry-forward rules, are appropriate in certain industries with long economic cycles.

311. Under the local tax carry-forward rule, the excess taxes for a jurisdiction that do not create an IIR tax credit create a local tax carry-forward. A local tax carry-forward may be included in the ETR computation in any subsequent year in which the local tax paid by the Constituent Entities in the same jurisdiction falls below the minimum tax rate on their aggregate GloBE tax base. The local tax carry-forwards can only be used to compute the ETR for the jurisdiction in which they arose and are used in chronological order. Local tax carry-forwards are reduced by the amount used to increase the local tax to the minimum tax rate in any year. The local tax carry-forward is illustrated in Annex, Example 4.2.1A.

312. If a Parent is potentially subject to IIR tax liability with respect to multiple jurisdictions in the same year, it may allocate its IIR tax credits, if any, among those jurisdictions as it chooses. However, if there are multiple Parent's in the same MNE Group applying an IIR, a Parent may not use another Parent's IIR tax credit.

313. The IIR tax credit may be used against a Parent's IIR tax liability arising in respect of any jurisdiction in the period the credit arises or a subsequent period.[4] At first blush, the ability to credit the IIR tax in one jurisdiction against IIR tax liabilities arising in respect of another jurisdiction may seem tantamount to worldwide blending. It is not the same, however. An IIR tax credit only arises when IIR tax is paid in respect of a jurisdiction, and subsequently, tax is paid in that same jurisdiction in excess of the minimum tax rate. Conceptually, a shareholder becomes eligible for a credit of IIR tax paid in respect of a jurisdiction when it can demonstrate that the tax was paid in respect of a temporary difference in the jurisdiction that reversed after the tax payment. The carry-forward approach uses the payment of tax in excess of the minimum tax rate as a proxy for the reversal of a temporary difference.[5]

314. If the timing of the income under the local tax base matched the timing of income under the GloBE tax base, there would have been no IIR tax liability in the first instance and no need for a subsequent IIR tax credit. From the taxpayer's perspective, the credit mechanism is functionally equivalent to a refund of IIR tax previously paid. However, instead of getting a cash refund from the tax administration and separately paying another IIR tax liability, the shareholder uses the credit to pay that tax liability. The fact that the credit can be used to satisfy an IIR tax liability arising in respect of a different jurisdiction does not change the analysis. Eligibility for the IIR tax credit is always rooted in a temporary difference arising and reversing with respect to the same jurisdiction or the interaction of two offsetting permanent differences in the same jurisdiction. In contrast, allowing excess taxes paid in respect of the income in one jurisdiction to create an IIR tax credit for IIR tax paid in respect of another jurisdiction would be tantamount to global blending.

Transitional rules and adjustments

315. There are a number of events that could trigger the application of the GloBE rules to an MNE Group for the first time. Where an MNE Group already has revenues in excess of the revenue threshold, it will become subject to the GloBE rules once they have been introduced into the domestic law of a jurisdiction in which the MNE Group operates. Smaller MNE Groups, however, will become subject to the GloBE rules for the first time if they grow their revenues above the threshold, either organically or as a result of a merger or acquisition.

316. At the point an MNE Group becomes subject to the GloBE rules, it will be required, under a jurisdictional blending approach, to compute the ETR on its income in each jurisdiction where it operates and compare it to the agreed minimum tax rate. Failure to take appropriate account of operating losses that the MNE Group has suffered in the period or periods immediately prior to becoming subject to the GloBE rules could, however, result in a distorted picture of the MNE Group's tax position in that jurisdiction and may subject the MNE Group to taxation in excess of its economic profit. For example, a Constituent Entity may have incurred operating losses in the years immediately prior to the MNE Group becoming subject to the GloBE rules. Frequently, the operating losses of the Constituent Entity will also be recognised for local tax purposes and these losses may be eligible to be carried forward and be available to reduce taxable income arising in a future period in the same jurisdiction. Ignoring the effect of these prior period losses could result in an immediate GloBE tax on profits arising in subsequent periods despite the fact that, the local tax jurisdiction is otherwise a high-tax jurisdiction and that the income subject to charge under the GloBE rules, represents, from the MNE Group's perspective, a recovery of recent losses. Failure to take appropriate account of pre-regime losses could therefore result in the MNE Group being overtaxed, by converting what was essentially a timing difference into a permanent difference based on the mere fact that the MNE Group was brought within the scope of the GloBE rules after those losses arose.

317. A similar transition-related issue in relation to timing differences that straddle the applicability date of the GloBE rules. Of particular concern are those timing difference that result in the acceleration of income and hence taxes paid prior to an MNE Group being subject to the GloBE rules, which then reverse after the MNE Group is subject to the GloBE rules. These situations may arise, for example, when local law taxes pre-payments of contractual fees upon receipt rather than over the term of the contract or prohibits deductions for estimates of future bad debts or warranty expenses (i.e. reserves for bad debts or warranty expenses). Absent a corrective rule, the result would be a lower GloBE ETR in the year(s) of reversal and thus potential GloBE top-up tax in those years, despite the fact that the local tax jurisdiction is otherwise a high-tax jurisdiction. Similarly, timing differences that defer tax on income arising before the GloBE rules apply would, absent a special rule, reduce the GloBE tax liability on GloBE income arising within the GloBE applicability period.

318. The Inclusive Framework on BEPS considers that transition rules are needed to minimize the GloBE tax liability effects of losses and timing differences that straddle the applicability date of the GloBE rules. The most accurate approach to addressing these transition issues would be to identify an applicable start date for the transitional period and require MNE Groups to compute an opening balance of its loss carry-forward and local tax carry-forward as if the GloBE rules had applied during the transitional period. However, applying the GloBE rules retroactively to prior years could be unduly complex and burdensome. A simplified method could be developed that could produce results that reasonably approximate this approach with less complexity and administrative burden. Further technical work will be necessary to develop a workable solution that provides for appropriate outcomes without imposing undue compliance or administrative burdens.

Adjustments for acquisition and disposal of Constituent Entities

319. In addition to rules dealing with what happens when an MNE Group enters the GloBE regime for the first time, further rules are required to address the situation where Constituent Entities join or leave an

MNE Group that is already subject to the GloBE rules. These transactions may be taxable or non-taxable and may include, for example, acquisitions of the equity or assets of Constituent Entities, or acquisitions by one MNE Group of the equity of the Ultimate Parent Entity of another MNE Group, or a spin-off by one MNE Group of Constituent Entities that following the spin-off become another MNE Group. The ability to transfer the benefit of carry-forwards from one MNE Group to another can be expected to be more restricted under the GloBE rules than ordinary tax rules because the GloBE carry-forwards are determined and applied on a jurisdictional basis. Thus, under the GloBE rules the carry-forwards are strongly associated with the MNE Group as a whole rather than with a Constituent Entity. Nevertheless, there are cases where part of the consideration for the sale of a Constituent Entity can include the benefit of certain deferred tax assets such as carry-forward losses or the benefit of taxes paid in advance of income which are available to reduce tax on future income.

320. The ability to carry-over the tax attributes of a Constituent Entity on a sale or disposal is a question of local law design. Many jurisdictions have shareholder continuity rules that prevent a company from carrying forward the benefit of a credit, loss, or other relief where there is a change in control. However, these rules are not comprehensive. They may require a significant change in shareholding before they apply and they would not, for example, typically prevent a company carrying forward the benefit of tax pre-payment or the tax paid on accelerated income. The ability to carry over the target company's local attributes in a sale transaction could, in the absence of a corresponding adjustment under the GloBE rules give rise to the risk of double, over-or under-taxation.

321. For example this situation could arise where a Constituent Entity such as a company, that is entitled to retain certain accrued tax benefits (such as carry-forward losses), is sold to an independent purchaser. If the target company derives income in a period subsequent to the transfer then that income will be sheltered by the carry-forward losses that are available under local law. Unless the GloBE rules recognise the transfer tax benefits that are permitted for local law purposes then:

a. The seller could effectively double dip on the value of the transferred tax losses through increased consideration for the sale of the target shares and by using the losses that it is treated as retaining under the GloBE rules to shelter other low-tax income
b. The buyer could suffer economic double taxation in the form of an increased purchase price for the target company shares and a tax charge under the GloBE.

322. The Inclusive Framework on BEPS considers that an adjustment to carry-forwards is appropriate when a Constituent Entity is sold outside the MNE Group. One approach under consideration would require the buyer and the seller to adjust the amount of any carry forward losses or excess taxes by the amount of the related deferred tax asset retained by the target company (or inherited by a successor entity, such as in the case of a merger) immediately following the sale. The deferred tax assets retained by the target company may represent a reasonable approximation of the amount of the carry-forwards that left the MNE Group along with the target company. The target company (or successor entity) may be expected to retain (or inherit) a deferred tax asset in transactions involving the sale and acquisition of equity of the company or in non-taxable acquisitions of the assets of the company (such as through a merger). The buyer and seller would be further required to identify those deferred tax assets that are in fact transferred to the buyer under local law and to make a corresponding adjustment to the amount of the carry-forward to recognise the effect of the transfer. Further technical work will be undertaken with regard to adjustments to carry-forwards when a Constituent Entity leaves the MNE Group. The outputs from this work will be incorporated into the model rules to be developed in accordance with Section 10.5.1.

4.2.2. Post-filing adjustments to tax liability and the GloBE *tax base*

323. The ETR for a jurisdiction under the carry-forward approach is determined by dividing the covered taxes in the jurisdiction with respect to that year by the GloBE tax base for the jurisdiction. However, an MNE Group's liability for covered taxes may increase or decrease after the tax return for the year is filed

due to various reasons. This could include a change in the amount of income recognised for local tax purpose due to an examination of the returns by the local tax authority, a review of the returns by the entity's management or tax advisers, or a loss in a subsequent period that is allowed to be carried back under applicable tax law, or a refund of tax to the taxpaying entity or its shareholder upon distribution of dividends. Increases would normally result in additional tax paid and decreases would normally result in a refund of tax (either in cash to, or as a reduction of another tax liability of, the taxpaying entity or its shareholders) after the IIR tax return for the relevant year was filed. The tax underpayments or overpayments may have impacted the shareholder's IIR tax liability and the amount of one of its carry-forwards for the corresponding tax year or its IIR tax credits. In other words, if the final tax liability had been correctly determined when the tax return was filed, the shareholder may have paid more or less IIR tax and may have established a larger or smaller local tax carry-forward or IIR tax credits.

324. The GloBE rules incorporate a carry-forward adjustment mechanism to address the effect of post-filing tax increases and decreases in subsidiary jurisdictions on the IIR tax liability and carry-forwards. This mechanism is much simpler than an alternative approach of requiring an amendment of the return to which the adjustment relates (and in some cases intervening year tax returns (i.e. tax years between the date of the adjustment and the date to which the adjustment relates)).

325. Under the carry-forward adjustment mechanism, the effects of a post-filing tax increase or decrease would be taken into account prospectively by adjusting the balances of the relevant carry-forwards when the increase or decrease is determined with finality. For this purpose, "determined with finality" means that the period for disputing the tax adjustment has expired either due to the passage of time or due to an administrative or judicial determination. For example, a payment of tax based on an administrative assessment to avoid additional interest expense while a claim is being litigated is not a final determination, but the judicial determination is a final determination when the time for appealing the decision expires without an appeal. Although the post-filing tax increase or decrease is primarily treated as an adjustment to the carry-forwards that arose in prior periods, the effect of those adjustments will be on the MNE's current and future tax liability under the GloBE rules.

326. Under the carry-forward adjustment mechanism, a tax decrease or refund in a jurisdiction would be treated as reduction in the amount of the relevant local tax carry-forward. Because local tax carry-forwards are limited in duration, they will need to be tracked based on the year in which they were created. Sometimes, a local tax carry-forward created for a year will have been used to reduce IIR tax liability in a subsequent year before it is discovered that the carry-forward was overstated. Rather than sifting through and unwinding all of the effects of the over-stated carry-forward in subsequent years, a local tax decrease should be treated as:

a. a decrease in the outstanding balance of the local tax carry-forward for the year to which the refund relates, if any;

b. a decrease in the outstanding balance of local tax carry-forwards established for subsequent years, to the extent thereof;

c. and then, a reduction to the tax expense for the year in which the decrease becomes final, to the extent thereof.

327. If the tax decrease exceeds the local tax carry-forwards described in (a) and (b) and the tax expense for the year, the excess should be treated as a current liability for IIR tax because it represents IIR tax that should have been due in respect of a prior year. If a tax decrease or refund does not relate to a specific taxable year, for example because it arises upon distribution of a dividend, the decrease or refund should be treated as a reduction of the current year tax liability to the extent thereof, and then a reduction of excess taxes paid in prior years. Any amount in excess of taxes paid in prior years should be treated as a current liability for IIR tax. Application of the rules in the case of a post-filing reduction in local tax liability is illustrated in Annex, Example 4.2.2A.

328. Under the carry-forward adjustment mechanism, a tax increase in a jurisdiction creates IIR tax credits to the extent of IIR tax paid in the look-back period that had not already given rise to an IIR tax credit. The excess, if any, is treated as a local tax carry-forward in respect of the year to which it relates or the last year in which IIR tax was paid. The period for using such local tax carry-forwards runs from the year in respect of which the carry-forward is established rather than the year in which the tax increase becomes final. Application of the rules in the case of a post-filing increase in local tax liability is illustrated in Annex, Example 4.2.2B.

329. Generally, the adjustments described above are only required with respect to post-filing increases or decreases in local tax liabilities with respect to tax years in which the MNE Group was subject to the GloBE rules or a tax year included in the determination of any carry-forward established in connection with a transition rule.

330. In addition to errors in the computation of annual tax liability, an MNE Group may occasionally make an error in the computation of its profit (or loss) before tax for financial accounting purposes that carries over into the GloBE tax base. For financial accounting purposes, the MNE Group generally must correct material "prior period errors" retrospectively by restating the comparative amounts for the prior period(s) presented in which the error occurred. "Prior period errors" are omissions from, and misstatements in, the consolidated financial statements for one or more prior periods. A prior period error that requires a restatement for prior periods in the MNE Group's consolidated financial statements should be corrected in the GloBE tax base by including the cumulative difference in income or expense in the GloBE tax base computation for each jurisdiction in the year in which the error is corrected for financial accounting purposes.

331. Furthermore, an MNE Group may change accounting method or principles used in the preparation of its financial statements. The change could be to the treatment of a single item or a category of transactions and could be voluntary, for example, due to an elective treatment of a particular type of transaction, or required, for example, due to a newly promulgated accounting standard. The MNE Group may also change from one acceptable accounting standard to another, such as from U.S. GAAP to IFRS. These changes may result in a cumulative change to the equity of the MNE Group based on the application of the different standards. In such cases, the cumulative change to equity attributable to each jurisdiction should be included in the GloBE tax base computation for the jurisdiction in the year in which the accounting method or principle is adopted for financial accounting purposes.

4.3. Formulaic substance-based carve-out

Formulaic substance-based carve-out

The carve-out amount is equal to the sum of the payroll component and the tangible asset component. If the carve-out amount exceeds the GloBE income in the relevant period, the excess amount cannot be carried-forward to reduce future GloBE income.

Payroll component

The payroll component is equal to [x]%[6] of the eligible payroll costs of eligible employees.

Eligible employees includes all employees of the MNE, including part-time employees. Eligible employees would also include independent contractors participating in the ordinary operating activities of the MNE.

The payroll component of the carve-out is computed on a jurisdictional basis focused on where the actual activity is performed. The CbCRrules, which are based on the residence jurisdiction of the Constituent Entity paying the employee's salary (i.e. the employer), can be used for determining this in most cases. However, where the residence jurisdiction of the Constituent Entity paying the employee's salary differs from the jurisdiction where the employee's activities or services are performed, the residence of the employee should be used as an indicator of the place of actual activity, unless there is strong evidence that the actual activity is performed in another jurisdiction.

Eligible payroll cost is determined based on a general test of whether the expenditure of the employer gives rise to a direct and separate personal benefit to the employee. Eligible payroll costs include expenditures for salaries and wages as well as for other employee benefits or remuneration such as medical insurance, payments to a pension fund or other retirement benefits, bonuses and allowances payable to eligible employees and stock-based compensation. Eligible payroll costs also includes payroll taxes (or other employee expense-related taxes such as fringe benefits taxes), as well as employer social security contributions.

Tangible asset component

The tangible asset component is equal to the sum of[7]:

(a) [x]% of the depreciation of property, plant and equipment;

(b) [x]% of the deemed depreciation of land;

(c) [x]% of the depletion of natural resources; and

(d) [x]% of the depreciation of a lessee's right-of-use tangible asset.

Buildings and land that are held as investment properties are excluded from the carve-out. Assets held for sale, rather than use, are also excluded from the carve-out.

The calculation of depreciation of property, plant and equipment, depletion of natural resources and depreciation of a lessee's right-of-use tangible asset, must conform with the calculation used for the same asset for financial accounting purposes, specifically the financial accounts used to compute the GloBE tax base for the relevant Constituent Entity. However, any incremental increase in depreciation or depletion resulting from revaluation increases, or related party asset sales are disregarded. And, to avoid double-counting, the labour costs and depreciation included in the carrying cost of a self-constructed asset are disregarded.

Depreciation and depletion charges that are accounted for as product costs are included in the carve-out base in the year incurred regardless of when the related product is sold.

For purposes of calculating the deemed depreciation of land, the depreciable base is equal to the original acquisition cost of the land, i.e., without regard to revaluation increases/decreases. The useful life is deemed to be [x][8] years. The depreciation method is deemed to be straight-line.

Impairment charges on depreciable property, plant and equipment, land, natural resources and a lessee's right-of-use tangible asset, are treated as equivalent to depreciation for purposes of the carve-out, thus included in the carve-out base in the year of impairment, and the post-impairment decrease in depreciation for financial accounting purposes is regarded.

A lessor is not allowed a carve-out in respect of the depreciation of leased assets.

The tangible asset component is computed on a jurisdictional basis.

332. The policy rationale behind a formulaic carve-out based on expenditures for payroll and tangible assets is to exclude a fixed return for substantive activities within a jurisdiction from the scope of the GloBE

rules. The use of payroll and tangible assets as indicators of substantive activities is justified because these factors are generally expected to be less mobile and less likely to lead to tax induced distortions. Conceptually, excluding a fixed return from substantive activities focuses GloBE on "excess income", such as intangible-related income, which is most susceptible to BEPS risks. Furthermore, a carve-out based on expenditures for payroll and tangible assets should help to shield low-margin businesses from what would otherwise be disproportionately negative outcomes under the GloBE as a result of expenditure based tax credits and other forms of government subsidy based on expenditure, such as government grants.

333. The carve-out will only benefit those MNEs with operations in jurisdictions that are taxed at below the minimum rate. However, provided the amount of the carve-out is limited to a modest return (sometimes colloquially referred to as a "routine return") on expenditures for payroll and tangible assets, then the MNE will not generally be able to use the carve-out to shelter other low-tax returns in a particular jurisdiction. An MNE can increase the amount of the carve-out by shifting more payroll and tangible assets into the jurisdiction, but, all other things being equal, increasing investment in these production factors would result in a corresponding real increase in the routine returns attributable to those factors and will not allow the carve-out to shelter excess returns or returns attributable to other factors such as intangible assets.

334. By acknowledging the contributions of both employees and tangible assets, a combined carve-out for payroll and tangible assets provides for a more level playing field by allowing a meaningful carve-out for MNEs with varying substance profiles, including labour-intensive and asset-intensive businesses. Whereas a carve-out based on a single factor, either payroll or tangible assets, would end up favouring one set of industries over another. Therefore, a combined carve-out provides greater neutrality between different industries.

335. Further consideration will be given, in light of the policy rationale behind the formulaic substance-based carve-out, to the effect of the carve-out on the calculation of the ETR and top-up taxes under the GloBE, particularly whether an MNE group that claims the benefit of the carve-out should be required to make a corresponding and proportional adjustment to the covered taxes. A decision on this tax adjustment will impact on the ETR and the top-up taxes payable under the GloBE and will be considered together with other questions such as the determination of the fixed percentage mark-up to be applied in a formulaic substance-based carve-out.

336. The Sections below set out more detail on the operation of the carve-out, starting with the payroll component and then turning to the tangible asset component.

4.3.1. Payroll component

337. The payroll component of the carve-out removes from the GloBE tax base a fixed return on activities performed in that jurisdiction calculated by reference to the taxpayer's employment costs. Such a carve-out design recognises a Constituent Entity's payroll expense as an appropriate proxy for substantive activities carried out by employees of the taxpayer in the relevant jurisdiction. In applying such a carve-out it is necessary to identify relevant employees (eligible employees), the situs of those employees as relevant for jurisdictional blending, and the relevant payroll expenses of those eligible employees (eligible payroll costs).

Eligible employees

338. For the purposes of the payroll component of the carve-out, eligible employees includes all employees of the MNE, including part-time employees. Eligible employees also includes independent contractors participating in the ordinary operating activities of the MNE, which is both consistent with country-by-country (CbC) reporting and avoids what would otherwise be a difficult line-drawing exercise of distinguishing an employee from an independent contractor.[9] Independent contractors include only natural persons and may include natural persons who are employed by a staffing or employment company but

whose daily activities are performed under the direction and control of the Constituent Entity. Independent contractors do not include employees of a corporate contractor providing goods or services to the Constituent Entity.

339. The payroll component of the carve-out is computed on a jurisdictional basis focused on where the actual activity is performed. The CbCR rules, which are based on the residence jurisdiction of the Constituent Entity paying the salary, can be used for determining this in most cases. However, where the residence jurisdiction of the Constituent Entity paying the employee's salary (i.e. the employer) differs from the jurisdiction where the employee's activities or services are performed, the residence of the employee should be used as an indicator of the place of actual activity[10], unless there is strong evidence that the actual activity is performed in another jurisdiction. The ordinary or normal residence of its employees should be information that an MNE can easily access and so this should not constitute a significant additional compliance burden. The approach for determining where eligible employees' activities or services are performed should be applied consistently across the MNE Group and from year to year.

Eligible payroll costs

340. A broad approach for determining eligible payroll costs is used for the payroll component of the carve-out based on a general test of whether the expenditure of the employer gives rise to a direct and separate personal benefit to the employee. Eligible payroll costs include expenditures for salaries and wages as well as for other employee benefits or remuneration such as medical insurance, payments to a pension fund or other retirement benefits, bonuses and allowances payable to eligible employees, and stock-based compensation. Eligible payroll costs also includes payroll taxes (or other employee expense-related taxes such as fringe benefits taxes), as well as employer social security contributions.

341. Consistent with the broad approach for determining eligible payroll costs, the payroll component of the carve-out is based on the total amount of the payroll expenditures in the current year, rather than the amount treated as an expense in the income statement as per financial accounting rules. This also avoids the additional administrative burden of taxpayers sorting payroll costs based on whether it was currently expensed or capitalised for financial accounting purposes.[11] It is also consistent with BEPS Action 5 approach to computing qualified R&D expenditures for the purposes of the modified nexus ratio.

4.3.2. Tangible asset component

342. The tangible asset component of the carve-out is equal to the sum of:

(a) [x]% of the depreciation of property, plant and equipment;

(b) [x]% of the deemed depreciation of land;

(c) [x]% of the depletion of natural resources; and

(d) [x]% of the depreciation of a lessee's right-of-use tangible asset.

343. The tangible asset carve-out base includes the annual cost of using depreciable property, plant and equipment, land, natural resources, and a lessee's right-of-use assets that are used in the production of income. Including a broad range of tangible assets in the carve-out base recognises that all such assets are indicative of substantive activities. Moreover, it helps to level the playing field across industries that use varying types of tangible assets in their business. Including leased tangible assets neutralises the difference between owning and leasing assets and recognises that the business decision to own or lease typically has no bearing on the intensity of substantive activities.

344. While the carve-out generally seeks to recognise a broad range of tangible assets, an MNE should not be allowed to generate a larger cave-out by purchasing investment property in a jurisdiction. This risk is particularly relevant as it relates to buildings and land, which are commonly held as investments. To

neutralise this risk, buildings and land that are held to earn rental income or for capital appreciation (or both), not owner-occupied; not used in production or supply of goods and services, or for administration; and not held for sale in the ordinary course of business are excluded from the carve-out. This rule is not expected to materially increase complexity or compliance costs because many accounting standards already require that such assets be separately identified and accounted for. For example, in the case of IFRS, investment properties are separately accounted for under IAS 40 – Investment Property.

345. Similarly, an MNE should not be allowed to generate a larger carve-out via tangible assets whose carrying amount, i.e., cost, will be recovered principally through a sale transaction instead of through continuing use in the business. Since such assets are held for sale, not use, they are a poor proxy for substantive activities. Consequently, assets held for sale are excluded from the carve-out. In order to be considered held for sale, the asset must be available for immediate sale in its present condition subject only to terms that are usual and customary for sales of such assets and its sale must be highly probable.[12] This rule is also not expected to materially increase complexity or compliance costs because many accounting standards already require that such assets be separately identified and accounted for. For example, in the case of IFRS, assets held for sale are separately accounted for under IFRS 5 – Non-current Assets Held for Sale and Discounting Operations.

346. The Sections below provide additional rules on the individual elements of the tangible asset carve-out, starting with property, plant and equipment.

Property, plant and equipment

347. Property, plant and equipment are tangible items that are held for use in the production or supply of goods or services or for administrative purposes and are expected to be used during more than one period. Assets in this category include: buildings, machinery, computers and other office equipment, motor vehicles, furniture and fixtures, and land improvements with a limited useful life. Land is also technically part of property, plant and equipment. However, because land is non-depreciable it is excluded from the definition of property, plant and equipment, for purposes of the carve-out, and considered separately.

348. Property, plant and equipment is initially recognised on the balance sheet at its costs, including its purchase price and any costs directly attributable to bringing the asset to the location and condition necessary for it to be capable of operating in the manner intended by management. After initial recognition as an asset, an item of property, plant and equipment is carried at its cost less any accumulated depreciation and any accumulated impairment losses (referred to as the "cost model"). Depreciation refers to the systematic allocation of the cost of an asset, less its residual or "salvage" value, over its useful life. An impairment loss is the amount by which the carrying amount of an asset exceeds its recoverable amount.[13]

349. Therefore, calculating depreciation of property, plant and equipment requires three factors be established: (i) the depreciable base of the asset, which is the cost of the asset less its residual value, (ii) the useful life of the asset, and (iii) the depreciation method, such as straight-line, diminishing balance and units of production. For purposes of the carve-out, all three factors are required to conform with those used for the same asset for financial accounting purposes, specifically the financial accounts used to compute the GloBE tax base for the relevant Constituent Entity (referred to as the "conformity rule"). For example, if the parent prepares its consolidated financial accounts in accordance with IFRS, then the factors used to compute depreciation, for purposes of the carve-out, must follow IAS 16 – Property, Plant and Equipment.

350. However, there are three exceptions to the conformity rule. The first relates to the revaluation model, which is permitted by some financial accounting standards as an alternative to the cost model. The second relates to asset sales between GloBE group members. The third relates to self-constructed assets.

(a) *Revaluation model.* Under some financial accounting standards, including IFRS, an entity can elect either the cost model or the revaluation model as its accounting policy. Under the revaluation model, an asset is carried at a revalued amount, which is its fair value at the date of the revaluation less any subsequent accumulated depreciation and subsequent accumulated impairment losses. Revaluation increases are generally recognised in OCI, rather than profit or loss. Revaluation decreases, on the other hand, are generally recognised in profit and loss. Absent a corrective measure the revaluation model would impact the quantum of the carve-out because depreciation expense is determined based on the revalued amount. This result is not appropriate because revaluation increases/decreases have no connection to substantive activities. Therefore, to eliminate the effect of the revaluation model for purposes of the carve-out, any subsequent incremental increase in depreciation resulting from revaluation increases are disregarded. And, any revaluation loss recognised in profit and loss is treated as additional depreciation in the year of the loss, and the subsequent decreased financial accounting depreciation is included in the carve-out base annually. In both cases, i.e., revaluation increases and decreases, the result of this rule is that the total depreciation charge included in the carve-out base over the life of the asset is the same as what it would have been without the revaluation. Such a result recognises that revaluation increases/decreases have no connection to substantive activities. It also eliminates a key difference across accounting standards: those that allow the revaluation model and those that do not.

(b) *Intercompany transaction.* Under the GloBE rules, transactions between Constituent Entities in different jurisdictions are not eliminated as they would be in the MNE's consolidated financial statements. Thus, when an asset is sold between Constituent Entities, the buyer may recognise the asset for purposes of the GloBE rules based on the purchase price of the asset, rather than the carrying value of the asset that is in the consolidated financial accounts. This creates the risk of MNEs engaging in intra-group asset sales designed to "refresh" the carrying value of assets and generate a larger carve-out. To prevent this type of planning, any incremental depreciation resulting from an asset acquired in a related party transaction is not allowed in the carve-out base.[14] If, however, the gain on the asset sale is recognised in the GloBE tax base, then the resulting increase in depreciation is regarded for purposes of the carve-out.

(c) *Self-constructed assets.* The cost of a self-constructed asset includes the labour costs, i.e., payroll, of the employees that constructed it. Absent a corrective measure, the labour-related costs of a self-constructed asset would be counted once in the payroll component of the carve-out and again in the tangible asset component. To eliminate such double-counting, the labour-related costs included in the carrying cost of a self-constructed asset are disregarded for purposes of computing the asset's depreciation. To avoid a further instance of double counting, the carrying costs of a self-constructed asset excludes the depreciation of assets used in its construction.

351. The depreciation charge of property, plant and equipment is recognised in financial profit or loss, and, by extension, the GloBE tax base, unless it is included in the carrying amount for another asset. For example, depreciation on manufacturing equipment is included in inventory. Eventually, when the product is sold, the depreciation charge becomes part of cost of goods sold. For purposes of the carve-out, depreciation includes both depreciation charges that are recognised in profit and loss in the period it is incurred (often referred to as "period costs"), and depreciation charges recognised in profit and loss in the period when the related product is sold (often referred to as "products costs"). Depreciation that is a product cost is included in the carve-out base in the year it is incurred regardless of when the related product is sold. This rule recognises that the timing of the recognition of the depreciation charge in the income statement has no bearing on substantive activities.

352. Most financial accounting standards, including IFRS, require firms to test property, plant and equipment for impairment when events or changes in circumstances indicate book value may not be recoverable. When an asset is in fact impaired, an impairment loss is recognised in profit and loss and the

carrying value of the relevant asset is reduced. The post-impairment carrying value then serves as the revised basis for subsequent depreciation. Consequently, absent a corrective measure, impairments would reduce the quantum of the carve-out amount. This result is not appropriate because impairments are typically caused by deteriorating market conditions, poor management, new competition or technological innovations, and are generally not indicative of a reduction in substantive activities. To eliminate the effect of impairments on the carve-out amount, impairment losses are treated as equivalent to depreciation for purposes of the carve-out, thus included in the carve-out base in the year of impairment, and the subsequent decrease in depreciation for financial accounting purposes is regarded.

353. For purposes of computing the carve-out on a jurisdictional basis, depreciation of property, plant and equipment is treated as having nexus in the jurisdiction of the Constituent Entity (which includes a permanent establishment) that uses the asset. As explained in the right-of-use asset Section below, a lessor is not allowed to include assets that it has leased to customers in its tangible asset carve-out base.

Land

354. Land is technically part of property, plant and equipment, however, unlike other property, plant and equipment, land is non-depreciable. As a non-depreciable tangible asset, land does not naturally "fit" in a depreciation-based tangible asset carve-out. Nonetheless, land is considered an indication of substantive activities and a significant non-mobile factor of production, and, on that basis, is included in the tangible asset carve-out base. The mechanic for doing so is a deemed depreciation charge for land, which requires establishing the same three depreciation factors as are required for depreciable property, plant and equipment, that is: (i) the depreciable base (ii) the useful life, and (iii) the depreciation method.

355. For purposes of calculating the deemed depreciation of land, as relevant to the carve-out, the depreciable base is equal to the original acquisition cost of the land, i.e., without regard to revaluation increases/decreases and with an assumed residual value of nil. The useful life is deemed to be [x] years. The depreciation method is deemed to be straight-line. Taken together, this implies that each year the deemed depreciation amount will be [x]% of the original acquisition cost of the land.

356. As previously provided, land that is an investment property is not included in the carve-out base. All other land is included, including land on which a building rests and land used in an agricultural business. The acquisition cost of land should be computed separately from the building and agriculture produce. Separating the value of land from a building or agriculture produce is not expected to materially increase complexity or compliance costs because many financial accounting standards already account for these assets separately. For example, IAS 16 – Property, Plant and Equipment, provides that land and buildings are separable assets and are accounted for separately. Similarly, IAS 41 – Agriculture Assets, scopes out the land related to agriculture activity, and requires the land be separately accounted for under IAS 16 and IAS 40 – Investment Property.

357. Like property, plant and equipment, land is tested for impairment. In the case of land, an impairment could arise when, for example, the area where the land is located experiences a natural disaster such as flooding, an earthquake or a tornado. If the land is in fact impaired, an impairment loss is recognised and the carrying value of the land is reduced. Consistent with the impairment rule for property, plant and equipment, impairment losses on land should be treated as equivalent to deemed depreciation for purposes of the carve-out, thus included in the carve-out base in the year of impairment.

358. For purposes of computing the carve-out on a jurisdictional basis, land is treated as having nexus in the jurisdiction in which the land is located.

Natural resources

359. Natural resources include oil and gas deposits, timber tracts and mineral deposits. These assets are accounted for similarly to depreciable property, plant and equipment. That is, natural resources are

initially recognised at cost, including acquisition, exploration-related, and restoration costs. After initial recognition, the asset is carried at its cost less any accumulated depletion and any accumulated impairment losses, i.e., the cost model. [15] Depletion is the allocation of the cost of natural resources, and has a number of similarities to depreciation accounting. Because the usefulness of a natural resource is generally directly related to the amount of resources extracted, the units of production method is widely used to calculate depletion. Service life is therefore the estimated amount of resources to be extracted, e.g., tons of minerals or barrels of oil.

360. For purposes of the carve-out, the assumptions used to compute depletion are required to conform with those used for the same asset for financial accounting purposes, specifically the financial accounts used to compute the GloBE tax base for the relevant Constituent Entity. For example, if the parent prepares its consolidated financial accounts in accordance with IFRS, then the factors used to compute depletion must follow IFRS 6 – Exploration for and Evaluation of Mineral Resources. However, as with property, plant and equipment, an exception applies with respect to the revaluation model. In particular, any incremental increase in depletion resulting from revaluation increases are disregarded. And, any revaluation loss recognised in profit and loss is treated as additional depletion in the year of the loss, and the decreased financial accounting depletion determined after the revaluation is included in the carve-out base annually. Additionally, the depletion charge should be computed without regard to restoration-related costs, which are not incurred until after the natural resource has been extracted from the site.

361. Depletion, being a product cost, is included in the cost of inventory, just as the depreciation on manufacturing equipment is included in inventory. The depletion charge is recognised as cost of goods sold in the income statement when the inventory is eventually sold. Consistent with the rule provided for property, plant and equipment, depletion is included in the carve-out base in the year it is incurred regardless of when the inventory is sold. This rule recognises that the timing of the recognition of the depletion charge in the income statement has no bearing on substantive activities.

362. Natural resources are tested for impairment under financial accounting rules. In the case of a natural resource, an impairment could arise when, for example, exploration for and evaluation of mineral resources in the specific area have not led to the discovery of commercially viable quantities of mineral resources.[16] If the asset is in fact impaired, an impairment loss is recognised in profit in loss and the carrying value of the relevant asset is reduced. The post-impairment carrying value then serves as the revised basis for subsequent depletion. Consistent with the impairment rule for property, plant and equipment and land, impairment losses on natural resources are treated as equivalent to depletion for purposes of the carve-out, thus included in the carve-out base in the year of impairment, and the subsequent decrease in depletion for financial accounting purposes is regarded.

363. For purposes of computing the carve-out on a jurisdictional basis, depletion is treated as having nexus in the jurisdiction in which the natural resource is located.

Right-of-use tangible assets

364. A carve-out based on the ownership of tangible assets would lead to a difference between owning and leasing assets. In order to avoid this distortion, the carve-out treats an appropriate portion of the expense of leasing a tangible asset, including buildings and land, in the same way as depreciation of property, plant and equipment.

365. In a lease arrangement a lessee recognises a "right-of-use" asset on its balance sheet representing its right to use the underlying asset and a lease liability representing its obligation to make lease payments. A lessee accounts for right-of-use assets similarly to an owner of property, plant and equipment. Specifically, a lessee initially recognises right-of-use assets based on the present value of the lease payments, and subsequently recognises depreciation and impairment losses i.e., the cost model.[17] The depreciation method is typically straight-line and the useful life is generally the earlier of the end of the

useful life of the asset or the end of the lease term. The lessee also recognises interest expense on the lease liability.

366. For purposes of the carve-out, the assumptions used to compute depreciation of a lessee's right-of-use asset must conform with the assumptions used for the same asset for financial accounting purposes, specifically the financial accounts used to compute the GloBE tax base for the relevant Constituent Entity.[18] For example, if the parent prepares its consolidated financial accounts in accordance with IFRS, then the assumptions used to compute the depreciation of the lessee's right-of-use asset must follow IFRS 16 – Leases. However, an exception applies with respect to the revaluation model. In particular, any incremental increase in depreciation resulting from revaluation increases are disregarded. And, any revaluation loss recognised in profit and loss is treated as additional depreciation in the year of the loss, and the decreased financial accounting depreciation determined after the revaluation is included in the carve-out base annually.

367. As with property, plant and equipment, land, and natural resources, a lessee must test the underlying asset for impairment for financial accounting purposes. A leased asset could be impaired for the same reasons property, plant and equipment is impaired: deteriorating market conditions, poor management, new competition, technological innovations, etc. If a right-of-use asset is in fact impaired, an impairment loss is recognised and the carrying value of the relevant asset is reduced. The post-impairment carrying value then serves as the revised basis for subsequent depreciation. Consistent with the impairment rule for property, plant and equipment, land, and natural resources, impairment losses on right-of-use assets are treated as equivalent to depreciation for purposes of the carve-out, thus included in the carve-out base in the year of impairment, and the subsequent decrease in depreciation for financial accounting purposes is regarded.

368. The lessor of an asset is not allowed a carve-out in respect of the depreciation on that asset. This rule reflects the fact that the lessor is not actively using the underlying asset to earn income. It is therefore not a reliable measure of substantive activities of the lessor.

369. For purposes of computing the carve-out on a jurisdictional basis, a lessee's depreciation of a right-of-use asset is treated as having nexus in the jurisdiction of the Constituent Entity lessee that uses the property in its business.

4.3.3. Low margin businesses

370. The impact of expenditure based tax credits on a taxpayer's ETR is more significant for low margin businesses. This is due to the fact that low margin businesses have more credits as a proportion of their total income. However, the formulaic substance-based carve-out based on payroll and tangible assets is designed, in part, to accommodate to some extent the provision of tax credits and other incentives for low margin businesses. Low margin businesses have more expenses as a percentage of their income and thus would secure a relatively larger carve-out. The carve-out will therefore limit the impact of GloBE rules on low margin businesses that are entitled to tax credits for local expenditures.

4.4. Computation of the ETR and top-up tax

Computation of the ETR for the Jurisdiction

The ETR[19] for a jurisdiction is equal to:

$$Adjusted\ Covered\ Taxes\ /\ Adjusted\ GloBE\ Income$$

Where,

(a) Adjusted Covered Taxes means the covered taxes assigned to the jurisdiction, except taxes attributable to income excluded from the GloBE tax base, increased by the lesser of the total local tax carry-forward or the amount of the local tax carry-forward necessary to achieve an ETR that is equal to the minimum rate; and

(b) Adjusted GloBE Income means the combined income and loss of all Constituent Entities located in the jurisdiction for the year decreased by the loss carry-forward for the jurisdiction.

Computation of the top-up tax for each Constituent Entity

The amount of top-up tax for each Constituent Entity in a jurisdiction is equal to:

$$Adjusted\ GloBE\ Income\ of\ the\ Constituent\ Entity\ x\ Top\ up\ Tax\ Percentage$$

Where,

(a) Adjusted GloBE Income of the Constituent Entity means, in respect of the income of a Constituent Entity in the relevant period, the income of that entity as calculated for the purposes of the GloBE rules reduced by its share of any loss carry forward and of any loss suffered by other Constituent Entities in the same jurisdiction in the same period and the proportionate share of any carve-out for the jurisdiction.

(b) Top-up Tax Percentage means the excess of the minimum ETR over the ETR as calculated for that jurisdiction in the relevant period.

371. The computation of the ETR for each jurisdiction and the top-up tax for each Constituent Entity in the jurisdiction is set forth in the preceding Sections. This Section describes the three-step process to compute the ETR for each jurisdiction and the top-up tax applicable to each Constituent Entity in a low-tax jurisdiction.[20] The ETR for the jurisdiction is computed first. Second, if the ETR is below the minimum rate, a top-up tax percentage is calculated. Third, the top-up tax for each Constituent Entity in the jurisdiction is determined. After each Constituent Entity's top-up tax is computed under the rules of this chapter, the liability to tax is then determined by the application of the operational rules discussed in the following chapters. For purpose of computing the jurisdictional ETR, the income or loss of a Constituent Entity is the total income or loss of the entity, irrespective of whether the MNE Group owns 100% of the entity. If the adjusted GloBE income for a jurisdiction is zero or a loss, there is no GloBE tax liability for the jurisdiction, and any loss is carried forward under the loss carry-forward rules described in Section 4.2.1

372. For purposes of the ETR computation, the adjusted covered taxes are the covered taxes assigned to the jurisdiction pursuant to the rules in Section 3.4.2, except taxes attributable to income excluded as a permanent adjustment from the GloBE income of the Constituent Entities located in the jurisdiction, increased by the lesser of the total local tax carry-forward or the amount of the local tax carry-forward necessary to achieve an ETR that is equal to the minimum rate. The amount of the local tax carry-forward necessary to achieve the minimum rate is equal to the excess of the adjusted GloBE tax base for the jurisdiction multiplied by the minimum rate over the covered taxes assigned to the jurisdiction. The amount of local tax carry-forward included in the adjusted covered taxes of the ETR computation for any year reduces the amount of the local tax carry-forward available in subsequent years.[21]

373. If, after taking into account local tax carry-forwards, the ETR remains below the minimum rate, the top-up tax percentage must be computed for the jurisdiction. The top-up tax percentage is the excess of the minimum rate over the ETR for the jurisdiction.

374. Finally, the top-up tax for each Constituent Entity that has positive net income for the year in the jurisdiction is computed by multiplying the adjusted GloBE income of each such Constituent Entity by the top-up tax percentage. The adjusted GloBE income of the Constituent Entity is equal to the entity's income for the year reduced by its share of:

(a) the current year losses of other Constituent Entities resident or located in the jurisdiction;

(b) the loss carry-forward for the jurisdiction; and

(c) the carve-out determined for the jurisdiction.

375. The current year losses, the loss carry-forward allowed, and the carve-out for a jurisdiction are allocated to Constituent Entities proportionally based on their net income. Specifically, current year losses, the loss carry-forward allowed, and the carve-out amount determined for the jurisdiction are allocated to a Constituent Entity with positive net income based on the ratio of that entity's net income to the total net income of Constituent Entities in the jurisdiction that have positive net income for the year.

References

OECD (2015), *Transfer Pricing Documentation and Country-by-Country Reporting, Action 13 - 2015 Final Report*, OECD/G20 Base Erosion and Profit Shifting Project, OECD Publishing, Paris, https://dx.doi.org/10.1787/9789264241480-en. [1]

Notes

[1] IIR tax paid in respect of a preceding taxable year includes IIR taxes that were paid or satisfied through the use of a pre-existing IIR tax credit.

[2] Further consideration will be given to permitting IIR tax credits to reduce other tax liabilities of the shareholder.

[3] If an IIR tax liability is offset against other domestic tax liabilities, this should not reduce the MNE's ETR in the jurisdiction

[4] It could not be claimed in connection with a liability in another jurisdiction arising pursuant to the other jurisdiction's application of the undertaxed payments rule.

[5] The references to temporary differences in this paragraph are not meant to limit the creation or use of an IIR tax credit to situations involving a temporary difference.

[6] While all fixed percentage mark-ups are indicated with an [x], that should not be interpreted to mean the mark-up necessarily has to be the same for each item.

[7] Further consideration is required to determine if the tangible asset component should be reduced to account for debt-financed property.

[8] Further consideration is required to determine the deemed useful life of land for purposes of the carve-out.

[9] See page 34 of Action 13 Report (OECD, 2015[1]): "In the tenth column of the template, the Reporting MNE should report the total number of employees on a full-time equivalent (FTE) basis of all the Constituent Entities resident for tax purposes in the relevant tax jurisdiction. The number of employees may be reported as of the year-end, on the basis of average employment levels for the year, or on any other basis consistently applied across tax jurisdictions and from year to year. For this purpose, independent contractors participating in the ordinary operating activities of the Constituent Entity may be reported as employees. Reasonable rounding or approximation of the number of employees is permissible, providing that such rounding or approximation does not materially distort the relative distribution of employees across the various tax jurisdictions. Consistent approaches should be applied from year to year and across entities."

[10] If an employee's employment activities and services are not performed in the jurisdiction of the employer, it is likely that the employee generally performs a substantial portion of their employment activities and services in the jurisdiction in which they are resident.

[11] For example, the direct labour costs of manufacturing related employees are capitalised into work-in-process inventory, then finished goods inventory and subsequently recognised as part of cost of goods sold, which may not be until a year or more after the payroll expenditure was initially incurred.

[12] IFRS 5 – Non-current Assets Held for Sale and Discontinuing Operations.

[13] IAS 16 – Property, Plant and Equipment.

[14] This rule also applies to assets sold to third parties as part of a structured back-to-back transaction.

[15] Under some financial accounting standards timber tracts are accounted for the same as other natural resources, i.e., cost model. However, under IFRS, specifically IAS 41 – Agriculture, "biological assets", which includes timber tracts, are valued at their fair value less estimated costs to sell, with changes in fair value included in profit or loss. For purposes of the carve-out, a deemed depletion charge for timber tracts must be derived using the cost model.

[16] IFRS 6 – Exploration for and Evaluation of Mineral Resources.

[17] Some financial accounting standards require lessee's to distinguish between "operating leases" and "finance leases". Other standards, including IFRS, have a single lessee accounting model which requires a lessee to recognise assets and liabilities for all leases with a term of more than 12 months, unless the underlying asset is of low value.

[18] For the financial accounting standards requiring lessee's to distinguish between "operating leases" and "finance leases", the rental costs for "operating leases" can be treated as depreciation costs for the calculation of the carve-out base for the GloBE rules.

[19] As noted in Section 4.3, further consideration will be given to the effect of the carve-out on the calculation of the ETR and top-up taxes under the GloBE, including whether an MNE group that claims the benefit of the carve-out should be required to make a corresponding and proportional adjustment to the covered taxes.

[20] Attributing a portion of the top-up tax to the each low-tax Constituent Entities Entity is necessary in situations where the profits made by some of these low-tax Constituent Entities are subject to the UTPR or are subject to IIRs applied by separate Parents, for example, due to split-ownership. As explained under

sections 6.3 and 7.2 this can be the case if an IIR applies to the profits made by some (but not all) Constituent Entities located in the low-tax jurisdiction. For example, if the Ultimate Parent Entity is not subject to an IIR but a sub-holding parent entity that owns some but not all low-tax Constituent Entities located in a given jurisdiction is subject to an IIR, another Parent's IIR or another CE's UTPR may apply with respect to the other Constituent Entities in the jurisdiction.

[21] In the event that a UTPR taxpayer has a UTPR tax amount that is carried-forward from a prior year (see Section 7.7.4), such amount should not be taken into account for purposes of the ETR computation.

5 Simplification options

5.1. Overview

376. During the December 2019 Public Consultation (OECD, 2019[1]), many MNEs stressed that simplification measures are needed to reduce the complexity and administrative burden associated with complying with the GloBE rules, particularly in the context of jurisdictional blending.

377. Several submissions pointed out that large MNEs often operate in more than 100 jurisdictions and would be required to undertake the same number of ETR calculations under a jurisdictional blending approach. Other submissions expressed concern that, under jurisdictional blending, it would be necessary to compute the ETR in jurisdictions that are likely to be above the agreed minimum rate year-after-year, given the base and tax rate in these jurisdictions.

378. Against this background, the Inclusive Framework has explored several potential simplification measures, as set out below. These simplification measures would benefit from future public consultations with business and therefore no decision has been taken on which, if any, of these simplification measures to incorporate into the final design of the GloBE rules.

379. The simplification measures that have been considered in the Inclusive Framework, include:

a. Country-by-country reporting ETR safe-harbour;

b. De minimis profit exclusion;

c. Single jurisdictional ETR calculation to cover several years; and

d. Tax administrative guidance.

380. These simplification measures could be applied at the election of the taxpayer and could be layered on top of one-another such that multiple simplification measures could be applied simultaneously. It also may be the case that different aspects of the simplification measures could perhaps be combined.

5.2. Country-by-country reporting ETR safe-harbour

381. This simplification measure would allow MNEs to leverage the work done to prepare their annual CbC report. Large MNEs are required to file a CbC report containing, among other things, certain financial information pertaining to their allocation of global profits and tax liability. A CbC report contains jurisdictional financial information in two columns that could be useful for purposes of computing jurisdictional ETRs for the GloBE rules: (i) Profit (Loss) before Income Tax; and (ii) Income Tax Accrued (Current Year).

382. This simplification measure would likely best operate as a safe-harbour. For example, if the jurisdictional ETR based on the CbC report was above a certain threshold, which could be set above the agreed minimum rate, then no further work would be required for that jurisdiction. In other words, the filing of the CbC report would be all that is required for that jurisdiction for purposes of the GloBE rules.

383. At least two restrictions would be required. First, the simplification measure would only be available for MNEs that prepare their CbC report based on the parent's consolidated financial accounts, which is an option, but not a requirement, under the CbCR rules. Based on initial consultations, a large majority of MNEs use the parent's consolidated accounts as their CbC data source. Assuming that to be the case, restricting the use of this simplification measure based on CbC data source would not be expected to materially reduce its reach and impact. Furthermore, MNEs that do not currently use the parent's consolidated accounts could change their data source and avail themselves of the simplification measure. If this simplification measure was to create an incentive for MNEs to converge to the parent's consolidated accounts as their CbC data source it would result in the attendant benefit of improving CbC risk assessment for tax administrations.

384. The second restriction is that several adjustments would need to be made which relate to differences between the financial information reported in CbC reports and the financial information required for calculating a jurisdictional ETR in accordance with the GloBE rules. Ideally, a jurisdictional ETR could be computed by simply dividing Income Tax Accrued (Current Year) by Profit (Loss) before Income Tax as reported for each jurisdiction in the CbC report. However, the unadjusted information in these two columns will not suffice for an accurate jurisdictional ETR computation. Nonetheless, adjustments could be made to produce a reasonably reliable approximation of the jurisdictional ETR, as described below.

5.2.1. Required adjustments

385. Profit (Loss) before Income Tax could be adjusted as follows:

(a) Any income or loss of non-group members reported in Profit (Loss) before Income Tax under the equity method of accounting would need to be removed;

(b) Permanent adjustments required under the GloBE rules to financial accounting income would need to be added to or subtracted from Profit (Loss) before Income Tax; and

(c) Subject to ongoing public consultation and further discussion in the Inclusive Framework, other adjustments may also be required.

386. Income Tax Accrued (Current Year) could be adjusted as follows:

(a) Withholding taxes and net basis taxes paid in respect of dividends from a group member would need to be moved from the shareholder's jurisdiction to the jurisdiction where the underlying income arose or to the distributing subsidiary's jurisdiction;

(b) CFC taxes should be assigned, where possible, to the jurisdiction in which the underlying income arises (i.e. to the jurisdiction of the CFC) and should be excluded from the ETR computation if the underlying income is excluded.[1]

(c) Withholding taxes paid in respect of dividends received from a corporation accounted for using the equity method would need to be removed;

(d) Covered taxes that are not income taxes for financial accounting purposes would increase Income Tax Accrued (Current Year);

(e) Refunds of tax would need to be treated as a reduction of Income Tax Accrued (Current Year); and

(f) Subject to further discussion in the Inclusive Framework, other adjustments may also be required.

387. It is possible that some of the adjustments, as described above, could be incorporated into the actual CbCR rules. However, several of the necessary adjustments may not; and they would then need to be made in addition to what is required for CbCR.

388. Notwithstanding the required adjustments described above, starting with the CbC report and making adjustments would likely be simpler for an MNE compared to the alternative of computing the jurisdictional ETR from the ground-up. MNEs already have the systems and processes in place to efficiently and reliably compile their CbCR information. Further, some of the required adjustments may not be difficult to determine. For example, it should be relatively straightforward to determine the amount of withholding taxes on dividends paid to a jurisdiction as well as the amount of income tax refunds received from a jurisdiction. Some of the other adjustments may not be necessary to compute a "conservatively-low" jurisdictional ETR.

389. One further option could be to incorporate deferred tax accounting information into the determination of an ETR safe-harbour. This option would combine the information presently provided in the CbC report with the information on the MNE's deferred tax accounting position in each jurisdiction where it operates, in order to provide a more accurate picture of the MNE's expected tax liability in each jurisdiction without the burden of computing and tracking carry-forwards and tax credits. The BEPS Action 13 report includes specific instructions that Income Tax Accrued (Current Year) "should not include deferred taxes or provisions for uncertain tax liabilities" (OECD, 2015[2]) (page 34). This is appropriate in the CbCR context as it focuses on the current tax in a jurisdiction for the fiscal year. However, in calculating an ETR for a particular jurisdiction, this can create a mismatch between the calculation of Profit (Loss) before Income Tax, which is calculated under financial accounting principles, and Income Tax Accrued (Current Year), which is essentially based on taxable profits calculated under tax rules in the relevant jurisdiction. The GloBE rules for addressing temporary differences compensate for this mismatch using carry-forwards and a tax credit mechanism. This option would eliminate the need to compute and track the carry-forwards and tax credits for jurisdictions in which the MNE consistently reports an ETR in excess of the safe-harbour ETR. Consideration would be required for instances in which the MNE is above the safe-harbour ETR for one or more prior years, but below the safe-harbour ETR in the current year and whether this would require the MNE to go back and compute its carry-forward attributes for the prior years.

390. As part of the CbCR 2020 review, consideration is being given to including movements in deferred tax as an additional column alongside Income Tax Accrued (Current Year). If an additional column is not added, the definition of Income Tax Accrued (Current Year) could potentially be amended, so as also to include movements in deferred tax.

5.3. De minimis profit exclusion

391. Another simplification measure could consist of excluding jurisdictions from the GloBE rules which have less than a certain percentage of the MNE Group's pre-tax profit. This may result in a significant reduction of compliance costs, while continuing to ensure that the GloBE rules remain effective in addressing some of the most important tax planning structures using low taxed principal or entrepreneurial IP structures.

392. Under these structures, an MNE shifts the ownership of valuable IP into a vehicle that is subject to low effective rates of taxation. The vehicle then exploits the IP and/or enters into manufacturing and/or sales and marketing arrangements with other group entities which often allow the IP vehicle to capture the full return from the exploitation of that IP. The net effect of these arrangements is that significant amounts of profits are rolled-up into the IP vehicle with the other entities in the group deriving only nominal returns.

393. The changes to the transfer pricing guidance that were introduced under Actions 8-10 of the BEPS Action Plan prevent MNEs from shifting intangible income into such IP vehicles unless they perform relevant functions in respect of the development, enhancement, maintenance, protection and exploitation of the transferred intangible (commonly referred to as DEMPE functions). The requirement imposed on the IP holding vehicle under Actions 8-10 to undertake the related DEMPE functions impedes the MNE from splitting the ownership of its valuable IP amongst a large number of different low taxed IP vehicles.[2]

394. A de minimis profit exclusion rule would build on these operational constraints imposed on MNEs by Actions 8-10. It would operate by targeting the GloBE rules at only those jurisdictions above a certain de minimis profit threshold.[3] Because IP vehicles will generally be the most profitable within the group, a low de minimis threshold, such as 2.5% of the group's pre-tax profit, would ensure the GloBE rules applied to all the MNE's IP vehicles while avoiding the compliance burden associated with applying the rule to every jurisdiction.

395. Effectively, this simplification measure puts a ceiling on the number of jurisdictional ETR calculations. For example, if the de minimis threshold were to be set at 2.5% of the group's pre-tax profit, then a maximum of 40 jurisdictional ETR calculations would be required, rather than the 100 or more calculations that may otherwise be required. In order to apply this simplification measure, MNEs would still be required to compute the pre-tax profit for every jurisdiction; however, MNEs would only need to compute covered taxes for jurisdictions with profits above the de minimis threshold. To reduce the compliance burden of computing pre-tax profit for every jurisdiction, it may be possible to use unadjusted CbC data (or potentially adjusted for the same items described in the context of the CbCR ETR safe-harbour), assuming the CbC data source was the parent's consolidated financial accounts.

396. Setting the de minimis threshold at a relatively low percentage should prevent an MNE from fragmenting its IP holdings among a large number of low tax structures in order to avoid the GloBE rules. Given the nature of the DEMPE functions required to support the transfer of the IP, it would not seem likely or commercially practical, at an operational level, for an MNE to divide its IP amongst a sufficiently large number of jurisdictions to reduce the profitability of each IP vehicle below the de minimis threshold.

397. In order to be implemented, further technical work would be required in several areas, including:

a. Whether the denominator of the de minimis calculation would be global pre-tax profit (i.e., including the parent jurisdiction) or foreign pre-tax profit (i.e., excluding the parent jurisdiction);

b. The treatment of losses, which absent an adjustment could upset the ceiling feature of the simplification measure;

c. How to best coordinate this rule with the management of temporary differences, in particular how to deal with jurisdictions that bounce in and out of scope from year-to-year;

d. Whether further rules are necessary to neutralise the risk of fragmentation; and

e. Where to set the de minimis percentage balancing simplification with other considerations, including the overall effectiveness of the GloBE rules.

398. A de minimis based simplification measure could also be structured as a fixed de minimis threshold, such as EUR 100,000, rather than a relative de minimis threshold, such as 2.5% of group profit. The benefit of the relative threshold is it puts a ceiling on the number of jurisdictional ETR calculations for every MNE whereas a fixed threshold would apply differently across MNEs and in some cases may not result in material simplification. These two approaches could also perhaps be combined, for example, the lesser of 2.5% of group profit and EUR 100,000.

5.4. Single jurisdictional ETR calculation to cover several years

399. This simplification measure would be designed to require an MNE to perform the jurisdictional ETR calculation for every jurisdiction in the base year. But, in the case that the ETR of a particular jurisdiction exceeded a certain threshold rate (in the base year or any subsequent year) then the MNE would not be required to compute the ETR for that jurisdiction for the next 3-5 years (the grace period). The threshold rate could be set above the agreed minimum rate.

400. A key element of this simplification measure would be balancing simplification with accuracy and potential for distortions. On the one hand, the grace period would need to extend for several years in order to provide material simplification. On the other hand, the longer the grace period the more likely it is to hide or overlook inaccuracies and distortions.

401. Certain restrictions would be required to make this simplification measure acceptable to governments. An example of such a restriction is to require MNEs to make an annual representation that no business change occurred over the grace period. Special anti-abuse rules may also be required. For example, rules may be needed to address situations whereby an MNE structures intercompany transactions designed to spike the ETR in the base year in order to escape the GloBE rules in the grace period. Special rules may also be needed to address situations whereby a jurisdiction could introduce a regime with balloon tax payments designed to spike the ETR in the base year, with no-tax or low-tax in the grace period.

402. A key disadvantage of this simplification measure is that MNEs would be required to establish all the necessary processes and systems in every jurisdiction in order to compute the base year ETR. Therefore, an MNE with operations in 120 jurisdictions would still be required to undertake 120 jurisdictional ETR calculations in the base year. Once an MNE has established all the necessary processes and systems, it may not be significantly more work to compute the jurisdictional ETR every year. In other words, this simplification measure may not deliver meaningful simplification.

403. If this option were to be pursued, it may be preferable to compute the base year ETR based on covered taxes and income data from multiple consecutive years rather than a single year, to safeguard against inappropriate exemptions. A multi-year approach should not be particularly onerous from a compliance perspective, since the MNE would have already configured its systems to compile all relevant data, and performed all the relevant calculations, in respect of the first year, which should facilitate doing so in respect of a multiple years.

5.5. Tax administrative guidance

404. This simplification measure seeks to reduce instances where MNEs prepare and tax administrations need to review a large number of ETR calculations that consistently show that the ETR exceeds the agreed minimum rate year-after-year. For these "low-risk jurisdictions", tax administrations that were following a risk-based approach would eventually stop reviewing an MNE's ETR for operations in these jurisdictions and MNEs that were required to continue determining their ETR for compliance purposes would legitimately question the associated compliance costs. Therefore, the question is whether this ex-post result could be avoided by establishing a structured and transparent ex-ante process with overall lower costs for businesses and tax administrations alike.

405. This simplification measure would establish an ex-ante process whereby tax administrations (via the Inclusive Framework) would work together with stakeholders, for instance, via a business advisory group, to identify jurisdictions where the tax base does not materially depart from the GloBE tax base (other than in areas where different accounting-tax approaches are common and low-risk, for example dividends may be taxable under local tax rules) and the tax rate is sufficiently high. For instance, this work could determine that Jurisdiction X, given its tax base and tax rate, would almost always result in an ETR above the minimum tax rate and hence absent a change in that jurisdiction's tax rules, MNEs would enjoy a presumption that their ETR in that jurisdiction exceeded the agreed minimum rate. Further work would be required to identify all the relevant factors that would be considered in the determination process.

406. The mechanism could work such that tax administrations would publish guidance (developed within an Inclusive Framework process) that set out jurisdictions deemed to be low-risk and then MNEs would not be required to perform the ETR calculation for those jurisdictions, unless a tax authority

specifically requested it within a certain period of time, potentially by reference to the statute of limitation rules in the respective jurisdictions. If the ETR calculated at the tax authority's request was below the agreed minimum rate, the MNE would be subject to tax under the GloBE rules on the relevant income but would not be subject to underpayment or other tax penalties with respect to the income that benefitted from the presumption. To be most effective, tax administrations participating in such an ex-ante process and working alongside relevant stakeholders, could focus their effort in the period after the GloBE rules are finalized, and before the rules are effective or the first filing obligation deadline.

407. The determination of "low-risk" could apply to all MNEs operating within a certain jurisdiction, or it could be restricted to MNEs within or without certain sectors. For example, it may be the case that in a certain jurisdiction virtually every MNE is likely to be above the agreed minimum rate, except MNEs in a certain sector because of sector-specific tax incentives. In such a case, the low-risk determination could apply to every MNE, except for MNEs in that particular sector. In the case of a sectoral approach, consideration would be required for the treatment of firms that operate across multiple sectors.

408. In general, the low-risk determination would apply every year (i.e., without a time restriction), but would require a re-determination in the case of tax law revision or reform that materially changed the jurisdiction's tax base and/or tax rate. For this purpose, a notification process could be set.

409. This option may require tax authorities to dedicate significant resources to understanding the design and potential impact of different countries' tax systems. However, it is recognised that tax authorities would need to undertake a risk assessment process even in the absence of this simplification measure and that there would be benefits in terms of synergies and certainty in developing definitive guidance, and that the key challenge therefore would be to design a technical, non-political and transparent process to achieve it.

References

OECD (2019), *Global Anti-Base Erosion Proposal ("GloBE") - Pillar Two*, OECD Publishing, Paris, https://www.oecd.org/tax/beps/public-consultation-document-global-anti-base-erosion-proposal-pillar-two.pdf.pdf. [1]

OECD (2015), *Transfer Pricing Documentation and Country-by-Country Reporting, Action 13 - 2015 Final Report*, OECD/G20 Base Erosion and Profit Shifting Project, OECD Publishing, Paris, https://dx.doi.org/10.1787/9789264241480-en. [2]

Notes

[1] See Section 3.4.2 on *Assignment of income and taxes of entity to each jurisdiction* for the approach for the treatment of CFC income and related taxes in the ETR calculation under the GloBE.

[2] Since this simplification measure relies on DEMPE concepts to protect against fragmentation risk, it would only be available in jurisdictions that follow the guidance provided in BEPS Actions 8-10.

[3] Consideration may be given to different mechanisms (e.g., profit-size threshold) to achieve a same or similar result.

6 Income Inclusion and Switch-Over Rules

6.1. Overview

410. The IIR effectively operates by requiring a parent entity (in most cases, the Ultimate Parent Entity) to bring into account its share of the income of each Constituent Entity located in a low-tax jurisdiction and taxes that income up to the minimum rate (after crediting any covered taxes on that income). The IIR imposes a top-up tax only on that portion of the low tax income of a foreign Constituent Entity which is beneficially owned (directly or indirectly) by the member of the group that applies the IIR (the Parent).

411. The IIR operates in a way that is similar to a CFC rule in that it subjects a domestic taxpayer to tax on its share of the foreign income of any controlled subsidiary The IIR is designed to be co-ordinated with the GloBE rules that apply in other jurisdictions where the MNE Group operates to ensure that, in aggregate, these rules do not result in incremental taxation on low taxed profit that is above the agreed minimum rate. The IIR is intended to be implemented consistently in every jurisdiction and operate in a way that produces the same overall result in order to ensure that an MNE Group is subject to a minimum level taxation in each jurisdiction that it operates regardless of where it is headquartered and without giving rise to the risk of double or over taxation.

412. Both the IIR and the UTPR are based on the same effective tax rate calculation. As described in Chapters 3 and 4, the ETR computation is determined on a jurisdictional blending basis taking into account the profits, losses and covered taxes paid by all the Constituent Entities of the MNE Group in the jurisdiction and adjusted for substance carve-outs and the carry-forward of losses and excess tax credits. As described in those Chapters:

a. the ETR is first computed at the jurisdictional level to determine whether the jurisdiction is, in fact, a "low-tax jurisdiction" (i.e. a jurisdiction where the MNE's jurisdictional ETR is below the agreed minimum rate) and to compute the top-up tax percentage necessary to bring the aggregate amount of tax on the income of that jurisdiction up to the minimum rate.

b. This top-up tax percentage is then applied to the income of each Constituent Entity in that low tax jurisdiction, adjusted for losses of other entities for the same period, loss carry-forwards, and any carve-out amount, thereby ensuring that the total amount of top-up tax arising in that jurisdiction is allocated to each Constituent Entity in proportion to its adjusted income.

413. The computation of the top-up tax in respect of each Constituent Entity is, therefore, undertaken prior to, and independently of, the mechanisms for allocating liability for such top-up tax under IIR (and UTPR) as described in this Chapter. Importantly, when the parent entity applying the IIR is not the Ultimate Parent Entity, the ETR of a jurisdiction is not computed solely by reference to the Constituent Entities owned by that parent entity; instead, the ETR is computed by reference to all the Constituent Entities controlled by the MNE Group in that jurisdiction. See Example 6.1A. of the Annex. The implication of determining the top-up tax in respect of each Constituent Entity based on a group-wide average ETR for

the jurisdiction is that top-up tax may be computed for an entity that would not be a low-taxed Constituent Entity on a standalone basis. See Example 6.1B of the Annex. In this sense, the IIR can be contrasted with the usual structure of CFC rules which typically apply to subsidiaries on a standalone entity basis based on the profits, losses and taxes paid by each controlled-foreign-corporation. The fact that the taxpayer and the controlled foreign corporation are part of a larger MNE Group is not usually relevant to the calculation of income or creditable taxes under a CFC rule.

414. The ETR computation and the mechanism for collecting the top-up tax are separate design features of the GloBE rules. The IIR provides for a mechanism to collect the top-up tax based on the parent entity's direct or indirect ownership of the low-taxed Constituent Entities. The UTPR serves as a backstop to the IIR by providing a mechanism to collect any remaining top-up tax in relation to foreign profits that are not in scope of an applicable IIR.

415. Liability for the amount of top-up tax computed for a low-taxed Constituent Entity is allocated to the parent entity in proportion to the parent entity's equity interest in the income of that entity. As described below, liability for the top-up tax usually falls on the Ultimate Parent Entity of the MNE Group. However, under certain circumstances, the GloBE rules are designed so that the liability for the top-up tax shifts to one or more other Constituent Entities of the MNE Group. This coordination of income inclusion rules among jurisdictions is part of the design of the GloBE rules, whereas CFC rules, though they may have tax credit rules designed to avoid double taxation, typically don't have this level of co-ordination.

6.2. Operation of the Income Inclusion Rule (IIR)

416. The IIR requires a taxpayer that is the "parent" of the MNE Group (or part of the MNE Group) to pay top-up tax on its proportionate share of the income of any low-tax Constituent Entity in which that taxpayer has a direct or indirect ownership interest.

417. The IIR includes an ordering rule that is designed to ensure that the IIR in different jurisdictions cannot be applied to the same interest in low-taxed income. The primary mechanism for co-ordinating the application of the IIR in each jurisdiction is through the top-down approach. This approach gives priority to the application of the income inclusion rule in the jurisdiction of the Constituent Entity that is at or near the top of the ownership chain in the MNE Group, starting with the Ultimate Parent Entity. In the event the Ultimate Parent Entity is not located in a jurisdiction that has implemented the IIR, then responsibility for applying the IIR falls to the Constituent Entity that is directly owned and controlled by that Ultimate Parent Entity, and so on, down the chain of ownership.

418. The application of the top-down approach is subject to a further rule that specifically addresses the application of the IIR in the case of "split-ownership structures". Split-ownership structures are those where a significant portion (e.g., 10% or more) of the equity interests in a Constituent Entity are held by persons outside the MNE Group. This rule pushes the obligation to apply the IIR down to the partially-owned "intermediate" parent. The intermediate parent then applies the IIR to its share of the income of any low-taxed Constituent Entity in which that Intermediate Parent has a direct or indirect ownership interest. This split ownership rule ensures that the IIR captures all the income of the low-taxed Constituent Entity that is beneficially owned by the Intermediate Parent, without imposing a disproportionate tax burden on the MNE Group in relation to income that is beneficially owned by entities outside the group. The operation of the IIR and the ordering rules is set out in the box below.[1]

1. Income Inclusion Rule

A Parent (including a Partially Owned Intermediate Parent) that owns (directly or indirectly) an equity interest in a foreign low-taxed Constituent Entity at the end of a reporting period shall be subject to a top-up tax under the income inclusion rule in respect of its proportionate share of the income of that Constituent Entity for that period.

2. Top-down approach

A Parent is a Constituent Entity that:

- owns (directly or indirectly) an equity interest in another Constituent Entity in the same MNE Group;
- is located in a jurisdiction that has adopted an income inclusion rule; and

is not controlled, directly or indirectly, by another Constituent Entity or Entities that are subject to the income inclusion rule; and also includes a Partially Owned Intermediate Parent.

3. Split-ownership structures

A Partially Owned Intermediate Parent is a Constituent Entity that is located in a jurisdiction that has adopted an income inclusion rule, other than the Ultimate Parent Entity, and X% or more of its equity interests are held directly or indirectly by persons that are not Constituent Entities of the MNE Group. A Constituent Entity that is a Partially Owned Intermediate Parent as a result of indirect ownership by persons that are not Constituent Entities shall not apply the income inclusion rule if all of its equity interests are held directly or indirectly by Constituent Entities required to apply the income inclusion rule.

If the Parent holds all or any portion of its equity in the low-taxed Constituent Entity through a Partially Owned Intermediate Parent, then the Parent will not apply the income inclusion rule to the income of that Constituent Entity to the extent such income has already been brought into account under the income inclusion rule that applies in the jurisdiction where the Partially Owned Intermediate Parent is located.

6.3. Top-Down Approach

419. If each Constituent Entity in the ownership chain were required to apply the income inclusion rule, the rules of multiple jurisdictions could apply to the same low-taxed Constituent Entities, which could give rise to double taxation. Thus, the GloBE rules require a coordination mechanism to prevent overlapping application of the income inclusion rules of different jurisdictions from giving rise to double taxation of income attributable to the same equity interests in low-taxed Constituent Entities. The primary mechanism for co-ordinating the interaction between different income inclusion rules in different jurisdictions is the top-down approach.

420. The top-down approach arises from the interplay of two rules.

a. The first rule is the general income inclusion rule. Under this rule, any Constituent Entity that meets the definition of a Parent is obligated to apply the income inclusion rule but only to its proportionate share of the income of any Constituent Entity in which it holds (directly or indirectly) an equity interest.

b. The second rule defines the term "Parent" in such a way that the income inclusion rule of Constituent Entities that are beneath the Parent applying the income inclusion rule in the ownership chain are not applicable.

421. Together, these two rules ensure that the Ultimate Parent Entity of the MNE Group has the first priority to apply the income inclusion rule and provides for an orderly determination of which Constituent Entity or Entities in the MNE Group will apply their income inclusion rules when the Ultimate Parent Entity is located in a jurisdiction that has not adopted the income inclusion rule. The operation of the top-down approach prevents the application of multiple income inclusion rules to a Parent's equity interest that is indirectly owned through another Constituent Entity or Entities.

422. Starting with the jurisdiction of the Ultimate Parent Entity, the top down approach requires the Ultimate Parent Entity to apply the income inclusion rule in the jurisdiction where it is located. The application of the rule at the Ultimate Parent Entity level will de-activate the income inclusion rule in jurisdictions where the other Constituent Entities are located. If the Ultimate Parent Entity does not apply the income inclusion rule, then the next Parent down the ownership chain applies the rule. The Parent is only required to apply its income inclusion rule and pay top-up tax with respect to the Low-Taxed Constituent Entities in which it has a direct or indirect equity interest. The top-up tax computed with respect to a Low-Taxed Constituent Entity is allocated to the Parent based on its ownership percentage of that entity.

423. Applying the IIR to the Ultimate Parent Entity as part of a top-down approach has a number of benefits from a design perspective:

a. ***Reduces compliance burdens and coordination issues.*** The top-down approach reduces the number of jurisdictions where the IIR can potentially apply and thereby reduces the complexity associated with applying the rule in multiple jurisdictions. This, in turn, reduces the administrative and compliance burden for both tax administrations and the different Constituent Entities within the MNE Group.

b. ***Use of a single accounting standard.*** The top-down approach is compatible with the policy decision to use the accounting standards of the Ultimate Parent Entity of the group for calculating the effective tax rate. The consolidated financial statements of the MNE Group are prepared by the Ultimate Parent Entity as defined by the accounting rules. A top-down approach is compatible with this design element of the GloBE rules because it significantly reduces the instances where the income inclusion rule is applied by an entity other than the one that has prepared the consolidated financial statements.

c. ***Consistent with jurisdictional blending.*** Jurisdictional blending allows that all the profits, losses and taxes of the Constituent Entities of the MNE Group located in the same jurisdiction are blended for purposes of the effective tax rate calculation. Giving priority to the Ultimate Parent Entity to apply the income inclusion rule is conceptually more consistent with jurisdictional blending because the blending is based on the income of all entities in the jurisdiction directly or indirectly owned by the Ultimate Parent Entity, which will in many cases include entities that are not owned or controlled by lower-tiered entities that might apply the income inclusion rule.

6.3.1. Two or more Parents within the same MNE Group applying the income inclusion rule

424. Under the top-down approach, when the Ultimate Parent Entity is not subject to an income inclusion rule, then two or more Constituent Entities in different ownership chains of the same MNE Group may meet the definition of a Parent, and each of these Parent entities can be required to apply the income inclusion rule to Low-Taxed Constituent Entities in which they own an equity interest. Example 6.1B

illustrates this situation in which two intermediate Parents are required to apply their income inclusion rules because the Ultimate Parent Entity of the MNE Group is located in a jurisdiction with no income inclusion rule. In the example, each Parent applying its income inclusion rule separately owns the low-taxed Constituent Entities to which it is applying the rule.

Allocation of top-up tax based on proportionate ownership

425. In some cases two or more intermediate Parents in different ownership chains within the same MNE Group may hold equity interests in the same low-taxed Constituent Entity. The GloBE rules coordinate the simultaneous application of more than one jurisdiction's income inclusion rule to the same low-taxed entity through the top-up tax allocation methodology. Under the ordinary terms of the income inclusion rule, the top-up tax computed for a Constituent Entity is allocated to the Parent based on its proportionate share of the income of the low-taxed Constituent Entity, determined by reference to its equity interest. Accordingly, each Parent applying an income inclusion rule with respect to the income of the same low-taxed Constituent Entity is allocated a proportionate share of the top-up tax of that entity.

426. A Parent applies this income inclusion rule with respect to each Low-Taxed Constituent Entity of its MNE Group that it directly or indirectly owns, regardless of whether, on a standalone basis, it controls that Constituent Entity. In other words, as long as the low-taxed entity and the intermediate Parent are directly or indirectly controlled by the Ultimate Parent Entity of the same MNE Group, the intermediate Parent applies its income inclusion rule in respect of its interest in the Low-Taxed Constituent Entity. However, a Parent does not apply its income inclusion rule in respect of minority interests in entities that are not Constituent Entities of its MNE Group. This rule is illustrated in Example 6.3.1A in which a Parent is required to apply its income inclusion rule even though it directly holds only 40% of the interests of the low-taxed Constituent Entity because the remaining 60% is owned by the Ultimate Parent Entity (located in a jurisdiction with no income inclusion rule). The top-up tax computed in respect of a given Low-Taxed Constituent Entity could be allocated among one, two, or more non-controlling Parents under this rule to the extent those Parents own independent interests in the entity.

Co-ordination with the UTPR where no controlling Parent entity can apply the IIR

427. Generally, the top-up tax allocated to the Parent is based on its proportionate share of the income of the low-taxed Constituent Entity, determined by reference to its equity interest. When all of the equity interests in the Low-Taxed Constituent Entity are owned by a Parent or Parents, all of the top-up tax determined with respect to that entity will be allocated under the income inclusion rule. When some of the equity interests of a Low-Taxed Constituent Entity are owned by Parents and the remainder is owned by Constituent Entities that are not subject to an income inclusion rule, however, all of the top-up tax cannot be allocated under the general rule. In these circumstances, some of the top-up tax that is not allocated under the general rule will be allocated to other Constituent Entities pursuant to the Undertaxed Payments Rule if the Low-Taxed Constituent Entity is not controlled by a Constituent Entity located in a foreign jurisdiction that has adopted the income inclusion rule. Thus, when the Low-Taxed Constituent Entity is not controlled by a single Parent, the undertaxed payments rule applies to the entity. In cases where the income inclusion rule and the undertaxed payments rule apply to the same Low-Taxed Constituent Entity, the undertaxed payments rule provides a credit for taxes paid under the income inclusion rule.

428. Example 6.3.1A illustrates the application of both the income inclusion rule and the undertaxed payments rule to a single Low-Taxed Constituent Entity. In Example 6.3.1A, 60% of the equity interests of a subsidiary in a low tax jurisdiction are directly owned by the Ultimate Parent Entity (which is not subject to an income inclusion rule) and 40% of the equity interests are owned by a Parent. In this case the Low-Taxed Constituent Entity is not controlled by a Parent. Accordingly, the top-up tax of the Low-Taxed Constituent Entity is subject to allocation under the UTPR; however the UTPR provides for a credit for the

taxes allocated to any Parent under the income inclusion rule. This mechanism is further discussed below in Section 7.2.2.

429. Thus, where a Low-Taxed Constituent Entity is subject to the income inclusion rule of non-controlling Parent Entities, all of its top-up tax is subject to allocation under the GloBE rules – part under the income inclusion rule and part under the undertaxed payments rule. Accordingly, no special rule is needed to prevent avoidance of top-up tax in this situation because the normal operation of the income inclusion rule and undertaxed payments rule ensure that the MNE Group's entire share of the top-up tax is within the GloBE rules.

430. However, when a Parent controls the Low-Taxed Constituent Entity, the undertaxed payments rule does not apply in respect to the income of the Low-Taxed Constituent Entity. Thus, under this general rule, if the other equity interests of that Low-Taxed Constituent Entity are owned directly or indirectly by the UPE but are not subject to an income inclusion rule, the related top-up tax attributable to the income arising in respect of that equity interest will not be subject to the GloBE rules. Accordingly, to address this situation, a special rule will be further developed to ensure that this income does not escape taxation under the GloBE rules. In these circumstances, the intermediate Parent that owns a controlling interest in the Low-Taxed Constituent Entity and is tax resident in a jurisdiction that has adopted the income inclusion rule could be required to increase its share of the top-up tax by the untaxed amount. Alternatively this untaxed amount could be subject to adjustment under the undertaxed payments rule. Under either option, all of the top-up tax attributable to low tax income owned beneficially by the UPE will be subject to charge under either the income inclusion or undertaxed payments rule.

Integrity measures to ensure the neutrality of the IIR

431. The GloBE rules are intended to operate in a consistent and coordinated way to ensure a level playing field under the rules regardless of where an MNE Group is headquartered. However, further special rules may be necessary to ensure that the integrity and neutrality of the GloBE rules is not undermined, for example, through structures involving the use of passive holding companies at the top of the ownership chain. Inclusive Framework on BEPS members will explore the development of such special rules that will be designed to preserve the integrity of the GloBE rules while avoiding undue compliances costs and administrative burdens.

432. The overall integrity of the GloBE rules would be undermined if a jurisdiction offered incentives to an MNE Group to move its UPE from one jurisdiction to another where those incentives were directly linked to the application of the IIR. For example, if the jurisdiction of the Ultimate Parent Entity provides a preferential rate of tax for MNE Groups headquartered in its jurisdiction, to compensate them for the additional tax payable under the Income Inclusion Rule, then that jurisdiction should not be treated as having an IIR that was in line with the GloBE rules. Accordingly these types of incentives would be taken into account as part of a determination made under a multilateral review process described in Section 10.5.2 below.

433. Furthermore, as part of a general review of the operation of the GloBE rules, Inclusive Framework on BEPS members could further consider the consequences of GloBE rules on tax motivated inversions and whether further measures are required to address any risk of material competitive distortion arising out of the implementation or application of the GloBE rules.

6.3.2. Split-ownership

434. The preceding Section explained the rules for the top-down approach, which de-activates the income inclusion rule of a Constituent Entity when that entity is controlled by another Constituent Entity that is subject to an income inclusion rule. This Section provides an exception to the top-down approach

in split-ownership structures and requires a Partially Owned Intermediate Parent Entity to apply its income inclusion rule in priority to the income inclusion rule of its controlling Parent.

435. In some cases, not all the income of the MNE Group belongs to the Ultimate Parent Entity because equity interests of the other Constituent Entities of the MNE Group could be held by third parties. One approach to addressing these cases would be to continue to apply the IIR under a top down approach and limit the application of the income inclusion rule to the share of income belonging to the Ultimate Parent Entity. However this approach has two particular problems.

436. The first problem is that it could result in horizontal inequities and economic distortions since the income of two or more entities that operate in the same circumstances would be taxed differently depending upon how their equity interests are held. Specifically, an MNE Group that is structured so that its equity holders own all of the group's equity through a single corporation will be liable for more top-up tax under the GloBE rules than a similarly situated MNE Group where a portion of the equity interests in its subsidiaries is held directly by some of its shareholders. This disparity creates an economic distortion because it makes a minority interest in a holding company below the Ultimate Parent Entity more valuable, after tax, than an equivalent equity interest in the Ultimate Parent Entity. This horizontal inequity further suggests that in an acquisition, the acquiring MNE Group can reduce the overall tax burden of the MNE Group by acquiring a target corporation or group of corporations (that is otherwise outside the scope of the GloBE rules) with stock of a subsidiary rather than stock of the parent. The existing shareholders of the Ultimate Parent Entity will bear the same level of top-up tax on their interests in the target corporations, the new minority shareholders of the acquiring subsidiary will avoid the top-up tax on their interest in those same target corporations. There are, of course, many factors considered in an acquisition structure. Moreover, the horizontal inequity creates tax planning incentives that conflict with the overall design of the GloBE rules. For example, an MNE Group can simply distribute or spin off a minority interest in its subsidiaries to its existing shareholders and reduce the Ultimate Parent Entity's top-up tax liability without changing the owners' economic interests in the underlying corporations. See Example 6.3.2A of the Annex. Split-ownership rules reduce the cases where these horizontal inequities and economic distortions can occur.

437. The second problem is that if Ultimate Parent Entity is located in a jurisdiction that has not adopted the income inclusion rule, the next intermediate parent entity down the ownership chain would need to apply the rule based on Ultimate Parent Entity's share of the low-taxed income. If the rule was applied by an intermediate parent entity that is not wholly-owned by the Ultimate Parent Entity, then the later would be indirectly subject to a lower tax burden. This outcome would also impact the income belonging to minority interest holders of the intermediate parent entity applying the rule even if the policy was to exclude these minority interests. Example 6.3.2B of the Annex illustrates this situation. Under the top-down approach, an intermediate parent entity (B Co) is required to apply the income inclusion rule with respect to the income of a low-taxed entity (C Co). The Ultimate Parent Entity of the Group (Hold Co) holds 60% of the shares of B Co, while the remaining 40% is owned by minority shareholders. If the top-up tax imposed by B Co.'s jurisdiction is limited to the Ultimate Parent Entity's ownership percentage of C Co, then Hold Co would not bear the full burden of the top-up tax on the low tax income of the Constituent Entity because it only owns a portion of the intermediate parent entity paying the tax (60% x 60% = 36%). A way to solve this problem would be by applying the income inclusion rule based on the intermediate parent's proportionate share of the low-taxed income. This ensures that the Ultimate Parent Entity is indirectly subject to the income inclusion rule based on its proportionate share of the low-taxed income. However, the effective tax rate and top-up tax computation cannot be changed depending on which parent entity or entities apply the income inclusion rule because the GloBE rules are based on a single effective tax rate and top-up tax computation for the reasons described at the beginning of this Chapter.

438. To address these issues, the split-ownership rules require Partially Owned Intermediate Parents to apply the income inclusion rule. This avoids any competitive advantages and other distortions in situations where an intermediate parent entity through which the low-taxed entity is held is not wholly-

owned by the Ultimate Parent Entity. It also ensures that the GloBE rules work properly because it ensures that the effective tax rate and top-up tax computation are always computed the same way and that the MNE Group's GloBE liability does not change regardless of whether the Ultimate Parent Entity is located in jurisdiction that has adopted the GloBE rules. These rules also allow the low-tax income of the MNE Group that is beneficially owned by the minority to be taxed at the minimum rate. The split-ownership rules apply to situations where there is a Partially Owned Intermediate Parent that has equity interests in the low-taxed Constituent Entity. It does not apply to the income of a low-taxed Constituent Entity that is directly owned by the minority shareholders. The difference between these two situations is illustrated in Example 6.3.2J.

439. The split-ownership rule operates as an exception to the top-down approach as it gives priority to apply the income inclusion rule to the partially owned intermediate parent entity. This rule ensures that the income inclusion rule applies more comprehensively to the low-taxed income of the MNE Group where a significant portion of that income is not beneficially owned by the Ultimate Parent Entity. By pushing the taxing obligation down to the Partially Owned Intermediate Parent the rule taxes the income belonging to the minorities owners without requiring the Ultimate Parent Entity to pay top-up tax on income that it does not beneficially own and without requiring minorities owners that are not Constituent Entities to apply the income inclusion rule.

440. The Partially Owned Intermediate Parent would apply the income inclusion rule based on that entity's ownership share of low-taxed Constituent Entity. Where the income of the low tax Constituent Entity is subject to tax under an IIR at the level of a Partially Owned Intermediate Parent, the split-ownership rule exempts that income from further taxation further up the ownership chain. This mechanism ensures that the GloBE tax burden is borne proportionally by the Ultimate Parent Entity and the minority owners of the Partially Owned Intermediate Parent based on their ownership percentage.

Methodology

441. This rule applies in cases where a Partially Owned Intermediate Parent holds equity interests of a Constituent Entity located in a low-tax jurisdiction as determined in accordance with Chapter 3. The rule operates by allowing the Partially Owned Intermediate Parent to apply the income inclusion rule in priority to any other parent entities located further up the ownership chain (including the Ultimate Parent Entity).In these situations, the Partially Owned Intermediate Parent is required to apply the rule with respect to its ownership percentage of the low-taxed Constituent Entities. In other words, the Partially Owned Intermediate Parent calculates its top-up tax liability based on the group-wide formula in Section 4.4. This ensures that the low-taxed income is subject to tax at the minimum rate in accordance with the principles of the GloBE rules while avoiding a disproportionate burden on the Ultimate Parent Entity or its shareholders.

442. This rule would not be applied to situations in which the Ultimate Parent Entity holds more than a certain percentage (e.g. 90% or more) of the equity interests of an intermediate parent entity. This limitation is designed to limit the need to co-ordinate the interaction between the IIRs in different jurisdictions in those cases where a relatively small number of equity interest in a group company are held by minority shareholders (such as employees, legacy shareholders from a prior acquisition or financing counterparties) and ensures that the additional complexity only applies in situations where an important percentage of profits would otherwise remain undertaxed. The application of this rule depends on the corporate structure of the MNE Group at the end of the accounting period.

443. The equity interests referred in this rule are those that give rights to the profits of the Partially Owned Intermediate Parent. For example, if minority shareholders outside the MNE Group have no voting rights on the Partially Owned Intermediate Parent but have the right to collect 30% of the profits distributed by such entity, then it should be considered that 30% of the equity interests are held by persons that are not Constituent Entities of the MNE Group.

444. In certain cases, equity holders interest could have a preferred right to collect a specific amount of the distributed profits in preference to that of the other interest holders. For example, minority shareholders could hold cumulative preferred shares that give the right to the first one million euros of profits. The percentage of profits attributable to preferred shareholders will fluctuate annually based on the total earnings of the relevant corporations. For purposes of determining whether a minority shareholder of preferred stock holds a sufficient share of the equity interests to invoke the application of the split ownership rule, the measurement of profit entitlement should be assessed over an average of three years rather than on a year-by-year basis. This average computation will made only with respect to Constituent Entities that issue this kind of equity interests.

445. Although the Partially Owned Intermediate Parent applies the income inclusion rule to its proportionate share of the income of its subsidiary Constituent Entities, the Ultimate Parent Entity or another intermediate parent entity may still be required to apply the income inclusion rule. If the Ultimate Parent Entity wholly owns other Constituent Entities, it would be required to apply the income inclusion rule with respect to the income of such entities. In these cases, the parent entity is required to exclude the income already subject to an income inclusion rule of the Partially Owned Intermediate Parent.

446. The operation of this rule is illustrated in Example 6.3.2C of the Annex. In this example, the Ultimate Parent Entity (Hold Co) owns 60% of an intermediate parent entity (B Co), while the remaining 40% is owned by minority shareholders. This makes B Co a Partially Owned Intermediate Parent because more than a certain percentage of its equity interests are held by persons that are not Constituent Entities. B Co holds 100% of the interests of a Constituent Entity (C Co 1) in a Low-Tax Jurisdiction. The Ultimate Parent Entity (Hold Co) also owns 100% of another Constituent Entity (C Co 2) in a Low-Tax Jurisdiction, through another intermediate parent (B Co 2). The rule requires the Partially Owned Intermediate Parent to apply the income inclusion rule with respect to the income of its subsidiary (C Co 1). The Ultimate Parent Entity (Hold Co) is still required to apply the income inclusion rule with respect to its wholly-owned subsidiary (C Co 2). To avoid double taxation, the Ultimate Parent Entity's income inclusion rule excludes the income of C Co 1.

447. There could be two or more Partially Owned Intermediate Parents in the same ownership chain. These rules give priority to the Partially Owned Intermediate Parent closest to the Constituent Entity in the Low-Tax Jurisdiction provided that all of its equity interests are not held by another Constituent Entities subject to the income inclusion rule. This ensures that the tax burden is distributed appropriately between the Ultimate Parent Entity and the minority shareholders of all the intermediate parent entities in the ownership chain. This also follows the top-down approach because it gives priority to the Constituent Entity in the upper part of the ownership chain when both of them are in the same situation (both of them hold, directly or indirectly, the same equity interests of the low-taxed Constituent Entity and their equity interests are held directly or indirectly by the same persons). This is illustrated in Example 6.3.2D of the Annex. Example 6.3.2E of the Annex illustrates this rule in a situation where one of the Partially Owned Intermediate Parents is itself a low-taxed Constituent Entity.

448. This rule applies where two Partially Owned Intermediate Parents are applying the income inclusion rule with respect to the same income and equity interests of the low-taxed entity. If this is not the case, the Partially Owned Intermediate Parent in the upper tier has to still apply the income inclusion rule to the income that was not subject under the income inclusion rule of the Partially Owned Intermediate Parent of the lower tier. This is illustrated in Example 6.3.2F of the Annex. The same result would follow if the Ultimate Parent Entity or another intermediate parent is required to apply the income inclusion rule with respect to income not subject to the income inclusion rule applied by the Partially Owned Intermediate Parent. This is illustrated in Example 6.3.2G of the Annex.

449. In cases where the Partially Owned Intermediate Parent required to apply the rule is located in a jurisdiction that has not adopted the income inclusion rule, then the next Partially Owned Intermediate Parent down the ownership chain located in a jurisdiction that has adopted the income inclusion rule (if

one exists) is required to apply the income inclusion rule provided that part of its equity interests are held indirectly by persons outside the MNE Group. This is illustrated in Example 6.3.2H of the Annex.

450. If there is no such intermediate parent entity below, then the next Partially Owned Intermediate Parent above the first Partially Owned Intermediate Parent located in a jurisdiction that has adopted the income inclusion rule applies its income inclusion rule. This is illustrated in Example 6.3.2I of the Annex.

451. The rule set out in this Section does not require the Partially Owned Intermediate Parent to have control over the low-tax Constituent Entity. It only requires that the Partially Owned Intermediate Parent owns equity interests that give rights to the profits of the low-tax Constituent Entity. The absence of control by the Partially Owned Intermediate Parent is not relevant because the low-taxed Constituent Entity is already under the control of the MNE Group. This is illustrated in Example 6.3.2F.

452. Further work will need to be undertaken on the design and methodology of the split-ownership rule described above in light of the top-down approach and the development of rules for taxation of Associates and joint ventures in Chapter 8.

6.4. Switch-over rule

453. A jurisdictional blending approach will require each member of the multinational group to determine the appropriate portion of the income derived, and taxes paid, by that group entity in each jurisdiction where that entity operates. Accordingly, a jurisdictional blending approach would require each foreign subsidiary of the multinational group to allocate an appropriate portion of its income (together with the taxes on that income) to a permanent establishment (PE) that may be maintained by that foreign subsidiary in another jurisdiction. The logic of the design of the GloBE proposal means that where the Parent derives PE income that benefits from a tax exemption under the laws of the parent jurisdiction, then the income of that exempt PE should be allocated to the PE jurisdiction (together with any tax on that income) in order to accurately calculate the jurisdictional ETR in the parent and PE jurisdictions.

454. Allocating the income of the parent between the parent and PE jurisdiction will align the measurement of the PE's income and taxes under the GloBE proposal with the domestic tax outcomes under the laws of the parent jurisdiction and ensure equality of treatment of exempt PEs and foreign subsidiaries under the GloBE proposal. Failure to apply such an approach to a parent's exempt PE income would create an unintended difference between the treatment of a parent's PEs and directly-owned foreign subsidiaries. It would allow low-tax income arising in the PE jurisdiction to be blended with high tax income in the parent jurisdiction, thereby understating the amount of low-tax income in the PE jurisdiction and allowing the MNE to avoid a GloBE tax liability by sheltering such low tax income with excess taxes paid in the parent jurisdiction.

455. A parent that seeks to apply the income inclusion rule to the income of an exempt PE will, however, be prevented from doing so where the parent jurisdiction has entered into a bilateral tax treaty that obliges the parent jurisdiction to exempt the income of the PE. A switch-over rule is therefore required in order to allow the state of the parent's residence to tax the income of the PE up to the minimum rate as provided for under the income inclusion rule. Accordingly the Programme of Work calls on the Inclusive Framework to explore options and issues in connection with the design of a switch-over rule in cases where a contracting state had agreed in a tax treaty to use the exemption method. Such a rule would allow a contracting state to limit the application of the exemption method where the profits attributable to a PE in the other contracting state are low tax profits of a Constituent Entity under the GloBE rules. The rule also applies to income derived from immovable property subject to a treaty provision equivalent to Article 6 of the OECD Model Tax Convention (OECD, 2017[8]) if such income is attributable to a PE and subject to the exemption method in accordance with the tax treaty.[2]

456. The aim of the switch-over rule would allow the state of the parent's residence to apply an income inclusion rule to tax the income of the PE in those cases where the income inclusion rule would apply as a matter of domestic law. The switch-over rule would permit the residence state to tax the low-tax profits of a PE up to the agreed minimum rate, using the same ETR test as the income inclusion rule. The rule would, by virtue of its domestic law trigger, only apply when and to the extent that the head office was required to apply the income inclusion rule to the PE.[3]

References

OECD (2017), *Model Tax Convention on Income and on Capital*, OECD Publisher, Paris, https://doi.org/10.1787/mtc_cond-2017-en. [1]

Notes

[1] Coordination between different jurisdiction to apply the top-down approach and split-ownership rules are discussed in Chapter 6.

[2] See Paragraph 9 of the Commentary on Article 5 of the OECD Model Tax Convention (OECD, 2017[8]).

[3] The Inclusive Framework may explore a switch-over rule that is not limited to the situations where the parent jurisdiction is seeking to apply the income inclusion rule to its (direct) foreign permanent establishments but could more broadly be developed on a standalone basis where the income of permanent establishment is subject to an effective tax rate below the minimum rate.

7 Undertaxed Payments Rule

Undertaxed Payments Rule (UTPR)

The UTPR applies in respect of the income of low-tax Constituent Entities

The UTPR requires a UTPR taxpayer that is a member of an MNE Group to make an adjustment in respect of any top-up tax that is allocated to that taxpayer from a low-tax Constituent Entity of the same group.

The IIR has priority over the UTPR

No top-up tax shall be allocated under the UTPR if that low-tax Constituent Entity is controlled, directly or indirectly by a foreign Constituent Entity that is subject to an IIR which has been implemented in accordance with the GloBE rules. A top-up tax may be allocated under the UTPR from Constituent Entities located in the UPE jurisdiction if the MNE's ETR in that jurisdiction is below the agreed minimum rate.

Allocation of the top-up tax

The top-up tax is allocated to a UTPR Taxpayer in two steps as follows:

(a) First, if the UTPR Taxpayer makes any deductible payments to the low-tax Constituent Entity during the relevant period, the top-up tax of such Constituent Entity is allocated to the UTPR Taxpayer in proportion to the total of deductible payments made to that entity by all UTPR Taxpayers;

(b) Second, if the UTPR Taxpayer has net intra-group expenditure, in proportion to the total amount of net intra-group expenditure incurred by all UTPR Taxpayers.

The top-up tax allocated to a UTPR Taxpayer under each step is limited to an amount equal to the domestic covered tax rate multiplied by the gross amount of deductible intragroup payments taken into consideration in calculating its portion of top-up tax.

No top-up tax is allocated to UTPR Taxpayers that are located in jurisdictions where the MNE's jurisdictional ETR is below the agreed minimum rate.

Maximum amount of top-up tax that can be allocated under UTPR

The total top-up tax allocated under the UTPR from all low-tax Constituent Entities located in the UPE jurisdiction cannot exceed the top-up tax percentage multiplied by the total amount of deductible intragroup payments received by these low-tax Constituent Entities from foreign Constituent Entities.

Definition of UTPR Taxpayer

A UTPR taxpayer is any Constituent Entity that is located in a jurisdiction that has implemented the UTPR in accordance with the GloBE rules (a UTPR Jurisdiction).

Adjustment to be made under the UTPR

A taxpayer that is allocated top-up tax under the UTPR shall be denied a deduction for an intra-group payment or required to make an equivalent adjustment under domestic law that results in the taxpayer having an incremental tax liability equal to the allocated top-up tax amount.

7.1. Overview

457. The Undertaxed Payments rule (UTPR) has the same general purpose as the income inclusion rule (IIR). More specifically, the policy rationale of the UTPR is to protect jurisdictions against base erosion through intra-group payments to low-taxed entities while ensuring that, in aggregate, the application of the GloBE rules does not result in the MNE Group being subject to tax on its income in those jurisdictions where it operates in excess of the minimum rate. While the IIR and the UTPR have the same general purpose they have a different function and operate in a very different way. The IIR provides for a mechanism to collect the top-up tax based on a Parent's[1] direct or indirect ownership of the low-tax Constituent Entities. The UTPR serves, in part, as a backstop to the IIR and reduces the incentives for tax driven inversions by providing a mechanism for making an adjustment in respect of any remaining top-up tax in relation to profits of a Constituent Entity that is not in scope of an applicable IIR. The UTPR also has the purpose of addressing base erosion through deductible intra-group payments. By operating as a backstop and targeting base eroding payments the UTPR serves a hybrid purpose and different aspects of the rules in this chapter may serve one or the other purpose, depending on the situation. The UTPR operates through an allocation key that is based on, and therefore limited in its application to the extent of, intra-group payments.

458. Because the UTPR has the potential to apply in any jurisdiction where a Constituent Entity makes an intra-group payment and because the outcomes under UTPR will vary based on the amount of intra-group payments made by each entity, the UTPR is a more complex rule to apply and requires a greater amount of co-ordination between jurisdictions than the IIR. In practice, however, the scope for the application of the UTPR is expected to be relatively narrow. This is because the UTPR only applies to the income of a low-tax Constituent Entity when that low-tax Constituent Entity is not otherwise subject to an IIR that is implemented in accordance with the GloBE rules under the laws of another jurisdiction.[2] To simplify both the compliance with and the administration of the GloBE rules the taxpayer has the opportunity under the UTPR compliance procedures, described in Section 7.8 below, to certify that the UTPR does not apply because, for example, there are no low-tax Constituent Entities within the MNE Group or that all these entities are under the control of another Constituent Entity that applies an IIR that has been implemented in accordance with the GloBE rules.

7.2. The IIR has priority over the UTPR

459. The top-up tax computed in relation to the MNE's profits is either collected through the application of the IIR in a "Parent jurisdiction" or gives rise to a corresponding adjustment under the UTPR in a "UTPR jurisdiction". As mentioned previously, the IIR takes priority over the UTPR. Therefore, no top-up tax may be treated as giving rise to an adjustment under the UTPR in respect of a Constituent Entity that is controlled, directly or indirectly by a foreign Constituent Entity that is subject to an IIR in accordance with the GloBE rules. When the UTPR applies, the UTPR of several other jurisdictions could, however, apply in relation to the income of a single low-tax Constituent Entity and this Chapter explains how these UTPRs are to be coordinated so as to minimise complexity and avoid double taxation.

7.2.1. Interaction between IIR and UTPR when IIR applied at level of Intermediate Parent

460. In the situation where no IIR applies at the Ultimate Parent Entity (UPE) level, the IIR can apply at a sub-holding level.[3] Under these circumstances, and as discussed in Chapter 6 above, it is possible that the low-tax Constituent Entities located in a given jurisdiction are not all owned by the same Parent applying the same IIR. In this situation, some of the low-tax Constituent Entities will be within the scope of an applicable IIR while others may be in the scope of the UTPR. An example of this structure is illustrated in Example 6.3.1A. Whether the income of a low-tax Constituent Entity is covered by an IIR or a UTPR is therefore determined on an entity-by-entity basis, for each of these low-tax Constituent Entities. The test for determining whether the IIR will be the mechanism for taxing the income of a low-tax Constituent Entity (or whether that amount gives rise to an adjustment under the IIR) is based on a control test. The low-tax income of a Constituent Entity will be subject to adjustment under the IIR where there is another Constituent Entity in the ownership chain that controls this low-tax Constituent Entity and is subject to the IIR. Where there is no such Constituent Entity in the ownership chain, then that amount gives rise to an adjustment under the UTPR. Therefore the determination of whether the UTPR applies to the profits of a low-tax Constituent Entity should generally be a binary one that depends on whether or not such low-tax Constituent Entity is controlled by another foreign Constituent Entity that is subject to an IIR in accordance with the GloBE rules.

7.2.2. Excluding IIR tax imposed by a minority shareholder

461. It is expected that in most cases either the low-tax Constituent Entities will be controlled by another Constituent Entity that is subject to the IIR (and the UTPR will not apply) or their shares will be wholly owned by other Constituent Entities that are not subject to an IIR (and the UTPR will apply). There may be situations, however, where no Constituent Entity that controls the low-tax Constituent Entity is subject to an IIR but a foreign Constituent Entity owns a minority interest in the low-tax Constituent Entity and applies the IIR in respect of its (minority) share of the income of such low-tax Constituent Entity, as described in Section 6.3.1. The UTPR applies under such circumstances, because the low-tax Constituent Entity is not controlled, directly or indirectly, by another Constituent Entity in another jurisdiction which applies an IIR.[4]

462. To avoid taxation of the same low-tax income both in the hands of the UTPR Taxpayers and of the Constituent Entity that applies the IIR (because of the minority interest it owns in the low-tax Constituent Entity), the top-up tax allocated under the UTPR excludes the portion of the top-up tax that has already been imposed under the IIR.[5] This mechanism ensures that the IIR has priority over the UTPR, while avoiding multiple taxation of the same low-tax income as a result of the GloBE rules.

7.2.3. Application of the UTPR to low-tax profits in the UPE Jurisdiction

Low-tax outcomes in the UPE jurisdiction

463. When the IIR and UTPR are introduced into domestic law, they will *not* apply to capture the domestic low-tax income from the perspective of the taxpayer (i.e. low-tax profits that arise in the same jurisdiction as the taxpayer). These domestic low-tax profits will however be covered by the rules of Constituent Entities located in other jurisdictions.

464. In the case of a subsidiary that is located in a different jurisdiction than its Ultimate Parent Entity, the jurisdictional scope of the UTPR will therefore include low-tax income that arises in the jurisdiction of the Ultimate Parent Entity in a relevant period. This application of the UTPR results from the fact that:

a. the profits made in the jurisdiction of the Ultimate Parent Entity are out of scope of any applicable IIR since any IIR that would apply in the parent jurisdiction would only cover "foreign" profits, i.e. profits made in all other jurisdictions than the parent jurisdiction, and

b. the jurisdiction of the Ultimate Parent Entity is a foreign jurisdiction from the perspective of the subsidiary jurisdiction applying the UTPR.

465. Therefore, in the situation where (i) the ultimate parent jurisdiction has implemented an IIR in accordance with the GloBE rules and (ii) the MNE's jurisdictional ETR falls below the minimum rate in the ultimate parent jurisdiction for a given period, both the IIR and the UTPR could apply within the group, but they would not apply in relation to the same low-tax income. The IIR would cover the MNE's low-tax income in all the subsidiary jurisdictions, while the UTPR only would apply to the profits made in the jurisdiction of the Ultimate Parent Entity ('the UPE jurisdiction'), and only if the MNE's jurisdictional ETR is below the agreed minimum rate in such jurisdiction in a relevant period.

Policy and design questions

466. The UPE jurisdiction is not expected to apply the IIR to its own domestic companies therefore, strictly from a technical perspective, the UTPR does not operate as a backstop to the IIR in this context but rather directly addresses the risk of base erosion in those cases where the UPE jurisdiction is subject to tax at below the minimum rate. Applying the UTPR to low tax profits of the UPE jurisdiction raises a number of policy and design challenges that do not arise when the rule is applied to subsidiaries of the MNE group. The application of the UTPR to the UPE jurisdiction could have a disproportionate impact on certain MNE Groups with de-minimis foreign operations. These adverse consequences could apply in circumstances where the UPE cannot structure out of the additional tax and compliance costs associated with the application of the UTPR by bringing itself within the scope of the IIR. Some of these challenges are addressed through the use of caps as discussed in Section 7.5.2 below. Technical work will explore further options for addressing these challenges. This could include options such as a credit for UTPR taxes paid due to timing differences in the UPE jurisdiction and a top-up tax mechanism for in-scope taxpayers.[6] The outcomes from this work will be incorporated into the development of model rules as described in Section 10.5.1.

7.3. Calculation of the top-up tax

467. The UTPR uses the same mechanics as the IIR for determining the MNE's jurisdictional ETR and the amount of top-up tax allocable under the rule. This includes the same definition of covered taxes and the application of any substance based carve-out.[7] Equally, the exclusions to the definition of Constituent Entity (for example, in respect of government entities) would apply under the UTPR and no top-up tax would arise, or be allocable under the UTPR, in respect of these entities.[8] Equally, the application of loss carry-forwards and excess taxes used to address timing differences apply in the same way to determine the ETR of each jurisdiction under both the IIR and UTPR.

468. Example 4.2.1A illustrates the application of a local tax carry-forward rule. In that example, a subsidiary pays excess taxes of 40 in year 1 which creates a local tax carry forward in that amount (assuming that this subsidiary is the only Constituent Entity in the relevant jurisdiction). While the subsidiary paid less than the minimum rate on its GloBE tax base in the subsequent year, it can carry forward the excess tax paid to increase its tax expense in year 2 up to the minimum rate. Accordingly, there would be no top-up tax liability under either the IIR or the UTPR in relation to this subsidiary's profits in year 2. Similarly, the loss carry-forward mechanism described in Section 4.2 would apply for the purpose of calculating the top-up tax under the UTPR.

469. Having the same mechanism to compute the top-up tax under the IIR and the UTPR improves co-ordination and reduces implementation and compliance costs, while ensuring that any adjustment does not result in over-taxation or in taxation in excess of economic profits. In addition, using the same top-up tax calculation mechanic under both the IIR and the UTPR aligns the expected outcomes under both rules, which allows the UTPR to operate as a meaningful backstop to the IIR, subject to certain limitations in

recognition of the UTPR's additional purpose of targeting base erosion outcomes. In order to operate as a meaningful backstop to the IIR, the UTPR needs to apply in situations where the IIR would have applied if it was introduced in the Parent jurisdiction. Failing to align the mechanics for computing the top-up tax under both the IIR and the UTPR would either lead to less effective or harsher outcomes under the UTPR than under the IIR. For instance, a rule that only applied to direct payments made to recipients located in jurisdictions that have a nominal CIT rate that is below the agreed minimum rate would be less effective than the IIR. On the other hand, a rule that would fail to apply the same blending approach, the same substance based carve-out and mechanisms to address timing differences as provided under the GloBE rules could produce outcomes that are harsher than those provided for under the IIR.

470. The UTPR uses the same calculation mechanic as the IIR to determine the corresponding amount of top-up tax allocable in relation to the profits in scope of the rule. Thus, for example, a withholding tax paid in relation to a particular payment made by a UTPR Taxpayer is taken into account for the computation of the ETR of the jurisdiction where the recipient Constituent Entity is located and does not reduce the amount of top-up tax allocated to this taxpayer under the UTPR. In accordance with the methodology described in Section 4.4, the amount of top-up tax that is allocable under the UTPR is determined in respect of each Constituent Entity located in a jurisdiction where the MNE's jurisdictional ETR is below the minimum rate (the "low-tax Constituent Entity"). The top-up tax attributed to a low-tax Constituent Entity under this mechanic is then allocated amongst the UTPR Taxpayers in accordance with the mechanisms set out in Section 7.4 below.

7.4. Allocation of the top-up tax

471. The top-up tax is allocated among entities that are subject to a UTPR in their jurisdiction. In general, the allocation of the top-up tax does not entail taxation of the profit of one entity in the hands of another. Rather the allocation of top-up tax operates as a co-ordinated way to connect the deductible intragroup payments made in one jurisdiction with low-tax outcomes in another jurisdiction. This connection is not, however, made by tracking through chains of intra-group deductible payments in order to connect the payment made by one Constituent Entity with the low tax outcomes of another. Rather the allocation keys applied by the UTPR apply an aggregate, proportionate approach that takes into account:

a. base-eroding intra-group payments made by those Constituent Entities within the MNE Group that are subject to the UTPR;[9] and

b. low-tax outcomes arising in those jurisdictions where that income is not subject to an IIR.

472. The UTPR then allocates the top-up tax arising in the low tax jurisdiction against the base eroding intra-group payments on a proportionate basis using a mechanical rule that is common to each jurisdiction applying the UTPR. To ensure a coordinated application of the rule, this allocation requires a common definition of its key components. This Section focusses on the design and the mechanics of the allocation keys, and the definition of the factors taken into account for the computation of the allocation keys (i.e. intra-group payments).

7.4.1. Overview – two-step approach

473. The top-up tax is allocated to a UTPR Taxpayer that is a member of the same MNE Group as the low-tax Constituent Entity as follows:

- First, if the UTPR Taxpayer makes any deductible payments to the low-tax Constituent Entity during the relevant period, the top-up tax that applies to the income of such Constituent Entity is allocated in proportion to the total of deductible payments made directly to the low-tax Constituent Entity by all UTPR Taxpayers;

- Second, if the UTPR Taxpayer has net intra-group expenditure, the remaining top-up tax is allocated in proportion to the total amount of net intra-group expenditure incurred by all UTPR Taxpayers.

Both allocation keys apply on a period by period basis. Section 7.7 describes the rules used to determine the timing in the recognition of these payments.

7.4.2. Purpose and design of the allocation keys

474. A two-step approach based on related party payments and expenditures is consistent with the hybrid function of the UTPR. The UTPR is designed to operate as a back-stop to the IIR while also providing jurisdictions with a tool to protect themselves from the effect of base eroding transactions.

Purpose and design of the first allocation key

475. The first allocation key allocates the top-up tax to entities that make direct payments to a low-tax Constituent Entity. This allocation key ensures that the UTPR allocates top-up tax in priority to those jurisdictions where there is a readily identifiable and direct connection between the payment and shifting of intra-group profit. An allocation key that prioritises adjustments in respect of deductible intra-group payments made directly to a low-tax Constituent Entity is designed to capture the most obvious and straight-forward intra-group profit stripping arrangements. Direct payments to a low-tax Constituent Entity are the easiest to identify, which limits the number of potential adjustments under the rule and makes the rule simpler from a compliance and administration perspective.

Purpose and design of the second allocation key

476. Adjustments made under the first allocation key may not result in an allocation of the full amount of top-up tax. In such a case, the remaining top-up tax, after the application of the first allocation key, is allocated to the UTPR Taxpayers under the second allocation key in proportion to their net intra-group expenditures.

477. The second allocation key fulfils part of the UTPR's function in providing a back-stop to the IIR and seeks to neutralise any advantage an MNE Group may obtain from structuring around the first allocation key. A rule that allocated the top-up tax only in proportion to direct payments made by UTPR Taxpayers could be circumvented by routing intercompany transactions through an entity that is not subject to the UTPR so that there are no direct payments made to any low-tax Constituent Entity from a UTPR Taxpayer. The second allocation key provides a relatively simple way to address these conduit structures by allocating a proportionate share of the top-up tax of a low tax Constituent Entity against a Constituent Entity's net related party expenditure without the need to trace the destination of all the payments made by UTPR Taxpayers within the MNE Group.

478. The second allocation key is therefore intended in part to operate as a backstop to the first one by targeting intragroup funding structures that indirectly shift profit into low-tax jurisdictions. It further, however, operates as a simplified anti-conduit rule that uses a fungibility of money approach that effectively deems the amount of net profit shifted out of each UTPR Taxpayer as funding a proportionate share of the remaining low-tax profit on the MNE without having regard to the specificities of intra-group payment flows. This proxy is premised on the supposition that profit shifting risks are generally greater for those entities that have net related party expenditure and is generally expected to have the effect of pushing the taxing obligation into those entities that derive a more significant proportion of their income from third party sales. The second allocation key does not require the tax administration to establish a connection between an item of deductible expenditure and a pool of low tax income. The second allocation key aggregates the remaining pools of low tax income and allocates them in proportion to net related party expenditures. This aggregate / proportional approach seeks to protect the integrity of the GloBE outcomes while striking a

balance between a rule that is comprehensive and relatively simple to apply and avoiding the complexity associated with tracking flows of intragroup payments through chains of connected intragroup payments. In practice the net related party expenditure actually incurred by an entity may be manipulated. An MNE Group could seek to reduce net related party expenditure of a particular UTPR Taxpayer by pushing third party expenditure into that entity (such as interest on a bank loan) and recharging that expense intra-group (such as through a loan to another group member). However, provided there is a critical mass of jurisdictions that have adopted the UTPR, the effect of such a strategy may simply be to shift the resulting liability under the UTPR to another entity or jurisdiction.

479. The second allocation key, when applied in combination with the first one, operates as an effective backstop to the IIR without triggering the risk of over-taxation since it can only result in an adjustment to the extent that a top-up tax was computed in the first place, as explained in Section 7.3.

7.4.3. Mechanics of the allocation keys

Mechanics of the first allocation key based on direct intra-group payments

480. Perhaps the simplest way of shifting profit from a high-tax to a low-tax jurisdiction is to make an intra-group deductible payment from a high-tax to a low-tax entity. The first allocation key, which allocates the top-up tax in proportion to deductible intra-group payments made directly by UTPR Taxpayers to such entities, therefore aims at neutralising one of the most obvious ways of shifting profits into such jurisdictions.

481. For the first allocation key, the payments that are taken into consideration are the payments made directly by a UTPR Taxpayer to a low-tax Constituent Entity (i.e. a Constituent Entity located in a jurisdiction where the MNE's jurisdictional ETR is below the agreed minimum rate). Each UTPR Taxpayer is allocated a portion of the top-up tax that is computed in relation to the income of each low-tax Constituent Entity on an entity-by-entity basis in accordance with the following formula:

$$\frac{Direct\ intragroup\ payments\ from\ UTPR\ Taxpayer\ A\ to\ Low\ Tax\ Constituent\ Entity\ Z}{All\ direct\ intragroup\ payments\ from\ all\ UTPR\ Taxpayers\ of\ the\ group\ to\ Low\ Tax\ Constituent\ Entity\ Z}$$

482. For the purpose of this formula:

- "Direct intragroup payments from UTPR Taxpayer A to low-tax Constituent Entity Z" is the amount of deductible intra-group payments made directly by UTPR Taxpayer A to the low-taxed Constituent Entity Z; and
- "All direct intragroup payments from all UTPR Taxpayers of the group to low-taxed Constituent Entity Z" is the sum of all deductible intra-group payments made directly by any UTPR Taxpayer in the group to that entity.

Example 7.4.3A provides an illustration of the operation of the first allocation key.

Mechanics of the second allocation key based on net intra-group expenditure

483. The application of the first allocation key may not be enough to achieve the function of the UTPR as a backstop to the IIR. First, a low-tax Constituent Entity may not be in direct receipt of any payments received from UTPR Taxpayers, and in such circumstances, no top-up tax at all would be allocated to any UTPR Taxpayers under the first allocation key.[10] Second, even when direct payments are made, the top-up tax allocated to UTPR Taxpayers that made direct payments may be limited by the operation of the caps described below and some top-up tax would then remain unallocated.[11]

484. For those situations where a top-up tax is identified but is not (fully) allocated under the first allocation key, a second allocation key applies after the first one and allocates any remaining top-up tax. This second allocation key allocates such remaining top-up tax to UTPR Taxpayers in proportion to their

net intra-group expenditures. The UTPR Taxpayers with net related-party income are therefore excluded from this second allocation key.

485. For the second allocation key, all payments and receipts to and from other Constituent Entities (both domestic and foreign Constituent Entities) are taken into consideration in order to determine a UTPR Taxpayer's net intra-group expenditure. The payments taken into account for the first allocation key are included for the purpose of the second allocation key when they both apply. Including all deductible payments is simpler from a compliance and administration perspective. Including both foreign and domestic payments recognises that payments made to another UTPR Taxpayer (even if it is resident or established in the same jurisdiction) can be used as a conduit to fund the low-tax profits of an offshore entity.[12] Each UTPR Taxpayer is allocated a portion of the total remaining top-up tax that was not allocated under the first allocation key, in accordance with the following formula:

$$\frac{Net\ intragroup\ expenditure\ of\ UTPR\ Taxpayer\ A}{Sum\ of\ all\ net\ related\ party\ expenditure\ of\ UTPR\ Taxpayers}$$

486. For the purpose of this formula:

- "Net intra-group expenditure of UTPR Taxpayer A" is the difference between: (i) the sum of all deductible intra-group payments made by UTPR Taxpayer A and (ii) the sum of all related party income derived by such UTPR Taxpayer from deducible intra-group payments made by other Constituent Entities of the MNE Group, when such difference is positive; and
- "Sum of all net intra-group expenditure of UTPR Taxpayers" is the sum of all net intra-group expenditure of any UTPR Taxpayers.

487. Example 7.4.3B provides an illustration of the operation of the second allocation key. Example 7.4.3C provides an illustration of the operation of the second allocation key when one UTPR taxpayer has net related party income.

No allocation of top-up tax to a low-tax Constituent Entity

488. Among those entities that are subject to a UTPR, the allocation of the top-up-tax is limited to those Constituent Entities located in jurisdictions where the MNE's jurisdictional ETR is at or above the agreed minimum rate. In other words, no top-up tax is allocated under the UTPR to low-tax Constituent Entities.[13] When a low-tax Constituent Entity is not allocated any top-up tax, both the direct payments made by and the net intra-group expenditure of such low-tax Constituent Entity are disregarded for the application of the allocation key under the UTPR. Example 7.4.3D provides an illustration for this specific feature.

489. The MNE's jurisdictional ETR in a jurisdiction where it has suffered a loss for GloBE purposes is not computed (as it has no income in that jurisdiction). Allocating top-up tax to Constituent Entities located in jurisdictions where the MNE has suffered losses is justified as jurisdictions may be in a loss position because of base eroding transactions. For the purpose of applying the UTPR, Constituent Entities that are located in a jurisdiction where the MNE has suffered losses are not considered as low-tax Constituent Entities and therefore may apply the UTPR, provided a mechanism is applicable in that jurisdiction to impose, if necessary, an incremental amount of tax on loss-making companies as a result of the application of the UTPR in that jurisdiction.[14] This latter mechanism may not be necessary in practice if the relevant UTPR taxpayers that are allocated top-up tax are profitable whereas other Constituent Entities in the UTPR jurisdiction have incurred a loss.

490. The restriction on allocating top-up tax to Constituent Entities in low tax jurisdictions simplifies the application of the rule. In particular it prevents a cross-allocation of top-up tax between two low tax jurisdictions. The restriction prevents top-up tax being allocated away from high tax jurisdictions (where the profit shifting risks are greater) towards low tax jurisdictions, contrary to the purpose of the rule. Allocating top-up tax to low-tax jurisdictions could also undermine the effectiveness of the rule as a back-

stop to the IIR if it resulted in top-up tax being allocated to a Constituent Entity that is unable to make an equivalent adjustment under its domestic UTPR mechanism.

491. Jurisdictions that introduced the UTPR may, for a given MNE Group and a given year, be a jurisdiction where an MNE's jurisdictional ETR is below the agreed minimum rate due to the operation of certain tax incentives or other specific features in the tax system that result in the MNE's operations in that jurisdiction being subject to an ETR falling below the agreed minimum rate in a certain period. However, jurisdictions that wish to ensure that they can apply the UTPR in every year could ensure the jurisdictional ETR of every MNE operating in their jurisdictions is at least at the agreed minimum rate by introducing an annual domestic minimum tax on income with the same tax base and tax rate as the GloBE rules. Introducing such a minimum tax on income would make the exclusion ineffective for their jurisdiction.

7.4.4. Identification of intra-group payments

Overview

492. Both the amounts of payments and of net intra-group expenditure taken into account for the application of the UTPR are identified at the level of each UTPR Taxpayer. This Section provides more details on the identification of the amounts of intra-group payments taken into account for the purpose of the allocation keys of the UTPR.

Definition of deductible payments

493. A consistent and coordinated application of the UTPR requires a common definition of which payments are to be taken into account in applying the allocation keys. Building on the definition of deductible payments used in the BEPS Action 2 Report (OECD, 2015[1]), the definition of payments for the UTPR covers any expenditure that is paid or payable (including in respect of any future or contingent obligation to make a payment) during the relevant period. Payments are taken into account on an accrual basis.[15] The definition includes all current expenditure and receipts including rents, royalties, interest and fees paid for services and would also include amounts included as inventory costs.

494. The definition of payment only includes, however, payments that are generally deductible under the tax laws of the payer jurisdiction. Payments that do not meet the general criteria for being deductible in the jurisdiction where the payer is located are disregarded. For this purpose, specific limitations on deductibility or the application of anti-abuse provisions are not taken into account. If a payment meets the general criteria for being deductible in the jurisdiction where the payer is located, then the full amount of this payment is used for the allocation key. This approach could result in a top-up tax being allocated to a UTPR taxpayer for the full amount of a payment that is otherwise subject to deduction limitations under other rules that are applicable in the relevant jurisdiction, such as interest limitation or anti-avoidance rules for instance.[16] Adjusting the allocation to reflect specific limitations on deductibility of certain payments would not be consistent with the overall design of the UTPR. While the allocation keys are based on intragroup payments, they are intended to be readily comparable proxies for profit shifting rather than providing an accurate measure of the actual tax saved by each UTPR Taxpayer in respect of such payments. For example, the allocation keys are not adjusted for other factors that have a direct bearing on profit shifting such as the tax rate at which they were actually deducted. In addition, measuring the extent to which each payment effectively eroded the tax base of the UTPR Taxpayer would represent significant compliance and administration costs as well as increase the risk of disputes among jurisdictions.

Identification of intra-group payments and net intra-group expenditure

495. Intra-group payments are any deductible payments made by a Constituent Entity to another Constituent Entity of the MNE Group.[17] The net intra-group expenditure of a Constituent Entity is the

positive difference (if any) between: (i) the sum of all deductible intra-group payments made by such Constituent Entity to other Constituent Entities of the MNE Group and (ii) the gross amount of income derived by such Constituent Entity from deductible intra-group payments made by other Constituent Entities of the MNE Group.

496. Both the intra-group payments used for the first allocation key and the net intra-group expenditure of a Constituent Entity used for the second allocation key are identified on the basis of the information available in its financial books and records (adjusted for items that are not generally deductible under the laws of the payer jurisdiction).[18] For the purpose of the first allocation key, intra-group payments are identified on the basis of the financial books and records of the Constituent Entities located in the jurisdictions where the MNE's jurisdictional ETR is below the minimum rate.[19] In practice, these intra-group payments correspond to the related party revenues that these entities receive from UTPR Taxpayers. For the purpose of the second allocation key, the net intra-group expenditure of each UTPR Taxpayer is determined on the basis of income and expenses that are identified in each taxpayer's financial books and records.[20] The flow of intra-group payments will change from one period to the next so that, in different years, top-up tax may be allocated to different jurisdictions in each year depending on the mixture of net related party expenditures in that year. In order to provide certainty for MNE Groups in applying the rule on a consistent basis and to prevent the need for subsequent adjustments, the income and expenses that are identified in each taxpayer's financial books and records for the relevant period will be treated as definitive for the purposes of determining the allocation of top-up tax under the allocation keys.

Application of the UTPR to deemed payments made by or to permanent establishments

497. As explained in Section 2.2.2, permanent establishments are treated as separate Constituent Entities for the purpose of the GloBE rules. Deemed or notional payments from a permanent establishment to its head office or from the head office to its permanent establishment, as well as deemed payments between permanent establishments of the same head office that are recognised for tax purposes should be included in the definition of payments, provided they meet the general criteria for being deductible in the payer jurisdiction.[21] This applies to payments taken into account under either the first allocation key or the second allocation key.

7.5. Maximum amount of top-up tax that can be allocated (caps)

498. The UTPR is designed to operate as a backstop to the IIR. As such, the aggregate adjustments made under the UTPR in each jurisdiction cannot exceed the amount of top-up tax that is necessary to bring the MNE's ETR up to the minimum rate in each jurisdiction the MNE operates. In addition to the overall cap on the adjustments that can be made under the UTPR there are two further caps:

a. The first cap applies to the amount of top up tax that can be allocated to a UTPR Jurisdiction and it is based on the domestic covered tax rate applicable in that jurisdiction;

b. The second cap limits the total top-up tax that can be allocated in respect of the low tax income of the UPE jurisdiction and is based on the gross amount of deductible intra-group payments.

499. These two caps are described in further detail below.

7.5.1. Limitation on top-up tax allocable to a UTPR Jurisdiction

500. The first cap is applied by the jurisdiction making the adjustment under the UTPR. The total amount of top-up tax that can be allocated under the first allocation key in respect of direct payments to a low tax Constituent Entity cannot exceed the domestic covered tax rate applicable in the jurisdiction of the UTPR

Taxpayer[22] multiplied by the amount of the deductible direct payments that are taken into account to apply the rule (numerator of the first allocation key).

501. The second allocation key allocates the amount of top-up tax between UTPR Taxpayers in proportion to the amount of their net related party expenditure. The total amount of top-up tax that is allocated in respect of this allocation key is also subject to a limitation. This top-up tax cannot exceed the domestic covered tax rate applicable in the jurisdiction of the UTPR Taxpayer[23] multiplied by the gross amount of the deductible intragroup payments that are taken into account to apply the rule (without deducting intragroup income). These payments are all intragroup payments made by UTPR Taxpayers, except those that were already taken into account for computing the cap under the first allocation key.

7.5.2. Limitation of top-up tax that can be allocated from UPE jurisdiction

502. The low-tax Constituent Entities located in the subsidiary jurisdictions can be covered either by the IIR (in priority) or the UTPR (as a secondary mechanism) however the low-tax income of the Constituent Entities located in the UPE jurisdiction cannot be subject to any IIR, and only the UTPR can apply in respect of such low-tax income. As the entity at the top of the ownership chain, the UPE cannot structure itself out of the UTPR and into the IIR in order to limit compliance costs or access the full benefits of timing adjustments such as the IIR tax credit. This may leave the MNE that is headquartered in a low tax jurisdiction with a proportionately larger tax burden than a subsidiary of an MNE Group operating in the same jurisdiction. As explained above, a domestic minimum tax on income, however, could be introduced in the jurisdiction of the UPE for in-scope taxpayers. Such a domestic minimum tax on income would aim at ensuring that the MNE's jurisdictional ETR in the ultimate parent jurisdiction is at least equal to the agreed minimum rate and would prevent the application of the UTPR in other jurisdictions in relation to profits made in the ultimate parent jurisdiction.

503. The application of the UTPR to the parent may have a disproportionate impact on certain MNE Groups that have little foreign operations outside the UPE Jurisdiction. Where the UPE is subject to a low level of taxation in the parent jurisdiction then its limited offshore operations could be significantly and adversely impacted by the application of the UTPR, potentially making it uneconomic for the group to expand offshore. The application of the UTPR could be triggered even in those cases where low-tax domestic profits of the Parent do not raise any BEPS risks. Therefore, the cap discussed in this section is designed to mitigate the impact of the UTPR on the UPE jurisdiction by limiting the application of the UTPR in these cases to the foreign intragroup income of the Constituent Entities located in the UPE jurisdiction. The cap applies when the low-tax income in the UPE jurisdiction exceeds the total amount of intragroup payments received by all Constituent Entities located in the UPE jurisdiction.

504. This cap limits the total amount of top-up tax to be allocated ("allocable top-up tax") in respect of the UPE Jurisdiction by reference to the foreign intra-group revenue of all Constituent Entities located in that Jurisdiction. The basis for computing the top-up tax allocable in respect of low-tax outcomes arising in the UPE Jurisdiction is therefore the minimum of:

- the GloBE income of the Constituent Entities located in the UPE Jurisdiction, computed in accordance with the rules described in Chapters 3 and 4, and
- the total amount of foreign intragroup revenue of all Constituent Entities located in that jurisdiction.

Calculation of the limited amount of top-up tax when the cap applies

505. When the GloBE income of the Constituent Entities located in the UPE Jurisdiction that is computed in accordance with the rules described in Chapters 3 and 4 exceeds the total amount of foreign intragroup revenue of all Constituent Entities located in that jurisdiction, the maximum top-up tax allocable in respect of the Ultimate Parent Jurisdiction is computed as per the following formula:

$$Top\ up\ Tax\ Percentage\ x\ Foreign\ intragroup\ revenue\ of\ all\ LTCE\ in\ the\ Ultimate\ Parent\ Jurisdiction$$

506. For the purpose of this formula:

- "Top-up Tax Percentage" means the difference between the minimum ETR and the ETR as calculated for that jurisdiction in the relevant period under the GloBE rules after adjusting for any excess taxes in that jurisdiction (same as for the general case described above); and
- "Foreign intragroup revenue of all LTCE in the Ultimate Parent Jurisdiction" is the sum of intra-group revenue received from any foreign Constituent Entity (including UTPR Taxpayers and other Constituent Entities) by all low-tax Constituent Entities located in the UPE jurisdiction (see further details below).

507. For the purposes of determining the amount of Foreign intra-group revenue of all low-tax Constituent Entities, all foreign intragroup sources of revenue would be taken into account, regardless of whether the payer was a UTPR Taxpayer or not. The Foreign Intragroup revenue is identified in accordance with the rules described Section 7.4.4 on the identification of intragroup payments.[24] This revenue would not include, however, domestic revenue (both intragroup and third party) or foreign third party sources of revenue. In order to avoid MNEs structuring their intragroup transactions to maximise the effect of this limitation, the rule could contain an anti-avoidance feature that treated an MNE that made direct sales from a low-tax jurisdiction to customers using related party agency structures including commissionaire arrangements (rather than buy-sell structures) as making those sales through a buy/sell company (and thereby recognising a payment to a low-tax Constituent Entity, which would decrease the impact of the cap). Further technical work will be necessary to explore the need for a targeted rule that provides for appropriate outcomes without imposing undue compliance or administrative burdens. Example 7.5.2A provides an illustration of the operation of this limitation.

508. When such a cap applies, the maximum amount of top-up tax is computed on an entity-by-entity basis, similarly to what is described above under the general case. Therefore, when the cap applies, the Adjusted GloBE income of each low-tax Constituent Entity subject to the UTPR is further adjusted, in accordance with the following formula:

$$\frac{Adjusted\ GloBE\ income\ of\ LTCE\ A}{Adjusted\ GloBE\ income\ of\ all\ LTCE}\ x\ Foreign\ intragroup\ revenue\ of\ all\ LTCE$$

509. For the purpose of this formula:

- "Adjusted GloBE income LTCE A" is the Adjusted GloBE income of a given low-tax Constituent Entity (A)
- "Adjusted GloBE income of all LTCE" is the sum of all Adjusted GloBE income of all low-tax Constituent Entities in the UPE jurisdiction, irrespective of the source of such income; and
- "Foreign intragroup revenue of all LTCE" is the sum of intra-group revenue received from any foreign Constituent Entity (including UTPR Taxpayers and other Constituent Entities) by all low-tax Constituent Entities located in the UPE jurisdiction (see further details above).

510. The amount of top-up tax that is allocable under the UTPR in respect of a low-tax Constituent Entity would then be equal to:

$$Adjusted\ GloBE\ Income\ of\ low\ tax\ Constituent\ Entity\ A\ after\ limitation\ x\ Top\ up\ Tax\ Percentage$$

511. For the purpose of this formula:

- "Adjusted GloBE Income of low tax Constituent Entity A after limitation" is the Adjusted GloBE income of a given low-tax Constituent Entity (A) after it has been further adjusted as per the mechanism described above; and

- "Top-up Tax Percentage" means the difference between the minimum ETR and the ETR as calculated for that jurisdiction in the relevant period under the GloBE rules after adjusting for any excess taxes in that jurisdiction (same as for the general case described above).

Impact of the cap on the UTPR

512. The UTPR is designed to operate as a back-stop to the IIR while also providing jurisdictions with a tool to protect themselves from the effect of base eroding transactions. This cap on the amount of tax that can be allocated in respect of the jurisdiction of the Ultimate Parent strikes an appropriate balance between these two functions.

513. First, this cap does not affect the ability of the UTPR to operate as a backstop to the IIR because it only applies in respect of low-tax income of Constituent Entities that are located in the Ultimate Parent Jurisdiction. The UTPR still mirrors the outcomes of the IIR in respect of low-tax outcomes arising in subsidiary jurisdictions. Therefore, the cap still reduces the incentives for tax driven inversions. In addition, as the IIR would not have applied to the profits made in the UPE jurisdiction, applying a cap to these low-tax profits under the UTPR does not provide for a better outcome than what applies under the IIR.

514. Second, this cap does not affect the UTPR as providing jurisdictions with a tool to protect themselves from the effect of base eroding transactions. If the MNE's ETR in the Ultimate Parent Jurisdiction is below the agreed minimum rate, three scenarios could occur:

- If the low-tax Constituent Entities in the UPE jurisdiction have not received any intra-group revenue from foreign Constituent Entities, the cap would result in the UTPR not applying at all. Indeed, the intragroup revenue would be zero and no top-up tax would be allocated, even if the MNE Group has made low-tax profits in that jurisdiction
- If the amount of all foreign intragroup revenue received by the low-tax Constituent Entities in the UPE jurisdiction was lower than the amount of their profits, this cap would limit the amount of top-up tax allocated under the UTPR
- Finally, if the Foreign intra-group revenue of all low-tax Constituent Entities located in the UPE jurisdiction exceeded the amount of Adjusted GloBE income made by such low-tax Constituent Entities, then this cap would not apply.

515. In the first and second scenarios (where there is either no foreign intragroup revenue in the parent jurisdiction or when such revenue does not exceed the amount of low-tax income of Constituent Entities located in the UPE jurisdiction), the cap limits the effect of the UTPR to the gross amount of the foreign intragroup revenue. However, under the second scenario, the potential base eroding transactions that could be used in the group to fund low-tax profits in the Ultimate Parent Jurisdiction are still subject to an adjustment under the UTPR. In the third scenario (where the foreign intragroup revenue exceeds the amount of low-tax income of Constituent Entities located in the UPE jurisdiction), the cap has no effect at all. In this case, the MNE does not derive any competitive advantage from a GloBE perspective in being headquartered in a jurisdiction that is low-tax and that did not introduce the IIR.

7.6. Definition of UTPR taxpayer

516. Only the Constituent Entities of the group that are subject to a UTPR in the jurisdiction where they are located are (required and) eligible to apply the rule ("UTPR Taxpayers"). Therefore, the top-up tax is allocated only among Constituent Entities that are subject to a UTPR in the jurisdiction where they are located. Constituent Entities that are not subject to a UTPR in the jurisdiction where they are located are not allocated any top-up tax.[25]

517. Allocating the top-up tax to entities that are not subject to a UTPR would significantly reduce the effectiveness of the rule, because the top-up tax allocated to those entities would not be collected. Therefore, Constituent Entities that are not subject to a UTPR in the jurisdiction where they are located are not allocated any top-up tax in respect of their own deductible payments. Consequently, both the payments made by (and the net intra-group expenditure of) Constituent Entities that are not subject to a UTPR in the jurisdiction where they are located are disregarded for the computations of the allocation keys.

518. A UTPR Taxpayer may consist of only one Constituent Entity or several Constituent Entities that are located in the same jurisdiction. Several Constituent Entities can form only one UTPR Taxpayer, for instance, if they belong to a tax consolidated group under the tax laws of that jurisdiction. Combining several Constituent Entities into a single UTPR Taxpayer has the effect of aggregating the amounts of intra-group payments that these Constituent Entities made to or received from any other Constituent Entities. In addition, this also results in disregarding the intragroup payments made between the Constituent Entities that form the same UTPR Taxpayer. Combining these Constituent Entities should not affect the total amount of top-up tax that is allocable to the UTPR Taxpayers. This should also not affect the top-up tax that these Constituent Entities would be allocated under the first allocation key. This could, however, affect the amount of top-up tax that they would be allocated under the second allocation key if, for instance the only intragroup payments that these entities were involved in were intragroup payments that are between them and that would be disregarded. The possibility to combine or not several Constituent Entities in a given jurisdiction to form one single UTPR Taxpayer depends on the domestic law of this jurisdiction.

7.7. Adjustment to be made under the UTPR

7.7.1. Domestic law mechanism

519. The rules set out above describe a coordinated mechanism which allocates top-up tax among the UTPR Taxpayers of the MNE Group. This allocation provides UTPR jurisdictions with the basis for calculating the amount of the adjustment to be made under the UTPR in these jurisdictions. The GloBE rules do not, however, prescribe the mechanism by which this adjustment must be made. This is a matter of domestic law implementation that is left to the jurisdictions that choose to adopt the UTPR. The adjustment could be through a limitation or a denial of a deduction for payments made to related parties or could be in the form of an additional tax. The form in which the adjustment is made will depend on the existing design of the domestic tax system and should be co-ordinated with other domestic law provisions and a jurisdiction's international obligations including those under tax treaties. For example, a jurisdiction that provides an allowance for corporate equity could choose to reduce that allowance to reflect an allocation of top-up tax. Another jurisdiction may require a taxpayer to make an adjustment under the UTPR by including an additional amount of deemed income representing a reversal of related party expenses incurred in current or prior periods.

520. In certain cases, the jurisdiction may allow the adjustment to be made by a taxpayer other than the UTPR Taxpayer that is allocated the top-up tax. For example, taxpayers in a UTPR jurisdiction may be consolidated for tax purposes or form part of a local tax group that allows members of the group to share the benefit of expenditure, credits or taxes paid. For such jurisdictions, the most straight-forward way of making the adjustment could be at the level of the local tax consolidated group rather than on an entity by entity basis.[26] In every case, however, the adjustment should result in the imposition of additional tax in the jurisdiction that is calculated by reference to intragroup payments (as provided for under the allocation key) and the adjustment should take effect within the same period that the top-up tax is allocated. In the event that it is not possible to make a full adjustment in that period then the adjustment should be made in the following period or as soon as reasonably practicable (see below Section 7.7.4 on the timing of the UTPR adjustment). The domestic design of the UTPR should ensure that the rules operate as an effective

backstop to the IIR by imposing an additional tax that is incremental to the tax that the taxpayer would otherwise have paid under the ordinary domestic rules for calculating taxable income.

7.7.2. Extent of the denial of a deduction or deduction limitation

521. If the UTPR adjustment takes the form of a denial of a deduction (or a limitation of the deduction of intragroup payments), the extent to which it applies depends on the top-up tax allocated to a UTPR Taxpayer. The amount of deduction that needs to be denied is obtained by dividing the amount of top-up tax allocated to the UTPR Taxpayer by the CIT rate to which this entity is subject. For instance, if a UTPR Taxpayer is allocated a top-up tax of 10 and is subject a 25% CIT rate, denying this entity the deduction of a payment of 40 (= 10 / 25%) results in the same incremental tax cost (40 x 25% = 10).[27]

522. The maximum top-up tax allocated to an entity will de facto be capped if the UTPR operates as a denial of a deduction. The denial of a deduction results in an incremental tax burden on the payer that is equal to the CIT rate on the total amount of expenses that are treated as non-deductible under the rule. However, a jurisdiction can introduce a carry-forward mechanism that would ensure that the tax liability is carried forward if the top-up tax allocated to the payer did not result in an adjustment in the current year. See below the Section 7.7.4 on the Timing of the UTPR adjustment.

7.7.3. Information requirement

523. Most of the information necessary to apply the UTPR relates to foreign entities and foreign transactions from the perspective of the jurisdiction applying the UTPR and may not be directly available in the tax return of the UTPR Taxpayer or to the tax administration. Therefore, it is necessary to ensure that the UTPR Taxpayers and the MNE will provide the information necessary to compute and allocate the top-up tax. Section 7.8 below provides further details about standardised mechanisms that can be contemplated to obtain such information from the taxpayer. [28]

7.7.4. Timing of the UTPR adjustment

524. The UTPR is calculated based on the intra-group payments made during the relevant period. Under the first allocation key, the allocation is determined based on the total intra-group payments received by the low-tax Constituent Entity in the period for which top-up tax has been allocated. Under the second allocation key, the allocation is determined based on the net intra group expenditure for the accounting period of the UTPR Taxpayer that ends during the period for which top-up tax has been allocated.

525. Absent an MNE having staggered year-ends for its Constituent Entities, the UTPR adjustment could be made in the same year as when the jurisdictional ETR of the MNE is below the agreed minimum rate in the relevant low-tax Jurisdiction. As mentioned above (Section 7.7.1), it is acknowledged that, if the top-up tax allocated to a UTPR Taxpayer cannot be imposed in the year of adjustment (for example, because the taxpayer does not have a sufficient amount of deductible related party expenses to support the adjustment) the adjustment could be carried over and imposed in a subsequent year provided the rule is likely to result in an incremental tax liability within a reasonable period of time [2 to 3 years]. Under such circumstances, the UTPR Taxpayer should not suffer any penalties for not being imposed the top-up tax in the previous years.

7.8. Compliance and administration of the UTPR

7.8.1. Overview

526. The UTPR will apply as a backstop to the IIR. This means the UTPR will not apply to the low-tax income of a Constituent Entity where that entity is owned directly or indirectly by another Constituent Entity that applies the IIR to those low-tax Profits.[29] To simplify both the compliance with the UTPR and the administration of the rule in instances where the UTPR should not apply, the taxpayer would be offered the possibility to certify that such an IIR applies and/or that the structure of the MNE it belongs to does not leave any low-tax profits that could be subject to the UTPR.[30] This Section describes the content of the relevant certifications that the taxpayer would be expected to provide to the tax administration for that purpose.

527. On the other hand, when the UTPR is applied, it is likely that the operation of the rule may need to be coordinated with the UTPRs in several other jurisdictions where the MNE operates. This co-ordination is necessary to ensure that the total amount of the top-up taxes does not exceed the amount necessary to bring the aggregate tax in respect of UTPR adjustments up to the agreed minimum rate. As explained above, the top-up tax computed and then allocated to a given UTPR Taxpayer depends on the amount of profits made in such jurisdictions, the tax paid on such profits and the total volume of intra-group payments that are potentially subject to adjustment under the UTPR. Both from a compliance and administration perspective, there will be benefits in applying a coordinated approach. Most of the information required to identify these amounts and to apply the rule will be the same for each jurisdiction applying the UTPR. In addition, the consistent application of the UTPR in each jurisdiction is critical to ensure that it does not result in the MNE being subject to an aggregate tax burden that is above the minimum rate. To simplify both the compliance with the UTPR and the administration of the rule, the taxpayer would provide this information in a standardised format to the tax administration in the jurisdictions where the UTPR applies. This Section further describes the content of standardised self-assessment returns that the UTPR Taxpayer would be expected to provide for that purpose.

7.8.2. Certification requirements in instances where the UTPR should not apply

528. There are several instances where the UTPR should not apply, either as a result of the prior application of an IIR rule or because the conditions required to apply the UTPR are not met. The basis for excluding the UTPR will depend on the structure of the MNE Group, the jurisdictions where it operates and its tax profile (e.g. the absence of low-tax profits). For example, the UTPR will not apply in any jurisdiction where the MNE operates if:

- the Ultimate Parent Entity of MNE Group is resident in a jurisdiction where an IIR applies and the MNE's jurisdictional ETR in the parent jurisdiction is at or above the agreed minimum rate;
- the MNE's jurisdictional ETR is at or above the agreed minimum rate in every jurisdiction where its Constituent Entities are located; or
- the nature of the intra-group payments of the UTPR taxpayer cannot lead to any top-up tax being allocated to that taxpayer.

529. The content of the certification required to avoid the application of the UTPR in each jurisdiction are further described below for each of those instances. Most of the information necessary to apply the UTPR relates to foreign entities and foreign transactions from the perspective of the jurisdiction applying the UTPR and may not be directly available to the Constituent Entities although they can be prepared at the Ultimate Parent level. Therefore, these certifications could be provided by the Constituent Entity itself or by the MNE's Ultimate Parent Entity.[31]

530. The type of information contained in the certifications is the same for all UTPRs to which the UTPR Taxpayers of the MNE Group are subject. Therefore, the compliance with the rule and its administration can be simplified by requiring those taxpayers to provide such certification under a single format. The format and content of the certificate would be developed as part of the work on implementation. In any instances, however, the tax authorities in UTPR jurisdictions would be able to assess the facts and computations underlying such certifications.

Certification that no adjustment required under UTPR due to prior application of IIR

531. If the low-tax Constituent Entities (or, a fortiori, all members) of the group are controlled by a Constituent Entity located in another a jurisdiction where an IIR applies, the IIR mechanism ensures that the MNE Group is liable for a top-up tax on the profits made in the low-tax jurisdictions where it operates (except from the parent jurisdiction). For this exception from the UTPR to apply, the applicable IIR(s) should be designed in accordance with the principles described in this report, which is further discussed in Chapter 10. As a matter of simplification, it is contemplated that part of the work on implementation could include compiling and publishing a list of the IIRs that have been designed in accordance with the principles described in this report.

532. As discussed in Section 7.2.3, any applicable IIR would not cover the profits made in the parent jurisdiction. Therefore, to be exempted from the application of the UTPR, the taxpayer would also need to certify that the ETR in the parent jurisdiction is at or above the agreed minimum rate. Such certification could be based on the simplifications that are discussed in Chapter 5 and that will be further developed as part of the work on implementation.

Certification that no adjustment required because ETR is at or above the agreed minimum rate

533. If the MNE's jurisdictional ETR is at or above the agreed minimum rate in every jurisdiction where its Constituent Entities are located, neither the IIR nor the UTPR apply. Therefore, if the taxpayer certifies that this is the case, the UTPR should not apply, even in the absence of any applicable IIR within the group.[32] For that purpose, the certification will also incorporate the simplifications that are discussed in Chapter 5 and that will be further developed as part of the work on implementation.

Certification that intra-group payments cannot result in allocation of top-up tax

534. The nature of the intra-group payments of a given UTPR Taxpayer does not lead to any top-up tax being allocated to that taxpayer when (i) it has not made any intra-group payments to entities located in jurisdictions where the MNE's jurisdictional ETR is below the agreed minimum rate and (ii) it has net related party income (and not net related party expenses) for the purpose of applying the rule. Under such circumstances, the top-up tax that may be due because of low-tax profits arising in the MNE Group would be allocated to other taxpayers. Certifying that this is the case is likely to operate at the Constituent Entity's level and involves the jurisdiction where this Constituent Entity is located only. It would not avoid the application of the UTPR in other jurisdictions where the MNE operates. However, the information necessary for this certification would be required in other jurisdictions as it affects the operation of the allocation keys.

7.8.3. Standardised self-assessment return to apply the UTPR

535. The information required to apply the UTPR will need to be provided by the taxpayer to the relevant tax administrations. As most of the information required to apply the UTPR in each jurisdiction is the same, a standardised self-assessment return that the MNE would prepare and use in order to comply with the UTPR could be developed as part of the work on implementation. These standardised self-assessment

returns could be provided by the UTPR Taxpayer itself or by the MNE's parent entity under the same format.[33] A number of benefits for MNEs and tax administrations in using such standardised information have been identified:

- It would reduce the burden on MNEs which would be able to provide the same documentation in each jurisdiction where they operate
- It would facilitate a consistent application of the rule
- It would facilitate the review by tax administrations that would gain experience in working with standardised templates
- It would facilitate the multilateral working by tax administrations
- It would be possible to develop guidance to support tax administrations and MNEs in completing and using standardised templates.

536. The format and content of the forms that could be part of the standardised self-assessment return will be developed as part of the work on implementation. This information is likely to include, for each period:

- A list of all jurisdictions in which the MNE has Constituent Entities and the MNE's jurisdictional ETR in each of these jurisdictions, as well as the balances in the pools of carry-forwards for losses, local taxes and IIR tax credits;
- The total amount of top-up tax arising in that period for jurisdictions where the MNE's jurisdictional ETR is below the agreed minimum rate, which would be computed based on the net income and taxes paid in each jurisdiction where the MNE operates;
- The total amount of intra-group payments made by each UTPR Taxpayer to each low-tax Constituent Entity;
- The total amount of top-up tax imposed in the year as a result of the first allocation key;[34]
- If there is top-up tax remaining after this first allocation, the net intra-group expenditure of each UTPR Taxpayer.

7.8.4. Local filing of the relevant information

537. Requiring each UTPR Taxpayer to provide the certifications or standardised self-assessment returns described previously implies that it is able to collect such information either from its Ultimate Parent Entity or from other group entities. However, the UTPR Taxpayer may not be in the best position to collect such information. The Ultimate Parent Entity would be in a better position to collect such information from all the group entities and may collect some of this information for consolidation purposes already. Although the UTPR Taxpayer will be required to provide the self-assessment return or certifications, the Ultimate Parent Entity could in practice prepare these documents and provide them to each tax administration in jurisdictions where it has a Constituent Entity, on behalf of its Constituent Entity. This could be compared with the approach currently adopted with respect to an MNE's master file which (assuming requirements correspond with the BEPS Action 13 recommendations) may be prepared centrally but is filed separately in each jurisdiction where required. In order to facilitate administration the local UTPR Taxpayer would, in any event, remain jointly responsible for providing the local tax administration with the information needed in order to apply the rule including the determination of the top-up tax allocated to that UTPR Taxpayer.

References

OECD (2015), *Neutralising the Effects of Hybrid Mismatch Arrangements, Action 2 - 2015 Final Report*, OECD Publishing, https://doi.org/10.1787/9789264241138-en. [1]

Notes

[1] The definition of Parent is set out in Section 6.2 and may include a Partially Owned Intermediate Parent.

[2] See also section 7.2 on the priority of the IIR over the UTPR

[3] See section 6.3 on the Top-Down Approach

[4] An example of this type of structure is illustrated in Example 6.3.1A of the Annex.

[5] See above Section 4.4 on the Computation of the ETR and the top-up tax

[6] In most cases the tax rate in the UPE jurisdiction will be above the minimum rate. However this could also be achieved by the UPE Jurisdiction adopting an alternative domestic minimum tax which uses the same tax base calculation mechanics as the GloBE. Further technical work would need to be done however in setting out the precise interaction between the GloBE rules (for example in relation to the application of the carve-out amount).

[7] As described in Section 4.3, the carve-out is intended to operate as a mechanical adjustment to the calculation of the ETR in a jurisdiction and is not intended to have further consequences for applying the allocation mechanisms under the IIR or UTPR. The fact, for example, that an intra-group payment could be considered, in whole or in part, as a return on the use of tangible assets or payroll, does not mean that the payment (or a portion of that payment) should be excluded from the intra-group payments taken into account under the UTPR allocation keys described in Section 7.4 below.

[8] See, however, section 7.5 on the limitations that are specific to the UTPR.

[9] The term "base-eroding intragroup payments" used in this section is a generic term that does not suggest a motive to such payments or a purpose test that would be needed in order to identify those payments that should be subject to the UTPR. See section 7.4.4 for further details about the identification of intragroup payments.

[10] See Section 7.6 on the Definition of UTPR Taxpayer.

[11] See Section 7.5 below on the Maximum amount of top-up tax that can be allocated

[12] However, as noted below, intra-group payments made by a Constituent Entity to another Constituent Entity in the same jurisdiction will be disregarded if both Constituent Entities form a single UTPR Taxpayer under the domestic tax law of this UTPR jurisdiction. See Section 7.6 on the definition of UTPR Taxpayer.

[13] One of the simplification options discussed above in Chapter 5 is to explore further the use of deferred tax assets/liabilities to compute the ETR. If these simplification options are further developed, the UTPR taxpayers would also be covered by such a mechanism. For instance, if a jurisdiction was considered to

be a high-tax jurisdiction in application of these simplifications, the UTPR taxpayers located in such a jurisdiction would be allocated top-up tax.

[14] As mentioned in Section 7.7, the top-up tax allocated to a UTPR Taxpayer that is in a loss-making position could be collected in a subsequent period.

[15] See paragraph 242 of BEPS Action 2 Report and 423-424 of BEPS Action 2 Report (OECD, 2015[1]).

[16] The interaction with existing domestic rules is expected to be treated under domestic law, as clarified under Section 7.7.

[17] Intra-group payments made by a Constituent Entity to another Constituent Entity in the same jurisdiction are disregarded if both Constituent Entities (possibly with other Constituent Entities located in the same jurisdiction) form a single UTPR Taxpayer under the domestic tax law of this UTPR jurisdiction. See Section 7.6 on the Definition of UTPR Taxpayer.

[18] Section 7.7 describes the rules used to determine the timing in the recognition of these payments.

[19] A reconciliation may be needed in the case where there are differences between entity-level accounts and consolidated accounts, or between payments recorded in the entity-level accounts of entities in different jurisdictions. This reconciliation process could be done as part of the self-assessment process described in Section 7.8, and involve the Ultimate Parent Entity as referred to in the section on Local filing of the relevant information.

[20] The Constituent Entities may not be held to the same extent by the same controlling entities. This, however, is not relevant for the identification of the amount of intra-group payments to be used in the allocation keys under the UTPR. Assuming the UTPR Taxpayer is wholly owned by an Ultimate Parent Jurisdiction that controls 80% of a low-tax Constituent Entity, for instance, the amounts of intra-group payments used for the allocation key are not adjusted to reflect the difference in the ownership of those entities.

[21] If the profit allocation between the head office and its permanent establishment does not rely on deemed payments, and no such deemed payments are recognised for tax purposes, then no deemed payments are recognised between the head office and its permanent establishment for the purpose of the UTPR.

[22] The domestic covered tax rate applicable in the UTPR jurisdiction is the combined rate of the relevant UTPR jurisdiction's covered taxes, which includes the CIT as well as other taxes such as sub-national taxes provided they are a covered tax (see Section 3.2).

[23] The domestic covered tax rate applicable in the jurisdiction of the UTPR taxpayer is the combined rate of the relevant UTPR jurisdiction's covered taxes, which includes the CIT as well as other taxes such as sub-national taxes provided they are a covered tax (see Section 3.2).

[24] Consistently with these rules, the Foreign Intragroup revenue does not include, for instance, payments made by Constituent Entities that are not generally deductible under the tax laws of the payer jurisdiction.

[25] The rules for determining the location of a Constituent Entity are set out in Chapter 2.

[26] Alternatively, under the domestic law of a UTPR Jurisdiction, the tax consolidated group itself could be the UTPR Taxpayer. Under such circumstances, the payments made by Constituent Entities would be aggregated for the purpose of applying the UTPR and the payments that occurred within the tax consolidated group would be disregarded for the application of the UTPR. See Section 7.6 on the Definition of UTPR Taxpayer

[27] The UTPR could also take the form of an additional tax. An additional tax could be achieved either by collecting the top-up tax directly or, for instance, by recognising an additional taxable income at the level of the UTPR Taxpayer.

[28] Each jurisdiction could design an appropriate mechanism (e.g. penalties) under its own domestic law to ensure it is provided with the relevant information.

[29] See above Section 7.2 on the priority of the IIR over the UTPR

[30] Such an IIR would need to be designed in accordance with the GloBE rules.

[31] See Section 7.8.4 about the local filing of the relevant information.

[32] For instance, if the MNE Group is subject to a domestic minimum tax based on the same base as the GloBE rules in a given jurisdiction, the MNE's jurisdictional ETR in that jurisdiction is at the agreed minimum rate and there will be no top-up tax allocated under the UTPR in respect of that jurisdiction.

[33] See Section 7.8.4 about the local filing of the relevant information.

[34] A record should also be kept of whether any top-up tax allocated but not imposed is imposed in a later year.

8 Special rules for Associates, joint ventures and orphan entities

8.1. Overview

538. This sets out rules dealing with Associates and joint ventures and with "orphan entities." The first rule applies a simplified IIR to the income of an MNE Group that is attributable to ownership interests in entities or arrangements that are reported under the equity method. The second rule is designed to extend the application of the UTPR to "orphan" entities or arrangements that could otherwise be used to extract profit from the MNE Group for the benefit of the controlling shareholders, giving rise to a BEPS risk.

8.2. Associates and joint ventures

539. The income inclusion rule applies to the income of Constituent Entities directly or indirectly owned by the Parent applying the rule. The MNE Group's share of the income of Associates and Joint Ventures (JVs) in which it has an equity interest is included in the group's financial accounting income under the equity method but is excluded from the GloBE tax base as a permanent difference.

540. Excluding the MNE Group's income from Associates and JVs, however, creates a risk of leakage and unfairness. An MNE Group could often arrange to acquire its minority interest in another MNE Group through an entity whose income is not subject to an IIR rule (including an IIR rule applicable under the split-ownership rules). Moreover, an interest in a Joint Venture represents a serious risk of leakage under the GloBE rules because the owner's share of the JV's income is excluded from the owner's income. If an Associate or JV is a Parent that applies the IIR, the income of its subsidiaries will be subject to the GloBE rules. However, in many cases, a JV will be a stand-alone entity or will not have foreign subsidiaries. Thus, the income of the entity or arrangement itself will escape taxation under the GloBE rules absent a special rule to deal with interests in these entities and arrangements. Finally, while the difference between control and joint control may have some significance for financial accounting purposes, it does not seem appropriate for taxation or full exemption under the GloBE rules should turn on that distinction.

8.2.1. Not possible to require MNE Group to apply IIR on standalone basis

541. It would be very challenging, however, to apply the full set of IIR rules to the income of Associates and JVs for a variety of reasons. The MNE Group would need to get detailed information about the income and covered taxes reported in the tax returns of the entity in which it directly holds an equity interest and the subsidiaries of that entity in order to compute jurisdictional ETRs. It would also need the information necessary to compute any carve-out for the jurisdictions in which those entities are tax resident. Because the MNE Group jointly controls a JV and has significant influence over an Associate, it may be able to secure relatively detailed financial information on the Associate or JV operations. However, this information is not contained in its own financial accounts and it may have difficulty getting the jurisdiction-by-jurisdiction

information in the format and detail necessary to incorporate that information into its own GloBE computations. Moreover, it may not be appropriate to include all the income of the Associate or JV in the MNE Group's ETR computations for a jurisdiction because the minority interest could significantly affect the MNE Group's ETR in the jurisdiction. Rather, it would be more appropriate to only include the MNE Group's share of the income and covered taxes attributable to the interest in the Associate or JV in its ETR computations.

8.2.2. Simplified IIR

542. Accordingly, a simplified income inclusion rule (the Simplified IIR) may apply to the income attributable to interests in Associates and JVs. Generally, the rule would apply to the income of an MNE Group attributable to ownership interests in entities or arrangements that are reported under the equity method. The simplified IIR follows the top-down approach, where the Ultimate Parent Entity would have the priority to apply the rule. The rule does not apply, however, in the case of an entity or arrangement in which the MNE Group has a direct ownership interest and that:

a. is organised in a jurisdiction that has adopted the GloBE rules; and

b. has an ETR at or above the minimum rate

543. The second requirement is necessary because often substantially all of the income of a JV will be derived from operations in the JV's tax jurisdiction, rather than through foreign subsidiaries. Without the second requirement, the income of a JV would escape the GloBE rules if it were organised in a low-tax jurisdiction that nonetheless had adopted the GloBE rules.

544. The simplified IIR determines the ETR for the interest in each Associate or JV as a whole. Specifically, it determines the ETR for the income attributable to each entity based on the MNE Group's equity method income attributable to each investment in the entity and the MNE Group's proportionate share of the income taxes accrued by the Associate or JV and its subsidiaries, if any, for the year. This computation departs from the general IIR in three respects.

545. First, the ETR computation under the simplified IIR is effectively based on worldwide blending of the income and taxes of the Associate or JV and all subsidiaries of that entity. In many cases, the Associate or JV will not own foreign subsidiaries and the simplified IIR will not result in cross-jurisdictional blending. In other cases, however, it would be extremely complex and burdensome to apply jurisdictional blending in the context of the Simplified IIR.

546. Second, the income taxes are determined based on the financial accounting rules, including deferred tax accounting. This simplification eliminates the need to determine the amount of cash taxes paid by each Associate or JV and its subsidiaries. It also eliminates the need for the local tax carry-forward and IIR tax credits.

547. Third, the simplified IIR only takes into account taxes that are treated as income taxes for financial accounting purposes. This simplification means that the MNE Group does not have to re-compute the income and taxes of each subsidiary to determine the ETR. The applicable accounting principles are the accounting principles used to determine the amount of the MNE Group's income reported under the equity method.

548. If the ETR computed for an Associate or JV is below the minimum rate, the MNE Group's equity method income attributable to the ownership interest in the entity is multiplied by the top-up tax percentage (the difference between the minimum rate and the ETR) to determine the top-up tax attributable to that ownership interest.

549. The Simplified IIR computes the tax liability for purposes of computing the ETR based on deferred tax accounting and worldwide blending. Therefore, carry-forwards generally are not necessary and indeed would be duplicative. However, a loss carry-forward or similar adjustment is needed for Associates and

JVs organised in jurisdictions that do not have an income tax or that have an income tax rate below the minimum ETR. Therefore, the Simplified IIR could allow for a loss carry-forward in respect of an Associate or JV that is organised in jurisdiction that does not impose an income tax on the entity's income annually. In the case of an entity organised in a jurisdiction that has a tax rate below the minimum, the deferred tax asset arising in connection with a loss is determined for purposes of the Simplified IIR based on the minimum tax rate.

550. Finally, the Simplified IIR does not allow a carve-out for a fixed return. This simplification is appropriate because, because the simplified IIR is a stand-alone tax imposed on an equity investment which simply measures the overall return on that investment and (expected) the tax liability on that return. It is also expected that, in practice, the MNE Group may have significant difficulty of getting and auditing the relevant information to apply the carve-out.

551. While the scope and overall operation of simplified IIR is described in the previous paragraphs further technical work is required to develop a more detailed rule to ensure that the rule is comprehensive and effective without giving rise to undue compliance burdens for taxpayers and is co-ordinated with the operation of the GloBE rules.

8.3. Orphan entities

552. The GloBE rules apply only in respect of low-tax Constituent Entities that are members of the same MNE Group as the taxpayer. Some entities or arrangements may not meet the criteria for being part of the MNE Group (and, therefore, are not "Constituent Entities") as defined in Chapter 2, even though they may be controlled by the same shareholder or group of shareholders as the Constituent Entities forming the MNE Group. The most common situation where this could arise is where the underlying shareholder or group of shareholders of the MNE Group and the entity or arrangement consists of a fund or foundation or a group of connected individuals (such as a family) that does not, itself, form part of the MNE Group.

553. These entities or arrangements ("Orphan Entities") are non-Constituent Entities that could be used to extract profit from the MNE Group for the benefit of the common controlling shareholders, giving rise to a BEPS risk. Including the profits made by Orphan Entities in the scope of application of the UTPR would mitigate this risk. An Orphan Entity rule would define the circumstances under which these profits should be included in the scope of application of the UTPR with the aim of limiting compliance and administration costs when this risk is the most acute. Excluded Entities listed in Section 2.3 would not be considered as Orphan Entities.

554. The BEPS risks posed by these Orphan Entity structures are likely to be most significant when (i) such an Orphan Entity is connected with some or all the Constituent Entities of the MNE Group and (ii) it derives a significant revenue or a significant portion of their revenues from payments that are made directly by Constituent Entities. Therefore, as an exception to the general definition of the scope of the MNE Group, the Orphan Entity rule would treat an entity or arrangement as a Constituent Entity for the purposes of the UTPR, if the entity is a connected person and it derives more than a certain amount or a certain percentage of its annual turnover from deductible intra-group payments that were made directly by Constituent Entities of the MNE Group.

8.3.1. Connected persons

Definition of Connected Persons

"Two persons shall be "connected persons" if, based on all the relevant facts and circumstances, one has control of the other or both are under the control of the same person or persons.

In any case, a person or enterprise shall be considered to be connected to another person if:

(a) one possesses directly or indirectly more than 50% of the beneficial interests in the other (or, in the case of a company, more than 50% of the aggregate vote and value of the company's shares or of the beneficial equity interest in the company) or

(b) if another person possesses directly or indirectly more than 50% of the beneficial interests (or, in the case of a company, more than 50% of the aggregate vote and value of the company's shares or of the beneficial equity interest in the company) in each person."

555. The definition of connected persons is based on the approach taken in the definition of "closely related" persons and enterprises in Article 5(8) and 5(9) respectively of the OECD and UN Model Tax Conventions, for the purposes of applying the independent agent and anti-fragmentation provisions in those Articles[1]. The test is the same as used for the STTR in Section 9.2 below and is similar to the control test used in consolidated accounting.

De facto control test

556. The first part of the definition sets out the general definition of "connected persons". It provides that there is a connection between persons where there is a *de facto* control relationship between them. In line with similar requirements set out in accounting standards, a de facto control test looks to the facts and circumstances between the parties in the context of other arrangements and seeks to determine whether the person has sufficient power over the entity to affect that person's investment return in that entity.

557. Factors that are relevant to the application of the de facto control test include the size of the person's shareholding relative to the size and dispersion of other shareholders, other potential voting rights held by that person through instruments such as options, warrants or convertible notes and rights arising from other contractual arrangements such as lending arrangements that provide the lender with de facto control over the business. This de facto control test means that an investor without a majority stake in a company could still be a controlling person if there are arrangements in place that provide that person with the ability to acquire a majority stake or the other shareholdings are widely dispersed and the investor holds significantly more voting rights than any other shareholder. The de facto test ensures that, in practice, a controlling investor in a company cannot sever that connection by putting in place arrangements designed to retain control but shift ownership of the equity into the hands of others. The *connected persons* test also extends to situations where a person has joint control over the parties involved in the transaction. For example, a joint venturer owns 50% of the equity interests of a joint venture. The joint venture company receives a payment from another company that is controlled by the joint venturer. In this case, both companies are considered to be connected persons for purposes of the Orphan Entity rule because they are controlled by the same person, even if one of those companies is not unilaterally controlled.

Group of persons

558. The definition set above states that two persons are connected if both of them are controlled by the same person or persons. The term "persons" refers to an identifiable group of persons that have

entered into an agreement in respect of the equity of the company or that habitually act together to exercise control over the entity. A control agreement is an agreement concerning the ownership or exercise of voting or equity interests that can be expected to have a material impact on the value of those interests. It would include, for example, shares held by different funds but under the control of a common manager. Persons who habitually act together to control an entity would include members of a family that hold a controlling stake in a company. The definition does not, however, seek to capture those situations where there is simply a set of otherwise independent shareholders that, in aggregate, hold a majority of the equity interests of two different companies.

559. The group of persons requirement means that a controlling shareholder cannot lose control of its equity holding in a company by transferring ownership to or among members of the shareholder's family. It also ensures that an entity that is spun-out of the MNE Group to a group of controlling shareholders will generally remain under common control even if that entity is no longer consolidated.

Deemed control test

560. The second part of the definition provides that the connection requirements are automatically met in certain circumstances. Under that second part, a person is considered to be connected to another person if either one possesses directly or indirectly more than 50% of the beneficial interests in the other or if a third person possesses directly or indirectly more than 50% of the beneficial interests in both. A person is therefore deemed to be connected to another person where the first person holds directly or indirectly more than 50% of the aggregate votes and value of a company's shares or of the beneficial equity interest in that company. The deemed control test means that a majority shareholder does not fall outside the scope of the rule simply because there are arrangements in place that mean that the de facto control test does not apply. For example, there may be legal or regulatory requirements in a jurisdiction that prevent a majority shareholder from fully exercising its rights over the subsidiary. While the majority holder may consider that it does not have de facto control over the entity it will be treated as a controlling shareholder by virtue of its majority stake in the subsidiary.

8.3.2. Revenue test

561. The amount or share of the annual revenue of an orphan entity that is derived from deductible intra-group payments made by Constituent Entities would be determined on the basis of the financial accounts of such an Orphan Entity, with the same methodology as the one that applies under the UTPR.

8.3.3. Application of the UTPR to Orphan Entities

562. An Orphan Entity may be included in the scope of the UTPR if treating such an entity as an Orphan Entity would result in an increase in the total amount of top-up tax that can be collected under the UTPR. Therefore, an Orphan Entity would be included only if including its income and covered taxes under the methodology described in Chapters 3 and 4 results in either:

- adding a new jurisdiction to the scope of jurisdictions for which the MNE Group computes its ETR (in the absence of any Constituent Entity being located in the same jurisdiction as the Orphan Entity) and the MNE's ETR in that jurisdiction being below the minimum rate as a result of taking into account the income and covered taxes of the Orphan Entity, or
- the MNE's ETR in the jurisdiction where the Orphan Entity is located becoming or remaining below the minimum rate after taking into account the income and covered taxes of the Orphan Entity.

563. In accordance with the methodology described in Section 8.3, the income and covered taxes of the Orphan Entity may be taken into account to compute a (revised) top-up tax percentage for the jurisdiction where it is located. Subsequently, this top-up tax percentage is applied to the Adjusted GloBE income of the Orphan Entity in order to determine the amount of top-up tax attributed to the Orphan Entity.

Such top-up tax may then be allocated to UTPR Taxpayers in accordance with the methodology described in Section 7.4. For that purpose, the payments that such an Orphan Entity receives from or makes to Constituent Entities are taken into account to allocate the top-up tax. If the Orphan Entity is located in the Ultimate Parent Jurisdiction, the overall cap provided in Section 7.5.2 applies by including the intragroup revenue of such an Orphan Entity. The data that relates to the computation of the income and the covered taxes of the Orphan Entity as well as the amounts and structure of intra-group payments involving the Orphan Entity would be subject to the same filing and documentation requirements as those that are provided for any Constituent Entity that is located in a low-tax jurisdiction for the purpose of applying the UTPR.

564. An Orphan Entity that would be located in a jurisdiction that introduced the UTPR, however, would not be allocated any top-up tax. This results from the condition described previously under which an Orphan Entity is included in the scope of the UTPR on the condition that the MNE's ETR in the jurisdiction where the Orphan Entity is located is below the minimum rate after taking into account the income and covered taxes of the Orphan Entity.

565. While the scope and overall operation of a rule for Orphan Entities is described in the previous paragraphs, further technical work is required to develop a more detailed rule to ensure that the rule is comprehensive and effective without giving rise to undue compliance burdens for taxpayers and is co-ordinated with the operation of the GloBE rules. For instance, further technical work needs to be done with regard to the determination of a revenue test that would ensure the rule applied to those entities that are more likely to present BEPS risks. The outcomes from this work will be incorporated into the development of model rules as described in Section 10.5.1.

Note

[1] It is noteworthy that the same approach – a two component rule with a de facto control test and deemed control above a 50% participation level – is also adopted in paragraph 6 of the alternative fees for technical services article provided for in paragraph 26 of the Commentary on Article 12A of the 2017 UN Model Tax Convention. A similar control test could also be applied in the context of rules for addressing the profit shifting risks raised by orphan entities in the context of the undertaxed payments rule.

9 Subject to tax rule

9.1. Overview

566. The GloBE rules focus on the remaining BEPS issues and seek to develop rules that would provide jurisdictions with a right to "tax back" up to the agreed minimum rate where other jurisdictions have not exercised their primary taxing rights or the payment is otherwise subject to low levels of effective taxation. The STTR complements these rules. It is a treaty based rule that specifically targets risks to source jurisdictions posed by BEPS structures relating to intragroup payments which take advantage of low nominal rates of taxation in the other contracting jurisdiction (that is, the jurisdiction of the payee).

567. The STTR is not premised on concerns (such as those addressed under Pillar One, or underlying the inclusion of the Article 12A technical service fees provision in the 2017 UN Model) that the current allocation of taxing rights between jurisdictions needs to be revisited. Rather it is based on the rationale that a source jurisdiction that has ceded taxing rights in the context of an income tax treaty should be able to apply a top up tax to the agreed minimum rate where, as a result of BEPS structures relating to intragroup payments, the income that benefits from treaty protection is not taxed or is taxed at below the minimum rate in the other contracting jurisdiction. Specifically the STTR targets those cross-border structures relating to intragroup payments that exploit certain provisions of the treaty in order to shift profits from source countries to jurisdictions where those payments are subject to no or low rates of nominal taxation. By restoring taxing rights to the source state in these cases, the STTR is designed to help source countries to protect their tax base, notably those with lower administrative capacities.

568. As discussed more fully in section 9.2.3 below, the STTR will therefore apply to certain categories of payments that present a greater risk of base erosion (covered payments). The work so far has entailed consideration of interest, royalties and a defined set of other payments that present BEPS risks because they relate to mobile capital, assets or risk.

569. Although BEPS risks associated with mobile capital, assets and risk may arise in relation to interest, rents, and certain other deductible payments between connected persons, similar concerns may also arise in respect of gains that would otherwise be taxable in the source state and are shifted into the residence jurisdiction in order to escape taxation. These structures may exhibit comparable mobile features to those targeted by covered payments. Further consideration will therefore be given to whether the STTR should also apply to these arrangements. This work will focus on strategies giving rise to a greater risk of base erosion (which, in relation to capital gains, may not be dependent on a connected persons relationship between the parties). Any such rules should minimise the burdens for both tax administrations and taxpayers and avoid double taxation or taxation in excess of economic profit such as taking into account the operation of participation exemption regimes.

570. The STTR does not seek to address broader tax treaty policy questions regarding the allocation of taxing rights between jurisdictions. Jurisdictions legitimately adopt differing positions on these questions, which are a matter for bilateral negotiations. None of the elements making up the design of the STTR –

which has a particular focus on addressing certain base erosion risks in the context of the wider GloBE proposal – either informs or prejudices those broader tax treaty policy positions.

571. Accordingly, the STTR will not be implemented via changes to the Articles of the OECD Model Tax Convention (OECD, 2017[1]) governing the allocation of taxing rights over business profits (Article 7), interest (Article 11) or royalties (Article 12), or the equivalent provisions included in existing treaties, but will be explored through a separate standalone treaty provision codifying the STTR and each of its design elements.

572. As with other elements of Pillar Two, Inclusive Framework members acknowledge the importance of developing rules that meet the objectives set out above while minimising burdens for both tax administrations and taxpayers and avoiding double taxation or taxation in excess of economic profit.

573. Drawing all of this together, work on the STTR will address the following design components:

a. **Applied to payments.** The STTR is a standalone treaty rule and, consistent with the way bilateral tax treaties operate, will apply to payments between residents of two contracting states. This payments-based approach means that the rule will not apply jurisdictional or entity blending, but will instead operate by reference to the tax applicable to an item of income. Consistent with the scope of application of the GloBE proposal, however, it will not apply to payments made to or by individuals.

b. **Applied between connected persons**. The STTR will apply to payments between connected persons. The definition of connected persons is based on the definition of "closely related" persons in Article 5(8) and 5(9) respectively of the OECD and UN Model Tax Conventions. Under this test, two persons are treated as "connected" if one has control of the other or both are under the control of the same person or persons. While the test is based on a de facto control relationship, these control requirements are automatically met where one person possesses directly or indirectly more than 50% of the beneficial interests in the other or if a third person possesses directly or indirectly more than 50% of the beneficial interests in both.

c. **Covered payments.** The STTR will apply to a defined set of payments giving rise to base erosion concerns. Further consideration will also be given to whether the STTR should also apply to certain structures that are designed to shift gains from the source to the residence state where they are subject to low nominal rates of taxation.

d. **Excluded entities.** Consistent with the scope of application of the GloBE, the STTR will not apply to certain entities that are outside the scope of the income inclusion and undertaxed payments rules (where certain conditions are met). The entities that are currently envisaged as being excluded from those rules are: investment funds; pension funds; governmental entities (including sovereign wealth funds); international organisations, and non-profit organisations.

e. **Materiality threshold**. In order to ensure that the STTR is both focused on those structures that pose the most material profit shifting risks and simpler to administer and comply with, consideration will be given to a materiality threshold based on one or a combination of the size of the MNE group, a tiered EUR-value of covered payments, and the ratio of covered payments to total expenditures.

f. **Adjusted nominal rate trigger**. The STTR will be triggered when a payment is subject to a nominal tax rate in the payee jurisdiction that is below the minimum rate, after adjusting for certain permanent changes in the tax base that are directly linked to the payment or the entity receiving it. This approach is consistent with the design of a payments-based rule; applying an effective tax rate test to each payment would be prohibitively complex to administer and comply with.

g. **Using a top-up approach.** The effect of the STTR will be to allow the payer jurisdiction to apply a top-up tax to bring the tax on the payment up to an agreed minimum rate and that interacts in a coordinated manner with any existing withholding rate in the treaty. Because the rule applies to the gross amount of the payment, the top-up tax will be limited to avoid excessive taxation.

574. The first five of these components frame the scope of the standalone treaty rule; and the last two determine the conditions under which it applies and the effect of its application. The elements identified above are described in further detail below.

9.2. Scope

575. Consistent with the nature of bilateral tax treaties, the STTR will apply at the entity (person resident in a contracting jurisdiction) level and to individual payments (items of income). Consistent with the overall design of Pillar Two, and subject to further consideration of the risks associated with certain types of capital gains, the STTR will only apply to payments between parties that are under common control and will not apply to payments made to (or by) residents who are individuals.

9.2.1. Connected persons requirement

576. Limiting the scope of the rule to covered payments between connected persons is in line with the policy and purpose of the STTR, as articulated in section 9.1 above. A connected persons requirement ensures that the rule focuses on those cross-border tax planning arrangements that are designed to shift an amount from the source state into a low-tax offshore structure without a corresponding change in the ownership of the underlying profit. An STTR that applied to all covered payments, regardless of the payer's connection with the payee, would push the policy of the rule, contrary to its agreed purpose, away from targeting BEPS risks.

577. Limiting the STTR to payments between connected persons limits the scope of the rule to those transactions which IF members consider raise the most significant BEPS risks. A connected person requirement ensures that there is a sufficient degree of common control between the payer and the payee such that the parties have both the ability to engineer the type of low-tax outcomes covered by the rule and sufficient economic connection to benefit from such profit shifting.

578. On the other hand, expanding the STTR to cover all covered payments, regardless of the degree of connection between the parties, could result in the over-taxation of transactions that do not raise any BEPS concerns. Absent concerns about treaty abuse,[1] payments made by a third party customer for the acquisition of services would not, in isolation, be considered profit-shifting from the payer to the payee jurisdiction in the sense contemplated by the STTR, even if those payments benefitted from low rates of taxation under the domestic laws of the payee jurisdiction. On these facts the payment of services fees to an unrelated party is not the shifting of profit but expenditure incurred in determining the amount of that profit. Limiting the STTR to payments between connected persons guards against the real risk that the imposition of gross-basis taxation may make the supply of those services uneconomic, thereby distorting pricing and purchasing decisions to the detriment of the payer.

579. The connected persons test is consistent with other design features of the STTR such as the definition of covered payments, which focuses on certain categories of transactions involving an intragroup transfer of risk, assets or capital and which are difficult to price from a transfer pricing perspective[2]. It is also in line with the operation of the other GloBE rules such as those applied to Orphan Entities.

Practical and administrative concerns

580. A STTR that did not incorporate a connected persons requirement could be difficult to apply and could lead to volatile and unpredictable outcomes for taxpayers due to the fact that the payer may not have

the information necessary to determine whether (and to what extent) the rule will apply and would not have the ability to control its liability for any withholding tax under the rule.

Documentation requirements

581. In order to comply with the STTR the payer needs to know, prior to making the payment, whether the payment is subject to tax above the minimum rate in the hands of the counterparty. While in certain cases it may be relatively simple for a payer to know whether the payee is subject to a nominal rate of tax on a payment, there are likely to be a number of situations where the nominal rate of taxation on a payment is not obvious.[3] These challenges are more significant in the case of payments to unrelated parties where it may be difficult for the payer to obtain the information necessary to comply with the rule but also because the compliance and economic incentives of the payer and payee may not be aligned.

582. Even if it were possible to address some of these concerns – for example by requiring the payee to communicate to the payer, whenever a payment was made, whether that payment was subject to tax at above the minimum rate – this would involve documentation requirements that do not currently exist for most service contracts. And it is not clear to what extent the payer can or should be able to rely on information provided by a payee located in a different jurisdiction. An alternative would be for the payer to withhold on all payments and require the payee to file for a refund. However this would impose a significant additional tax burden on cross-border supplies of services and would be contrary to the policy behind the STTR which focuses on defined transactions that give rise to significant BEPS concerns.

Inability of payer to control risk

583. While, as discussed further below, there may be a number of domestic mechanisms that the source state could use to levy the tax provided for under the STTR, in most cases it is expected that the compliance and payment obligations are likely to fall, as least in part, on the local payer. Furthermore in situations where the parties are independent persons acting at arms-length with divergent economic interests, then the payee may seek to shift the additional cost of tax payable in the source state onto the payer in the form of a tax indemnity or gross-up. This is commonly the case, for example, in relation to third-party lending transactions. Therefore, particularly in the case of payments between unconnected parties, the economic and compliance burden of the tax falls on the local payer.

584. The risk of the payer being exposed to unexpected liabilities pursuant to the operation of the STTR will be exacerbated in cases where the payer and payee have divergent interests and are not under common control. For example, the payer would not necessarily know (or expect to be notified) that the underlying IP licensed from a third party has been shifted into a low tax preferential regime. The payer could not protect itself from the resulting change in the tax treatment of license payments without inserting onerous provisions into the service agreement that restricted the counterparty's right to manage its own IP.

9.2.2. Definition of Connected Persons

Connected Persons

"Two persons shall be "connected persons" if, based on all the relevant facts and circumstances, one has control of the other or both are under the control of the same person or persons.

In any case, a person or enterprise shall be considered to be connected to another person if:

(a) one possesses directly or indirectly more than 50% of the beneficial interest in the other (or, in the case of a company, more than 50% of the aggregate vote and value of the company's shares or of the beneficial equity interest in the company) or

(b)	if another person possesses directly or indirectly more than 50% of the beneficial interest (or, in the case of a company, more than 50% of the aggregate vote and value of the company's shares or of the beneficial equity interest in the company) in each person.".

585. The definition of connected persons adopts (with the necessary adaptations) the approach taken in the definition of "closely related" persons and enterprises in Article 5(8) and 5(9) respectively of the OECD and UN Model Tax Conventions, for the purposes of applying the independent agent and anti-fragmentation provisions in those Articles[4]. This rule is based on a de facto control test but includes a back-up rule that deems there to be control where there is a direct or indirect participation of 50% or more. This test is the same as control test used for Orphan Entities in Section 8.3 above which, in turn, is similar to the control test used in consolidated accounting.

586. As set out in Section 8.3, the connected persons test looks to the facts and circumstances between the parties in the context of its other arrangements and seeks to determine whether the person has sufficient power over the entity to affect that person's investment return in that entity. The test takes into account a broad range of factors affecting control which ensure that, in practice, a controlling investor in a company cannot sever a connection with an entity by putting in place arrangements that are designed to retain control but shift ownership of the equity into the hands of others. The connected persons test also extends to joint venture interests. The connected persons test applies to groups of controlling persons. The controlling persons requirement means that shares in an entity that are held by members of the shareholder's family or received as part of a spin-off of a business to controlling shareholders will generally remain under common control even if that entity is no longer consolidated with the group. The de facto test is supplemented by a deeming rule that treats one person as connected to another where the first person holds directly or indirectly more than 50% of the beneficial interest in the second person. The deemed control test means that a majority shareholder does not fall outside the scope of the rule simply because it is de-consolidated for other reasons. Together these three elements of the connected persons test (de facto control, groups of persons and deeming rules) ensure that two parties to arrangement that have a significant economic connection and the ability to structure arrangements between them to the advantage of one or the other are likely to fall within the scope of the connected persons test.

587. Whilst the de facto control test provides a robust defence against arrangements designed to shift the ownership of equity in order to reduce participation to minority levels, consideration will be given during the development of the detailed rules to supplementing the control test with mechanical anti-abuse rules targeting conduit structures designed to circumvent the connected persons condition. For example, an MNE might enter into back-to-back arrangements through which payments of covered income are routed through one or more intermediate unconnected person(s) with the prima facie result that the connection between each payer and payee is severed. Purpose-based general anti-abuse rules, such as the principal purpose test codified in Article 29(9) of the OECD and UN Model Tax Conventions, offer an effective remedy to such arrangements, but the Models and their Commentaries include a number of mechanical anti-abuse rules that may be used in addition to those general rules to target particular arrangements (such as the anti-contract splitting rule provided in paragraph 52 of the Commentary on Article 5 of the OECD Model) and these can be attractive especially to tax administrations that may have limited capacity to resource more fact-intensive approaches. Such mechanical provisions, however, require more detailed drafting to ensure that they effectively describe and remedy the targeted abuse, without being too widely-drawn, and risk adding complexity to the design of the rules. The further technical work in this area will therefore balance these considerations with a view to designing rules that are appropriately focused and administrable.

9.2.3. Categories of covered payments

588. As outlined in section 9.1 above, the STTR will apply to a defined list of payments. Work so far has entailed consideration of interest,[5] royalties and a defined set of other payments designed to capture categories of payments that present BEPS risks because they exhibit features such as being susceptible to transfer pricing abuse or uncertainty and arise in respect of mobile risk, ownership of assets, or capital. The rule will include a definitive list of the categories of payment to which it will apply. Further work is required to refine this list to ensure that the rule is targeted and effective without giving rise to undue compliance burdens for taxpayers and the outcomes from this work will be incorporated into the development of a model provision.

Interest and royalties

589. The STTR will apply to payments of interest and royalties.

Other covered payments

590. Other payments are considered to present a greater BEPS risk if the value of the payment is primarily compensation for mobile factors such as capital, assets, or risks that are owned or assumed by the person entitled to the payment. Conversely, payments present a lower risk from a BEPS perspective where their value is primarily linked to functions performed by the person entitled to the payment. Whilst the latter type of payment may, in certain cases, be equally difficult to price from a transfer pricing perspective they might not be expected to give rise to the same base-eroding opportunities as payments that are primarily compensation for the provision of capital, assets or risk. This is because the functions performed by personnel are less mobile than the ownership or assumption of capital, assets and risk and therefore less susceptible to BEPS strategies.

591. In addition to payments of interest and royalties, the STTR would therefore apply to the following categories of payments primarily based on these mobile features:

a. A franchise fee or other payment for the use of or right to use intangibles in combination with services;

b. Insurance or reinsurance premium;

c. A guarantee, brokerage or financing fee;

d. Rent or any other payment for the use of or the right to use moveable property;

e. An amount paid to or retained by the payee that is consideration for the supply of marketing, procurement, agency or other intermediary services.

592. These payments were identified by applying the principles set out above and aim at providing jurisdictions with a tool to deal with arrangements that are designed to shift profit to low tax structures within the group. These tax structures have been previously identified by their tax administrations. Each of these categories of payment is described in further detail below.

593. None of these categories apply to payments forming part of the income of a permanent establishment in the source state or for the use of an asset that forms part of the business property of a permanent establishment in the source state. This is because the source state has an existing and prior taxing right over the profits of the permanent establishment under Article 7. This would be codified in the text of the STTR.

594. A payment that does not fall in the categories (a) to (e) listed above would not be covered by the STTR. In addition, the STTR will not apply to payments falling within those categories where the payment generates a low return (see below the section on the exclusion of low-return payments).

595. Defining the list of covered payments by reference to the components that generate value and providing an exclusion based on the return generated for the payee ensures that the STTR targets relevant payments that are likely to present BEPS risk offers a number of advantages:

- it is relatively simple;
- the inclusion of payments the value of which derives from a significant asset is in line with the inclusion of royalties in the scope of covered payments;
- the inclusion of payments the value of which derives from a significant risk is in line with the fact that the assumption of increased risk would also be compensated by an increase in the expected return, although the actual return may or may not increase depending on the degree to which the risks are actually realised;
- the exclusion for low-return payments whose compensation, when expressed on a cost-plus basis, does not exceed a certain margin limits the risk of taxation in excess of economic profits if the rule applies as a withholding tax on the gross amount of the payment made;
- the exclusion for low-return payments is in line with the simplified approach provided in Chapter 7 of the OECD Transfer Pricing Guidelines (OECD, 2017[2]) as available for low-value adding services;
- the exclusion for low-return payments could leave the possibility for taxpayers and tax administrations to prove on an ex-post basis that the payment did or did not generate a low-return on costs, which is likely to facilitate the administration of the rule.

596. In developing the detailed rules, further work will be undertaken on the definition and delineation of each of the categories of payment included in the list. This will include an examination of the extent to which management fees and payments for knowledge-based technical services are covered.

(a) A franchise fee or other payment for the use of or right to use intangibles in combination with services

597. Under a franchise arrangement, one member of an MNE Group may agree to provide a combination of services and intangibles to an associated enterprise in exchange for a single fee (a "franchise fee").[6] The franchisor may have developed intangible assets (e.g. trademark, know-how) that it licenses to the franchisee together with additional services in return for a fee, such as a percentage of the franchisee's revenue.

598. Other similar arrangements could give rise to payments for the "use or right to use intangibles in combination with services". Such payments could, for instance, be made for the right to use a technology owned by a connected person that provides services to the payer based on the use of that technology. Another example is a payment for the use of software where the provider also provides ancillary support such as technical support, customisation and maintenance which is performed by the same connected person. The payer could pay a single fee for both the use of the software and the related services.

599. If related intragroup services can be rendered by a connected person that benefits from a low-tax regime, an MNE Group could organise its structure so that the ownership of such an intangible asset is transferred to such a low-tax connected person, which would then license the asset and render combined services in exchange for a single fee, which could generate a high return.

600. Where the payment is made under a mixed contract and includes a royalties[7] element, the contract may be able to be broken down into its constituent parts (i.e. royalty + payment for a service). In this case, the STTR will only apply to the constituent parts that are in scope of the rule.[8] Assuming that the payment can be broken down into a royalty and a payment for a service, the following will apply:

- Where the treaty allocates a source state taxing right over royalties, both the existing treaty provision and the STTR will apply to the royalty component and the source state will be permitted to tax the royalty element at the higher of the existing treaty rate or the top-up rate. This is consistent with the ordering rule described in Section 9.3.2 below.

- The remainder of the payment (the services element) will be in the scope of the STTR if it is, viewed in isolation, itself a covered payment that is not a low-return payment.

(b) Insurance or reinsurance premium

601. Insurance or reinsurance premiums are payments made in exchange for covering a risk that would otherwise be borne by the insured person. Through the insurance/reinsurance, the assumption of the insured risk is transferred to the insurer, so that if the risk materialises the insured person does not bear the financial consequences of that risk. Risks can therefore be transferred from one connected person to another through this arrangement. If the risk does not materialise, the insurance or reinsurance premium can generate a high return. Insurance or reinsurance services rendered by connected persons such as captive insurance tend to be more profitable than other insurance or reinsurance services. Furthermore, it can be hard to find comparable unrelated transactions to test whether the pricing of these transactions meets the arm's length principle.

602. In the situation where the insurance premium would form part of the taxable profits of a permanent establishment located in the source jurisdiction, these premiums would be taxable in the source jurisdiction and the STTR would not apply to them. The UN Model Tax Convention, for instance, provides that an insurance enterprise shall be deemed to have a permanent establishment in the state where it collects premiums or insures risks situated therein through a person.[9] An exception, however, is provided for reinsurance premiums. In this situation, the existence of a PE can be avoided by providing reinsurance services to local (possibly connected) insurers instead of insurance services directly to final customers. The STTR could apply to such reinsurance premiums if the other conditions to apply the rule are met.

(c) A guarantee, brokerage or financing fee

- Guarantee fee

603. A guarantee is a legally binding commitment of the guarantor to assume an obligation of the guaranteed debtor if the debtor defaults on that obligation. In an MNE Group context, a related party guarantor may provide a guarantee on a loan taken out by a connected person from an unrelated lender. By providing an explicit guarantee the guarantor is exposed to additional risk as it is legally committed to pay if the borrower defaults. While the guarantor can suffer a loss in case the risk materialises, the guarantee fee can generate a high return if the borrower does not default on its obligation. The risks assumed by the guarantor may be shifted into a low tax jurisdiction provided the guarantor has the financial capacity to assume the risk. .

- Brokerage fees

604. A broker acts as an intermediary to facilitate a transaction, in exchange for a commission or a brokerage fee. An underlying component of this transaction is the access to and use of an intangible asset (for instance the client and the supplier list). When a broker acts on behalf of connected persons, the development of the client or supplier list consisting of connected persons may not have required significant efforts. The broker may have been transferred such an intangible asset and benefit from a low-tax regime.

605. It may be difficult to find reliable comparable transactions to the intragroup brokerage service that is rendered, which makes it difficult to test whether the pricing of the intragroup transactions meets the arm's length principle. When the brokerage fee is a percentage of the underlying transaction (and not based on the costs of the service provider), the transaction may also generate a high return.

- Financing fees

606. When a company borrows money, either through a loan or a bond, it usually incurs financing fees. These are fees paid by the borrower to intermediaries or persons involved in arranging the financing. If a connected person was involved in arranging the financing, it could also charge intragroup financing fees.

607. It may be difficult to find reliable comparable transactions to the financing fee, which makes it difficult to test whether the pricing of the intragroup transactions meets the arm's length principle. When the financing fee is a percentage of the underlying transaction (and not based on the costs of the service provider), the transaction may also generate a high return.

(d) Rent or any other payment for the use of right to use moveable property

608. This category covers leasing or rental payments for moveable property and would apply, for instance, where such moveable property is held by a connected person that benefits from a low-tax regime and is used by another connected person. The ownership of such moveable property can be transferred within the group while it may be hard to find reliable comparable transactions for the use of such moveable property when it is relatively unique and essential to the business of the lessor. For instance, a company operating in the extractives sector could transfer the ownership of a drilling rig to a low-tax affiliate which would lease this property to other connected persons and receive a rent. When the rent is not based on the costs of the low-tax affiliates, the transaction may generate a high return.

(e) An amount paid to or retained by the payee that is consideration for the supply of marketing, procurement, agency or other intermediary services.

609. This category is aimed at covering agency and intermediary services such as marketing agency, procurement or other centralised intermediary services when their value primarily derives from the use of an intangible asset, such as a client list or a supplier list.

610. The payments covered by this category may either be paid to the intermediary (for instance in the case of a commission paid to a sales agent for the sales made to the customers that it introduced to the intragroup seller) or retained by the intermediary (for instance in the case of a procurement fee that is incorporated in the price of the products that are purchased on behalf of the other affiliates).[10] This difference in payment terms does not affect the characterisation of such payments as being covered by the STTR.

611. One of the underlying components of these payments is the access to and use of an intangible asset (e.g. client list or supplier list). When the related intermediary functions are mobile, an MNE Group could organise its structure so that the ownership of such an intangible asset is transferred to a low-tax connected person, which would then be entitled to the intermediary fee, which could generate a high return.

612. Other marketing agency, procurement and other intermediary services may primarily derive their value from functions performed, for example for market research. These services would be expected to generate a low-return and would be covered by the exclusion for low-return payments (see below).

Exclusion for low return payments

613. Although payments for the listed categories of covered payments, by their nature, present prima facie risks of base-erosion and profit-shifting, the STTR is designed to be targeted and to minimise administrative and compliance burdens. The rule will therefore provide an exclusion for payments falling within those categories where the payment generates a low return (low-return payments). A payment is a low-return payment where it is calculated by reference to the costs incurred by the payee in earning the payment[11], or can be calculated on a cost plus basis, and where the margin is no higher than an agreed percentage.

614. When combined with a materiality threshold as described later in this Section, this exclusion will ensure that the STTR is focused on cross-border tax planning structures that take advantage of particular low tax outcomes in the residence jurisdiction in order to shift material amounts of profit from the source to the residence jurisdiction.

615. The effect of the exclusion for low-return payments is to focus the STTR only on those payments that generate a high return. Activities that produce a low-return for the payee are the least likely to present a risk of base erosion for the payer jurisdiction. The STTR will not apply when the taxpayer demonstrates that payments generate a low return (i.e. when the mark-up of costs incurred by the payee is below a fixed percentage). This mark-up test will be applied independently of whether the transfer pricing method applied is a cost-plus method, or another method the result of which produces an equivalent mark-up on costs. The application of the mark-up test for the purposes of the low-return payments exclusion does not, however, displace or influence the normal requirement to apply the transfer pricing rules, as for any other intragroup payments, including the principles that govern the choice and the application of an appropriate transfer pricing methodology.

616. This limitation is generally expected to exclude payments that had already been subjected to a transfer pricing benchmarking analysis and would be consistent with existing transfer pricing safe-harbours used by Inclusive Framework members. In designing the detailed rules that will codify the STTR, further technical work will be undertaken to identify the circumstances under which this limitation would apply – including the determination of the cost base and mark-up percentage – and potential simplifications to the design of this rule component.

9.2.4. Excluded entities

617. For the purposes of the income inclusion and undertaxed payments rules, and where certain conditions are met, it is proposed that the following entities will not be treated as Constituent Entities of an MNE Group (and will therefore be excluded from the scope of those rules: investment funds, pension funds, governmental entities (including sovereign wealth funds), international organisations, and non-profit organisations. Consistent with the exclusion of these entities from the scope of the income inclusion and undertaxed payments rules the same exclusion could apply for the purposes of the STTR.

618. These excluded entities all have a particular purpose and status under the laws of the jurisdiction in which they are created or established. This status is likely to result in the entity not being exposed to domestic income tax in order to preserve a specific intended policy outcome under the laws of that jurisdiction. The domestic tax outcome may, for example, be designed to ensure a single layer of taxation on vehicles used by investors (e.g. funds) or on retirement plans used by employees, or because the entity is carrying out governmental or quasi-governmental functions. The tax policy objectives of the domestic tax exemption for these types of entities are neither inconsistent with the tax policy objectives of the GloBE rules nor create a competitive distortion that would undermine the tax policy objectives of the GloBE proposal. Subjecting the income of such entities to tax under the GloBE rules would undermine the policy objectives that the domestic jurisdiction is seeking to achieve by granting the exemption without furthering the tax policy objectives of the GloBE rules.

619. Similar considerations apply in the context of bilateral tax treaties and this is recognised in the OECD Model and Commentaries.

a. Paragraphs 22 to 48 of the Commentary on Article 1 address issues relating to collective investment vehicles and, recognising that under domestic law such arrangements may enjoy exemption from tax, be taxed on a reduced base (often reduced to nil) by being granted deductions for distributions to investors, or be taxed at special low rates, generally seek to clarify their entitlement to treaty benefits as persons who are liable to tax and the beneficial owners of their income.

b. In 2017, Article 4(1) of the Model was revised to expressly include a "recognised pension fund", which may be conditionally exempt from tax under domestic law, in the definition of a resident liable to tax and prima facie entitled to treaty benefits.

c. Paragraphs 49 to 53 of the Commentary on Article 1, and paragraph 8.5 of the Commentary on Article 4, discuss the treaty entitlement of entities set-up and wholly-owned by a state or its political subdivisions, including sovereign wealth funds, and note that these entities often enjoy exemption from tax and paragraph 8.11 of the Commentary on Article 4 considers similar issues in relation to charities and other organisations that may be exempted from tax.

620. Many states include provisions in, or interpret and apply, their bilateral tax treaties to treat these entities as residents. Those treaties may also include provisions to grant the benefit of exemptions from or reductions in source taxation of these entities, notwithstanding that they may be exempt in their state of residence, in recognition of the principles outlined above. In such cases, applying the subject to tax test to such entities would therefore run contrary to that policy objective.

621. Jurisdictions are, of course, free to determine their response to these issues in their bilateral negotiations and may, as is recognised in paragraph 8.12 of the Commentary on Article 4, take the view that entities that are exempt from tax under domestic law do not qualify as residents prima facie entitled to benefits or, as is recognised in paragraph 8.9 of the Commentary on Article 4, choose to omit the reference to a "recognised pension fund" in Article 4(1). In relation to the application of the principle of sovereign immunity to governmental entities, paragraph 52 of the Commentary on Article 1 notes that most states would not extend this to business activities carried on by such entities.

622. Consideration of these exclusions in the context of the STTR will be updated as the discussions develop further on sectoral carve-outs in relation to the broader GloBE rules, with the option to align the treatment of these entities.

9.2.5. Materiality threshold

623. In the absence of a threshold or filter an MNE would be required to identify and compute the adjusted nominal tax rate for every covered payment made to connected persons in each separate payee jurisdiction. For a large MNE this could be thousands of payments for which there is no distinct line item in the financial statements. As far as the tax policy context permits, and in line with aims of the wider Pillar, the design of the STTR should seek to minimise such compliance burdens. Moreover, the STTR is intended to serve as a tool to discourage MNEs from structuring themselves in a way designed to exploit the allocation of taxing rights under a treaty in order to make base-eroding payments that benefit from low tax outcomes in the other contracting jurisdiction. MNEs are unlikely to incur the costs of structuring themselves in this way unless the result would secure material tax advantages. A threshold or filter could exclude these de minimis outcomes from the scope of the rule.

624. Similar materiality considerations can underlie the allocation of audit resources by tax administrations to cases where the tax at risk best justifies costly interventions. For this reason, tax administrations build such thresholds into their domestic regimes including, for example, excluding small and medium sized enterprises from the scope of transfer pricing legislation or applying safe harbours for intra-group payments falling below a de minimis value. Chapter B.4.5.2 of the UN Transfer Pricing Manual sets out two safe harbours that may be used by tax authorities – a safe harbour for low-value services that are unconnected to an Associated enterprise's main business activity; and a minor expenses safe harbour – and notes as a rationale that the administrative costs and compliance costs may be disproportionate to the tax at stake.

625. One way of addressing these compliance and administration considerations would be to include a materiality threshold, below which the STTR would not apply, as part of the detailed rules underpinning the operation of the Rule. This approach would also provide greater tax certainty. However, it must also

be recognised that what is a materially significant risk can vary between small and large jurisdictions. And that the administration of a threshold test itself might introduce complexity and cost, especially for tax administrations with lower capacity.

626. There are a number of possible approaches to the design of a materiality threshold, which could be used in isolation or in combination, and three approaches are discussed below. The choice of an approach will be informed by views on the levels at which MNEs are likely to enter into structuring arrangements to take advantage of low tax outcomes and the appropriate allocation of tax administrations' resources to risk.

Threshold based on the size of the MNE

627. The income inclusion and undertaxed payments rules apply to MNE Groups that meet the EUR 750m threshold adopted by the Inclusive Framework under BEPS Action 13 (Country by Country Reporting). As a standalone treaty rule the STTR does not need to be limited to groups meeting that size threshold, but there are merits in considering a threshold based on the size of the MNE Group.

628. A threshold based on the size of an MNE Group is easy to administer and apply, especially in the context of a payments-based rule, because it does not rely on information that might not be available at the point of payment or during the period in which a payment is made. This clearly has advantages for both tax administrations and taxpayers. Although a size threshold applying for the purposes of the STTR does not need to align with the EUR 750m threshold applying for the purposes of the GloBE, it should not be set too low in recognition of the lower risk of material base-eroding payments in smaller groups. It seems clear, for example, that micro, small and medium sized enterprises (SMEs)[12] should be excluded from the scope of the rule. A number of jurisdictions provide exclusions for SMEs in their domestic transfer pricing and other rules, on similar materiality grounds.

629. The STTR focuses on a defined set of cross-border payments between connected persons other than individuals and is therefore addressing particular risks arising in an MNE Group context. A threshold based on the characteristics of an MNE Group would therefore be consistent with this focus and would serve to target the rule on those MNE Groups most likely and best equipped to enter into BEPS structures taking advantage of low-tax outcomes.

Threshold based on a tiered value of covered payments made to connected persons in other contracting state

630. Because the STTR focuses on particular categories of cross-border, connected-person payments giving rise to greater BEPS risks, the materiality threshold could be set by reference to the value of such payments in a year. Where the EUR-value of covered payments made to connected persons in the other contracting jurisdiction exceeded a fixed amount in a year, the STTR would apply. The test would apply to all covered payments irrespective of the tax treatment. Such a threshold could be tiered by reference to GDP, with a lower threshold amount for smaller economies, in a way that recognises that what is considered a significant risk can vary between small and large jurisdictions, and be informed by existing safe-harbour regimes. For example, the United Nations Transfer Pricing Manual discusses safe harbours for "minor expenses" and example 20 alludes to a $750,000 threshold.

631. An approach that relies on the value of payments in a year raises administrative and compliance questions, where the total value of payments in a year is not known and cannot be established at the point a particular payment is made. To address this, the determination of whether the threshold is crossed for a particular year could be made on the basis of the average value of covered payments to [connected persons in] the other contracting jurisdiction in the preceding three years. Where that average exceeds the threshold, the STTR would apply to all such payments in the current year. Such an approach may, however, result in both over- and under-withholding – where (although the threshold is crossed according

to the three year average) payments in a year ultimately fall below the threshold, or vice versa – and give rise to concerns about excessive contingent withholding and potential delayed repayment. Administrative approaches to minimising or eliminating these issues, including applying the top-up tax on an ex-post basis in the form of an annualised charge are discussed further in Section 9.3.4 below. Alternatively, the STTR could apply prospectively to subsequent payments once the level of payments in a period has crossed the threshold.

Threshold based on a ratio

632. Under this approach, the STTR will not apply where the total amount of covered payments the payer had made (or was expected to make) to any connected persons in the other contracting jurisdiction over the course of the payer's financial year, expressed as a proportion of total expenditures, were below a certain ratio. Building off a risk assessment concept, the threshold could be designed to measure whether the payer makes a sufficient amount of covered payments (as defined above) during the relevant period to connected persons in the other contracting jurisdiction to justify further intervention by the source jurisdiction and allow an efficient allocation of a jurisdiction's tax administration's resources to risk. The threshold is intended to focus the operation of the STTR by excluding from its scope those connected person arrangements that would not typically be expected to give rise to BEPS concerns. As with the EUR-value approach described above, this materiality test would capture all covered payments and apply irrespective of the tax treatment of each specific payment in the payee jurisdiction.

633. The threshold would be met when (i) the total amount of covered payments the payer had made (or was expected to make) to [any connected persons in] the other contracting jurisdiction over (ii) the payer's total expenditures except cost of goods exceeded a certain percentage. In order to be able to compute this ratio at the time when the payment is made, both the payments and expenditures taken into account could be an average calculated across the preceding three years. This raises similar administrative and compliance considerations as the EUR-value approach discussed above, and potential remedies are discussed in Section 9.3.4 below. Again, the STTR could apply prospectively to subsequent payments once the ratio of payments in a period has crossed the threshold.

634. Both the EUR-value and ratio approaches could also include an anti-fragmentation rule that prevented the MNE splitting payments under the same arrangement between multiple payers in the source state to avoid reaching the threshold.

Further technical work

635. Balancing these considerations, the Inclusive Framework will take forward further technical work on the design of a materiality threshold within a framework that will explore:

- an MNE size threshold;
- a tiered EUR-value payments threshold; and
- a ratio-based threshold,

which could be applied in isolation or combination.

636. The evaluation of these approaches will be informed by views on the levels at which MNEs are likely to enter into structuring arrangements to take advantage of low tax outcomes and the appropriate allocation of a tax administration's resources to risk. It will also recognise that a threshold would be intended to both simplify the operation of the STTR and focus its application on a risk-assessment basis, by excluding from its scope those connected person arrangements that would not typically be expected to give rise to audit concerns. Such a threshold should operate as an administrable filter to determine whether the STTR should apply in a particular case given the policy objectives of the rule that should be

straightforward for taxpayers and tax administrations to apply and avoid giving rise to undue compliance and administration costs.

9.3. Operation and effect

9.3.1. Subject to Tax Rule applies on a nominal basis

637. The STTR will be triggered where a covered payment is subject to a nominal tax rate in the payee jurisdiction that is below an agreed minimum rate, after adjusting for certain permanent changes in the tax base. A rule that sought to establish the effective tax rate on a particular payment or transaction (after taking into account relevant deductions) would be prohibitively complex both from an administrative and compliance perspective. Focusing on a nominal tax rate test makes the rule simpler to apply, particularly in the context of the other mechanics of the rule discussed further below (such as top-up withholding).

638. Using an effective tax rate test in the context of a withholding tax measure would be particularly difficult as an effective tax rate test measures the tax imposed on an entity's net income over a defined accounting period and it would not be possible to establish the effective tax rate in the payee jurisdiction at the time when a payment is made (and the withholding tax would need to be levied). A nominal tax rate test is easier for tax administrations to administer (particularly those with low capacity) and is more in line with the policy goal of the STTR to focus on specific low-tax outcomes in respect of specific payments.

639. Because the STTR is a treaty rule, the taxes that will be taken in account for the purposes of applying the nominal rate test will be those that are covered taxes for the purposes of the treaty, as defined in the treaty in provisions equivalent to Article 2 of the OECD Model Tax Convention (OECD, 2017[1]). These covered taxes may not align with the taxes that are covered taxes for the purposes of the GloBE, but this is consistent with the nature of bilateral tax treaties which include rules setting the scope of their application (e.g. to defined persons and taxes).

Nominal test applies on a payments basis

640. A rule that looked only to the statutory rate applied to a payment, however, and did not take account of specific provisions that alter the amount of the payment that is brought within the charge to tax, might fail to capture cases in which a payment is subject to low levels of taxation and leave countries exposed to BEPS risks. Such an approach would not, therefore, offer a credible response to targeting the base-erosion concerns that underpin the STTR. To balance these considerations, the determination of the adjusted nominal rate would start with the statutory rate applicable to the counterparty in the payee jurisdiction and adjust this by reference to any preferential rate or special exemptions, exclusions, reductions or expansions that are linked directly to the payment or the entity receiving it. Multiplying the actual tax rate on the payment by the proportion of the payment that is subject to tax in the payee jurisdiction would produce the adjusted nominal rate. For example, where a company in State X receives foreign source royalty income, State X might

(a) apply a preferential tax rate to that royalty payment;

(b) exclude a certain percentage of the royalty payment from taxation;

(c) apply tax at a low rate, but to an amount that is greater than the income;

(d) allow resident companies a deduction for deemed expenditure associated with payments of that character that is in addition to or calculated independently of the payee's actual expenditure.

In all these cases this approach would calculate the rate of tax on the payment by reference to the proportion of the payment that is subject to tax after taking into account the exclusion or deduction from the payment.

641. An adjusted nominal rate determined along these lines would, for example, apply to low or zero rate jurisdictions; payments to a territorial regime where such payments are not brought into account as income in the residence state; payments eligible for a preferential tax regime and regimes that provided for a full or partial exclusion from income.

No adjustment for general deductions against the tax base

642. This approach would not, however, take into account deductions from the tax base that were not directly linked to the item of income or category of payee. For example, adjustments such as super-deductions for certain categories of expenditure or notional interest or dividend deductions and other unilateral downward adjustments of profit would, therefore, not be covered by the STTR. And deductions, in computing profits of the payee, for costs that represent actual business expenditures incurred should not give rise to an adjustment of the nominal tax rate. Taking these types of general deductions from the tax base into account would raise prohibitive challenges from a design perspective, such as how to allocate the reduction in the tax base to particular payments, and would add another layer of complexity and controversy to the application of the rule. It would also raise questions about what account should be taken of the non-deductibility of certain expenditure, such as whether the nominal rate needed to be adjusted upwards to take account of the fact that some interest expenses might be non-deductible.

Tax base calculated otherwise than by reference to income

643. In developing the detailed rules that will codify and govern the operation of the adjusted nominal tax rate test, further work will be undertaken on the design of mechanisms that ensure that the test applies appropriately in relation to jurisdictions that calculate their tax base other than by reference to a resident's income. These mechanisms will be informed by, and could draw upon with suitable adaptations, the solutions developed for the purposes of the IIR and UTPR. For example the Zakat levied on corporations by the Kingdom of Saudi Arabia is a tax on both income and equity. The Zakat is levied at 2.5% but since it is imposed on income and equity it results in a higher effective rate. Equally certain members of the Inclusive Framework have income tax regimes that impose an income tax on a corporation when the corporation's income is distributed to its shareholders, rather than when it is earned. The statutory tax rates in these jurisdictions may equal or exceed the agreed minimum rate of tax, thereby ensuring that ultimately the income is not subject to a low rate of tax. Absent a distribution, however, the income is not subject to tax in the year it is earned. The design of a nominal tax rate test mechanism would need to be adjusted in these cases to reflect to specific features of these countries regimes. For example, for jurisdictions with a corporate tax base that is not calculated by reference to income, the payee may be able to certify that, notwithstanding the low nominal rate, the average tax burden on all income of the payee over an agreed period was in excess on the minimum rate.

Practical considerations

644. Subject to the application of a materiality threshold, as discussed in section 9.2.5 above, which would serve to remove the obligation in cases below that threshold, taxpayers, withholding agents and tax administrations will need to establish the adjusted nominal tax rate for all covered payments in determining whether the STTR applies and, where it does, the rate of top-up tax to be applied to the covered payment. If the primary mechanism for applying the STTR were to be an interim withholding tax at the point of payment, it is particularly important that this information is ascertainable by the payer, or a withholding agent, at that time, to determine whether and at what rate the withholding tax should be applied. Whilst information on the nominal tax rates, and details of special regimes, applying to categories of income in particular jurisdictions is generally available – either in material published by the relevant tax administration, or from third party sources – further work will be undertaken on how best to administer this in light of the specificities of each jurisdiction's tax regime.

No adjustment for exemption or credit under treaty elimination article

645. Under paragraph 1 of Article 23 A of the OECD Model, the residence jurisdiction is obliged to exempt an item of income from tax where the source jurisdiction is permitted to tax that item of income in accordance with the treaty. This treaty exemption is, prima facie, an exemption, exclusion, or reduction in the tax base that is linked directly to the payment or the entity receiving it. But taking the treaty exemption into account for the purposes of computing the adjusted nominal rate would produce outcomes that go beyond the intended functioning of the STTR, which is not to reallocate taxing rights between jurisdictions but to allow source jurisdictions to apply a top-up tax to covered payments that are subject to low nominal rates in the residence jurisdiction. This is illustrated by example 9.3.1A.

646. In order to address this issue, the entitlement to an exemption under provisions equivalent to Article 23 A of the OECD Model will not be taken into account when computing the adjusted nominal rate for the purposes of the STTR.

647. To the extent that similar considerations could arise in respect of the residence jurisdiction's obligation under paragraph 1 of Article 23 B and paragraph 2 of Article 23 B to provide a credit against its own tax on an item of income for the tax paid on that income in the source jurisdiction, the entitlement to credit under those provisions will also be disregarded when computing the adjusted nominal rate for the purposes of the STTR.

648. Disregarding the entitlement to exemption or credit under the elimination article in a tax treaty in this way for the purposes of computing the adjusted nominal rate raises questions about the interaction between the source jurisdiction's right to apply a top-up tax under the subject to tax test and the residence jurisdiction's obligation to provide relief by exemption or credit for that top-up tax. These questions are addressed in Section 9.3.3 below. In developing the detailed rules, further technical work will be undertaken in the Inclusive Framework on these two interlinked issues and the precise interaction with the residence jurisdiction's obligations under the elimination of double taxation provisions of tax treaties.

Setting nominal tax rate

649. Given that the nominal tax rate trigger applies to the gross amount of the payment, on a transaction by transaction basis and does not allow for blending, the STTR might, in certain cases, give rise to the risk of over-taxation. This over-taxation could arise, for example, where a covered payment is made to an entity that is subject to tax at a nil rate but which has incurred expenses in deriving that income. In this case, applying the minimum ETR determined under the income inclusion and undertaxed payments rules to the gross amount of the payment when computing the top-up rate to be applied to that payment under the STTR would give rise to an effective tax rate above that minimum rate and could even give rise to taxation in excess of economic profit. In order to limit this risk of over-taxation, Inclusive Framework members could decide to limit both the trigger rate and the amount of top-up tax under the STTR to a rate that is lower than the minimum ETR under the income inclusion and undertaxed payments rules.

9.3.2. Top-up to a minimum rate

650. The effect of the rule will be to allow the source jurisdiction to tax the gross amount of the payment up to an agreed minimum rate. That is, the payer jurisdiction would be able to impose a withholding tax on the covered payment at a rate that was equal to the difference between the minimum rate provided for under the STTR and the adjusted nominal tax rate applicable to the covered payment in the payee jurisdiction. As noted above, in order to mitigate this risk of over-taxation, it may be appropriate to limit both the trigger rate and the amount of top-up tax under the STTR to a rate that is lower than the minimum ETR set under the income inclusion and undertaxed payments rule. Having a lower trigger and top-up rate under the STTR would limit the risk of over-taxation and be intended to arrive at a net tax burden that is (after taking into account any tax levied on the gross amount of the payment) equal, or at least broadly similar,

to the minimum effective rate under the income inclusion and undertaxed payments rules. To address this and conform with the broader GloBE objective of avoiding double and excessive taxation, the top-up rate could be set at a rate that is lower than the minimum rate agreed for the income inclusion and undertaxed payments rules.

651. In general, no top-up tax would be imposed in circumstances in which the relevant treaty already provided for source taxation on the covered payment. But the treaty rule would include provision for applying top-up tax where the existing allocation of taxing rights was less favourable to the payer jurisdiction (for example, where the treaty provides for a low rate – say 5% – on the gross payment and the top-up mechanism would result in increased taxing rights). This will take the form of an ordering rule in the relevant provisions, the effect of which will be to allow the payer jurisdiction to apply the higher of the rate agreed in the treaty or the top-up rate provided for under the STTR.

9.3.3. Interaction with treaty elimination articles

652. This Section deals with a technical feature of the STTR that will need to be incorporated as part of the final design, in order to avoid unintended outcomes resulting from the interaction with other treaty provisions.

653. As discussed in Section 9.3.1 above, the computation of the adjusted nominal rate (and therefore the amount of top-up required to bring that rate up to the agreed minimum rate) will not take account of the obligation to provide exemption or credit in the residence jurisdiction under the elimination of double taxation provisions in a tax treaty between the payer and payee jurisdictions. This avoids an unintended reallocation of taxing rights between the jurisdictions that would go beyond the intended effect of the STTR. But questions also arise about the interaction between the source jurisdiction's right to apply a top-up tax under the STTR and the residence jurisdiction's obligation, under the elimination of double taxation provisions of a tax treaty, to provide relief by way of exemption or credit in those circumstances.

654. Under paragraph 1 of Article 23 A of the OECD Model, the residence jurisdiction is obliged to exempt an item of income where the source jurisdiction is permitted to tax that item of income in accordance with the treaty. Where the conditions are met for the STTR to apply, the source jurisdiction will be permitted, in accordance with the treaty, to apply a top-up tax and the residence jurisdiction will then be obliged under the provisions of the elimination article to exempt that income from tax. Even where that obligation is not taken into account for the purposes of determining the adjusted nominal rate, and therefore does not increase the top-up tax that can be applied in the source jurisdiction, the residence jurisdiction will nevertheless be deprived of its taxing right. The result of this will be that only the source jurisdiction will tax the affected payment; and only at the top-up rate. This effect can be illustrated by adapting example 9.3.1A in Annex A – see example 9.3.3A in Annex A.

655. This outcome can be considered to be at odds with the intended effect of the STTR, which is not to reallocate taxing rights away from the residence jurisdiction but to permit the source jurisdiction to apply a top-up tax to covered payments that are subject to low nominal rates in the residence jurisdiction, in order to bring the tax on those payments up to an agreed minimum rate.

656. Similar considerations arise where the residence jurisdiction is obliged to provide a credit under paragraph 1 of Article 23 B or paragraph 2 of Article 23 A of the OECD Model. Even where that credit is not taken into account in computing the adjusted nominal rate for the purposes of the STTR, the residence jurisdiction's taxing right is reduced by the credit it is obliged to give for the top-up tax applied in the source jurisdiction. This is illustrated by example 9.3.3B in Annex A.

657. In order to avoid these outcomes, the residence jurisdiction's obligation to provide exemption or credit under the elimination of double taxation provisions of a tax treaty could be switched-off where the source jurisdiction is only exercising a taxing right in accordance with the treaty because it is applying a top-up tax in accordance with the STTR. The effect of this approach is illustrated by example 9.3.3C in

Annex A. There would then be no reallocation of taxing rights away from the residence jurisdiction and, given the limitation imposed on the source jurisdiction to only apply a top-up to the agreed minimum rate, concerns about unrelieved double taxation might be minimal.

658. This approach could, however, result in a cliff-edge where a covered payment to which the STTR applies is subject to an existing source jurisdiction taxing right under the terms of the treaty at a rate above the top-up rate. This is illustrated in Example 9.3.3D in Annex A.

659. Although this outcome does not disturb the position obtaining before the STTR came into contemplation, it does mean that the combined residence and source taxation of a covered payment in respect of which all the conditions for the STTR to apply are met will be lower than it would be if the rule had applied to produce a top-up tax. To avoid this outcome, without depriving the source jurisdiction of its bilaterally agreed right to tax the income at a rate above the top-up, the residence jurisdiction's obligation to provide relief by way of exemption or credit would be proportionately limited. The effect of this will bring the combined rate in the residence and source jurisdictions up to the agreed minimum rate under the STTR (assumed to be 7.5%). This is illustrated in example 9.3.3E in Annex A.

660. In developing the detailed rules, further technical work will be undertaken in the Inclusive Framework on the precise interaction with the residence jurisdiction's obligations under the elimination of double taxation provisions of tax treaties in a range of scenarios, including where the treaty includes source taxation rights that are not conditioned upon the application of the STTR.

9.3.4. Administrative considerations

661. The STTR is intended to address remaining BEPS risks by restoring to source jurisdictions a limited right to apply a top-up tax to a defined set of connected person payments resulting in low tax outcomes in the other contracting jurisdiction, in order to bring the tax on those payments up to an agreed minimum rate. Because this top-up tax will be applied to the gross amount of the payment it may be appropriate, as discussed in Section 9.3.2 above, to limit both the trigger rate and the amount of top-up tax under the STTR to a rate that is lower than the minimum ETR set under the income inclusion and undertaxed payments rules, in order to limit the risk of over-taxation and arrive at a net tax burden that is equal, or at least broadly similar, to the minimum effective rate under the income inclusion and undertaxed payments rules.

662. However, although such an approach will mitigate the risk of covered payments ultimately being over-taxed, there remains a risk of temporary over-taxation if the source jurisdiction applies contingent withholding taxes at higher rates at the point of payment and requires the recipient entities to file claims for treaty relief and repayment after the year-end. Paragraph 109 of the Commentary on Article 1 of the OECD Model notes that jurisdictions are not prevented by the treaty from adopting this approach, but observes that delay in making refunds can result in a direct cost to taxpayers and that it is extremely important that refunds are made expeditiously. The Commentary goes on to say that, in order to ensure the expeditious implementation of benefits under a treaty, it is highly preferable for source jurisdictions to automatically limit the tax they levy in accordance with the relevant provisions of the treaty. In the context of the STTR, this would mean limiting the tax applied at the point of payment to the top-up rate.

663. Consistent with these aims, consideration will be given to administrative approaches facilitating as far as possible the application of the STTR in a way that: ideally, allows the tax applied to covered payments to be limited to the top-up tax that is due after computing the adjusted nominal rate and applying the materiality threshold; and in any event minimises the need for and delay in obtaining refunds of contingent withholding taxes in excess of the top-up.

664. Further technical work will be undertaken in the Inclusive Framework on administrative approaches that could deliver these aims. This will include work on:

- applying the top-up tax as an ex-post annualised charge;
- a certification system providing for reduced rates of withholding tax; and
- the application of contingent withholding taxes set at a level that would generally result in an annual ex-post balancing payment by the taxpayer (rather than a repayment).

Each of these approaches is briefly discussed in the remainder of this section.

Ex-post annualised charge

665. An advantage of applying the top-up tax as an ex-post annualised charge would be that both the taxpayer and tax administration would know at the point the charge is applied: the value of covered payments subject to adjusted nominal tax rates below the agreed minimum rate made in the relevant period; and that the materiality threshold had been crossed for that period. As well as addressing the risk of temporary over-taxation in the form of contingent withholding taxes, this approach would increase tax certainty. But it does give rise to administrative questions, particularly in relation to the person to whom the charge would be applied. Two possible approaches seem to present themselves. The first would be to apply the annualised charge to the non-resident payee.[13] The second would be a charge on the resident payor[14]. Adopting the first approach might be seen as less of a departure from withholding taxes, because the incidence of the tax is applied to the same legal person (the payee). It might also fit better with the income inclusion and undertaxed payments rules, because the top-up tax applied under the STTR will be included in the ETR of the payee (whereas a charge on the payor might require an allocation of the top-up tax to the payee). And imposing the charge on the recipient of the income might be less likely to give rise to issues about ability to pay. But this approach raises an obvious compliance issue, by requiring collection from a non-resident taxpayer. One potential remedy is domestic law collection machinery permitting the tax administration to serve a notice on companies within the same control group as the non-resident taxpayer.[15]

Certification system

666. Some jurisdictions operate administrative easements that allow non-resident taxpayers whose local source income is subject to withholding taxes in that jurisdiction to apply for certificates limiting the rate at which those withholding taxes are applied to that income. The effect of the granting of such certificates is that the withholding tax burden is reduced to a level that is commensurate with the expected final liability to local taxes in the source jurisdiction and therefore the need for the taxpayer to claim a refund after filing a return in that jurisdiction is reduced. The source jurisdiction may grant the certificate, and set the appropriate rate of withholding tax, when satisfied that the taxpayer's circumstances are likely to result in a final liability that is below the amount produced by applying withholding taxes at the full domestic rate to the gross amount of the income sourced in that jurisdiction. In the context of the STTR, such a system could allow taxpayers to apply for a reduction to zero in respect of income that is not covered income for the purposes of the STTR and a reduction to a rate that is limited to the agreed minimum rate or the top-up tax rate (net of the adjusted nominal rate) in respect of income that is covered income for the purposes of the STTR (provided that the income is not subject to an existing source jurisdiction taxing right at higher rates under the applicable treaty). The effect of the granting of a certificate in this context would be to reduce or eliminate the scope for income to be subject to excessive contingent withholding taxes, with the resulting need for repayment claims, as a result of the inclusion of the STTR in the applicable treaty. It would be important to design the information and evidential requirements associated with the making of applications for such certificates in a way that minimises the associated compliance and administrative burdens and provides for an efficient and timely process.

Low interim withholding with balancing payment

667. An alternative, or extension, to the certification system described above is to design, as part of the detailed rules codifying and supporting the application of the STTR, a system providing for the application of withholding taxes at rates that would generally result in an annual ex-post balancing payment by the taxpayer to the tax administration (rather than a repayment). In setting the appropriate rate for particular categories of covered income, the top-up tax could first be computed by reference to the known agreed minimum rate and the adjusted nominal rate for that category of income in the relevant residence jurisdiction (drawing upon the database discussed in section 9.3.1 or other publicly available sources); the amount of withholding tax applied to the income could then be set at an agreed proportion of the top-up tax to produce a rate of withholding tax that would result in an annual balancing payment to the tax administration. Such an approach would balance the revenue flow concerns of tax administrations with the cash flow concerns of businesses and is facilitated by the greater predictability of liabilities based on ascertainable nominal rates of taxation. It would also minimise the cash flow impact on business of the application of the resulting low rate of withholding tax to income that, on an ex-post examination of the facts, is determined not be within the scope of the STTR.

References

OECD (2017), *Model Tax Convention on Income and on Capital*, OECD Publisher, Paris, https://doi.org/10.1787/mtc_cond-2017-en. [1]

OECD (2017), *OECD Transfer Pricing Guidelines for Multinational Enterprises and Tax Administrations 2017*, OECD Publishing, Paris, https://doi.org/10.1787/tpg-2017-en. [2]

Notes

[1] An MNE Group may arrange to provide services to its customers through a subsidiary that is resident in a contracting state which has a tax treaty with the state where that customer is located (the source state). Where a principal purpose of that arrangement is to take advantage of the tax treaty between the two jurisdictions then, under the measures agreed in Action 6, the source state will not be required to extend treaty benefits to any covered payment made under that arrangement.

[2] The STTR does not, of course, displace the requirement to apply transfer pricing rules to the covered payments between connected persons to which the rule applies.

[3] There are a number of reasons why a payment could be subject to no or little tax in the counterparty jurisdiction. The payment may have a different character under the laws of the payee jurisdiction which means that it is not treated as income for tax purposes. The payee could have a special tax status or be eligible for special tax treatment in respect of the payments (e.g. because the payment is subject to tax under a preferential tax regime). The payee jurisdiction may impose tax at progressive rates and the payee may be eligible for an exclusion or lower rate on small amounts of income or the payee may be eligible for a lower rate of tax on income from certain sources or based on the way the payment is treated (i.e. whether it is remitted to the jurisdiction of the payer).

[4] It is noteworthy that the same approach – a two component rule with a de facto control test and deemed control above a 50% participation level – is also adopted in paragraph 6 of the alternative fees for technical services article provided for in paragraph 26 of the Commentary on Article 12A of the 2017 UN Model Tax Convention. A similar control test could also be applied in the context of rules for addressing the profit shifting risks raised by orphan entities in the context of the undertaxed payments rule.

[5] Further consideration could be given to the treatment of interest payments on intra-group regulatory capital or other regulated financing instruments where the imposition of withholding taxes could give rise to a significant risk of over-taxation making such funding arrangements uneconomic on an after-tax basis.

[6] See Paragraph 6.100 of the OECD Transfer Pricing Guidelines (OECD, 2017[2]): "One situation where transactions involving transfers of intangibles or rights in intangibles may be combined with other transactions involves a business franchise arrangement. Under such an arrangement, one member of an MNE group may agree to provide a combination of services and intangibles to an associated enterprise in exchange for a single fee."

[7] As defined in the relevant treaty.

[8] See Paragraph 6.100 of the OECD Transfer Pricing Guidelines (OECD, 2017[2]) in relation to the breakdown of the constituent parts of a business franchise arrangement: "If the services and intangibles made available under such an arrangement are sufficiently unique that reliable comparables cannot be identified for the entire service/intangible package, it may be necessary to segregate the various parts of the package of services and intangibles for separate transfer pricing consideration. It should be kept in mind, however, that the interactions between various intangibles and services may enhance the value of both."

[9] See Article 5(6) of the UN Model Tax Convention: "Notwithstanding the preceding provisions of this Article but subject to the provisions of paragraph 7, an insurance enterprise of a Contracting State shall, except in regard to re-insurance, be deemed to have a permanent establishment in the other Contracting State if it collects premiums in the territory of that other State or insures risks situated therein through a person."

[10] See paragraph 7.15 of the OECD Transfer Pricing Guidelines (OECD, 2017[2]).

[11] When the service provider is acting only as an agent or intermediary, the cost base will include only those costs incurred by the intermediary in performing its agency function. For example, the cost base of a company acting as a procurement agent and incurring costs for the purchase of goods on behalf of connected companies would not include the costs of those goods.

[12] SME is not a term defined at the international level, but there are existing examples of definitions. For instances SMEs are defined in the EU recommendation 2003/361. The main factors determining whether an enterprise is an SME under that approach are staff headcount and either turnover or balance sheet total. The size thresholds for SMEs are a staff headcount below 250 and either turnover below or equal to EUR 50m or a balance sheet total below or equal to EUR 43m.

[13] An approach taken in the United Kingdom's offshore receipts of intangible property (ORIP) regime.

[14] An approach taken in the United States' base erosion and anti-abuse tax (BEAT).

[15] Such collection machinery is available under UK domestic law and applies in relation to the ORIP regime there.

10 Implementation and Rule Co-ordination

10.1. Overview

668. This chapter first summarises the rule co-ordination and rule order framework within which the different elements of Pillar Two are intended to operate. It then discusses questions of implementation of each of the elements as well as mechanisms to ensure that effective co-ordination and tax certainty in practice. It also covers compatibility of the GloBE rules with existing tax treaty obligations, however it does not include an analysis on the compatibility of the GloBE rules with other international obligations, such as the EU fundamental freedoms.

10.2. Rule order

669. The preceding chapters of this Pillar Two Blueprint include recommendations for the design of an income inclusion rule (IIR) and an undertaxed payments rule (UTPR), complemented by a switch-over rule (SOR) that removes treaty obstacles from the application of the IIR to certain branch structures and applies where the treaty otherwise obligates the contracting state to use the exemption method.[1] They also contain a Subject to Tax Rule (STTR). The Policy Note and the Programme of Work (OECD, 2019[4]) call for the development of rules under Pillar Two that operate to co-ordinate these different elements in order to ensure that they interact in a way that minimises compliance and administration costs and avoids the risk of double taxation.

670. The co-ordination between these various elements of Pillar Two is already described in the previous chapters, but for ease of reference is also summarised below.

10.2.1. Subject to Tax Rule

671. Where the STTR permits the source jurisdiction to apply a top-up tax to a covered payment, for example in the form of a withholding tax, the effect of that additional tax will be taken into account in determining the effective tax rate under the GloBE rules.[2] Under the jurisdictional blending approach this top-up tax is assigned to the Constituent Entity that brings the payment into account as income.[3] By taking the tax charged as a consequence of the STTR into account in calculating the ETR of the payee, the GloBE rules effectively give priority to the application of the STTR. Example 10.2.1A provides an illustration of the interaction of the STTR with the IIR while Example 10.2.1B provides an illustration of the interaction of the STTR with the UTPR. These examples demonstrate that the STTR applies even if the MNE Group is subject to the IIR or the UTPR. These examples further illustrate that the withholding tax levied under the STTR is taken into account in order to determine the ETR (and, if relevant, the top-up tax) of the jurisdiction where the recipient is located.

10.2.2. GloBE rules

672. The mechanisms for calculating and allocating the tax base and covered taxes under GloBE rules are designed to take into account both domestic and foreign taxes imposed on each Constituent Entity's income.[4] Therefore, the effect of existing rules for taxing foreign income (such as under a CFC regime) or for taxing non-residents on domestic source income (such as through a withholding tax mechanism) are taken into account when determining a Constituent Entity's ETR under the GloBE on a jurisdictional basis. The effect of giving priority to withholding taxes and taxes imposed under a CFC regime is described in further detail in Chapter 3.

Income inclusion rule (IIR)

673. As described further in Chapter 5 of the Pillar Two Blueprint, the IIR applies in priority to the UTPR under the GloBE rules. However, the IIR includes further co-ordination rules that ensure that the IIR in different jurisdictions cannot be applied to the same interest in low-taxed income. The primary mechanism for co-ordinating the application of the IIR in each jurisdiction is through the "top-down approach" which gives priority to the application of the IIR in the jurisdiction of the Constituent Entity that is at or near the top of the ownership chain in the MNE Group, starting with the Ultimate Parent Entity. In the event the Ultimate Parent Entity is not located in a jurisdiction that has implemented the IIR, then responsibility for applying the IIR falls to the Constituent Entity that is directly owned and controlled by that Ultimate Parent Entity, and so on, down the chain of ownership.

674. The application of the top-down approach is subject to a further rule that specifically addresses the application of the IIR in the case of "split-ownership structures". Split-ownership structures are those where a significant portion of the equity interests in a Constituent Entity are held by persons outside the MNE Group (see Section 6.3.2). This rule pushes the obligation to apply the IIR down to the partially-owned "intermediate" parent. The intermediate parent then would apply the IIR to its share of the income of any low-taxed Constituent Entity in which that Intermediate Parent has a direct or indirect ownership interest.

Switch over rule

675. The IIR will apply where the parent of the MNE derives income attributable to a foreign permanent establishment (PE) that benefits from a tax exemption under the laws of the parent jurisdiction. In this case the income of that exempt PE will need to be apportioned between the PE jurisdiction and the parent jurisdiction (together with any tax on that income) under the GloBE rules in order to accurately calculate the jurisdictional ETR in the parent jurisdiction and the PE jurisdiction. A parent that seeks to apply the IIR to the income of an exempt PE will, however, be prevented from doing so where the parent jurisdiction has entered into a bilateral tax treaty that obliges the parent jurisdiction to exempt the income of the PE in the hands of its own resident. A jurisdiction that found itself in the position where it was unable to tax the low taxed income of a PE due to the operation of the treaty would not be able to implement an IIR that was compatible with the requirements of the GloBE rules. A switch-over rule is therefore required in order to allow the state of the parent's residence to tax the income of the PE up to the minimum rate as provided for under the income inclusion rule.[5]

Undertaxed payments rule (UTPR)

676. As noted above the IIR takes priority over the UTPR. Therefore, no top-up tax may be allocated under the UTPR in respect of a Constituent Entity that is controlled, directly or indirectly, by a foreign Constituent Entity that is subject to an IIR in accordance with the GloBE rules.[6]

10.3. Implementation

677. Both the STTR and SOR require changes to existing bilateral tax treaties. These could be implemented through bilateral negotiations and amendments to individual treaties. Consideration may also

be given to adopting these under the Multilateral Convention to Implement Tax Treaty Related Measures to Prevent Base Erosion and Profit Shifting (the MLI) (OECD, 2016[6]), emerging from BEPS Action 15. The MLI is a multilateral treaty that applies alongside existing bilateral treaties and modifies their application. It represents a significant efficiency gain compared to the alternative of multiple pairs of bilateral negotiations. The MLI requires one negotiation and allows countries to go through a single ratification procedure in their legislature covering all of their affected treaties. Using the MLI, or a new multilateral convention (see Section 10.5.3.), to give effect to the STTR and SOR in relevant treaties could offer a more efficient path to implementation of these rules. The MLI approach would allow for optionality and would not necessarily require all countries to adopt the STTR and SOR.

678. The IIR and UTPR can be implemented by way of changes to domestic law. Therefore, it is a matter for individual jurisdictions to decide to implement the IIR and UTPR in their domestic legislation, the implementation of which must be in accordance with the agreed terms of the GloBE rules. It is acknowledged that jurisdictions may want to retain their right to apply the IIR (or rules based on the IIR) to MNE Groups, headquartered in their jurisdiction, which do not meet the consolidated revenue threshold. However, there is a need to consider whether the right of a jurisdiction to apply the IIR rules to MNE Groups with a lower consolidated revenue should be restricted as part of the overall agreement, to ensure that they are applied consistently with the principles, agreed outcomes and co-ordination requirements of the GloBE rules. For example, a jurisdiction which has introduced the undertaxed payments rule cannot apply that rule to a Constituent Entity of an MNE Group if that group does not have consolidated revenues above the threshold. The mechanisms for ensuring effective overall co-ordination of the application of the IIR and UTPR across multiple jurisdictions are discussed in Section 10.5, including exploration of a multilateral convention for the IIR and UTPR which would be the only means to enshrine rule co-ordination in a legally binding form.

10.4. Treaty compatibility

10.4.1. General principles

679. The common starting point for an analysis of the compatibility of the IIR and UTPR with existing tax treaty obligations is the general principle that, with limited exceptions, tax treaties are not intended to restrict a jurisdiction's right to tax its own residents. This longstanding principle is now codified in Article 1(3) of the OECD Model (often referred to as the "saving clause"), and reads as follows:

> *This Convention shall not affect the taxation, by a Contracting State, of its residents except with respect to the benefits granted under paragraph 3 of Article 7, paragraph 2 of Article 9 and Articles 19, 20, 23 [A] [B], 24, 25 and 28.*

680. As a general matter, then, tax treaties should not present any obstacle to jurisdictions implementing an IIR and UTPR along the lines envisaged under the GloBE.

10.4.2. Income Inclusion rule (IIR)

681. The IIR operates by requiring a parent entity (in most cases, the Ultimate Parent Entity) to bring into account as income its proportionate share of the income of each Constituent Entity located in a low-tax jurisdiction in which it owns an equity interest. That income is then taxed in the parent entity's hands up to the GloBE minimum rate, after crediting any covered taxes (as defined for the purposes of the GloBE) on that income. In subjecting a domestic taxpayer to tax on its share of the foreign income of a controlled subsidiary, therefore, the IIR operates in a way that is closely comparable to a CFC rule and raises the same treaty questions. Although there are a number of differences between the IIR and the CFC rules of many jurisdictions, these do not alter the analysis.

682. The compatibility of CFC regimes with treaty obligations is addressed in paragraph 81 of the Commentary on Article 1 of the OECD Model Tax Convention (OECD, 2017[8]) (MTC), which concludes that they do not conflict with treaty obligations. Paragraph 81 reads as follows:

> *"A significant number of countries have adopted controlled foreign company provisions to address issues related to the use of foreign base companies. Whilst the design of this type of legislation varies considerably among countries, a common feature of these rules, which are now internationally recognised as a legitimate instrument to protect the domestic tax base, is that they result in a Contracting State taxing its residents on income attributable to their participation in certain foreign entities. It has sometimes been argued, based on a certain interpretation of provisions of the Convention such as paragraph 1 of Article 7 and paragraph 5 of Article 10, that this common feature of controlled foreign company legislation conflicted with these provisions. Since such legislation results in a State taxing its own residents, paragraph 3 of Article 1 confirms that it does not conflict with tax conventions. The same conclusion must be reached in the case of conventions that do not include a provision similar to paragraph 3 of Article 1; for the reasons explained in paragraphs 14 of the Commentary on Article 7 and 37 of the Commentary on Article 10, the interpretation according to which these Articles would prevent the application of controlled foreign company provisions does not accord with the text of paragraph 1 of Article 7 and paragraph 5 of Article 10. It also does not hold when these provisions are read in their context. Thus, whilst some countries have felt it useful to expressly clarify in their conventions, that controlled foreign company legislation did not conflict with the Convention, such clarification is not necessary. It is recognised that controlled foreign company legislation structured in this way is not contrary to the provisions of the Convention."*

683. For the same reasons, it can be concluded that an IIR along the lines envisaged under the GloBE is similarly compatible with the provisions of tax treaties that are generally based on the OECD Model.

10.4.3. Undertaxed payments rule (UTPR)

684. The UTPR serves as a backstop to the IIR. It operates when the IIR does not apply by providing jurisdictions with a tool to protect themselves from the effect of base eroding transactions. In order to do so, the UTPR takes the form of a limitation (or denial) of the deduction of intra-group payments, or an equivalent adjustment. The extent to which the deduction of an intra-group payment is affected by the UTPR depends on the amount of top-up tax that is allocated to a UTPR Taxpayer. As described in Chapter 7 the UTPR uses the same mechanics as the IIR for determining the MNE's jurisdictional ETR and the amount of top-up tax allocable under the rule. The UTPR, however, operates through an allocation key that is based on deductible intra-group payments.

685. The top-up tax is allocated to a UTPR taxpayer that is a member of the same MNE Group as the low-tax entity as follows:

- First, if the UTPR taxpayer makes any deductible payments to the low-tax entity during the relevant period, the top-up tax that applies to the income of such entity is allocated in proportion to the deductible payments made to such low-tax entity by all UTPR taxpayers;
- Second, if the UTPR taxpayer has net intra-group expenditure, the remaining top-up tax is allocated in proportion to the total amount of net intra-group expenditure incurred by all UTPR taxpayers.

686. The rationale for the two-step approach is that the full amount of top-up tax may not be allocated after application of the first allocation key. This can happen if there are no direct payments made to any low-tax entity from a UTPR taxpayer or if the adjustments on direct payments are not sufficient to soak up the computed top-up tax. In such a case, the remaining top-up tax after the first allocation key applied is allocated to the UTPR taxpayers in proportion to their net intra-group expenditures. The UTPR taxpayers with net related party income are disregarded for the purpose of the second allocation key. Both allocation keys only take into account the payments that were made in the same year as the year when the top-up tax arises.

687. The UTPR provides a coordinated mechanism to identify the maximum amount of top-up tax that can be allocated and that can be imposed on each UTPR Taxpayer. The top-up tax imposed on each UTPR taxpayer is capped by reference to the gross amount of deductible intra-group payments that are taken into account for the purpose of the allocation keys. The UTPR, however, does not provide any requirements as to how this top-up tax is collected. The adjustment in the payer jurisdiction could take the form of a denial or a limitation of a deduction for intra-group payments, or an equivalent tax computed by reference to those payments. The precise method under which the adjustment is made will be a matter of domestic law implementation left to the jurisdictions applying the UTPR (see Section 7.7).

688. Because the UTPR has the potential to apply in any jurisdiction where a UTPR taxpayer makes an intra-group payment, and because the outcomes under the UTPR will vary based on the amount of intra-group payments made by each entity, the UTPR is a more complex rule to apply and requires a greater amount of co-ordination between jurisdictions than the IIR. In practice, however, the scope for the application of the UTPR is expected to be relatively narrow. This is because the UTPR only applies where the entity is not otherwise subject to an IIR that is implemented in accordance with the GloBE rules under the laws of another jurisdiction (see Section 10.2 on rule order).

689. The UTPR would also, therefore, affect how a country taxes its own residents. Since a denial of a deduction under the UTPR could result in a higher taxable base than the base solely based on arm's length profits, some may question whether the denial could conflict with Article 9(1) (Associated Enterprises) or, where the UTPR applies to a PE, Article 7(2) MTC. It is generally recognised, however, that once the profits have been allocated in accordance with the arm's length principle, how they are taxed is a matter determined by the domestic law of each country. A frequently quoted illustration of this point, found in the domestic law of many countries, are rules denying a deduction for entertainment expenses. As mentioned above, this longstanding principle is now codified in Article 1(3) of the OECD Model (the "saving clause") and is further confirmed by paragraph 30 of the Commentary on Article 7 MTC, as follows:

> *"Paragraph 2 determines the profits that are attributable to a permanent establishment for the purposes of the rule in paragraph 1 that allocates taxing rights on these profits. Once the profits that are attributable to a permanent establishment have been determined in accordance with paragraph 2 of Article 7, it is for the domestic law of each Contracting State to determine whether and how such profits should be taxed as long as there is conformity with the requirements of paragraph 2 and the other provisions of the Convention. Paragraph 2 does not deal with the issue of whether expenses are deductible when computing the taxable income of the enterprise in either Contracting State. The conditions for the deductibility of expenses are a matter to be determined by domestic law, subject to the provisions of the Convention and, in particular, paragraph 3 of Article 24 [...]"*

Non-discrimination provisions

690. The general principle codified in Article 1(3) MTC is, however, constrained in some circumstances by Article 24 MTC (the non-discrimination provision). In relation to the UTPR two provisions of Article 24 need to be considered. Article 24(4) requires equal treatment to be given to payments made by a resident to a non-resident when compared to payments between resident taxpayers. In order to comply with Article 24(4), the conditions for deductibility should not be different merely because the payment is made to a non-resident. And, where the UTPR applies to deemed payments by a PE, Article 24(3) requires that the taxation on that PE shall not be less favourably levied than that on resident enterprises carrying on the same activities.

691. As described in Section 7.4.3, the UTPR will not apply where a payment is made from a jurisdiction that is characterised as a low tax jurisdiction for that group in a particular year (based on the local group's ETR profile in that jurisdiction in that year). The first step of the UTPR will also not apply to a payment from a jurisdiction that is characterised as a high tax jurisdiction for the group in a particular year to a group entity in a jurisdiction that is also characterised as a high tax jurisdiction for that group in that year. There is no denial of a deduction under the UTPR in either scenario. The first step of the UTPR will only apply

where a payment is made from a jurisdiction that is characterised as a high tax jurisdiction for that group in a particular year to a group entity in a jurisdiction that is characterised as a low tax jurisdiction for that group in that year. In this scenario, there may be a denial of a deduction under the UTPR. And, because a jurisdiction cannot be both a high tax and a low tax jurisdiction for a group in a particular year, this denial will only apply to certain cross-border payments. But in all of these scenarios, the conditions under which a deduction for a domestic or cross-border payment is permitted or denied are the same; the only relevant consideration is whether the payment is high tax to low tax. This demonstrates that the denial of a deduction under the first step of the UTPR is not determined by the residence of the recipient of the payment but by the jurisdiction's classification as high or low tax on the basis of the local group's effective tax rate profile in the relevant period.

692. Under the second step described above, deniability can arise in respect of any net related party expenditure, whether the payment is made to a domestic or foreign member of the group. The net related party expenditure is determined on an entity-by-entity basis. Under this step, therefore, the UTPR will apply in the same way to intra-group payments made to domestic and non-resident group entities without any distinction.

693. For these reasons, it can be concluded that a UTPR along the lines envisaged under the GloBE rules is compatible with the obligation not to discriminate on the basis of the residence of the recipient of a deductible payment set out in Article 24(4). A similar conclusion can be reached in relation to Article 24(3) for the reasons set out below.

694. PEs are treated as separate Constituent Entities for the purpose of the GloBE rules. Deemed or notional payments from a PE to its head office (HO) that are recognised for tax purposes will be included in the definition of payments, provided they meet the general criteria for being deductible in the payer jurisdiction. This applies to payments taken into account under either the first or second step described above. Such a PE could therefore be a UTPR taxpayer and be subject to a denial of deduction where the PE is in a jurisdiction characterised as high-tax and its HO is in a jurisdiction characterised as low-tax on the basis of the ETR profile in each jurisdiction in a particular year, in the same way as described above. The UTPR will then apply, using the same mechanics as the IIR for determining the MNE's jurisdictional ETR and the amount of top-up tax allocable under the rule and applying to the PE the two step allocation key based on the PE's deductible intra-group payments (that is, the deemed payments recognised for tax purposes). The effect is the same as for payments made by a group entity that is a UTPR taxpayer.

695. Article 24(3) requires that the taxation on a PE shall not be less favourably levied in the host jurisdiction as compared to a hypothetical enterprise resident in that jurisdiction and carrying on the same activities. In applying this test, as with the other tests in Article 24, paragraph 3 of the Commentary on Article 24 MTC sets out the following general principles:

> *"The various provisions of Article 24 prevent differences in tax treatment that are solely based on certain specific grounds [...] Thus, for these paragraphs to apply, other relevant aspects must be the same. The various provisions of Article 24 use different wording to achieve that result (e.g. "in the same circumstances" in paragraphs 1 and 2; "carrying on the same activities" in paragraph 3; "similar enterprise in paragraph 5). Also, whilst the Article seeks to eliminate distinctions that are solely based on certain grounds, it is not intended to provide foreign nationals, non-residents, enterprises of other States or domestic enterprises owned and controlled by non-residents with a tax treatment that is better than that of nationals, residents or domestic enterprises owned or controlled by residents."*

696. The UTPR applies to a PE that is a UTPR Taxpayer, in the same way as to a UTPR Taxpayer that is a group entity, as a mechanism to allocate top-up tax resulting from a low-tax outcome within an MNE. The mechanism takes the form of a limitation (or denial) of the deduction of intra-group payments, or an equivalent adjustment, based on deductible payments to a low-tax entity or net related party expenditures in the relevant period. It is a rule designed to serve as a backstop to the IIR by allocating top-up tax among the Constituent Entities in an MNE Group when the IIR does not apply. The UTPR, therefore, does not

discriminate against a PE situated in a state compared with a resident entity of that state which carries on the same activities merely because it is the PE of a non-resident entity.

10.5. Effective co-ordination of the GloBE rules

697. Further guidance and mechanisms will be developed to ensure consistent, comprehensive and coherent application of the IIR and UTPR, and effective overall coordination of their application across multiple jurisdictions. This will include model legislation and guidance together with a multilateral review process as well as the exploration of a multilateral convention containing the key elements of the IIR and UTPR.

698. Further consideration will be given to whether it would be appropriate for jurisdictions to agree to stagger the implementation of the rules, allowing the IIR to come into effect first and only activating the UTPR after a specified number of years following the finalisation of Pillar Two.

10.5.1. Model legislation and guidance

699. To enhance consistency and improve rule co-ordination, model legislation will be developed setting out the detailed rules for the IIR and UTPR. The model legislation will serve as a template that jurisdictions could use as the basis for domestic legislation.

700. Furthermore, as jurisdictions move into the implementation stage, questions of interpretation may arise. In the interest of consistent implementation and certainty for both tax administrations and taxpayers, the Inclusive Framework on BEPS will develop co-ordinated guidance to respond to those questions. This is similar to the approach used in connection with the implementation of BEPS Action 13.

701. Work on model legislation for the IIR and UTPR will proceed in parallel to the work on drafting the STTR and SOR.

10.5.2. Multilateral review process

702. To simplify both the compliance with the UTPR and the administration of the rule in instances where the UTPR should not apply, there is a need for a system that allows an MNE Group to certify that Constituent Entities of the MNE are parented in a jurisdiction which has implemented an IIR is in line with the GloBE requirements.

703. The determination of whether a jurisdiction's IIR is in line with GloBE can be facilitated through a multilateral review process. The multilateral process for determining whether a jurisdiction has introduced an IIR in line with GloBE requirements would be a collective assessment and would result in publication of an agreed compilation of jurisdictions that had implemented an IIR consistent with the rules contained in this Pillar Two Blueprint. The model legislation and guidance will serve as a consistent set of guidelines on what constitutes a Pillar Two-compliant IIR, and will form the basis of the multilateral review process.[7]

704. Separately, following implementation of the IIR and UTPR in jurisdictions' domestic law, Inclusive Framework on BEPS members will consider undertaking a general review of the operation of the GloBE rules to ensure that they are working as intended. This would be linked to the process that allows Inclusive Framework on BEPS members to consider whether the way the rules operate in a particular context "results in material competitive distortions in the application of the GloBE rules".[8] In the meantime, where Inclusive Framework on BEPS members identify specific issues or risks, the Inclusive Framework on BEPS could develop further guidance to address these. A multilateral review process will seek to minimise the resource burdens on tax administrations engaged in this exercise.

10.5.3. Multilateral convention

705. Although it is not a prerequisite, a multilateral convention would be the only means to enshrine rule co-ordination in a legally binding form. Inclusive Framework on BEPS Members will therefore develop provisions that could be included in a new multilateral convention and that would be designed to ensure consistency, certainty and co-ordination in the application and operation of the IIR and UTPR. This would supplement the model legislation, guidance and multilateral review process with a legal overlay that underpins the political agreement on Pillar Two.

706. The provisions could contain the key elements and high-level principles of the GloBE rules that are necessary to ensure consistent and coordinated application across multiple jurisdictions, in particular rule order and the top-down approach for the IIR. They could also contain the key design elements of the GloBE rules that require common defined terms, including tax base, definition of covered taxes, jurisdictional blending approach, and the allocation rules for the UTPR. The model legislation would contain the detailed rules for the IIR and UTPR, which would sit alongside the multilateral convention as a source of further guidance and interpretation.

707. Unlike the MLI used to implement the tax treaty related BEPS measures, the provisions would not seek to modify existing treaty provisions. Instead, the provisions could be included in a new multilateral convention, which would be a standalone international public law instrument designed specifically for the purposes of ensuring consistent, coordinated and comprehensive application of the GloBE rules, and which would coexist with the existing tax treaty network. It may also be possible to include the GloBE provisions in the new multilateral instrument considered under Pillar One, which could also have the benefit of setting out the interaction between Pillar One and Pillar Two.[9] Consideration could also be given to including the STTR and SOR in this new multilateral instrument.

708. A multilateral convention could also confirm the compatibility of the GloBE rules with existing double tax treaties providing further certainty for the operation of the GloBE rules. Furthermore it could contain exchange of information and dispute resolution mechanisms (see Section 10.6.2).

10.6. Dispute prevention and resolution

709. Ensuring tax certainty through dispute prevention and resolution mechanisms is a key component of Pillar Two. There are a number of tools within the existing international tax framework to mitigate the risks of a taxpayer potentially being exposed to double taxation.

10.6.1. STTR and SOR

710. The STTR and the SOR are treaty rules that could be incorporated into existing tax treaties. Therefore, they would benefit from the existing dispute resolution mechanisms in the relevant tax treaties. In accordance with the BEPS Action 14 Minimum Standard, all treaties involving the members of the Inclusive Framework on BEPS should include a MAP article that is in line with Article 25(1-3) of the OECD Model Tax Convention (OECD, 2017[8]). Therefore, a mutual agreement procedure could be initiated in case a taxpayer would consider that one jurisdiction has applied the STTR or the SOR in a way that resulted or will result in taxation is not in accordance with the tax treaty.

10.6.2. GloBE rules (IIR and UTPR)

711. The IIR and UTPR are new rules that would be incorporated into the domestic law of jurisdictions. The IIR and UTPR have been designed in a way to minimise the scope for disputes concerning their application across multiple jurisdictions primarily because of the rule order and the binary way in which they operate (i.e. the UTPR should not apply in situations where the low-tax Constituent Entity is controlled, directly or indirectly by a foreign Constituent Entity that is subject to an IIR which has been implemented in accordance with the GloBE rules). Other design features of the GloBE rules that will help to minimise

disputes include the application of the IIR at a single Parent level and the mechanism for identifying those jurisdictions that have implemented an IIR in line with the requirements of the GloBE rules as well as the standard mechanism for the MNE to certify that it is subject to these rules.[10]

712. In addition, the UTPR has been designed in a way to minimise the scope for disputes since (i) as a backstop, the UTPR is only expected to be applied in a limited number of situations and (ii) the UTPR calculation and allocation rules are largely mechanical and less subject to interpretation than other rules allocating taxing rights (such as transfer pricing rules). Furthermore, the development of model legislation and guidance together with the development of a multilateral legal instrument as well as standardised returns will help to prevent disputes arising by facilitating consistent application of the GloBE rules and multilateral working by tax administrations.[11]

713. If an inconsistent application of the GloBE rules would nevertheless result in a taxpayer potentially being exposed to double taxation, then there are a number of tools within the existing international tax framework to mitigate these risks. First, jurisdictions can rely on the Convention on Mutual Administrative Assistance in Tax Matters ("MAAC") to exchange information.[12] Furthermore, in the situations where a tax administration considers reassessing the UTPR return filed by the taxpayer in its jurisdiction, it could be required to inform or consult with other jurisdictions or to initiate simultaneous tax examinations across several jurisdictions potentially affected by the reassessment of the UTPR return.[13] The legal framework for simultaneous tax examinations is provided for in the MAAC.[14] Simultaneous tax examinations have proven to be an effective tool to ensure the right amount of tax is paid while minimising the risk of double taxation (OECD, 2019[13]).

714. Furthermore, in case a jurisdiction reassesses the UTPR return filed by the taxpayer, and this results in double taxation for the taxpayer (for example, because it affects the top-up tax that was allocated to another jurisdiction), a mutual agreement procedure could be initiated under existing treaties. For that purpose, competent authorities of the relevant jurisdictions could rely on the provision contained in Article 25(3), second sentence of the OECD Model Tax Convention (OECD, 2017[8]), which allows them to consult together for the elimination of double taxation in cases that are not provided for in the Convention. This would require, however, that the jurisdictions involved in the double taxation have entered into a tax treaty with each other, and that they have the authority to resolve the case, which may not be the case for all jurisdictions involved.

715. In addition, the Inclusive Framework on BEPS will also explore the development of a multilateral convention which could then also contain provisions for dispute prevention and resolution concerning the application of the GloBE rules as well as provisions for exchange of information between tax administrations – reflecting that ensuring effective compliance with the UTPR and IIR will require tax administrations to have access to information on constituent entities that are outside of the control of local resident companies (see Section 10.5.3). Further consideration could also be given as to whether this convention could be combined with the instrument that is under consideration for the purposes of Pillar One.

References

OECD (2020), *Tax Challenges Arising From Digitalisation – Report on the Pillar One Blueprint: Inclusive Framework on BEPS*, OECD Publishing, Paris. [5]

OECD (2019), *Joint Audit 2019 – Enhancing Tax Co-operation and Improving Tax Certainty: Forum on Tax Administration*, OECD Publishing, Paris, https://dx.doi.org/10.1787/17bfa30d-en. [4]

OECD (2019), *Programme of Work to Develop a Consensus Solution to the Tax Challenges Arising from the Digitalisation of the Economy, OECD/G20 Inclusive Framework on BEPS*, OECD Publishing, Paris, https://www.oecd.org/tax/beps/programme-of-work-to-develop-a-consensus-solution-to-the-tax-challenges-arising-from-the-digitalisation-of-the-economy.pdf. [1]

OECD (2017), *Model Tax Convention on Income and on Capital*, OECD Publisher, Paris, https://doi.org/10.1787/mtc_cond-2017-en. [3]

OECD (2016), *Multilateral Convention to Implement Tax Treaty Related Measures to Prevent Base Erosion and Profit Shifting*, OECD Publishing, Paris, https://www.oecd.org/tax/treaties/multilateral-convention-to-implement-tax-treaty-related-measures-to-prevent-BEPS.pdf. [2]

OECD, C. (2011), *The Multilateral Convention on Mutual Administrative Assistance in Tax Matters*, OECD Publishing, Paris, https://dx.doi.org/10.1787/9789264115606-en. [6]

Notes

[1] See Section 4.2.1.

[2] See Section 3.3.2.

[3] See Section 3.4.2.

[4] See Section 3.4.

[5] See Section 4.2.1.

[6] For the situation where no controlling Parent entity can apply the IIR, see above Section 6.3.1.

[7] Parallel with this process, tax administrations that have implemented an IIR could agree on simplified risk assessment procedures that could be applied in determining compliance with the IIR in each jurisdiction. Options for development of simplified risk assessment procedures are discussed further in Chapter 5. These simple procedures could also include a mechanism for demonstrating that the effective tax rate in the parent jurisdiction for GloBE purposes was above the agreed minimum rate.

[8] See the discussion on *'Other generally accepted financial accounting standards'* in Section 3.3.3.

[9] See Section 10.2.2. *Public international law implementation* of the Pillar One Blueprint (OECD, 2020[16]).

[10] See Section 7.8 on the Compliance and administration of the UTPR.

[11] See also Section 7.8.2 about certification mechanisms and standardised returns for the purpose of the UTPR. Further work could explore whether standardised returns could also be developed for the purpose of the IIR. In addition, as model legislation and guidance are developed, further technical work will be undertaken to explore potential simplification options associated with the exchange of the relevant certifications and standardised returns.

[12] The Convention on Mutual Administrative Assistance in Tax Matters as Amended by the 2010 Protocol (OECD, 2011[17]) (the MAAC) is a multilateral treaty aimed at assisting countries to better enforce their tax laws by providing an international legal framework for exchanging information and co-operating in tax matters with a view to countering international tax evasion and avoidance. As of June 2020, there are 137 participating jurisdictions in the MAAC.

[13] Simultaneous tax examinations refer to an arrangement between two or more tax administrations to examine simultaneously, each in its own territory, the tax affairs of a person or persons in which they have a common or related interest, with a view to exchanging any relevant information which they so obtain.

[14] Under the MAAC, two or more jurisdictions may consult together for the purposes of determining cases and procedures for a simultaneous tax examination (Article 8). One jurisdiction may also request its competent authority to be present during tax examinations that occur in another jurisdiction (Article 9).

Annex A. Examples

Chapter 2 Flow Chart and Example

Flow Chart 2.2.2.

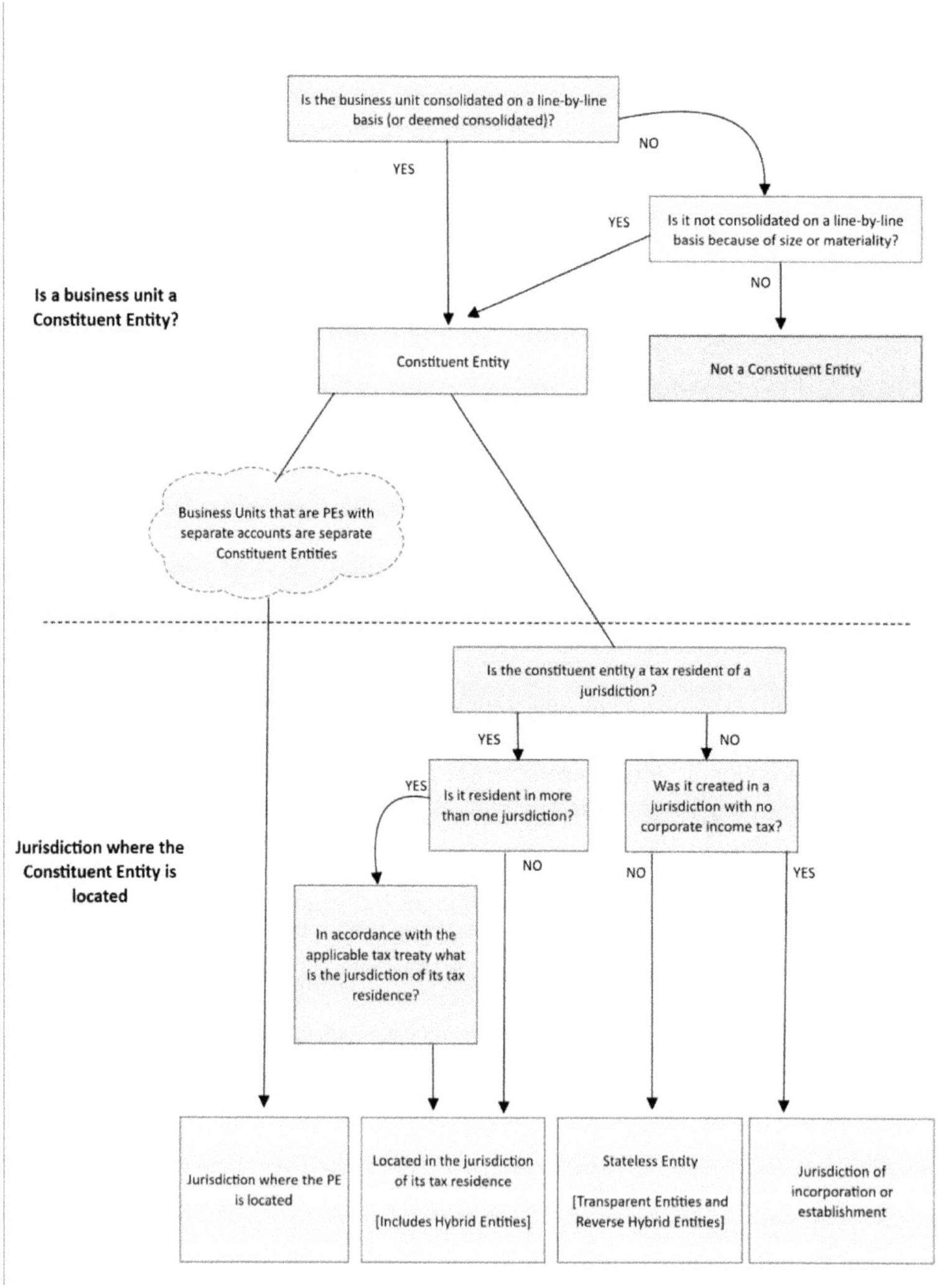

Example 2.4.3. Calculating consolidated revenue threshold for an MNE Group held by an Excluded Entity.

Facts

1. FUND is an investment entity that does not consolidate the accounts of its investments under IFRS 10. FUND is the majority shareholder of Hold Co 1 and Hold Co 2. These companies are the parent entities of two different MNE Groups whose consolidated revenue is EUR 500 million each. Separate consolidated financial statements are prepared for MNE Group 1 and MNE Group 2.

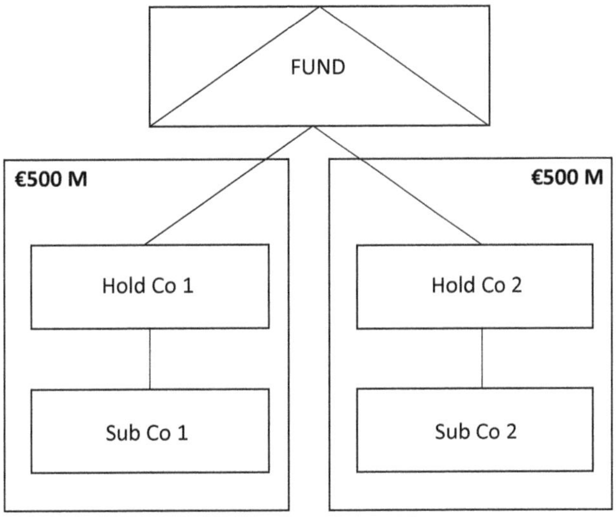

Question

2. Are MNE Group 1 and MNE Group 2 in the scope of the GloBE rules?

Answer

3. Both groups are out of the scope of the GloBE rules.

Analysis

4. MNE Group 1 and MNE Group 2 are considered to be separate groups because FUND is not required to consolidate with either of them on a line-by-line basis. Therefore, the consolidated revenue of MNE Group 1 and MNE Group 2 should be computed separately for purposes of the EUR 750 million threshold. The consolidated revenue of each MNE Group, i.e., MNE Group 1 and MNE Group 2, is below EUR 750 million.

5. If FUND were an entity required to consolidate Hold Co 1, Hold Co 2 and their subsidiaries on a line-by-line basis, but was an investment fund that fell within the definition of Excluded Entity under the GloBE rules then Hold Co 1 and Hold Co 2 would be treated as separate UPEs and, accordingly the computation of the threshold would be applied apply to the MNE Groups parented by Hold Co 1 and Hold Co 2.

Chapter 3 - Examples

Example 3.2.5- 1A.

Covered Taxes – Zakat

Facts

1. The Zakat levied on corporations by the Kingdom of Saudi Arabia is an example of a tax on both income and equity. The Zakat is levied at 2.5% on a Saudi's share of a resident company (also applies to citizens of Gulf Cooperation Council countries) but since it is imposed on income and equity it results in a higher effective rate. Corporate income tax is levied at 20% on a non-Saudi's share of a resident company or a non-resident's income from a permanent establishment in Saudi Arabia and a higher corporate income tax rate is imposed on Saudi working in the oil and gas industries. The corporate Zakat could be considered as an alternative to corporate income tax levied on a different basis.

2. The Zakat base is the total of the corporate taxpayer's current year's income and equity as calculated for financial accounting purposes after adjustments for certain items. In general terms these two elements of the Zakat base are determined as follows:

   a. The starting point for calculating the income portion of the Zakat base begins with the company's annual profit or loss as calculated for financial reporting purposes. This profit or loss is then adjusted by the changes to certain provisions or reserves, such as bad debts.

   b. The starting point for calculating the equity portion of the Zakat base begins by:

      i. calculating shareholder equity as determined under IFRS (excluding current year profit and any distributions); and

      ii. adjusting for the balance of certain provisions, including bad debts.

This amount is then increased by long-term liabilities and decreased by the cost of certain deductible assets to arrive at an adjusted net equity amount.

Question

3. Does the Zakat meet the definition of covered taxes under the GloBE?

Answer

4. The Zakat operates as a tax on income or equity or both and is therefore properly considered a covered tax for the purposes of the GloBE rules.

Analysis

5. Both components of the Zakat base meet the definition of a covered tax under the GloBE:

   (a) The first element of the Zakat base is on the company's income (i.e. adjusted profit or loss for the year). The adjustments for provisions and reserves is consistent with (but not a requirement of) the definition of an income tax for the purposes of the GloBE rules.

   (b) The second component of the Zakat base is a measure of adjusted equity. The equity component of the Zakat base is determined under financial accounting rules adjusted for certain provisions. This amount is then subject to a further adjustment that decreases the equity portion of the Zakat base to the extent that the company's deductible assets exceed its long-term debt.

6. Although this latter adjustment may have the effect of excluding a portion of the shareholder equity from the tax base, this feature of the Zakat does not disqualify it from being treated as a tax on the equity

of the corporation. The extent to which a corporation's liabilities are taken into account in determining equity under accounting and local law are a matter of domestic tax policy design which do not impact on the intended outcomes under the GloBE rules.

7. A company's liability for Zakat is calculated on the total of adjusted income and adjusted equity base or only on the income base (where the equity component is negative) or only the equity base (when the corporation has an operating loss). Thus, a profitable company will always be liable for Zakat on its income while a corporation that has an operating loss for the year will nonetheless be subject to Zakat on the adjusted equity portion of the Zakat base.

Example 3.3.6A. Distribution taxes modification with recapture.

Facts

1. The following example illustrates the methodology for addressing distribution taxes. X earns 100 of income in Year 1, 150 of income in Year 2, and 200 of income in Year 3. X distributes 50 of income in Year 3. Assume that the distribution tax rate in X's jurisdiction is 20%, the minimum tax rate is 12%, and the specified period for payment of distribution tax liability is two years.[1]

Question

2. How much of the accrued distribution tax is recaptured in Year 3?

Answer

3. Because X only paid 10 of distribution tax within the relevant period, 2 of accrued distribution tax is recaptured in Year 3.

Analysis

4. In Year 1, X accrues 12 of tax for GloBE purposes, which is the minimum tax on 100 of income. Accordingly, X's ETR for Year 1 is 12% and X's income is not subject to a top-up tax under the GloBE proposal. Similarly, in Year 2, X accrues 18 of tax for GloBE purposes on 150 of income and incurs no top-up tax liability. In Year 3, X accrues 24 of tax for GloBE purposes on 200 of income and X paid 10 of distribution tax in Year 3. As demonstrated in the table below, the 10 of distribution tax paid by X in Year 3 reduces the Year 1 outstanding balance of accrued minimum tax from 12 to 2. The 2 remaining balance of accrued minimum tax from Year 1 is treated as a reduction to the tax expense in the numerator of the ETR fraction in Year 3. Thus, X's ETR for Year 3 is 11% ([24 accrued minimum tax – 2 recapture of accrued minimum tax] / 200 GloBE tax base). X's GloBE tax liability for Year 3 is 2 ([200 GloBE tax base x 12%] - 22 tax expense), which equals the recaptured accrued minimum tax.

	Year 1	Year 2	Year 3
Income	100	150	200
Minimum Tax (12% tax rate)	12	18	24
Distribution tax paid	0	0	10
Distribution tax paid in excess of accrued tax outstanding balance (A)	0	0	0
Accrued tax for GloBE purposes (B)	12	18	24
Recapture of accrued tax in preceding tax year (C)	0	0	(2)
Total tax expense for ETR computation purposes (A + B – C)	12	18	22
Top-up tax (Min tax – Total tax expense for ETR computation purposes)	0	0	2

Example 3.3.6B. Distribution taxes modification with excess taxes paid.

Facts

1. Assume the same facts as in Example 3.7.4A, except that X distributed 200 in Year 3.

Question

2. How much distribution tax is accrued for purposes of GloBE in Year 3?

Answer

3. X accrues only 24 of distribution tax for GloBE purposes in Year 3.

Analysis

4. As demonstrated in the table below, X would accrue 14 of minimum tax that when added to the 10 of excess distribution tax paid in Year 3 would produce an ETR equal to the 12% minimum tax rate on 200 of income and no top-up tax liability.

5. The distribution tax of 40 (200 x 20%) would have eliminated the outstanding balances of accrued minimum tax for Year 1 (12) and Year 2 (18), and the excess (10) would have been included in the tax expense and numerator of the ETR fraction in Year 3. The minimum tax liability on 200 of income in Year 3 would be 24

	Year 1	Year 2	Year 3
Income	100	150	200
Minimum Tax (12% tax rate)	12	18	24
Distribution tax paid	0	0	40
Distribution tax paid in excess of accrued tax outstanding balance (A)	0	0	10
Accrued tax for GloBE purposes (B)	12	18	14
Recapture of accrued tax in preceding tax year (C)	0	0	0
Total tax expense for ETR computation purposes (A + B – C)	12	18	24
Top-up tax (Min tax – Total tax expense for ETR computation purposes)	0	0	0

Example 3.4.2A. Jurisdictional blending: Permanent establishments – assignment of income and taxes

Facts

1. Corp A (resident in jurisdiction A) is a Constituent Entity of an MNE Group whose Ultimate Parent Entity is tax resident in Jurisdiction X. Corp A has a permanent establishment located in jurisdiction B. Corp A has EUR 100 of profit before tax. Jurisdiction A exempts the income of foreign permanent establishments. Pursuant to the tax laws of jurisdiction B, Corp A is required to determine the portion of its income attributable to its permanent establishment located in jurisdiction B. Corp A determines that EUR 20 of its profit before tax is attributable to the permanent establishment and pays EUR 5 of tax in jurisdiction B on this basis.

Question

2. To which jurisdictions are the income of permanent establishments and the taxes on that income assigned?

Answer

3. Under the rule, EUR 20 of profit before tax would be allocated to jurisdiction B. Any tax on that income is assigned to jurisdiction B.

Analysis

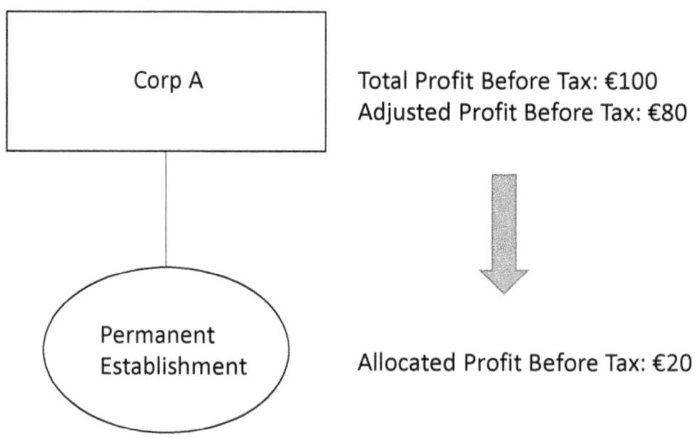

Example 3.4.2B. Jurisdictional blending: assignment of withholding taxes

Facts

1. Corp A (resident in jurisdiction A) owns Corp B (resident in jurisdiction B) and Corp C (resident in jurisdiction C). In Year 1, Corp B makes a EUR 100 royalty payment to Corp A. Jurisdiction B applies a 10% withholding tax to the payment. Also in Year 1, Corp C earns EUR 100 of profit before tax and pays EUR 20 of tax in jurisdiction C and pays a dividend to Corp A.2 Under the laws of jurisdiction A, Corp A includes the intra-group dividend in its taxable income, and after taking into account a foreign tax credit for the tax paid in jurisdiction C, Corp A pays EUR 5 of residual tax in jurisdiction A related to the intra-group dividend.

Question

2. To which jurisdictions are withholding taxes assigned?

Answer

3. Under the rule, EUR 10 of withholding tax is assigned to jurisdiction A and EUR 5 of tax is assigned to jurisdiction C.

Analysis

4. Each constituent entity's income is assigned to its tax jurisdiction of residence. The EUR 10 of withholding tax paid to jurisdiction B on the royalty received from Corp B is assigned to jurisdiction A because it is tax paid in respect of income assigned to jurisdiction A. The EUR 5 of tax paid in jurisdiction A with respect to the dividend from Corp C is assigned to jurisdiction C because it is paid in respect of income that was assigned to jurisdiction C.

Example 3.4.2C. Jurisdictional blending: CFC rule – assignment of taxes

Facts

1. Corp A (resident in jurisdiction A) wholly owns Corp B (resident in jurisdiction B). Corp B earns EUR 100 of profit before tax and pays EUR 5 of tax in jurisdiction B. Under the CFC rules of jurisdiction A, Corp A includes EUR 100 of income of Corp B computed pursuant to the jurisdiction A CFC rules in its taxable income, with a foreign tax credit for taxes paid in jurisdiction B. Assume the result is that residual CFC rule tax is paid in jurisdiction A.

Question

2. To which jurisdiction are CFC B's income and taxes on that income assigned?

Answer

3. Under the rule, the CFC regime tax paid in jurisdiction A is assigned to jurisdiction B, which results in the taxes being assigned to the same jurisdiction as the underlying income.

Analysis

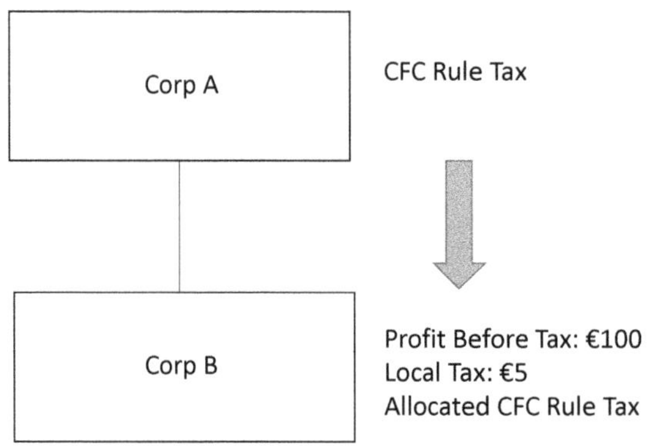

Example 3.4.2D. Jurisdictional blending: Hybrid entity – assignment of taxes

Facts

1. Corp A (resident in jurisdiction A) wholly owns Hybrid Entity B (resident in jurisdiction B). Hybrid Entity B is a corporation that is tax resident in jurisdiction B, but is tax transparent for purposes of jurisdiction A. Hybrid Entity B earns EUR 100 of profit before tax and pays EUR 20 of tax in jurisdiction B. Jurisdiction A does not exempt Corp A's share of the income of Hybrid Entity B and therefore Corp A includes the income of Hybrid Entity B in its taxable income, which is taxed in jurisdiction A less a foreign tax credit for taxes paid in jurisdiction B. Assume the result is that Corp A pays EUR 5 of residual tax in jurisdiction A.

Question

2. To which jurisdiction are Hybrid Entity B's income and taxes on that income assigned?

Answer

3. Hybrid Entity B's income is assigned to its tax jurisdiction of residence, jurisdiction B. The EUR 5 of tax paid in jurisdiction A with respect to the income of Hybrid Entity B is assigned to jurisdiction B.

Analysis

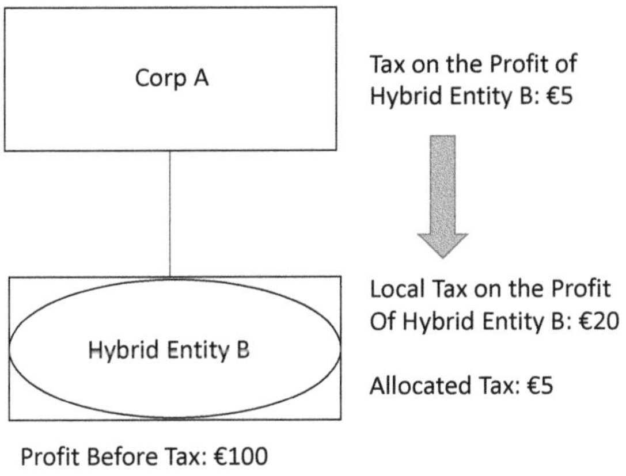

Example 3.4.2E. Jurisdictional blending: Reverse-hybrid entity – assignment of taxes

Facts

1. Corp A (resident in jurisdiction A) wholly owns Reverse-Hybrid B (organised in jurisdiction B). Reverse-Hybrid B is treated as tax transparent for purposes of jurisdiction B and has no jurisdiction of tax residence. However, Reverse-Hybrid B is not tax transparent for purposes of jurisdiction A. Reverse-Hybrid B earns EUR 100 of profit before tax in Year 1. Jurisdiction A imposes EUR 5 of net basis tax on a EUR 100 dividend paid from Reverse-Hybrid B to Corp A in Year 1. Jurisdiction B imposes no tax on the income of Reverse-Hybrid B or the distribution to Corp A.

Question

2. To which jurisdiction are reverse-Hybrid B's income and taxes on that income assigned?

Answer

3. Reverse-Hybrid B's income is assigned to stateless because it has no jurisdiction of tax residence and its owner's tax jurisdiction does not treat the entity as tax transparent. The EUR 5 of tax paid in jurisdiction A related to the underlying income earned by Reverse-Hybrid B is assigned to stateless.

Analysis

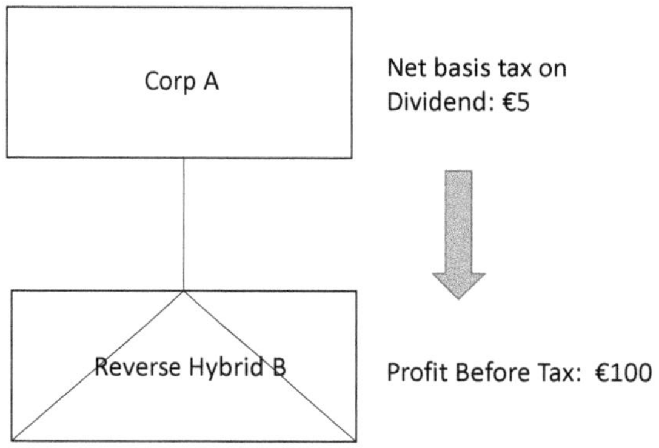

Example 3.4.2F. Jurisdictional blending: Partially tax transparent & partially hybrid entity– assignment of income

Facts

1. Corp A (resident in jurisdiction A), Corp B (resident in jurisdiction B), and Corp C (resident in jurisdiction C), are constituent entities of MNE Group ABC. They each own equal shares of an entity, Partnership D. Partnership D is organized under the laws of jurisdiction D and is treated as a tax transparent entity by jurisdictions A, B, and D. Corp A and Corp B do not have a permanent establishment in jurisdiction D as a result of their ownership interest in Partnership D or otherwise. Corp A and Corp B are subject to tax in their respective jurisdictions on their share of Partnership D's income. Jurisdiction C does not treat Partnership D as tax transparent and Corp C does not have a permanent establishment in jurisdiction D. Partnership D earns EUR120 of profit in Year 1 and is not subject to tax in jurisdiction D.

Question

2. To which jurisdictions are the income of Partnership D and the taxes paid in respect of that income assigned?

Answer

3. Corp A and Corp B's share of Partnership D's income is assigned to their respective jurisdictions. Covered taxes paid by Corp A and Corp B on such income is assigned to jurisdiction A and jurisdiction B, respectively. Corp C's share of Partnerships D's income is assigned to the stateless jurisdiction.

Analysis

4. Partnership D is a stateless entity because it has no tax jurisdiction of residence. However, Partnership D's income is allocated to some of its owners in accordance with the partnership agreement because Corp A's and Corp B's tax jurisdiction treats Partnership D as a tax transparent entity. Accordingly, Corp A and Corp B are each allocated EUR 40 of profit before tax. The remainder of Partnership D's income – Corp C's EUR 40 share – is allocated to the stateless jurisdiction. Corp A and Corp B are subject to tax in Year 1 in their tax jurisdiction of residence on their allocable share of the partnership income. The tax paid by each partner on its share of the partnership income is assigned to that partner's tax jurisdiction of residence. Corp C is not subject to tax on its allocable share of the partnership income in Year 1. Therefore, no covered taxes are assigned to Jurisdiction D in Year 1.

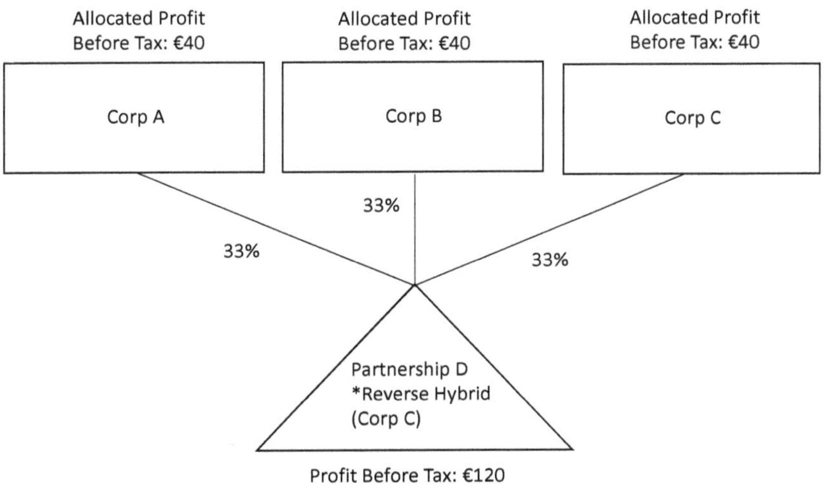

Example 3.4.2G. Jurisdictional blending: Partially tax transparent & permanent establishments of its owners

Facts

1. The facts are the same as Example 3.4.2F, except that Partnership D is managed and controlled in jurisdiction D and regularly conducts business operations in jurisdiction D. Partnership D is treated as a tax transparent entity by jurisdictions A, B, and D. Under the law of jurisdiction D, Corp A, Corp B, and Corp C each have a permanent establishment in jurisdiction D and are subject to jurisdiction D's income tax on their share of Partnership D's income. In addition, Corp A and Corp B are subject to tax in their respective jurisdictions on their share of Partnership D's income. Jurisdiction C does not treat Partnership D as tax transparent. Partnership D earns EUR 120 of profit in Year 1.

Question

2. To which jurisdictions are the income of Partnership D and the taxes paid in respect of that income assigned?

Answer

3. The permanent establishments of Corp A, Corp B, and Corp C are treated as Constituent Entities (PE-Constituent Entities) of MNE Group ABC. Each PE-Constituent Entity's share of Partnership D's income is assigned to jurisdiction D. Covered taxes paid by the PE-Constituent Entities are assigned to jurisdiction D. Covered taxes paid by Corp A and Corp B on their shares of Partnership D's income are also assigned to jurisdiction D.

Analysis

4. Partnership D is a stateless entity because it has no tax jurisdiction of residence. However, Partnership D's income is allocated to Constituent Entities that are permanent establishments of its owners under the law of jurisdiction D. Jurisdiction D allocates the income among the permanent establishments of Corp A, Corp, B and Corp C accordance with the partnership agreement. Accordingly, each PE-Constituent Entity is allocated EUR 40 of profit before tax. The jurisdiction D income tax is allocated to jurisdiction D. In addition, Corp A and Corp B are subject to tax in Year 1 in their tax jurisdiction of residence on their allocable share of the partnership income. The tax paid by each partner on its share of the partnership income is assigned to jurisdiction D.

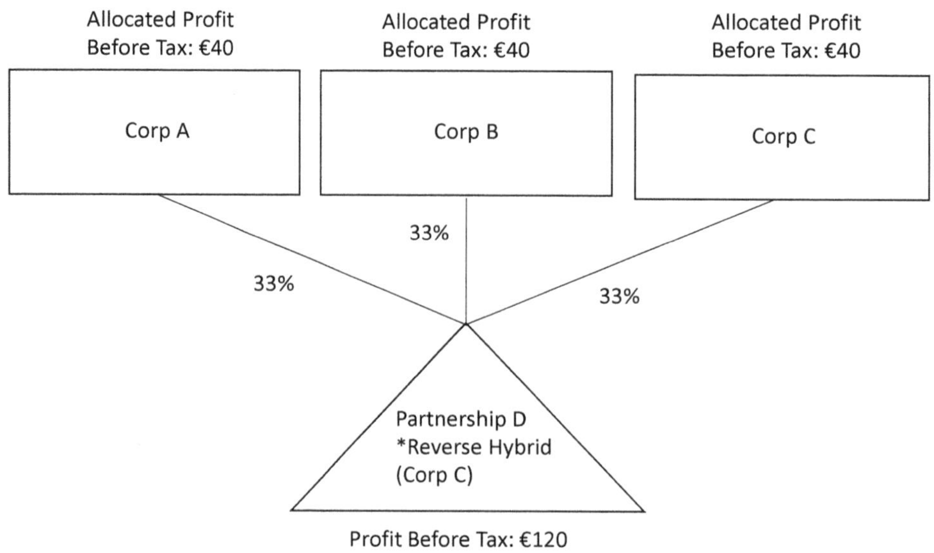

Chapter 4 – Examples

Example 4.2.1A. Local tax carry-forward

Facts

1. The following example illustrates the application of the local tax carry-forward rule where there was no IIR tax paid by the shareholder in a previous period. Assume that MNE-1 owns Subsidiary A, which is subject to tax in Jurisdiction A, and that the minimum tax rate is 10%. Subsidiary A's GloBE tax base is 1,000 in each of Year 1, Year 2, and Year 3. Subsidiary A pays 140 of tax in Year 1, 80 of tax in Year 2, and 50 of tax in Year 3. MNE-1 has never paid IIR tax in respect of Jurisdiction A.

Subsidiary A	Year 1	Year 2	Year 3
Income	1,000	1,000	1,000
Minimum tax (10%)	100	100	100
Local tax paid (Jurisdiction A)	140	80	50
Excess taxes	40	0	0
Local tax carry-forward used	0	20	20
Local tax carry forward remaining	40	20	0
GloBE Tax (top up to 10%)	0	0	30

Question

2. What is the GloBE tax liability and the GloBE tax carry-forward in Years 1-3?

Answer

3. The GloBE tax carry-forward at the end of Year 1 is 40, the end of Year 2 is 20 and the end of Year 3 is 0. The GloBE tax liability for Year 1 is 0, for Year 2 is 0, and for Year 3 is 30.

Analysis

4. As shown above, Subsidiary A paid excess taxes of 40 in Year 1, and MNE-1 creates a Year 1 local tax carry-forward in that amount. In Year 2, Subsidiary A paid less than the minimum tax on its GloBE tax base and used 20 of the local tax carry-forward to increase the tax expense in Jurisdiction A to the minimum rate. MNE-1 reduced its Year 1 local tax carry-forward by the amount used in Year 2. In Year 3, Subsidiary A increased its tax expense in Jurisdiction A by the remaining balance of the Year 1 local tax carry-forward to 70. However, even after adding the carry-forward to the Year 3 tax paid, the ETR computed for Subsidiary A's GloBE tax base is below the minimum tax rate (70 tax / 1,000 GloBE tax base = 7% ETR). Therefore, MNE-1 is subject to 30 of top-up tax (100 minimum tax – 70 tax expense) in respect of Jurisdiction A in Year 3.

Example 4.2.1B. IIR tax credit

Facts

1. The following example illustrates the application of the IIR tax credit. Assume that MNE-2 owns one subsidiary, Subsidiary A, in Jurisdiction A, and the agreed minimum tax rate is 10%. At the beginning of Year 4, MNE-2 had paid 100 of IIR tax in Year 2 and IIR tax of 20 in Year 3 in respect of Jurisdiction A. Prior to Year 4, Subsidiary A had never had excess taxes. In Year 4, Subsidiary A had 1,000 of income and paid 275 of tax in Jurisdiction A. In Year 5, Subsidiary A had 1,000 of income and paid 20 of tax in Jurisdiction A.

Subsidiary A	Year 2	Year 3	Year 4	Year 5
Income	1,000	1,000	1,000	1,000
Local tax paid (Jurisdiction A)	0	80	275	20
Minimum tax (10%)	100	100	100	100
IIR Tax (top up to 10%)	100	20	0	25
Excess taxes (local tax – min tax)	0	0	175	0
Local tax carry forward (excess tax – IIR tax credit created for year – excess taxes used to reduce top-up tax)	0	0	55	0
IIR tax credit used	0	0	0	25
IIR tax paid (aggregate)	100	120	0	0
IIR tax credit (aggregate)	0	0	120	95

Question

2. What is MNE-2's IIR tax credit in this scenario?

Answer

3. At the beginning of Year 6, MNE-2's IIR tax credit is 95, and its Year 4 Jurisdiction A local tax carry-forward is 0.

Analysis

4. As shown above, Subsidiary A paid 175 of taxes in excess of the minimum tax rate in Year 4. The excess taxes create IIR tax credits in respect of IIR taxes paid in years 2 and 3. The remaining 55 of excess taxes paid create a local tax carry-forward.

5. In Year 5, Subsidiary A paid 20 of IIR tax and increased its adjusted covered taxes by the 55 local tax carry-forward. Subsidiary A computed an ETR of 7.5% (i.e. below the minimum rate) and 25 of top-up tax. However, MNE-2 used its 25 of IIR tax credits to reduce the liability to 0. At the beginning of Year 6, MNE-2's local tax carry-forward is 0 and its IIR tax credits are 95.

Example 4.2.1C. Application of IIR tax credit to IIR tax arising in respect of a different jurisdiction

Facts

1. The following example illustrates how the IIR tax credit can be applied in respect of an IIR tax liability that arises in respect of a low-tax outcome in another jurisdiction. Assume that Parent is a corporation organized and subject to tax in Country A, which has adopted the GloBE proposal and the agreed minimum tax rate is 10%. Parent owns Subsidiary B in Country B and Subsidiary C in Country C. In Year 1, Subsidiary B earns 1,000 of income and pays no tax in Country B, and Subsidiary C earns 1,000 of income and pays 100 of tax in Country C. In Year 2, Subsidiary B earns 400 of income and pays 100 of tax in Country B, and Subsidiary C earns 1,000 of income and pays 20 of tax in Country C.

	Subsidiary B			Subsidiary C		
	Year 1	Year 2	Year 3	Year 1	Year 2	Year 3
Income	1,000	400	1,000	1,000	1,000	1,000
Local tax paid	0	100	100	100	20	100
Minimum tax (10%)	100	40	100	100	100	100
IIR Tax (top up to 10%)	100	0	0	0	80	0
IIR tax credit used	0	0	0	0	**60**	0
IIR Tax Paid	100	0	0	0	20	0
Excess taxes (local tax – min tax)	0	60	0	0	0	0
Local tax carry-forward (excess tax – IIR tax credit created for year)	0	0	0	0	0	0
IIR tax paid (aggregate)	100	40	40	0	20	20
IIR tax credit	0	**60**	0	0	0	0

Question

2. Can parent use an IIR tax credit arising with respect to Country B to reduce a subsequent IIR tax liability arising with respect to Country C ?

Answer

3. Yes.

Analysis

4. As shown above, Parent pays 100 of tax to Country A under the income inclusion rule in respect of income of Subsidiary B for Year 1 because the tax paid in Country B on Subsidiary B's income was below the minimum tax rate. In Year 2, Subsidiary B pays 60 of tax in Country B in excess of the minimum tax on income earned in Country B. Also in Year 2, Parent incurs 80 of income inclusion rule tax liability in respect of income earned by Subsidiary C that was subject to tax below the minimum rate.

5. At the end of Year 2, Parent creates an IIR tax credit of 60 as a result of the excess taxes paid in Year 2. Parent is eligible to use the IIR tax credit of 60 against its Country A IIR tax liability arising in respect of Country C in the same year. (The 60 IIR tax credit arising in Country B in Year 2 and used in Country C in Year 2 is highlighted in bold in the chart above.) After using the credit, Parent pays 20 of IIR tax with respect to Country C in Year 2. At the beginning of Year 3, Parent has 40 of IIR tax paid in Year 1 in respect of Country B and 20 of IIR tax paid in Year 2 in respect of Country C that has not given rise to an IIR tax credit.

Example 4.2.2A. Post-filing decrease in local tax liability.

Facts

1. The following example illustrates the application of the carry-forward adjustment approach to the treatment of post-filing decreases in local tax liability.

2. Assume that MNE1 is subject to an income inclusion rule in its jurisdiction of tax residence and owns a single entity, X Corp, that is tax resident in Jurisdiction X and that Local Tax Carry-forwards are allowed to be used to reduce the tax liability of the succeeding 10 years from the year in which they were created. X Corp's covered taxes in Jurisdiction X exceeded the minimum tax on its income by 100 in Year 1 and 80 in Year 2. Accordingly, X Corp established a Local Tax Carry-forward of 100 for Year 1 and 80 for Year 2.

3. In Year 3, X Corp initiated a refund claim with respect to 100 of tax paid to Jurisdiction X in Year 1. In Year 4, X Corp initiated a refund claim with respect to 30 of tax paid to Jurisdiction X in Year 2. In Year 6, X Corp and Jurisdiction X settled the Year 1 refund claim with a refund of 60 and Jurisdiction X refunded 30 with respect to the Year 2 refund claim. The refunds in Year 6 were a final determination of X Corp's refund claims in respect of Year 1 and Year 2. Prior to Year 6, X Corp had used 10 of its Local Tax Carry-forward from Year 1 in the computation of the Jurisdiction X ETR for a taxable year.

Question

4. What is the carry-forward adjustment in this scenario?

Answer

5. Beginning with the Year 6 ETR computation for Jurisdiction X, X Corp has 30 of Local Tax Carry-forward from Year 1 and 50 of Local Tax Carry-forward from Year 2 to increase the covered tax expense in the numerator of the ETR fraction to achieve a minimum tax rate in Jurisdiction X.

Analysis

6. The post-filing tax decreases in Jurisdiction X liability reduce X Corporation's Local Tax Carry-forwards for Year 1 and Year 2 by 60 and 30, respectively, as of the beginning of Year 6.

Example 4.2.2B. Post-filing increase in local tax liability.

Facts

1. The following example illustrates the application of the carry-forward adjustment approach to the treatment of post-filing decreases in local tax liability.

2. Assume that MNE2 is subject to an income inclusion rule in its jurisdiction of tax residence and owns a single entity, Y Corp, that is tax resident in Jurisdiction Y. In Year 1, MNE2 paid 80 IIR tax in respect of Jurisdiction Y. In Year 3, Jurisdiction Y asserted additional liability of 100 in respect of Year 1 and in Year 5, a Jurisdiction Y court determined, with finality, that Y Corp was liable for the additional 100 tax in respect of Year 1.

Question

3. What is the IIR tax credit and Local Tax Carry-forward in this scenario?

Answer

4. As of the beginning of Year 5, Y Corp first creates an IIR tax credit of 80 and then a Local Tax Carry-forward of 20 with respect to Year 1.

Analysis

5. MNE2 did not pay IIR tax in respect of Jurisdiction Y, and Y Corp did not pay excess tax in Jurisdiction Y, for any year subsequent to Year 1.

[1] The two year distribution period in the example is for illustrative purposes. The period that will apply for GloBE purposes has not yet been agreed by the Inclusive Framework.

[2] This sentence has been amended to reflect a comment made by Canada.

Chapter 6 - Examples

Example 6.1A. Computation of the ETR in cases where the UPE does not apply the IIR – High tax jurisdiction

Facts

1. The MNE Group consists of eight constituent entities located in jurisdictions A, B, C and D. Hold Co is a tax resident of Country A and is the Ultimate Parent Entity of an MNE Group subject to the GloBE rules. Hold Co owns directly the shares of B Co (tax resident in Country B), C Co (tax resident in Country C) and D Co 5 (tax resident in Country D). D Co 5 is subject to a tax rate of 5%.B Co owns the shares of D Co 1 and D Co 2 (tax residents in Country D) that are subject to a tax rate of 0%.

2. B Co owns the shares of D Co 1 and D Co 2 (tax residents in Country D) that are subject to a tax rate of 0%. C Co owns the shares of D Co 3 and D Co 4 (tax residents in Country D) that are subject to a tax rate of 25%.

3. Country B and Country C have adopted an income inclusion rule. Assume that the minimum rate is 11%.

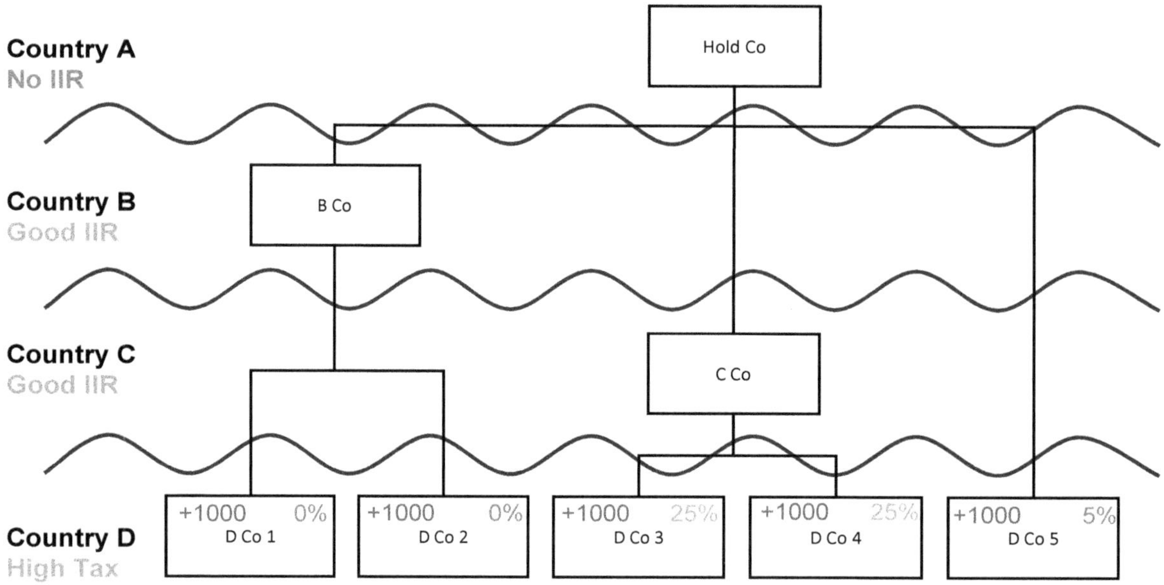

Questions

4. How should the ETR of the Constituent Entities located in Country D be computed? Should jurisdictional blending apply across all the Constituent Entities of the MNE Group, or only between the Constituent Entities controlled by the Parents applying the IIR?

5. In this case, are B Co and C Co required to apply the IIR with respect to the income earned by the Constituent Entities located in Country D?

Answers

6. The ETR is computed considering all the Constituent Entities of the MNE Group located in the same jurisdiction regardless of the Parents applying the IIR.

7. In this case, B Co and C Co are not required to apply their IIR because Country D is considered a high tax country.

Analysis

8. The ETR of the Constituent Entities of the MNE Group is computed based on a jurisdictional blending approach. Therefore, a GloBE tax liability will arise when the ETR of a jurisdiction in which the MNE Group operates is below the agreed minimum rate.

9. In this example, B Co and C Co would be required to apply the IIR under the top-down approach because Hold Co is located in a jurisdiction that has not adopted the GloBE rules. However, they are not required to apply their IIR because their subsidiaries are located in a jurisdiction with an ETR above the minimum rate.

10. In this case, the ETR of the Constituent Entities located in Country D is of 11% (55 of tax paid divided by 5,000 of profits). The computation of the ETR is not affected by the fact that the different Constituent Entities located in Country D are owned by different Parents required to apply the rule (B Co and C Co). Therefore, the ETR in Country D is not below the minimum rate.

11. If jurisdictional blending was computed depending on the Parent applying the IIR, B Co would be required to apply the IIR because its two subsidiaries (D Co 1 and D Co 2) are subject to an ETR below the minimum rate. However, jurisdictional blending takes into account all the Constituent Entities of the MNE Group located in a jurisdiction regardless of the entities under control of the Parent applying the IIR. Therefore, all the Constituent Entities located in Country D are not subject to an ETR below the minimum rate.

Example 6.1B. Computation of the ETR in cases where the UPE does not apply the IIR – Low tax jurisdiction

Facts

1. The facts are the same as Example 6.1.1A, except that income of D Co 5 is exempt from tax in Country D.

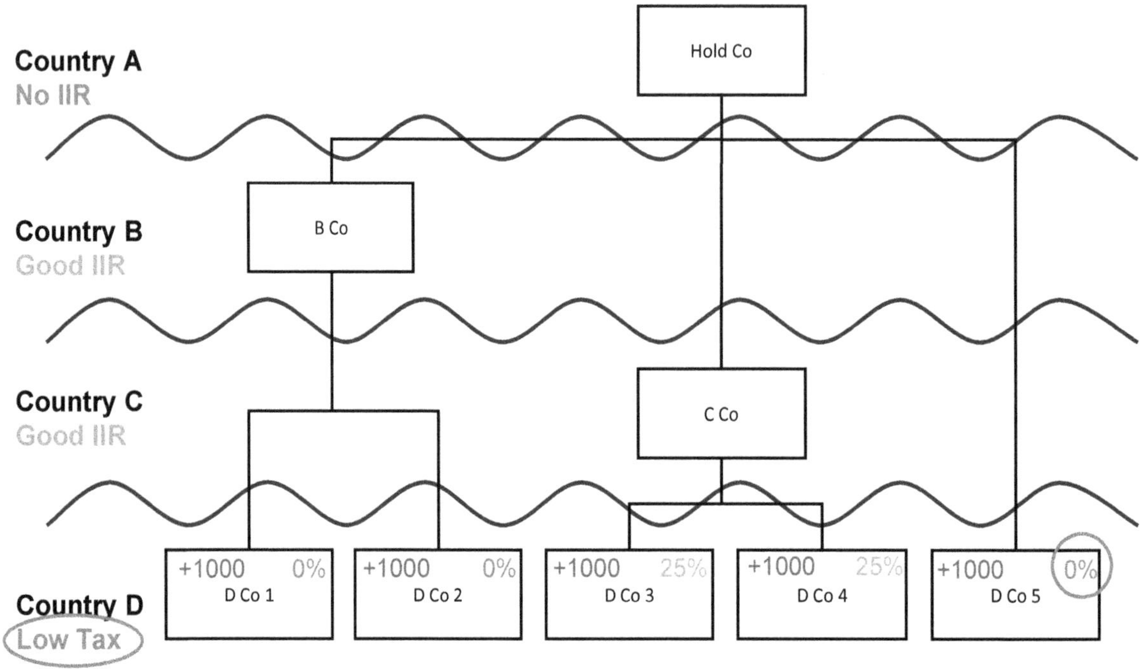

Questions

2. How should the ETR of the Constituent Entities located in Country D be computed? Should jurisdictional blending apply across all the Constituent Entities of the MNE Group, or only between the Constituent Entities controlled by the Parents applying the IIR?

3. In this case, are B Co and C Co required to apply the IIR with respect to the income earned by the Constituent Entities located in Country D?

Answers

4. The ETR is computed considering all the Constituent Entities of the MNE Group located in the same jurisdiction regardless of the Parents applying the IIR.

5. In this case, B Co and C Co are required to apply their IIR because Country D is considered a low tax country.

Analysis

6. Country D is a low tax jurisdiction because the ETR on the income of Constituent Entities located therein (500/5,000 = 10%) is below the minimum rate of 11%. Accordingly, B Co and C Co are Parents because they own equity interests in Constituent Entities located in a low-tax jurisdiction and they are not controlled by another Constituent Entity that is subject to an income inclusion rule. The top-up tax percentage is 1% (11% minimum ETR – 10% ETR). Therefore, the top-up tax allocated in respect of each Constituent Entity located in Country D is 10 (1,000 adjusted income x 1%), for a total of 50.

7. B Co and C Co are required to pay 20 each. In both cases, the Parent determines its share of the top-up tax by multiplying the top-up tax computed for each Constituent Entity by its ownership percentage of the entity (100% x 10).

8. D Co 5 is not controlled by a Parent. Therefore, the 10 of top-up tax computed in respect of D Co 5 is allocated to other Constituent Entities pursuant to the undertaxed payments rule.

Example 6.3.1A. Operation of the IIR in case of a non-controlling Parent

Facts

1. The facts are the same as Example 6.1B., except that shares of D Co 2 are owned by Hold Co (60%) and B Co (40%).

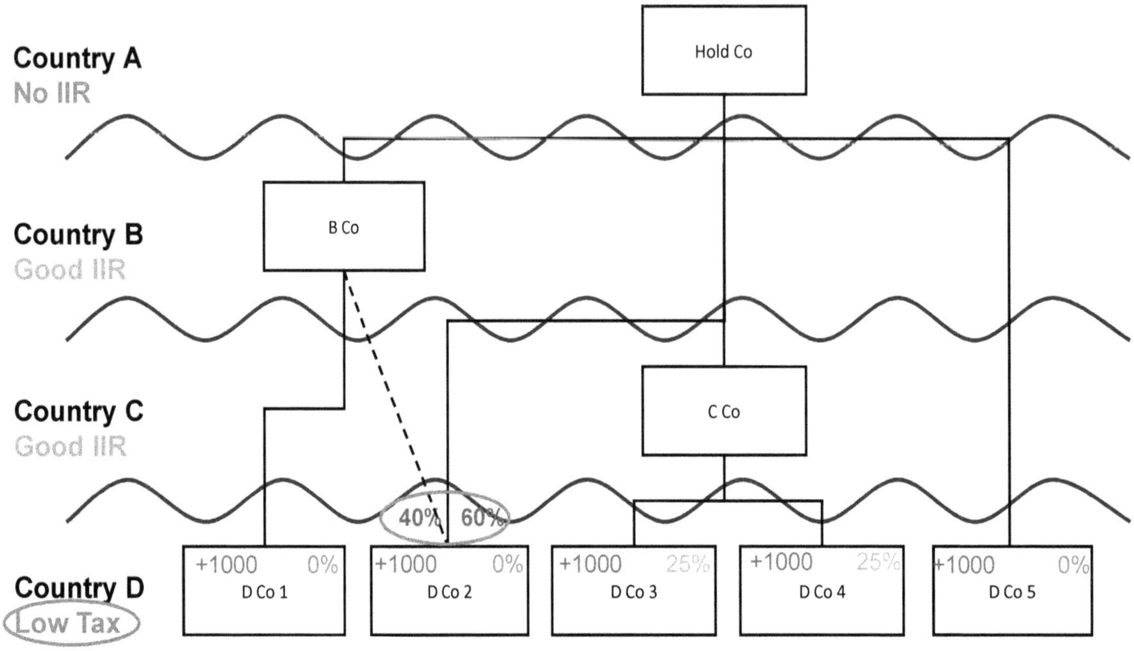

Questions

2. Are Parents required to apply the IIR to Constituent Entities that are not under their control?

3. In this case, is B Co required to apply the IIR with respect to the income of D Co 2?

Answers

4. Parents are required to apply the IIR to entities or arrangements even if they do not control them provided that they are both Constituent Entities of the same MNE Group.

5. B Co is required to apply the IIR with respect to 40% of the income of D Co.

Analysis

6. Country D is a low tax jurisdiction because the Constituent Entities located in such jurisdiction are subject to an effective tax rate test of 10%, which is below the minimum rate of 11%. The top-up tax percentage is 1% and the top-up tax computed under the rules of Chapters 3 and 4 for each Constituent Entity in Country D is 10 (1,000 adjusted income x 1%).

7. B Co's top-up tax liability is determined based on its ownership percentage. Therefore, B Co is required to pay 14. 10 with respect to the income of D Co 1 (100% x 10) and 4 with respect to the income of D Co 2 (40% x 10). B Co is required to apply the IIR to the income of D Co 2 because both entities are controlled by the UPE and are Constituent Entities of the MNE Group. The fact that B Co does not control D Co 2 is irrelevant for purposes of applying the IIR based on its ownership share.

8. As in Example 6.1B, C Co is required to pay $20 with respect to income of D Co 3 and D Co 4.

9. D Co 5 is not controlled by a Parent. Therefore, the 10 of top-up tax computed in respect of D Co 5 is allocated to other Constituent Entities pursuant to the undertaxed payments rule. In addition, the 10 top-up tax computed in respect of D Co 2 with a 4 credit for top-up tax allocated under the income inclusion rule is allocable to other Constituent Entities pursuant to the undertaxed payments rule.

Example 6.3.2A. Tax avoidance scheme using split-ownership structures

Facts

1. Hold Co is the Ultimate Parent of a family owned MNE Group subject to the GloBE rules. Hold Co owns all the shares of B Co, an entity located in Country B. B Co holds all the shares of C Co 1, an entity located in Country C. Hold Co also holds all the shares of C Co 2, an entity located in Country C.

2. The ETR of C Co 1 and C Co 2 is below the minimum rate. Therefore, Hold Co would be required to apply the income inclusion rule with respect to 100% of the income of C Co 1 and C Co 2. Assume that the split-ownership rules apply in cases where 10% or more of the equity interests of a Partially Owned Intermediate Parent are held directly or indirectly by persons that are not Constituent Entities of the MNE Group.

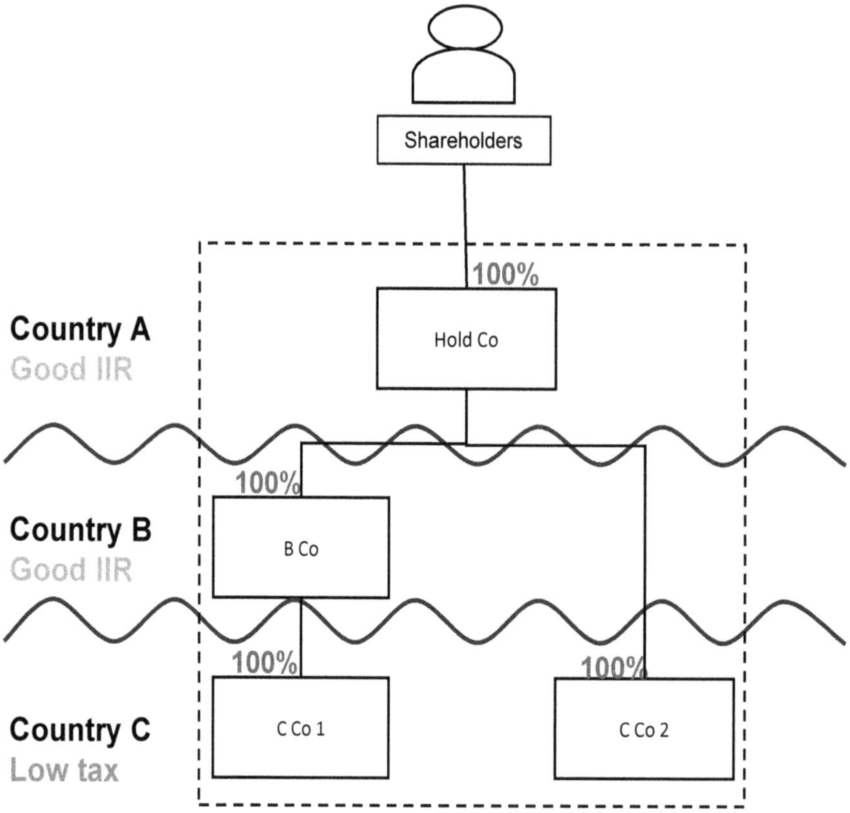

3. To avoid the GloBE rules, Hold Co spins-off 40% of its shares of B Co and C Co 2 to its own shareholders. If the ETR test and tax liability under the GloBE rules was based only in the Ultimate Parent's ownership percentage of C Co 1 and C Co 2, then this reorganization would cut GloBE tax liability by 40%.

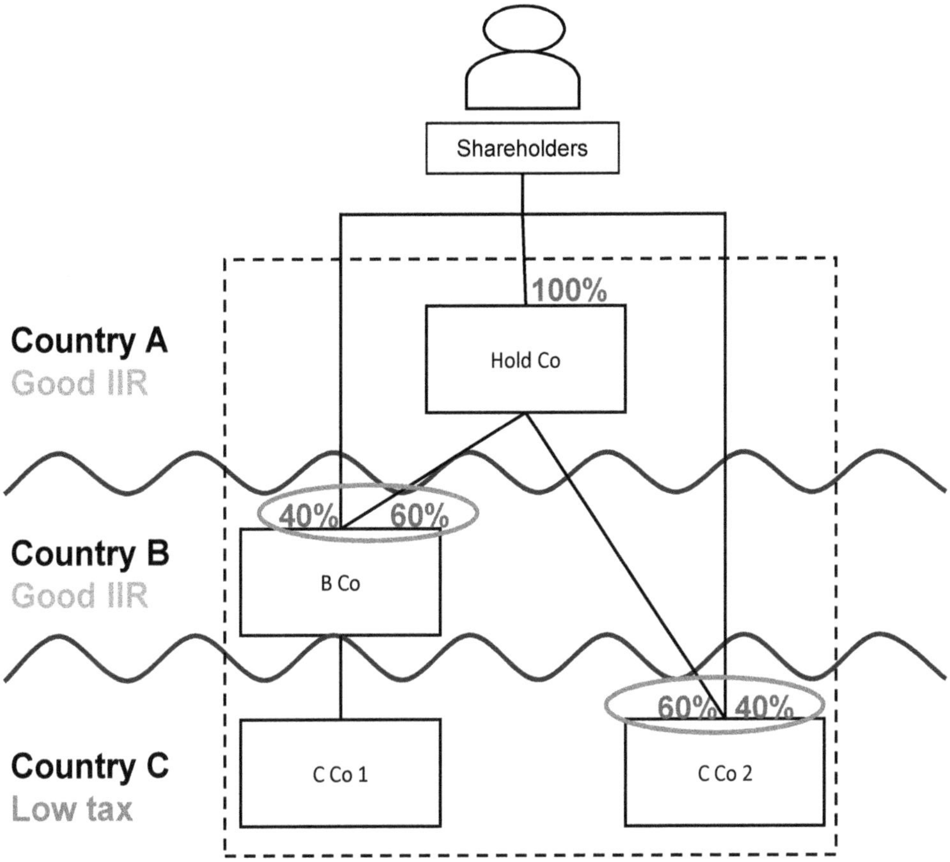

Question

4. How will the split-ownership rules deal with this tax planning scheme?

Answer

5. The split-ownership rules only deal with Partially Owned Intermediate Parents. They do not deal with partially owned low-tax entities.

Analysis

6. According to the split-ownership rules, B Co would be required to apply the IIR. Therefore, this reorganization would not have an effect on the top-up tax paid under the GloBE rules with respect to the income of C Co 1.

7. However, the split-ownership rules do not cover 40% of the income of C Co 2 because it is not a Partially Owned Intermediate Parent. In this case, the entity subject to low taxation is the partially owned Constituent Entity . This result would not change even if there was an intermediate entity between Hold Co and C Co 2 provided that the equity shares of the later are still owned by the shareholders of Hold Co.

Example 6.3.2B. Issues arising without split-ownership rules

Facts

1. The GloBE rules have not adopted split-ownership rules. The ETR and top-up tax of the low-taxed entities are computed based on the UPE's ownership share of the low-taxed income.

2. Hold Co is the UPE of an MNE Group subject to the GloBE rules. Hold Co is a tax resident of Country A, a jurisdiction that has not adopted the income inclusion rule. It owns 60% of the shares of B Co, a Constituent Entity of the group located in Country B that has adopted the GloBE rules. The remaining 40% of the shares of B Co are owned by minority shareholders that are not Constituent Entities of the MNE Group. B Co owns 100% of the shares of C Co, a Constituent Entity located in Country C. C Co has an effective tax rate of 0%. In this example, the minimum tax rate is 11%.

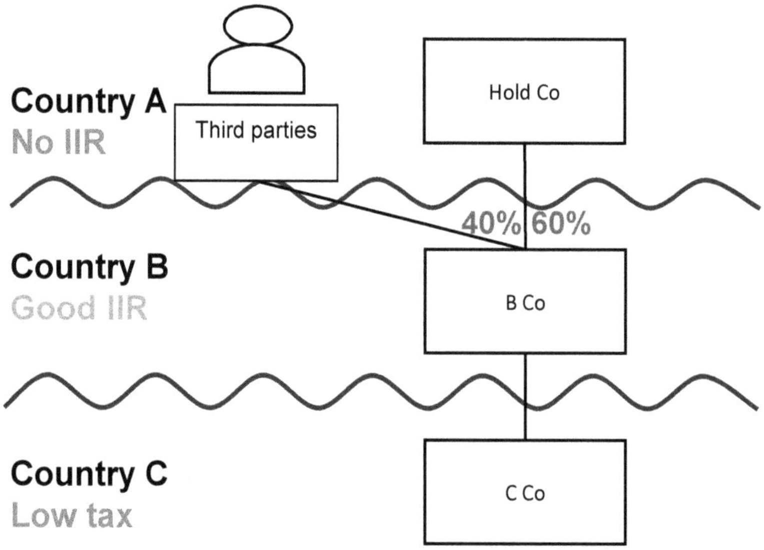

Questions

3. How would the GloBE rules operate without split-ownership rules in this situation?

4. What are the issues arising in the absence of split-ownership rules?

Answer

5. In this case, B Co would be required to apply the IIR because Hold Co is located in a jurisdiction that has not adopted the IIR. B Co would be required to apply the IIR with respect to 60% of the income of C Co because that it's the ownership percentage owned by the UPE. Hold Co would be effectively taxed at 36% because it owns 60% of the equity interests of the Parent applying the IIR, the remaining 24% would be borne by the minority interest holders.

6. The UPE would be subject to a lower IIR liability if the top-up tax is paid by an intermediate parent which is partially-owned. The minority interest holders would be impacted by part of the top-up tax that belongs to the UPE, even if the policy rationale was to exclude minorities.

Analysis

7. The GloBE could have adopted an approach in which the ETR and top-up tax are computed based on the UPE's ownership share of the low-taxed entity. If the UPE applies the IIR or if it is applied by an intermediate parent wholly owned by the UPE, then the rules work perfectly fine (regardless of exempting

income belonging to minorities) because the ETR and top-up tax are computed based on the UPE's ownership percentage on the low-taxed income.

8. However, if an intermediate parent entity that is not wholly-owned by the UPE is required to apply the rule, then a flaw in the IIR system would occur because the UPE would be subject to lower tax burden. In this case, the income belonging to minorities would be taxed even if the policy was to exclude these minority interests.

9. In this example, the top-up tax imposed by B Co's jurisdiction is limited to the Ultimate Parent Entity's ownership percentage of C Co. Therefore, B Co would apply the IIR with respect to 60% of the income of C Co. This means that Hold Co would effectively be paying top-up tax with respect to 36% of its ownership percentage (60% x 60% = 36%). The remaining 24% would indirectly impact the returns of the minority interest holders as they also own B Co, the entity subject to the IIR tax.

10. A way to solve this problem would be by applying the income inclusion rule based on the intermediate parent's proportionate share of the low-taxed income. This ensures that the Ultimate Parent Entity is indirectly subject to the income inclusion rule based on its proportionate share of the low-taxed income. In the example, this would mean that B Co would be required to apply the IIR with respect to 100% of the income of C Co. However, the effective tax rate and top-up tax computation would be changing depending on the parent entity or entities apply IIR, which would create another series of issues.

Adopted approach

11. Under the adopted approach the top-up tax percentage computed for Country C is 11% (11% minimum rate – 0% ETR). Accordingly, the top-up tax computed for C Co is 11 [(100 (income) x 11% (top-up tax percentage)]. B Co computes its share of the top-up tax of C Co based on its ownership percentage of C Co, 100%, and pays 11 of top-up tax. Consequently, Hold Co effectively pays 6.6, while the remaining 4.4 of the tax cost is borne by the minority shareholders of B Co.

12. The top-up tax percentage computed for Country C is 11% (11% minimum rate – 0% ETR). If the top-up tax under the GloBE rules was based on Hold Co's ownership percentage of C Co, then Hold Co would be required to pay 6.6 of top-up tax (100 x 60% x 11%). However, Hold Co is located in a jurisdiction that has not adopted the GloBE rules. Therefore, under the top-down approach, B Co is required to apply the income inclusion rule. If B Co were required to pay 6.6, then Hold Co would be effectively paying 3.96. The tax cost of the remaining 2.64 would be borne by the minority shareholders.

Example 6.3.2C. Coordination between the UPE and POIP to apply the IIR

Facts

1. The facts are the same as Example 6.2.2B, except the GloBE rules include the split-ownership rules, Country A has adopted an income inclusion rule, and Hold Co also owns 100% of the shares of B Co 2 (located in Country B), an entity that holds 100% of the shares of C Co 2 (located in Country C). The income of C Co 2 is subject to an effective tax rate of 0%. Assume that the split-ownership rules apply in cases where 10% or more of the equity interests of a Partially Owned Intermediate Parent are held directly or indirectly by persons that are not Constituent Entities of the MNE Group.

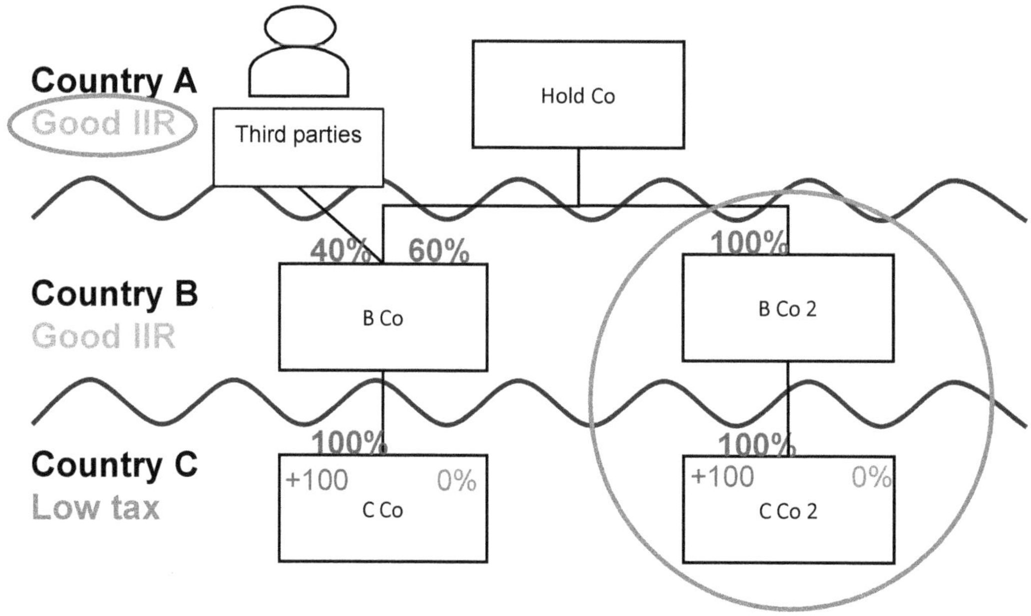

Question

2. How would the IIR be applied in this situation?

Answer

3. B Co would be required to apply the IIR with respect to the income of C Co because it is a Partially Owned Intermediate Parent, while Hold Co would be required to exempt such income from its IIR and apply it only with respect to the income of C Co 2.

Analysis

4. The ETR of Country C is of 0%, and therefore, the top-up tax percentage is 11% [11% (minimum tax rate) – 0% (ETR)]. The top-up tax computed for C Co and C Co 2 is 11 each [(100 (income) x 11% (top-up tax percentage)].

5. Under the top-down approach, Hold Co is required to apply the income inclusion rule. However, B Co is also required to apply the income inclusion rule with respect to the income of C Co in accordance with the split-ownership rules because it is a Partially Owned Intermediate Parent.

6. B Co is required to pay 11 (100% x 11) under its IIR.

7. Hold Co is also required to apply the IIR. However, to avoid double taxation, it will compute its top-up tax only with respect to its share of C Co 2's income and therefore, it would be required to pay a tax of 11 (100% x 11).

8. If there were no split ownership rules, Hold Co's tentative top-up tax for Country C Constituent Entities would be 17.6 [(60% x 11) + (100% x 11)] rather than the total of 22 top-up tax paid by the MNE Group (11 paid by B Co + 11 paid by Hold Co).

Example 6.3.2D. Coordination between two or more POIP

Facts

1. In this example, Hold Co is the Ultimate Parent Entity of an MNE Group subject to the GloBE rules. Hold Co is located in Country A. Hold Co holds 60% of the shares of B Co, an entity located in Country B. The remaining 40% of the shares of B Co are held by minority shareholders that are not Constituent Entities of the MNE Group. B Co holds 60% of the shares of C Co, an entity also located in Country C. The remaining 40% of the shares of C Co are held by minority shareholders that are not Constituent Entities of the MNE Group.

2. C Co owns 100% of the shares of D Co, an entity located in Country D. D Co holds 100% of the shares of E Co, an entity located in Country E and whose income is subject to an ETR below the minimum rate. The income of all other Constituent Entities is subject to tax above the minimum rate. The GloBE rules have been adopted by Countries A, B, C and D. Assume that the split-ownership rules apply in cases where 10% or more of the equity interests of a Partially Owned Intermediate Parent are held directly or indirectly by persons that are not Constituent Entities of the MNE Group.

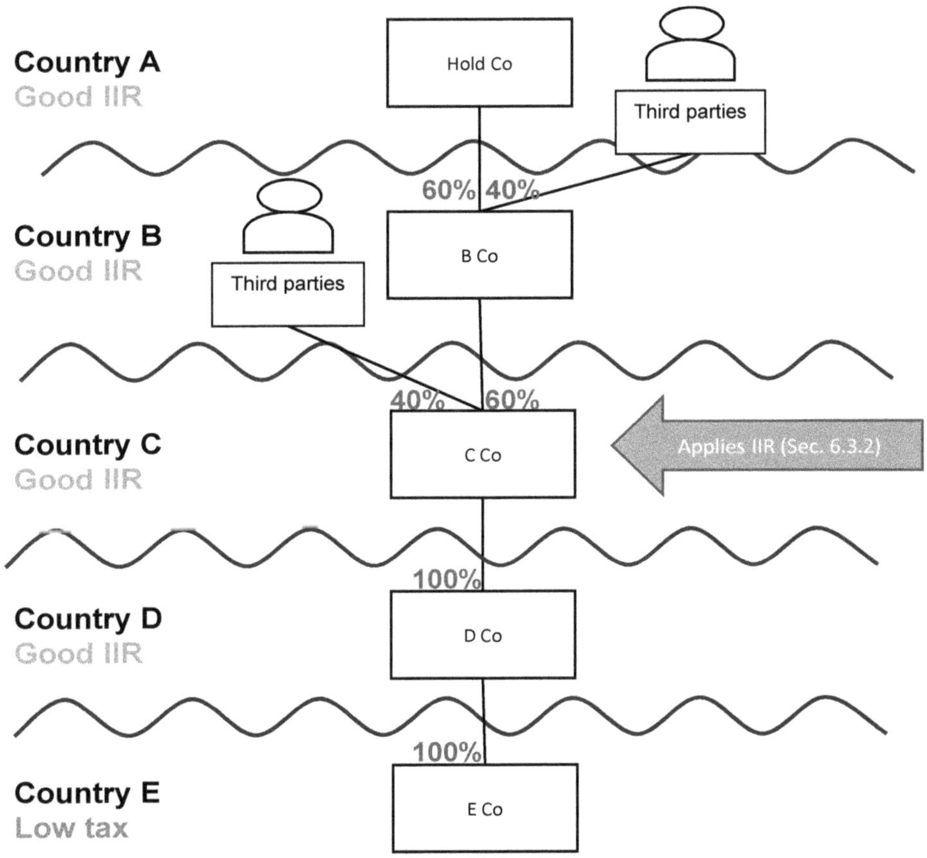

Question

3. Which of these Constituent Entities are Partially Owned Intermediate Parents and which of them should have the priority to apply the IIR?

Answer

4. B Co, C Co, and D Co are all Partially Owned Intermediate Parents because more than 10% of their equity interests are held directly or indirectly by persons that are not Constituent Entities of the MNE Group (third parties).

5. C Co is required to apply the IIR under the split-ownership rules (Section 6.3.2). B Co and D Co are not required to apply the IIR with respect to the income of E Co.

Analysis

6. B Co is a Partially Owned Intermediate Parents because more than 10% of its equity interests are held directly by persons that are not Constituent Entities of the MNE Group (third parties). Likewise, C Co is also a Partially Owned Intermediate Parents because 10% or more of its equity interests are held directly and indirectly by persons that are not Constituent Entities (its minority equity interest holders and the minority interest holders of B Co). D Co is also a Partially Owned Intermediate Parent because 10% or more of its equity interests are held indirectly by that are not Constituent Entities of the MNE Group (the minority equity interest holders of C Co and the minority interest holders of B Co).

7. The next question that arises is which of these entities is required to apply the IIR. The answer to this question is important to ensure coordination between jurisdictions and avoid double taxation.

8. In accordance with the definition of a Parent under the top-down approach, this includes a Partially Owned Intermediate Parent. Therefore, all Partially Owned Intermediate Parents are also "Parents" in accordance with the top-down approach. The second paragraph of the split-ownership rules establish an exception to the top-down approach because it states that a Parent that holds at least a portion of the equity interests in the low-taxed Constituent Entity through a Partially Owned Intermediate Parent, shall not apply the IIR to the extent such income has already been subject to the IIR of the Partially Owned Intermediate Parent.

9. In this example, B Co is a Parent of C Co, through which it holds interests in the low-taxed Constituent Entity (E Co). Moreover, the low-taxed income is already subject to the IIR of C Co Therefore, B Co shall not apply the IIR because it is already subject to the IIR of C Co. The same analysis exempts Hold Co from applying the IIR because it is a Parent of C Co.

10. A different analysis is needed to determine which of the remaining Partially Owned Intermediate Parents should apply the IIR. In accordance with the second sentence of the first paragraph of the split-ownership rules, a Partially Owned Intermediate Parent shall not apply the IIR if all of its equity interests are held directly or indirectly by Constituent Entities required to apply the income inclusion rule.

11. In this example, all the equity interests of D Co are held by C Co, a Constituent Entity subject to the IIR. Therefore, D Co shall not apply the IIR because C Co would apply the IIR to the low-taxed income. This follows the rationale of the top-down approach.

12. Therefore, C Co would be the only Partially Owned Intermediate Parent required to apply the IIR given that B Co and D Co are restricted to apply the IIR in this situation. Furthermore, Hold Co as a parent of C Co is also required not to apply the IIR.

Example 6.3.2E. Coordination between two or more POIP when one of them is subject to low taxation

Facts

1. The facts are the same as in Example 4.2.3D, except that the income of C Co is also subject to an effective tax rate below the minimum rate.

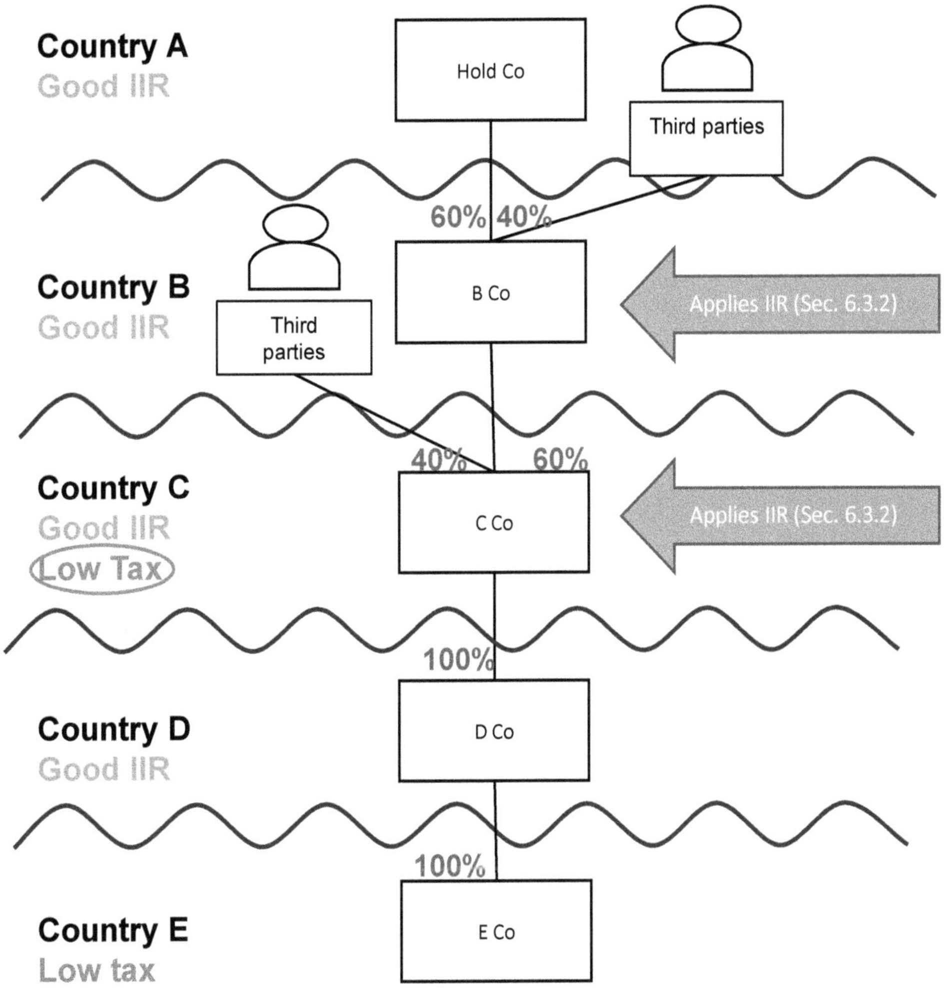

Question

2. Which of these Constituent Entities are Partially Owned Intermediate Parents and which of them should have the priority to apply the IIR?

Answer

3. As in Example 6.3.2D, B Co, C Co, and D Co are all Partially Owned Intermediate Parents because 10% or more of their equity interests are held directly or indirectly by persons that are not Constituent Entities of the MNE Group (third parties).

4. As in Example 6.3.2D, C Co is the only Parent and Partially Owned Intermediate Parent that is required to apply the IIR with respect to the income of E Co. However, B Co is a Partially Owned Intermediate Parent required to apply the IIR with respect to the low-taxed income of C Co.

Analysis

5. C Co is the only Parent and Partially Owned Intermediate Parent required to apply the IIR based on the analysis set out in Example 6.3.2D. given that the relevant facts are the same.

6. However, B Co is required to apply the IIR with respect to the income of C Co because it is a Partially Owned Intermediate Parent holding shares of a low-taxed entity. Hold Co has to exclude from its IIR the income of C Co because it was already subject to the IIR of B Co.

Example 6.3.2F. Coordination between two or more POIP in case they hold different equity interests of the low-taxed entity

Facts

1. The facts are the same facts as in Example 4.2.3D, except that C Co only holds 50% of the shares of D Co while the remaining 50% are held by B Co. Therefore, B Co owns indirectly 80% of the income of E Co (30% through its ownership of C Co and 50% through its ownership of D Co).

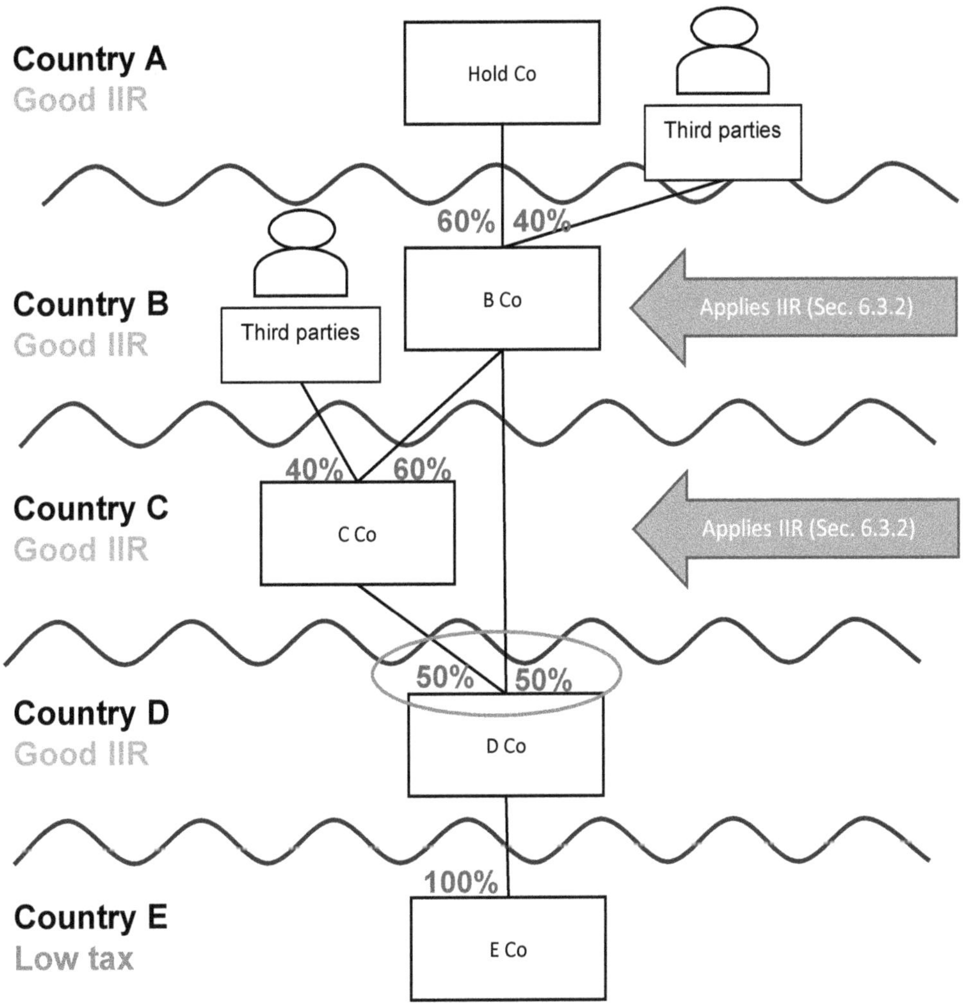

Question

2. Which of these Constituent Entities are Partially Owned Intermediate Parents and which of them should have the priority to apply the IIR?

Answer

3. As in Example 6.3.2D, B Co, C Co, and D Co are all Partially Owned Intermediate Parents because 10% or more of their equity interests are held directly or indirectly by persons that are not Constituent Entities of the MNE Group (third parties).

4. As in Example 6.2.3D, C Co still has priority to apply the IIR with respect to 50% of the income of E Co. However, B Co is still required to apply the IIR with respect to the other 50% of the low-taxed income.

Analysis

5. The analysis set out in Example 6.2.3D is the starting point with respect to 50% of the low-taxed income held through B Co, C Co and D Co. B Co is not required to apply the IIR because it is a Parent that owns this portion of the low-taxed income through a Partially Owned Intermediate Parent (C Co) that is required to apply the IIR.

6. The next question is what which Partially Owned Intermediate Parent should apply the remaining 50% held through B Co and D Co. In this case, D Co should not apply the IIR because is a Partially Owned Intermediate Parent whose all of its equity interests are held by Constituent Entities required to apply the IIR (B Co and C Co). Therefore, B Co would be required to apply the IIR with respect to the remaining 50% of the low-taxed income. This policy follows the rationale of the top-down approach and avoids indirectly taxing twice the income that belongs to the minority interest holders of C Co.

7. Hold Co is not required to apply the IIR with respect to the income of E Co because all of it has been subject to the IIR of a Partially Owned Intermediate Parents.

8. The fact that D Co is not controlled by B Co or C Co is not relevant because all of them are Constituent Entities of the same MNE Group as they are controlled by Hold Co.

Example 6.3.2G. Coordination between the UPE and a POIP when both are required to apply the IIR

Facts

1. The facts are the same as Example 4.2.3D except that 40% of the shares of B Co are held by A Co, a Constituent Entity of the MNE Group wholly owned by Hold Co.

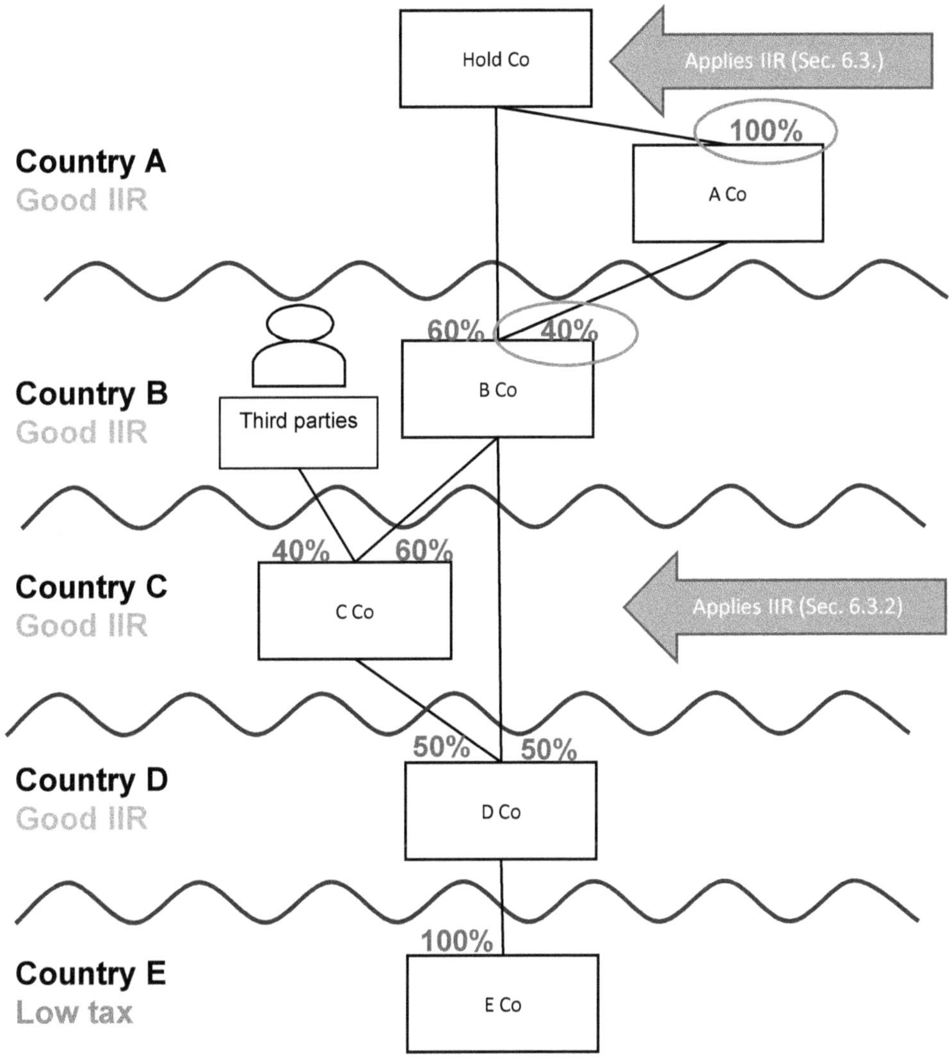

Question

2. Which of these Constituent Entities are Partially Owned Intermediate Parents and which of them should have the priority to apply the IIR?

Answer

3. C Co and D Co are all Partially Owned Intermediate Parents because 10% or more of their equity interests are held directly or indirectly by persons that are not Constituent Entities of the MNE Group (third parties). B Co is not a Partially Owned Intermediate Parent as in Example 6.3.2D because all of its equity interests are directly or indirectly held by Hold Co.

4. As in Example 6.2.3D and 6.2.3F, C Co still has priority to apply the IIR with respect to 50% of the income of E Co. However, Hold Co is required to apply the IIR with respect to the remaining 50%.

Analysis

5. In this example, C Co and D Co are Partially Owned Intermediate Parents. B Co is not a Partially Owned Intermediate Parent because all of its equity interests are held by the UPE.

6. As in Example 6.2.3F, C Co has the priority to apply the IIR with respect to 50% of the income of E Co.

7. However, unlike Example 6.2.3F, Hold Co has the priority to apply the IIR before B Co in accordance with the top-down approach because the latter is not a Partially Owned Intermediate Parent. Therefore, Country B has to deactivate its IIR. However, Hold Co would only apply its IIR with respect of 50% of the income of E Co because the other 50% is already subject to an IIR of a Partially Owned Intermediate Parent (C Co) based on the split-ownership rules.

8. D Co on the other hand, is not required to apply the IIR because all of its equity interests are held by Constituent Entities required to apply the IIR (Hold Co and C Co).

Example 6.3.2H. Coordination between two or more POIP and an intermediate parent located in a jurisdiction with no IIR

Facts

1. The facts are the same as in Example 4.2.3D, except that Country C has not adopted the income inclusion rule.

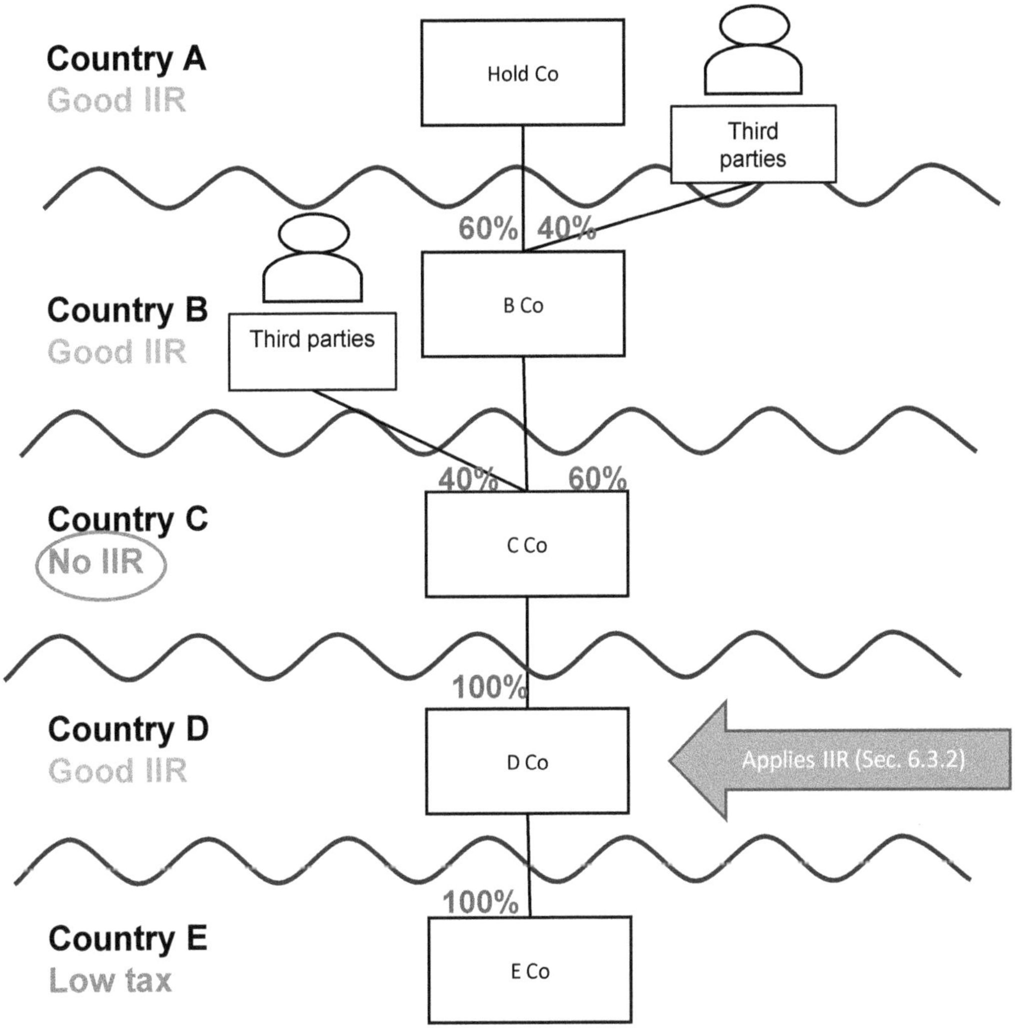

Question

2. Which of these Constituent Entities are Partially Owned Intermediate Parents and which of them should have the priority to apply the IIR?

Answer

3. B Co and D Co are Partially Owned Intermediate Parents because 10% or more of their equity interests are held directly or indirectly by persons that are not Constituent Entities of the MNE Group (third parties). C Co is not a Partially Owned Intermediate Parent in accordance with the split-ownership rules.

4. D Co is required to apply the IIR under the split-ownership rules (Section 6.3.2). B Co is not required to apply the IIR with respect to the income of E Co.

Analysis

5. Unlike Example 6.3.2D, C Co is not a Partially Owned Intermediate Parent because it is not located in a jurisdiction that has adopted an IIR. Therefore, this means that either B Co or D Co should be required to apply the IIR.

6. In this case D Co is not subject to the restriction stated in the second sentence of the first paragraph of the split-ownership rules because not all of its equity interests are held by a Constituent Entity required to apply the IIR. B Co only owns (indirectly) 60% of the equity interests of D Co. Therefore, D Co is required to apply the IIR.

7. B Co on the other hand cannot apply the IIR because it is a Parent that holds a portion of the equity interests of the low-taxed Constituent Entity (E Co) through a Partially Owned Intermediate Parent (D Co) that has applied the IIR in accordance with the second paragraph of the split-ownership rules. Therefore, B Co is required to exclude the income of E Co from the IIR.

8. Likewise, Hold Co is required to exclude from its IIR the income of E Co because it was already subject to the IIR of a Partially Owned Intermediate Parent (D Co).

9. The result of applying the rules ensures that all of the low-taxed income is subject to the GloBE rules. If B Co was required to apply the rule, it would only apply it with respect to 60% of the low-taxed income.

Example 6.3.2I. Coordination between a POIP and two intermediate parents located in a jurisdiction with no IIR

Facts

1. The facts are the same as in Example 4.2.3D except that Countries C and D have not adopted the income inclusion rule.

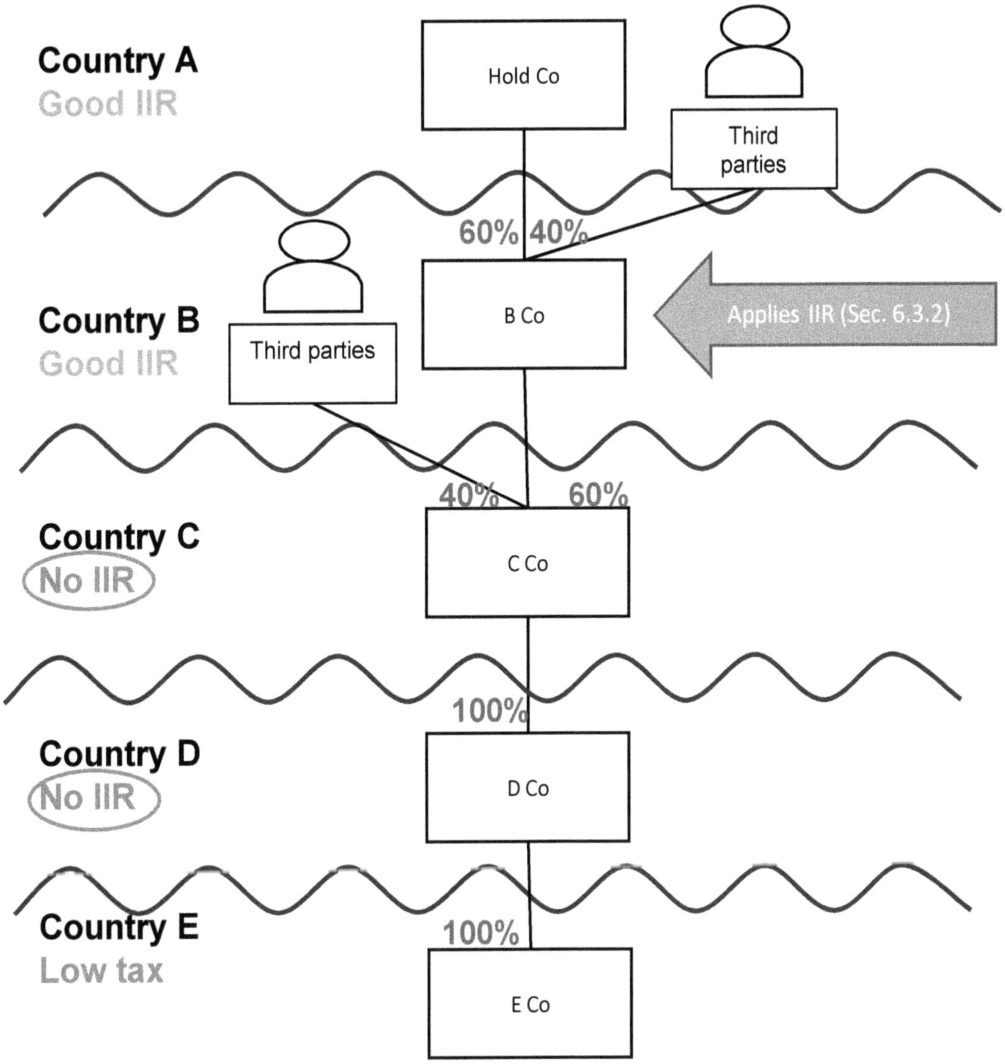

Question

2. Which of these Constituent Entities are Partially Owned Intermediate Parents and which of them should have the priority to apply the IIR?

Answer

3. B Co is the only Partially Owned Intermediate Parent and has priority to apply the IIR before Hold Co.

Analysis

4. In this example, only B Co is a Partially Owned Intermediate Parent. C Co and D Co do not meet the definition of a Partially Owned Intermediate Parent because they are located in jurisdictions that have not adopted the IIR. Therefore, B Co is required to apply the IIR with respect to E Co's income.

5. B Co would be required to collect 60% of the top-up tax for E Co because it only owns indirectly 60% of its equity interests. The remaining 40% would not be taxed under the GloBE rules because they are not subject to an IIR and because the UTPR would not apply because E Co is controlled by a Constituent Entity subject to an IIR.

6. Hold Co is required to exempt the income of E Co from its IIR because it is the Parent of an Intermediate Parent Entity applying the IIR.

Example 6.3.2J. Difference between a POIP and a partially owned low-taxed entity

Facts

1. Hold Co is the UPE of an MNE Group subject to the GloBE rules and is located in a jurisdiction that has adopted the IIR. Hold Co holds 60% of the shares of B Co, an entity located in Country B. The remaining 40% of the shares are held by minority shareholders that are not Constituent Entities of the MNE Group. Country B has adopted the IIR. B Co owns 100% of the shares of C Co 1, a Constituent Entity located in Country C.

2. Hold Co also holds 60% of the shares of C Co 2, an entity located in Country C.

3. The income of C Co 1 (100) is subject to a covered tax of 5, while the income of C Co 2 (100) is exempt. In this example, the minimum tax rate adopted by the GloBE rules is 10%. Assume that the split-ownership rules apply in cases where 10% or more of the equity interests of a Partially Owned Intermediate Parent are held directly or indirectly by persons that are not Constituent Entities of the MNE Group.

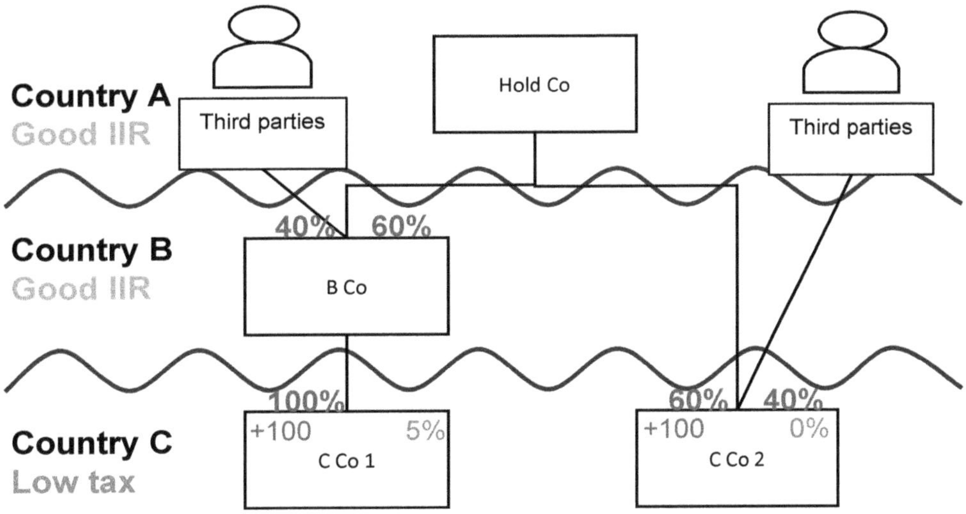

Question

4. What is the amount of income earned by the Constituent Entities located in Country C subject to the GloBE rules and the amount of top-up tax paid by the MNE Group?

Answer

5. The amount of income subject to the GloBE rules is 160 and the amount of top-up tax paid by the MNE Group is 12.

Analysis

6. The ETR of C Co 1 and C Co 2 is of 2.5%. Therefore, the MNE Group is required to pay a tax of 15. The top-up tax for C Co 1 and C Co 2 is 7.5 each [100 (income) x 7.5 ETR difference]

7. Hold Co is required to apply the IIR based on its ownership percentage in accordance with the top-down approach (Section 6.3). B Co is also required to apply the IIR based on the split-ownership rules (Section 6.3.2).

8. B Co is required to pay 7.5 (100% x 7.5). On the other hand, Hold Co applies the IIR only with respect to the income of C Co 2 because the income of C Co 1 was already subject to the IIR of B Co and therefore, is required to pay 4.5 (60% x 7.5).

9. The MNE Group paid a total top-up tax of $12 ($7.5 paid by B Co + $4.5 paid by Hold Co). The split-ownership rules do not apply to income of C Co 2 because the low-taxed entity is the partially owned entity (not the Partially Owned Intermediate Parent). Therefore, the remaining 3 of tax that corresponds to 40% of the income of C Co 2 would not be collected by the MNE Group. In certain situations, the simplified version of the IIR could apply to the income of C Co 2.

Example 7.4.3A. Example of operation of the first allocation key of the UTPR (without any cap)

Facts

1. An MNE is parented in jurisdiction P and operates in jurisdictions A, B, C and D. It is further assumed that the MNE's jurisdictional ETR in jurisdiction P (the Ultimate Parent jurisdiction), jurisdiction A and jurisdiction B is above the minimum rate. P Co directly owns all of the equity interests in A1 Co, B Co and C Co. A1 Co owns all of the equity interests in A2 Co and C Co owns all of the equity interests in D Co. A1 Co and A2 Co are tax resident in the same jurisdiction (jurisdiction A). B Co, C Co and D Co are tax resident of jurisdiction B, jurisdiction C and jurisdiction D respectively. Jurisdictions A and B introduced the UTPR.

2. This MNE's jurisdictional ETR in jurisdictions C and D are below the minimum rate. A top-up tax is computed in relation to the profits made in these two jurisdictions. The top-up tax amounts to 200 and 75 in relation to the profits made in jurisdictions C and D respectively.[1] There is no income inclusion rule that applies in relation to the profits made in jurisdictions C and D because jurisdictions P and C have not implemented the income inclusion rule.

3. The direct payments structure involving Constituent Entities established in jurisdictions where the MNE's jurisdictional ETR is below the minimum rate is as follows:

- A1 Co made payments to C Co. These payments amounted to 750.
- A2 Co made payments to D Co. These payments amounted to 100.
- B Co made payments to C Co and to D Co. These payments amounted to 250 and 200 respectively.

4. The following chart summarises these facts.

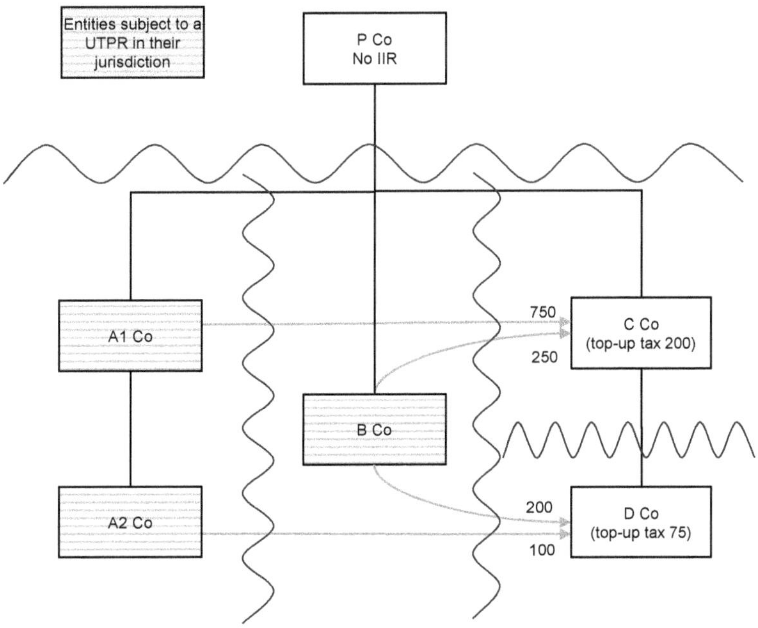

Question

5. How are the top-up taxes computed in relation to the profits made in jurisdictions C and D allocated under the first allocation key of the UTPR?

Answer

6. Each of the amounts of top-up tax (200 and 75) is allocated as follows:

- The top-up tax allocated to A1 Co amounts to 150 (75% x200)
- The top-up tax allocated to A2 Co amounts to 25 (33.33% x 75)
- The top-up tax allocated to B Co amounts to 100 (25% x 200 + 66.66% x 75)

7. The effect of a potential cap on the amount allocated under the first allocation key is disregarded for the purpose of this example. If a cap applied and limited the amount of top-up taxes allocated under the first allocation key, the remaining amount of top-up tax would be allocated under the second allocation key.

Analysis

8. If the MNE has an effective tax rate that is below the agreed minimum rate in several jurisdictions where it is operating, the first allocation key would be applied to the top-up tax owed in relation to the profits made in each jurisdiction separately. The example provided here aims at illustrating this mechanism. The effect of a potential cap on the amount allocated under the first allocation key is disregarded for the purpose of this example.

Allocation of the top-up tax computed in relation to the profits made by C Co

9. The top-up tax computed in relation to the profits made by C Co is allocated to UTPR Taxpayers established in jurisdictions A and B in proportion to the direct payments these entities made to C Co. The proportions of direct payments received by C Co are as follows:

UTPR Taxpayers	Amount of direct payments made to C Co	Proportion of direct payments
A1 Co	750	$\frac{\mathbf{750}}{\mathbf{1000}} = \mathbf{75\%}$
B Co	250	$\frac{\mathbf{250}}{\mathbf{1000}} = \mathbf{25\%}$
Total	1000	100%

10. The top-up tax computed in relation to the profits made by C Co amounts to 200. The top-up tax is allocated to UTPR Taxpayers established in jurisdictions A and B in proportion to the amount of direct payments computed above. This mechanism results in the following allocation:

UTPR Taxpayers	Proportion of direct payments	Allocated top-up tax
A1 Co	75%	$\mathbf{75\%\ x\ 200 = 150}$
B Co	25%	$\mathbf{25\%\ x\ 200 = 50}$
Total	100%	200

11. The effect of a potential cap on the amount allocated under this allocation key is disregarded for the purpose of this example. If there remains any unallocated top-up tax on the profits made in jurisdiction C after this cap applies, it will be allocated under the second allocation key.

Allocation of the top-up tax computed in relation to the profits made by D Co

12. The top-up tax computed in relation to the profits made by D Co is allocated to UTPR Taxpayers established in jurisdictions A and B in proportion to the direct payments these entities made to D Co. The proportions of direct payments received by D Co are as follows:

UTPR Taxpayers	Amount of direct payments made to D Co	Proportion of direct payments
A2 Co	100	$\frac{\mathbf{100}}{\mathbf{300}} = \mathbf{33.33\%}$
B Co	200	$\frac{\mathbf{200}}{\mathbf{300}} = \mathbf{66.66\%}$
Total	300	100%

13. The top-up tax computed in relation to the profits made by D Co amounts to 75. The top-up tax is allocated to UTPR Taxpayers established in jurisdictions A and B in proportion to the amount of direct payments computed above. This mechanism results in the following allocation:

UTPR Taxpayers	Proportion of direct payments	Allocated top-up tax
A2 Co	33.33%	$\mathbf{33.33\%\ x\ 75 = 25}$
B Co	66.66%	$\mathbf{66.66\%\ x\ 75 = 50}$
Total	100%	75

14. The effect of a potential cap on the amount allocated under this allocation key is disregarded for the purpose of this example. If there remains any unallocated top-up tax on the profits made in jurisdiction D after this cap applies, it will be allocated under the second allocation key.

Total amount of top-up tax allocated under the first allocation key

15. The top-up tax computed in relation to the profits made in jurisdictions C and D are cumulative. Therefore, UTPR Taxpayers established in jurisdictions A and B are allocated the following top-up tax:

UTPR Taxpayers	Top-up tax allocated in relation to the profits made in jurisdiction C	Top-up tax allocated in relation to the profits made in jurisdiction D	Total top-up tax
A1 Co	150	n.a.	150
A2 Co	n.a.	25	25
B Co	50	50	100
Total	200	75	275

16. As a result of the first allocation key, the total amount of top-up tax of is allocated as follows:

- The top-up tax allocated to A1 Co amounts to 150
- The top-up tax allocated to A2 Co amounts to 25
- The top-up tax allocated to B Co amounts to 100

17. The effect of a potential cap on the amount allocated under this allocation key is disregarded for the purpose of this example. If there remains any unallocated top-up tax on the profits made in jurisdiction C or D after this cap applies, it will be allocated under the second allocation key.

Example 7.4.3B. Example of the operation of the UTPR when the first allocation key does not apply

Facts

1. The same facts as for Example 7.4.3A are assumed for this example, except for the fact that no direct payments are made by entities subject to a UTPR to entities located in jurisdictions where the MNE's jurisdictional ETR is below the agreed minimum rate. Therefore, no top-up tax is allocated under the first allocation key and only the second allocation key applies.

2. The following chart summarises these facts.

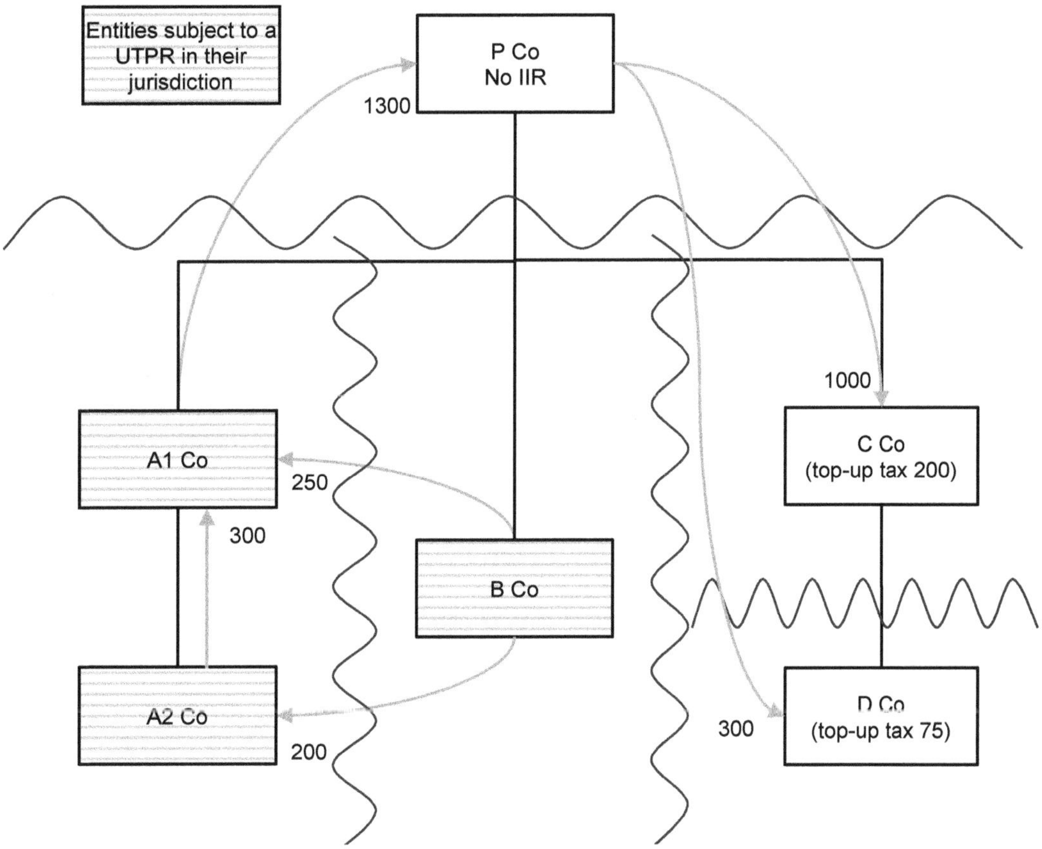

Question

3. How are the top-up taxes computed in relation to the profits made in jurisdictions C and D allocated under the UTPR?

Answer

4. The first allocation key of the UTPR does not apply in this fact pattern. The second allocation key applies to the remaining (i.e. total in this case) amount of top-up tax.

5. The second allocation key of the UTPR allocates such a total amount of top-up tax (200 + 75 = 275) in proportion to net intra-group expenditure of the UTPR Taxpayers. The net intra-group expenditure of A1 Co, A2 Co and B Co are respectively 58%, 8% and 34% of the aggregated amount of the sum of their net intra-group expenditures.

6. These entities are therefore allocated a portion of top-up tax as follows:

- The top-up tax allocated to A1 Co amounts to 159.5 (58% x 275)

- The top-up tax allocated to A2 Co amounts to 22 (8% x 275)
- The top-up tax allocated to B Co amounts to 93.5 (34% x 275)

Analysis

7. The first allocation key of the UTPR does not apply in this fact pattern. Under the second allocation key, all remaining top-up taxes (i.e. those that were not allocated under the first allocation key) are aggregated to form one pool of top-up tax that is allocated in proportion to each UTPR Taxpayer's net intra-group expenditure.

8. The set of related party transactions results in the following amounts of net intra-group expenditure:

UTPR Taxpayers	Related party Income	Related party expenses	Amount of net intra-group expenditure
A1 Co	300 + 250 = 550	1300	550 – 1300 = (750)
A2 Co	200	300	200 – 300 = (100)
B Co	-	250+200 = 450	(450)

9. The proportion of net intra-group expenditure can be computed on the basis of these net intra-group expenditures computed at the entity level.

UTPR Taxpayers	Amount of net intra-group expenditure	Proportion of net intra-group expenditure
A1 Co	(750)	$\frac{750}{1300} = 58\%$
A2 Co	(100)	$\frac{100}{1300} = 8\%$
B Co	(450)	$\frac{450}{1300} = 34\%$
Total	(1300)	100%

10. The total amount of top-up tax can then be allocated amongst A1 Co, A2 Co and B Co in proportion to their net intra-group expenditure.

UTPR Taxpayers	Proportion of net intra-group expenditure	Allocated top-up tax
A1 Co	58%	$58\%\ x\ 275 = 159.5$
A2 Co	8%	$8\%\ x\ 275 = 22$
B Co	34%	$34\%\ x\ 275 = 93.5$
Total	100%	275

11. The difference with the top-up tax allocated under the second allocation key in Example 4.3.2A results from the fact that, under the second allocation key, the top-up tax is aggregated before being allocated to all Constituent Entities in proportion to their net intra-group expenditure.

Example 7.4.3C. Example of the operation of the UTPR when the first allocation key does not apply and one entity has net related party income for the purpose of the second allocation key

Facts

1. The same facts as for Example 7.4.3B are assumed for this example. It is further assumed that B Co received an intragroup payment for an amount of 500 from P Co.

2. The following chart summarises these facts.

Question

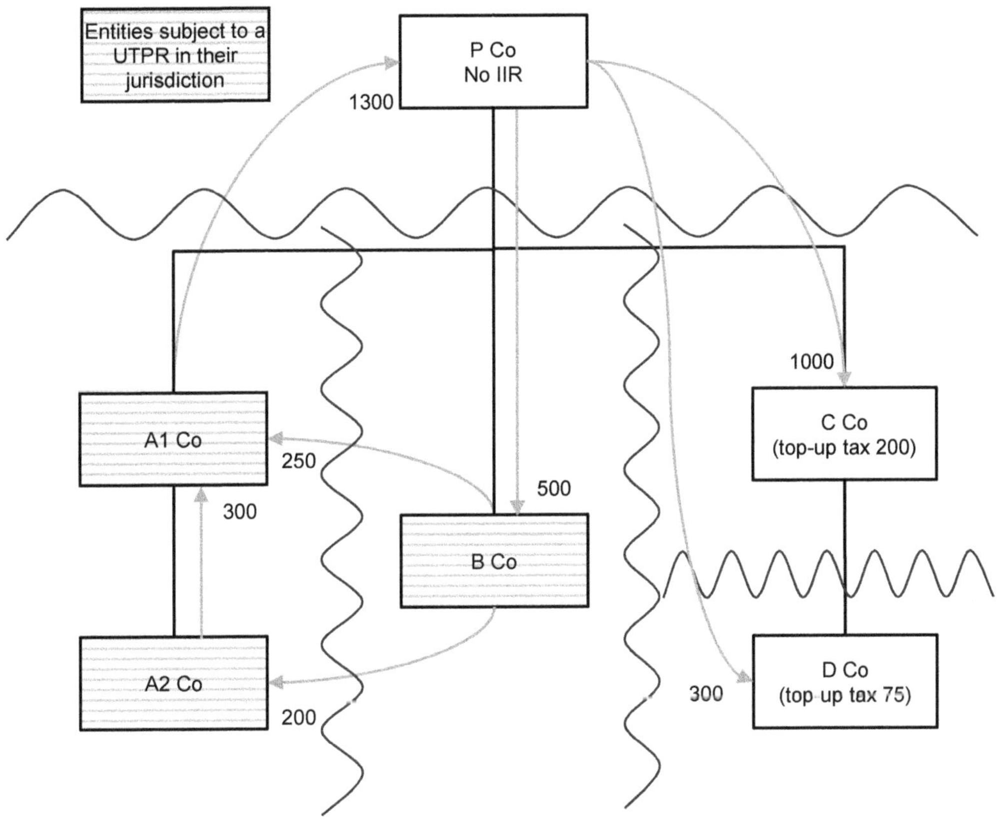

3. How are the top-up taxes allocated in relation to the profits made in jurisdictions C and D under the UTPR?

Answer

4. The first allocation key of the UTPR does not apply in this fact pattern. The second allocation key applies to the total amount of top-up tax.

5. The second allocation key of the UTPR allocates such a total amount of top-up tax (200 + 75 = 275) in proportion to net intra-group expenditure of the UTPR Taxpayers. The net intra-group expenditure of A1 Co and A2 Co are respectively 88% and 12% of the aggregated amount of the sum of their net intra-group expenditures. The net related party income of B Co is disregarded for this purpose.

6. These entities are therefore allocated a portion of top-up tax as follows:

- The top-up tax allocated to A1 Co amounts to 242 (88% x 275)
- The top-up tax allocated to A2 Co amounts to 33 (12% x 275)

Analysis

7. The first allocation key of the UTPR does not apply in this fact pattern. Under the second allocation key, all remaining top-up taxes (i.e. those that were not allocated under the first allocation key) are aggregated to form one pool of top-up tax that is allocated in proportion to each UTPR Taxpayer's net intra-group expenditure.

8. The set of related party transactions results in the following amounts of net intra-group expenditure:

UTPR Taxpayers	Related party Income	Related party expenses	Amount of net intra-group expenditure
A1 Co	300 + 250 = 550	1300	550 – 1300 = (750)
A2 Co	200	300	200 – 300 = (100)
B Co	500	250+200 = 450	Net related party income

9. The proportion of net intra-group expenditure can be computed on the basis of these net intra-group expenditures computed at the entity level. Entities with net related party income are disregarded for this purpose.

UTPR Taxpayers	Amount of net intra-group expenditure	Proportion of net intra-group expenditure
A1 Co	(750)	$\frac{\mathbf{750}}{\mathbf{850}} = \mathbf{88\%}$
A2 Co	(100)	$\frac{\mathbf{100}}{\mathbf{850}} = \mathbf{12\%}$
B Co	Net related party income	n.a.
Total	(850)	100%

10. The total amount of top-up tax can then be allocated amongst A1 Co and A2 Co in proportion to their net intra-group expenditure.

UTPR Taxpayers	Proportion of net intra-group expenditure	Allocated top-up tax
A1 Co	88%	$\mathbf{88\%\ x\ 275 = 242}$
A2 Co	12%	$\mathbf{12\%\ x\ 275 = 33}$
Total	100%	275

Example 7.4.3D. Example of the operation of the UTPR when a Constituent Entity subject to the UTPR is resident in a jurisdiction where the MNE's jurisdictional ETR is below the minimum rate

Facts

1. The same facts as for Example 7.4.3B are assumed for this example. It is further assumed that B Co is established in a jurisdiction where the MNE's jurisdictional ETR for the current year is below the agreed minimum rate.

Question

2. How are the top-up taxes allocated in relation to the profits made in jurisdictions C and D under the UTPR?

Answer

3. The first allocation key of the UTPR does not apply in this fact pattern. The second allocation key applies to the total amount of top-up tax.

4. The second allocation key of the UTPR allocates such a total amount of top-up tax (200 + 75 = 275) in proportion to net intra-group expenditure of the UTPR Taxpayers. B Co is not eligible to apply the UTPR because it is established in a jurisdiction where the MNE's jurisdictional ETR is below the minimum rate. Therefore, the net intra-group expenditure of B Co is disregarded for this purpose.

5. The net intra-group expenditure of A1 Co and A2 Co are respectively 88% and 12% of the aggregated amount of the sum of their net intra-group expenditures.

6. These entities are therefore allocated a portion of top-up tax as follows:

- The top-up tax allocated to A1 Co amounts to 242 (88% x 275)
- The top-up tax allocated to A2 Co amounts to 33 (12% x 275)

Analysis

7. The first allocation key of the UTPR does not apply in this fact pattern. Under the second allocation key, all remaining top-up taxes (i.e. those that were not allocated under the first allocation key) are aggregated to form one pool of top-up tax that is allocated in proportion to each UTPR Taxpayer's net intra-group expenditure.

8. Only the Constituent Entities that are eligible to apply the UTPR are taken into account for this purpose. B Co is not eligible to apply the UTPR and is not a UTPR Taxpayer because it is established in a jurisdiction where the MNE's jurisdictional ETR is below the minimum rate. Therefore, the net intra-group expenditure of B Co is disregarded for this purpose.

9. The set of related party transactions results in the following amounts of net intra-group expenditure for the UTPR Taxpayers:

UTPR Taxpayers	Related party Income	Related party expenses	Amount of net intra-group expenditure
A1 Co	300 + 250 = 550	1300	550 – 1300 = (750)
A2 Co	200	300	200 – 300 = (100)

10. The proportion of net intra-group expenditure can be computed on the basis of these net intra-group expenditures computed at the entity level. UTPR Taxpayers with net related party income are disregarded for this purpose.

UTPR Taxpayers	Amount of net intra-group expenditure	Proportion of net intra-group expenditure
A1 Co	(750)	$\frac{750}{850} = 88\%$
A2 Co	(100)	$\frac{100}{850} = 12\%$
Total	(850)	100%

11. The total amount of top-up tax can then be allocated amongst A1 Co and A2 Co in proportion to their net intra-group expenditure.

UTPR Taxpayers	Proportion of net intra-group expenditure	Allocated top-up tax
A1 Co	88%	$88\%\ x\ 275 = 242$
A2 Co	12%	$12\%\ x\ 275 = 33$
Total	100%	275

Example 7.5.2A. Illustration of the operation of the limitation of top-up tax that can be allocated from UPE jurisdiction

Facts

1. P Co is the ultimate parent company of an MNE group in scope of Pillar Two rules and directly owns three subsidiaries: A Co, B Co and C Co.

2. P Co and its subsidiaries are located in jurisdictions P, A, B and C respectively.

3. P Co has a total revenue of 2 000m and expenses of 1 800m. P Co's profit is 200m and it is subject to a 9% ETR in jurisdiction P, while the minimum rate is 10%.

4. The MNE's ETR in jurisdictions A, B and C is above the minimum rate.

5. Only jurisdiction A has introduced the UTPR. A Co is subject to a 20% CIT rate in its jurisdiction.

6. A Co made a direct payment of 1m to P Co and another payment of 6m to B Co. B Co and C Co also made direct payments to P Co of 2m and 4m respectively.

7. This set of simplified assumptions and the relevant amounts are summarised in the chart below.

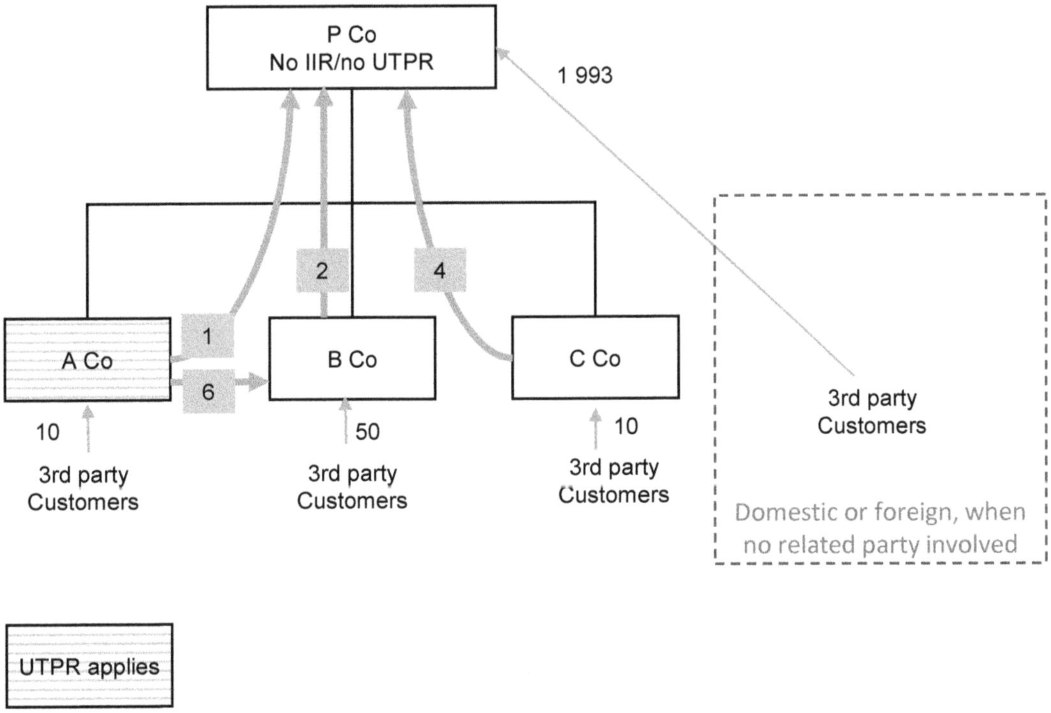

Question

12. What is the top-up tax allocated to A Co under the UTPR?

Answer

13. The top-up tax allocated to A Co, after taking into account the limitation of top-up tax that can be allocated from UPE jurisdiction, is 70,000.

Analysis

14. The top-up tax percentage is the difference between the minimum rate (assumed to be 10%) and the MNE's ETR in the low-tax jurisdiction (assumed to be 9%). The top-up tax percentage for Jurisdiction P under this fact pattern is 1%.

15. In this scenario, the foreign sources of intragroup revenue do not exceed the low-tax Income in the low-tax Jurisdiction.

- The foreign sources of intragroup revenue in Jurisdiction P amount to 1m + 2m + 4m = 7m
- The total amount of Adjusted GloBE income in Jurisdiction P is equal to P Co's income since there are no other Constituent Entities established in Jurisdiction P. This income amounts to 200m.

16. Since the foreign sources of intragroup revenue do not exceed the low-tax Income in the low-tax Jurisdiction, a limitation applies to the allocable top-up tax computed above.

17. The limitation is computed by applying the top-up tax percentage to the foreign sources of intragroup revenue in Jurisdiction P, i.e.:

$$1\% \text{ x } 7m = 70{,}000.$$

18. The top-up tax allocated in the group would therefore be limited to 70,000 in this example.

19. This limited amount of top-up tax would be allocated in full to A Co under the UTPR as a result of the first allocation key since A Co is the only entity of the group subject to the UTPR and it has made direct payments to P Co.

20. Assuming this subsidiary was subject to a 20% CIT rate in its jurisdiction, denying the deduction of the payment of 1m would result in a maximum top-up tax of 200,000. This cap would not be reached and A Co would be allocated the whole top-up tax of 70 000.

Chapter 9 - Examples

Example 9.3.1A. – Interaction between adjusted nominal rate computation and exemption under tax treaty elimination of double taxation provisions

Facts

1. Imagine that States R and S have a tax treaty including a royalty article following Article 12 of the OECD Model, but including the STTR; and that State R has adopted the Article 23 A exemption method in the elimination article. State R has a statutory rate of 20% but, under a special regime applying to certain royalty income, excludes 80% of the income from tax. Without any other adjustment, this will mean that only 20% of the income is subject to the 20% rate, producing an adjusted nominal rate of 4%.
2. Imagine also that the agreed adjusted nominal trigger rate for the purposes of the STTR is 7.5% and that all the other conditions for its application are met. SCO, a resident of State S, makes a covered royalty payment to RCO, a resident of State R.

Question

3. How would the STTR apply in these circumstances?

Answer

4. The effect of taking the treaty exemption into account would be to reduce the adjusted nominal rate to 0% and increase the top-up tax that can be applied in State S to 7.5%, depriving State R of its 4% taxing right and reallocating an exclusive taxing right to State S (up to the agreed minimum rate).

Analysis

5. Because the adjusted nominal tax rate applied to the royalty payment, before taking account of State R's obligation to provide an exemption under Article 23 A, is below the 7.5% trigger rate, State S is prima facie entitled to apply a top-up tax of 3.5% under the STTR. State R is only obliged to provide an exemption under Article 23 A where State S may tax in accordance with the treaty. Solely as a result of the STTR being triggered, State S is permitted to tax the income in accordance with the treaty. State R is then obliged to exempt the income in accordance with Article 23 A. The effect of taking account of this treaty obligation when computing the adjusted nominal rate is to reduce that rate to 0% and increases the top up rate to the full 7.5% trigger rate.

Example 9.3.3A – Interaction between the application of the STTR and tax treaty elimination of double taxation provisions (exemption)

Facts

1. The facts are the same as example 9.3.1A., apart from the obligation on State R to apply the exemption method under Article 23 A of the OECD Model is not taken into account in computing the adjusted nominal rate for the purposes of the STTR.

Question

2. How would the STTR apply in these circumstances?

Answer

3. The effect of disregarding the treaty exemption when computing the adjusted nominal rate is that the adjusted nominal rate in State R is 4%. This is the effect of the domestic law exclusion of 80% of the income from tax. The top-up rate that State S can apply is therefore 3.5%.

Analysis

4. State R has a statutory rate of 20% but, under a special regime applying to certain royalty income, excludes 80% of the income from tax. This will mean that only 20% of the income is subject to the 20% rate, producing an adjusted nominal rate of 4%. The adjusted nominal trigger rate for the purposes of the STTR is assumed to be 7.5% and all of the conditions for the rule to apply are met. SCO, a resident of State S, makes a covered royalty payment to RCO, a resident of State R. Because the adjusted nominal tax rate applied to the royalty payment is below the 7.5% trigger rate, State S is entitled to apply a top-up tax of 3.5% under the STTR. State R is now obliged to exempt the income in accordance with Article 23 A.

Example 9.3.3B. – Interaction between the application of the STTR and tax treaty elimination of double taxation provisions (credit)

Facts

1. The facts are the same as example 9.3.3A, except that State R applies the credit instead of the exemption method.

Question

2. How would the STTR apply in these circumstances?

Answer

3. As in example 9.3.3A, the adjusted nominal rate in State R will be 4% and the top-up rate that can be applied in State S is 3.5%. The result is that the payment is taxed at 4% (split between 0.5% net of credit relief in State R and 3.5% in State S).

Analysis

4. State R would now apply its tax at 4% and provide a credit against that tax for the 3.5% tax applied in State S. State S would apply a top-up tax of 3.5%.

Example 9.3.3C. – Effect of switching-off tax treaty elimination of double taxation provisions where the STTR applies

Facts

1. The same facts as examples 9.3.3A and 9.3.3B above.

Question

2. What is the effect of switching-off tax treaty elimination of double taxation provisions where the STTR applies?

Answer

3. The effect of this under both the exemption and credit methods would be that State R would tax the item of income at 4%, without providing any exemption or credit under Article 23 A or B, and State S would apply a top-up tax at 3.5%. There would be no reallocation of taxing rights away from the residence jurisdiction.

Analysis

4. In order to achieve these outcomes, the residence jurisdiction's obligation to provide exemption or credit under the elimination of double taxation provisions of a tax treaty could be switched-off where the source jurisdiction is only exercising a taxing right in accordance with the treaty because it is applying a top-up tax in accordance with the STTR.

Example 9.3.3D. – Effect of tax treaty elimination of double taxation provisions where the conditions for the STTR to apply are met, but the source jurisdiction is permitted to apply a higher treaty rate than the top-up rate (no restriction)

Facts

1. Imagine that a treaty permits the source jurisdiction to tax royalties at the rate of 5% and includes the STTR. Consistent with the ordering rule approach outlined in paragraph XX of the report, the source jurisdiction can apply the higher of that existing treaty rate and the top-up rate. Adapting the facts of example 9.3.3C, and because 5% is higher than the 3.5% top-up rate in that example, the source jurisdiction is permitted to apply the 5% rate.

Question

2. How would the STTR apply in this scenario?

Answer

3. In this scenario, the STTR is triggered (because all of the conditions for its application are met) but it is not applied (because the source jurisdiction is exercising an existing taxing right that does not depend upon those conditions and which results in a higher rate of source taxation). State S is therefore taxing in accordance with the treaty, other than solely because the STTR is triggered, and State R is obliged to eliminate double taxation by exemption or credit.

Analysis

4. If the residence jurisdiction's obligation to exempt the income or provide a credit under the elimination of double taxation provisions in the treaty were not restricted in this scenario, the residence state will either exempt the income or provide a credit for the tax applied in the source jurisdiction (up to the amount of the residence jurisdiction's tax on the same income). Applying the exemption method will result in no tax in the residence jurisdiction and a 5% tax in the source jurisdiction, with the result that the total tax is 5%. Applying the credit method will have the same result, with the residence jurisdiction providing a credit against its own tax for the tax applied on the income in the source jurisdiction. This will cover in full the 4% tax in the residence jurisdiction, leaving no net tax paid there, and the source jurisdiction will tax at 5%. In each case, the total residence and source jurisdiction tax is 5%, which is below the agreed minimum rate (assumed to be 7.5%).

Example 9.3.3E. – Effect of tax treaty elimination of double taxation provisions where the conditions for the STTR to apply are met, but the source jurisdiction is permitted to apply a higher treaty rate than the top-up rate (proportionate restriction)

Facts

1. The same facts as example 9.3.3D.

Question

2. How could the "cliff-edge" effect illustrated above be addressed?

Answer

3. Although the outcome illustrated in example 9.3.3D. does not disturb the position obtaining before the STTR came into contemplation, it does mean that the combined residence and source taxation of a covered payment in respect of which all the conditions for the STTR to apply are met will be lower than it would be if the rule had applied to produce a top-up tax. To avoid this outcome, without depriving the source jurisdiction of its bilaterally agreed right to tax the income at a rate above the top-up, the residence jurisdiction's obligation to provide relief by way of exemption or credit could be proportionately limited. The effect of this will bring the combined rate in the residence and source jurisdictions up to the agreed minimum rate under the STTR (assumed to be 7.5%).

Analysis

4. The effect of applying a proportionate restriction when applying the elimination of double taxation provisions in a tax treaty would be:

- Under exemption method – the residence jurisdiction would exempt 37.5% of the income over which it has taxing rights before the application of the elimination provisions in the treaty, bringing its rate down from 4% to 2.5%. (To achieve the target 2.5% rate, the proportion of the income taxable in the residence jurisdiction at 4% will need to be reduced to 2.5/4 x 100 = 62.5%, requiring an exemption of 37.5% of the income.)
- Under the credit method – the residence jurisdiction would provide a credit for the 5% source jurisdiction tax capped at 1.5% (instead of the full 4%), leaving the residence jurisdiction applying tax at 4% - 1.5% = 2.5%.

  In both cases, the combined residence and source jurisdiction tax would then be equal to the minimum rate under the STTR (assumed to be 7.5%).

[1] These top-up taxes are assumptions

Chapter 10 - Examples

Example 10.2.1A. - Interaction between the STTR and the income inclusion rule

Facts

10. The MNE Group consists of four constituent entities located in jurisdictions A, B and C. Hold Co is a tax resident of Country A and is the Ultimate Parent Entity of an MNE Group subject to the GloBE rules. Hold Co owns directly the shares of B Co (tax resident in Country B), C Co 1 (tax resident in Country C).

11. C Co 1 holds valuable intangible property of the group and licenses it to B Co, which made a payment of 100 to C Co 1. Country C has a corporate tax rate of 25% and a preferred regime that exempts 80% of royalty income. C Co 1 also receives other foreign source payments of 100 from third parties that are not taxable in Country C. It is assumed that Hold Co and B Co have no income.

12. Hold Co is subject to an Income Inclusion Rule in Country A.

13. Countries B and C have a tax treaty that follows the OECD Model Tax Convention (OECD, 2017[1]) and contains a STTR.

14. It is assumed that the minimum adjusted nominal tax trigger rate for the purposes of the STTR is 7.5% and that the minimum rate for the GloBE rules is 10%.

15. This set of simplified assumptions and the relevant amounts are summarised in the chart below.

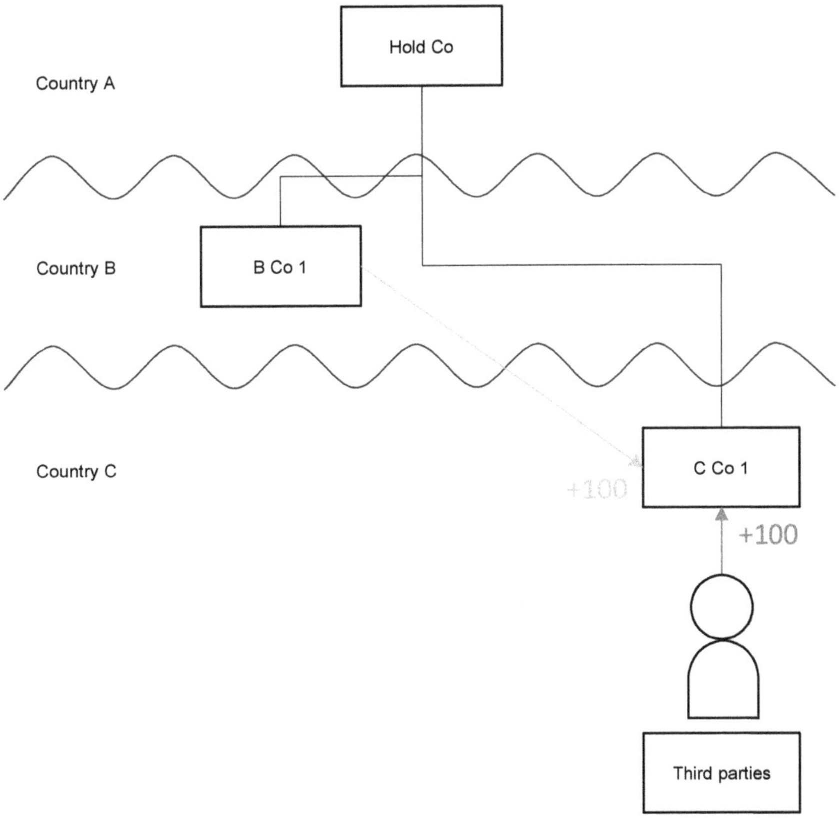

Question

16. How do the STTR and the income inclusion rule (IIR) interact under these assumptions?

Answer

17. The top-up tax imposed under the STTR is 2.5 and is levied in Country B, while the top-up tax imposed under the IIR after taking into account the tax imposed under the STTR is 12.5, levied in Country A.

Analysis

18. The STTR applies first, before any operation of the IIR. The payment received by C Co 1 is subject to an adjusted nominal tax rate of 5%, which is obtained by reducing the nominal CIT rate of 25% by 80% because of the exemption of 80% of the income.

19. Because the adjusted nominal rate is below 7.5%, and the payment is a covered payment under the STTR, the STTR applies in country B. B Co is required to withhold at the top-up rate of 2.5%, which is the difference between the minimum rate (7.5%) and the adjusted nominal tax rate (5%).

20. Hold Co is subject to an IIR in Country A. The IIR operates similarly to a CFC rule by requiring a parent company to bring into account and tax the profits of a subsidiary that are subject to an effective tax rate below the minimum rate.

21. The effective tax rate is determined by dividing the amount of covered taxes by the amount of profits. Covered taxes include withholding taxes imposed by source jurisdictions. The effective tax rate of C Co 1 is computed as follows:

- Covered taxes: 2.5 (2.5% of withholding tax under the STTR[1] x 100) + 5 (CIT imposed in country C) = 7.5
- Tax base (assumed to be equal to the amount of the income for the purpose of this example): 100+100 = 200.
- ETR = Covered tax / Tax base = 3.75%

22. The ETR of C Co 1 is below the minimum rate. Therefore, Hold Co is required to apply the IIR in respect of the income of C Co 1. The top-up tax percentage is 10% - 3.75% = 6.25%. The top-up tax imposed under the IIR is 6.25% x 200 = 12.5.

Example 10.2.1B. - Interaction between the STTR and the undertaxed payments rule

Facts

1. The facts are the same as in Example 6.2.1A, but Country A has not introduced the IIR, whereas Country B has introduced an undertaxed payments rule.

2. It is further assumed that the CIT rate applicable in Country B is 20%.

Question

3. How do the STTR and the undertaxed payments rule (UTPR) interact under these assumptions?

Answer

4. The top-up tax imposed under the STTR is 2.5 and is levied in Country B, while the top-up tax imposed under the UTPR after taking into account the tax imposed under the STTR is 12.5, levied in Country B as well.

Analysis

5. The STTR applies first, before any operation of the UTPR. The payment received by C Co 1 is subject to an adjusted nominal tax rate of 5%, which is obtained by reducing the nominal CIT rate of 25% by 80% because of the exemption of 80% of the income.

6. Because the adjusted nominal rate is below 7.5%, and the payment is a covered payment under the STTR, the STTR applies in country B. B Co is required to withhold at the top-up rate of 2.5%, which is the difference between the minimum rate (7.5%) and the adjusted nominal tax rate (5%).

7. Hold Co is not subject to an IIR in Country A. The undertaxed payments rule serves as a backstop to the income inclusion rule by allowing other subsidiaries of the MNE Group to make an adjustment to intra-group payments and collect the top-up tax that was not collected under the IIR.

8. The effective tax rate is determined under the UTPR with the same mechanics as under the IIR, by dividing the amount of covered taxes by the amount of profits. Covered taxes include withholding taxes imposed by source jurisdictions. The effective tax rate of C Co 1 is computed as follows:

- Covered taxes: 2.5 (2.5% of withholding tax under the STTR[2] x 100) + 5 (CIT imposed in country C) = 7.5
- Tax base (assumed to be equal to the amount of the income for the purpose of this example): 100+100 = 200.
- ETR = Covered tax / Tax base = 3.75%

9. The ETR of C Co 1 is below the minimum rate. Therefore, B Co is allocated a top-up tax in respect of the income of C Co 1. The top-up tax percentage is 10% - 3.75% = 6.25%. The top-up tax imposed under the IIR is 6.25% x 200 = 12.5. The amount of deduction that needs to be denied is obtained by dividing the amount of top-up tax allocated to the UTPR Taxpayer by the CIT rate to which this entity is subject. B Co is subject to a CIT rate of 20% and therefore Country B can deny the deduction of 12.5/20% = 62.5.

References

OECD (2017), *Model Tax Convention on Income and on Capital*, OECD Publisher, Paris, https://doi.org/10.1787/mtc_cond-2017-en. [1]

Notes

[1] The timing of recognition of the withholding tax is the same as that of the income, provided the payment is made no later than during the financial year that follows the one when the income was accrued for financial purposes. Therefore, even if the income was accrued for financial purposes the year preceding the one when the payment actually occurred (and the withholding tax was actually paid), the withholding tax would be considered as a covered tax during the same financial year.

[2] The timing of recognition of the withholding tax is the same as that of the income, provided the payment is made no later than during the financial year that follows the one when the income was accrued for financial purposes. Therefore, even if the income was accrued for financial purposes the year preceding the one when the payment actually occurred (and the withholding tax was actually paid), the withholding tax would be considered as a covered tax during the same financial year.

www.ingramcontent.com/pod-product-compliance
Ingram Content Group UK Ltd.
Pitfield, Milton Keynes, MK11 3LW, UK
UKHW051500290926
15471UKWH00008B/1310

9 789264 812390